To

Bob & Helene —

Best wishes.

Norman Sherwin

D1292151

ATLANTA

triumph of a people

an illustrated history
by Norman Shavin and Bruce Galphin

MAUD PRESTON PALENSKE
MEMORIAL LIBRARY
St. Joseph, Michigan 49085

*"ATLANTA: Triumph Of a People" is published by
Capricorn Corporation, 4961 Rebel Trail, NW, Atlanta,
Georgia 30327. Copyright 1982 by Capricorn
Corporation. All rights reserved.*
ISBN 0-910719-00-4
First Edition
Book design by Kathleen Oldenburg King
Mechanicals by Olio-2 Graphics
Typesetting by Clopton Typography & Graphics, Inc.
Printing by Perry Communications, Inc.
Binding by National Library Bindery

ACKNOWLEDGEMENTS

The creation of a book of this magnitude demanded the dedication and affection of skilled artisans and supportive spirits. *ATLANTA: Triumph Of a People* was aided by many to whom the authors hereby express their deep gratitude:

To Dan Sweat, executive director, and Grace Sherry of Central Atlanta Progress, and James Cumming, president, and Eileen Segrist of the Atlanta Preservation Center. The two important civic agencies cosponsored this book, and Sweat and Cumming were always responsive to our needs.

To John Kerwood, executive director; Jack Spalding, president, and Franklin Garrett, Historian, of the Atlanta Historical Society. They lent their support and encouragement. Garrett's role was essential: Not only was his two-volume *Atlanta and Environs* an absolute gold mine—as many writers of Atlanta history know—but he also read this entire history text, made important suggestions, saved us from embarrassing errors, and wrote the Introduction.

To Michael Chalverus, Director of Marketing for the book, who carried out a number of diverse chores, and to his sales associates: Gail Chalverus, Carole Golding, Ray Odom, Gene Talley, Mary Wilkes and Roy Wilkes. They performed extremely well under heavy pressure.

To Manning, Selvage & Lee/Atlanta, a preeminent public relations firm which was charged with developing the 91 corporate and institutional profiles in this volume. It was an enormous, sometimes maddening task, but handled with admirable professionalism. We are indebted to George Goodwin, president; Richard Dowis (whose calm was remarkable), and other agency staffers—Ann Howell, Corinne Adams, Candice Cohen, Janice Hoffman and Stan Fisher—plus the skilled writers under contract to the agency: Robert Johnson, John Knapp, Judith Schonbak and Paul Troop.

To Robert Fishman, of Georgia State University's Department of Anthropology, for assistance with the feature on Atlanta's ethnic communities.

To Linda Matthews and others of her staff at the Emory University Library Special Collections.

To Raleigh Bryans, who shared published and unpublished manuscripts, particularly of recent history.

To the very cooperative staff of the *Atlanta Journal-Constitution* library; editor Jim Minter, and Joe Coleman, head of the newspapers' photo department.

To Audrey Williams and Tom Tester of Clopton Typography—the former for her responses to, and patient tolerance of, our often-hectic demands; and the latter for his consistently cheerful and superior work as the typesetter for this volume.

To Chris Evans, president of Perry Communications, Inc., printer of this volume, for his enthusiasm for this project, and the unflappable manner of his British heritage. Our thanks also to others at Perry: coordinator Wanda Minter, who suffered quietly; T. W. (Willie) Owings and John ("Butch") Henley, painstaking craftsmen of the stripping department; and Charles Lee, the pressroom foreman whose personal concern for quality is much appreciated.

To the executives of those 91 entities profiled herein, for their expressions of confidence and support. We simply could not have achieved this work without them.

A special commendation is saved for last: Kathleen Oldenburg King. She designed the book, and was responsible for the mechanicals. Kathy met with us at ungodly times—days, nights, weekends—to shape the project, and give it her loving concern. We have worked with Kathy on other volumes, and her professionalism, her dedication and good humor make her the candidate for future labors—if she'll have us.

NORMAN SHAVIN
BRUCE GALPHIN

Atlanta's newest skyscraper, Georgia-Pacific's headquarters building, towers in the background.

In the foreground, the venerable English-American (Flatiron) Building, dating from 1897.

Introduction

By **FRANKLIN R. GARRETT**

Historian, Atlanta Historical Society

One hundred forty five years ago, for topographic reasons, the site of a future city was chosen as the terminus of a railroad. And during that century and a half transportation has been the keystone of the arch of its progress.

First, rails, then almost simultaneously in the present century, highway and air. Only in matters maritime has Atlanta played no significant role.

That lack has been insured by its elevation of 1,050 feet. But the same elevation, highest of all American cities save Denver, has been the chief factor in its year-round mostly salubrious climate.

The story of Atlanta has seen print before, in whole, or in part: Clarke in 1881; Reed in 1889; Pioneer Citizens and Martin 1902; Hornady in 1922; Allen in 1928; Garrett in 1954 and 1974. Various phases of its history have been set forth in monographs, theses, accounts of specific organizations, etc.

Here, however, is an illustrated, popular account of Atlanta, put together by two noted authors, Norman Shavin and Bruce Galphin. In fast moving prose, and with copious illustrations, it tells a straightforward story from Standing Peachtree to Hartsfield International Airport.

It makes no claim to absolute completeness. It is not a critique, nor does it attempt to carry the burden of special pleadings. There is no call to man the barricades. It is precisely what it started out to be—an illustrated popular history.

For the newcomer to Atlanta this account of the city's founding and progress, together with its generous use of pictures, should be just the prescription for making the new arrival interestingly informed as to what has gone before in his new surroundings. For the long-time resident it will recall just how fascinating local history can be.

A generous section of this volume is devoted to the history and development of corporate and business entities which, through the years, have been central to Atlanta's progress and well-being.

FOREWORD

That prolific author, "Anonymous," is credited with observing that "The only lesson history has taught us is that man has not yet learned anything from history."

Like all universal statements, that cynical observation is true and false. The volume you hold may help refute the sour quote, for it seeks—in part—to exhibit the origins and continuum of historical strengths which have become the wellsprings of this city's courageous and adventuresome spirit.

ATLANTA: Triumph of a People is an attempt to retrace some major and minor roads to self-discovery. It aims for comprehensiveness, not the impossible task of completeness in every detail. I hope it has succeeded.

It was constructed to be readable, anecdotal and well illustrated, so as to appeal to the young, to the more knowledgeable, to the longtime resident, to the newcomer, to the teacher, to the student. In short, it is meant to be a "popular" history, not a forbidding work of dull profundity. It is a work designed to be used and enjoyed, not shelved and ignored.

In planning its creation, I called upon the special talents of an admired professional, co-worker and longtime friend and author, Bruce Galphin. It was agreed that he would research and write the portion of the main text which begins with 1920, and that I would be responsible for all that preceded. Despite other severe demands on his time, Bruce accepted the challenge, for which I

am deeply grateful. Bruce, who has lived in Atlanta since 1954, drew upon firsthand experiences as a reporter and editor with *The Atlanta Constitution,* and mined numerous sources to shape his contribution. I am indebted to Bruce for his dedication, and the superior skill amply evident in this book.

In shaping th text, we read—and made suggestions—on each other's material. Each chapter was then reviewed by our consultant, Franklin Garrett, Historian for the Atlanta Historical Society. I am most thankful to Franklin for protecting us from oversights and errors; beyond that, his *Atlanta and Environs,* that two-volume work of such marvelous detail, was a major source for material, as were primary sources noted in that work.

it is not an uncomfortable confession to observe that, despite our best efforts, errors crept into this work. We spotted no serious ones, but it did offend us to realize that, for example, we once misnamed John A. Sibley, and once gave Robert F. Maddox the wrong middle initial. We beg the reader's understanding, and promise that any future editions will amend the faults.

ATLANTA: Triumph of a People is dedicated to those myriad men and women whose lives gave this city the character, the pulse, the energy which shaped its history.

But we owe lasting debts to family and friends who suffered our obsession in creating this work, and made their own

contributions by paying with the priceless coin of understanding.

My personal passion for history was ignited on onetime battlefields in and near my home, Chattanooga. As a boy, I played on the slopes of Missionary Ridge, Orchard Knob and Lookout Mountain, and on the plain of Chickamauga. As I did, the struggles of long-ago decades were no longer events frozen bloodless in the past: The participants came alive in individual, personal ways.

I read their letters and their reminiscences, was touched by their anger and their pain. The past became present; we were linked, and I understood more of my own brief time because I was made aware of, and shaped by, theirs.

Today, I read my late father's diaries, and I am part of the continuum. My children's diaries continue the process of remembrance.

Cicero, more generous than "Anonymous," capsuled it better, more than 2,000 years ago: "To be ignorant of what occurred before you were born is to remain always a child. For what is the worth of human life unless it is woven into the life of our ancestors by the records of history?"

That is the motive power of this book: understanding. From the threads of yesteryear, we have sought to weave today—and tomorrow.

NORMAN SHAVIN

CONTENTS

Tracking Atlanta

1782-1837

Long before James Oglethorpe brought his settlers to Georgia, the area was perceived by an early map-maker as little more than a wilderness. He was right.

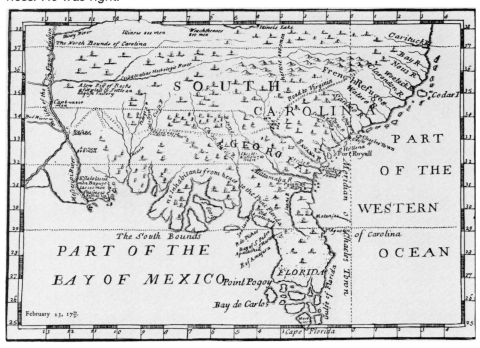

In the summer of 1839 the southern terminal of the just-launched Western & Atlantic Railroad was visited by Alexander H. Stephens and a companion. Stephens' eyes roamed the dense virgin forest thick with heat, and mused to his friend, "I was just thinking what a magnificent inland city will at no distant date be built here."

It was pure, unwarranted prophecy. Only a visionary watching a few workmen clear the woods would have dared such a prediction, for the nation was gripped by the vestiges of financial panic. The backwoods area where Stephens stood had few settlers for the last of the Cherokee Indians in Georgia had only recently migrated West on a forced march known as "The Trail of Tears."

When Stephens came through that summer, most of Georgia's development was coastal though three railroads had begun to stretch their iron fingers within the state. Decatur, east of the W. & A. terminus site, was emerging as a village, as were Lawrenceville, Athens and Columbus. But Stephens confirmed the inexorable movement west by land-hungry settlers—tradesmen and farmers.

What he foresaw was a great future for the point where a railhead would connect central Georgia lines with markets to the north. Once the Indians had been forced out, growth could be impeded only by the lack of a transportation system to move Georgia's raw materials to factories elsewhere, and return as finished products.

Stephens' prediction was not widely shared. A year after he made it, W. & A.'s chief civil engineer quit the state, declining an offer to buy half interest in nearby land. The place that engineer, Col. Stephen Long, had selected as the southern terminus of the W. & A. would never boast more than a tavern, a blacksmith shop and a grocery, he predicted. When Long departed in 1840, that's about what Terminus contained.

The rugged site Stephens predicted in 1839 would become a "great inland city" would emerge as Atlanta. It is an oddity of history that Stephens would nearly be killed in that city 10 years later, and die there as governor in 1883.

In 1782, when Savannah could celebrate its 49th year as a town, Atlanta's origins could be traced to its favorite place-name, Peachtree. The first documented references to that name emerged in 1782 when "the Talassee (Indian) King" warned Gov. John Martin that a war party of Coweta Indians "were to rendezvous at the Standing Peachtree," an Indian village on the Chattahoochee River near the present Atlanta water pumping station. On this advice, Martin pleaded with higher military authority, "For God's sake exert yourself and come to our timely aid..."

The reference to the Indian village indicated that the Standing Peachtree was of some backwoods importance in the Revolutionary War era, and the Indian threats—

TREATY BETWEEN OGLETHORPE AND TOMOCHICHI AT SAVANNAH MAY 21 1733

especially the Creek alliance with the British in the War in 1812—confirmed the need for frontier ports to protect Georgia's upcountry settlers.

Immediate conflict with the land-rich aborigines was avoided with James Oglethorpe's settlement of Savannah in 1733, when he made a peaceful pact soon after his arrival. The treaty allowed whites to sell goods to the Creeks, who agreed to let settlers have lands their nation did not want. The Creeks pledged peace "as long as the sun shines and the water runs." But boundaries were hazy, and the Creeks contended with the Cherokees of northwest Georgia for dominance over disputed lands.

First the British colonists contested with the Spanish for dominance over coastal areas. Soon after the Spanish were vanquished, colonists were divided in their allegiance to an emerging American nation and Mother England. There followed decades of struggle with the Indians, some of whom aligned themselves with the British in the War of 1812. For 25 years thereafter the westward movement of Georgians led to conflict with the Indians. The final Federal expulsion, by treaty of 1835, sealed off the confrontations in 1838 when 16,000 Cherokees were forced further west on "The Trail of Tears," a cruel migration in which 4,000 of them died.

Before this climactic episode of Indian sorrow, two forts relevant to Atlanta's history were established prior to end of the War of 1812: Ft. Daniel (at Hog Mountain in Gwinnett County), completed late in 1813, and Ft. Peachtree, at the Standing Peachtree. The 30-mile connector between them was known as Peachtree Road, a name it later surrendered.

George R. Gilmer was a 23-year-old lieutenant in 1813 when he was commissioned to build Ft. Peachtree at the Indian village. Gilmer (later a governor) knew nothing of how to erect a fort, but with a textbook called *Duane's Tactics*, he and 22 recruits—supervised by James M. Montgomery—constructed a $5,000 facility: a boatyard, two blockhouses, six dwellings and a store in 1814. Several months later the war ended and Gilmer left; the post fell into gradual disuse. Montgomery, who also departed, returned six years later, established his home, became a DeKalb County legislator, Standing Peachtree postmaster, and $1,000-a-year land surveyor appointed by Pres. Andrew Jackson. In 1837 Gilmer signed an act authorizing Montgomery to build a river ferry near the old fort they had constructed.

The continuing Indian difficulties brought Gen. Jackson to Gwinnett County in 1820 and there he issued a warning to whites that he would remove trespassers on Indian lands and destroy their crops, houses and fences. Jackson wrote the Secretary of War that he found "a great many numerous and insolent" white intruders "on the north of the Chattahoochey."

The force of legislation legitimatized the westward movement by creating new political subdivisions, such as Gwinnett County in 1818, and Lawrenceville in 1821. And when DeKalb County (named for the German baron who fought for the colonists) was created in December, 1822, one more outpost was fixed, if meagerly settled.

DeKalb then had about 2,500 residents,

The visionary James Oglethorpe led settlers from England to the site that was named Savannah in 1733. His treaty of friendship with the Indian Chief Tomochichi gave the new colony of Georgia a period of peace, but war with Spaniards to the south created turmoil. Oglethorpe prevailed, however, and when he left Georgia to make his report of the colony's progress, Indians went with him—to be presented to court.

Alexander H. Stephens foresaw a great city at the site of the new railroad—Atlanta—and decades later died there, as Georgia's governor.

Sequoyah (George Guess)

Before Decatur was a town, Cherokee Indian George Guess, better known as Sequoyah, had developed his 80-character alphabet (1821), and in 1828 the tribe began publishing a newspaper, *The Phoenix.*

William Carroll, who visited the Cherokee in 1829, was "astonished" by their "advancement...in morality, religion, general information and agriculture..."

A census of 1825 reported there were 13,563 Cherokees in Georgia—and among them were 1,277 slaves.

Cherokee Indian Chief William McIntosh was killed by other Cherokees in 1825; they believed he had betrayed them by signing a treaty ceding to Georgia certain lands.

mostly of English, Scotch and Irish descent —poor of possession, inadequately educated but temperate, industrious, and used to the hard frontier life they had always known. Most owned no slaves; some had one or two servants, and individual ownership of a dozen was rare since DeKalb had no large plantations. Women spun gingham and dyed cloth by boiling bark collected by the boys; the men farmed, raised cattle, hacked the woods for timber. The area was self-sufficient and in the 1820s only an occasional traveler brought news into the crude if bucolic isolation.

In 1824 Decatur (named for a War of 1812 naval hero) began to emerge as the county seat and most of DeKalb's 3,500 "free white" citizens lived in the town that then boasted an academy (for those who could pay for education), a crude jail (for those who had to pay for crime), and a number of stores and houses.

Life was generally stern, and morality demanded especially by the handful of churches which began to emerge as early as 1824: Macedonia Primitive, followed by Mount Gilead Methodist, Nancy Creek Primitive Baptist, Utoy Primitive Baptist, Decatur Presbyterian, Rock Chapel Methodist, Wesley Chapel Methodist, and Hardman Primitive Baptist. Blacks had no houses of worship but some white owners allowed some to attend services from segregated benches.

Church membership required strict obedience to rules. In one, no member could miss a congregational meeting without the pastor's approval, and worshippers were required to address each other as "Brother" or "Sister." In another, members could be cited for failure to commune, for drunkenness and for fighting. One member was excluded for "moving into the Indian country" and another for "running race paths," suggesting that competitive jogging was frowned upon.

Decatur Presbyterian sought to discipline an organizer, Joseph D. Shumate, for running his grist mill on the Sabbath, but exonerated him when he proved it was a necessity since rain fell that day after a long drought, and his neighbors needed his services.

Before 1830 at least three other churches had organized—Decatur Methodist, Mount Zion Methodist, and Fellowship Baptist—and the growth of religious institutions led to the formation of a Bible society to supply the destitute with Holy Scriptures. It had rough going: Some citizens were offended when asked if they owned a Bible, and others resisted because "some one may be making money by selling or printing" the Good Book.

But commerce found other expressions: Mason Shumate opened a hotel in Decatur, ferries were started, a $5,100 courthouse (replacing the original log structure) was completed in 1829, and following the arrival of small stores, Samuel Miner inaugurated the first print shop and newspaper, the *DeKalb Gazette,* in 1830. His venture lasted only briefly: Miner soon left after mistreatment by some unruly boys, and Decaturites were deprived the civilizing influence of journalism until the second paper, the *Decatur Watchman,* appeared.

Unruly boys weren't the only disturbers of the peace in the largely placid town. In 1824 several persons protested that the election announced for April 20 had been held on the 19th, and a new election was ordered. The same year blacksmith Nathan W. Wansley had a piece of his nose bitten off in a fight, and his unnamed protagonist was placed in the stocks.

In 1835 ferry operator John B. Nelson was murdered by John W. Davis. The assailant was jailed, escaped the noose, and 24 years later was adjudged a pauper lunatic and committed to an asylum. Among Nelson's bereaved family was a 3-year-old son, Allison, who became Atlanta's mayor in 1855 and died a Confederate general.

Decaturites were also abuzz in 1825 when Creek Chief William McIntosh was killed by dissident tribesmen after he signed a treaty ceding their Georgia territory for lands west. And when gold was discovered at nearby Dahlonega in 1828, bringing some 4,000 whites to the fields by 1830, Decaturites were among them, speculating on the riches to be found.

The Decatur Gold Mining Co.—which included Reuben Cone and William Ezzard —joined the hunt, led on by one Kenneth Gillis. But Decatur residents had a good laugh when it was discovered that someone had "salted" the Company's creek, and the firm promptly fell apart, "a much sadder but wiser set of men." Cone and Ezzard prospered later in Atlanta; the first as a judge, and Ezzard as mayor.

Not gold but prehistoric stone was the

George I. Parrish, J

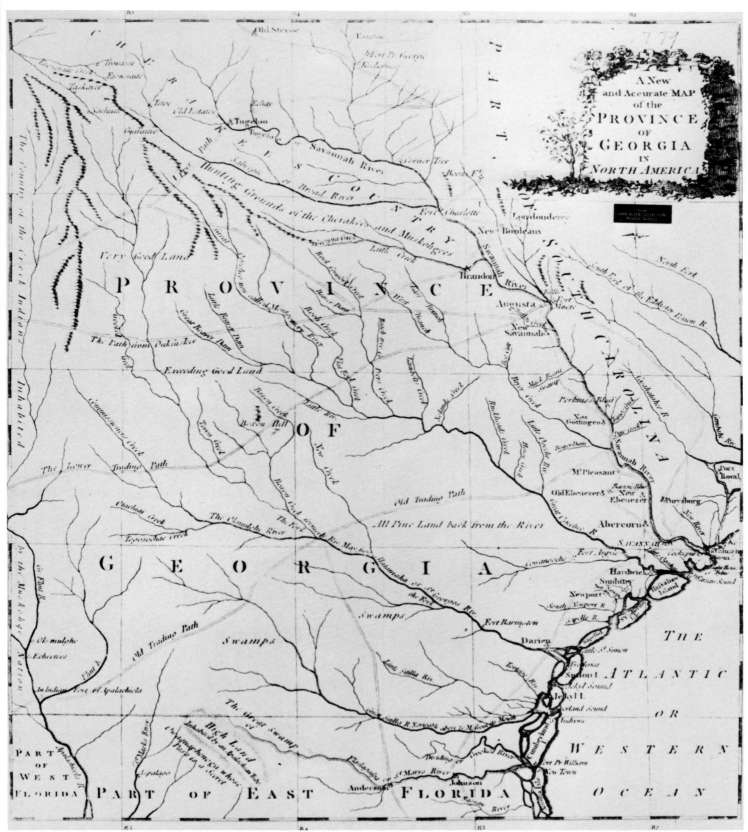

A 1779 map of the Georgia colony illustrates that only the coastal areas had settlements, notably Savannah, which had been founded 46 years before. The interior was marked with rivers, references to bountiful lands, and Indian villages. About this time the Cherokees had a village on the Chattahoochee River, called Standing Peachtree. There, 35 years after this map was published, Lt. George Gilmer built a fort, named for the village, as a buffer against the British and their Indian allies who sought to encroach upon the territory during the War of 1812. But there is no record that Fort Peachtree ever saw military action, and it fell into disuse. Gilmer, however, later became a governor.

This replica of Ft. Peachtree, dedicated in 1976, was placed near Peachtree Creek in the area of Ridgewood Road. The original Fort was about 50 yards southwest of the site of the replica.

Wilson Lumpkin was the transportation surveyor (later governor) of 1826, and the preeminent booster of a railroad system. Marthasville (later Atlanta) was named for his daughter.

natural wonder of DeKalb: Before 1830 the granite mass nearby was known as New Gibraltar, a tourist site with homes and a stage stop. It was incorporated in 1839, and the name changed in 1847 to Stone Mountain.

Emerging Decatur took little notice of two men involved in a state-ordered transportation survey in 1826: Wilson Lumpkin and Hamilton Fulton, who would both leave their imprints on history. The two examined the territory between Milledgeville and the future site of Chattanooga, reporting that a railroad would be practicable but not a canal, to connect Georgia with markets north. The state did nothing with the survey; public awareness of locomotive power and rails was dim, though Northern canals were emerging as a preeminent form of transport.

But 10 years after the Lumpkin-Fulton survey the legislature approved an act to establish a point at which a new railroad would connect privately owned middle Georgia lines with the Tennessee River. The point ultimately became the state capital and the city which Alexander H. Stephens forecast: Atlanta.

Lumpkin, as governor, was the great early proponent of internal improvements and was aware of the excitement created in Charleston, S.C., in 1830 when the locomotive "Best Friend" made its initial run.

Shortly after his inauguration, Lumpkin declared, "We may anticipate the day when...with pride we may point to (Georgia's) railroads, canals and turnpikes." Following his urging, the legislature in 1833

chartered three lines: The Central Railroad and Canal Company, the Georgia Railroad Company (later the Georgia Railroad and Banking Co.), and the Monroe Railroad (now part of the Central of Georgia). The Central planned to connect Savannah to the interior while the Georgia sought to run west from Augusta, and the Monroe company was to run north from Macon.

What was missing was a common, central connecting link to the North. That decision was near.

Before it came, Decatur plodded forward, some of its citizens unknowingly leaving marks on the future Atlanta.

The Lyricist Who Hoped To Aid the Cherokees

A champion of the Cherokees' cause visited them in October, 1835, to collect information on which to base a book.

But in early November John Howard Payne was arrested by the Georgia militia and confined near Dalton for 12 days, awaiting trial for sedition.

Payne was properly acquitted and left the state.

Twelve years earlier there had been the first performance—in London—of the song for which he wrote the verses: *Home Sweet Home.*

It was sung by opera star Adelina Patti at the funeral of Abraham Lincoln's son Willie in 1862. Payne, who served as American consul in Tunis, died 10 years before.

Hardy Ivy, the First To Farm 'Downtown'; His Grave Is Unknown

Pioneer Hardy Ivy, first to settle on land which became part of downtown Atlanta, paid $225 in produce for Land Lot 51, and moved there with his wife Sarah and five sons.

Hardy died in December, 1842, after breaking his neck in a fall from a horse. His wife survived until 1865.

Hardy left no will, but his estate was appraised at a value of $714.67—and his widow had to pay the 1843 property tax assessment: 55 cents. The estate included 800 pounds of salted pork valued at $30, 40 hogs worth $50, and a teaster bed, bedstead and furniture valued at $25.

Billings Socrates Ivy, Hardy's grandson (child of Henry P. Ivy, a blacksmith and dentist), arrived Nov. 2, 1844, and is said to have been the first white male child born in Atlanta (then known as Marthasville).

Ivy Street is named for Hardy, and three sons-in-law were honored by having streets—all within Land Lot 51—named for them: James M. Ellis, John J. Cain and Thomas Baker.

Where Hardy is buried is uncertain—but his widow's grave is in Oakland Cemetery.

MONTGOMERY'S FERRY 1840

Montgomery Ferry served the Standing Peachtree area. Its builder, James C. Montgomery, lived in that locale after helping construct Ft. Peachtree. Montgomery is honored in the name of an Atlanta street.

Hardy Ivy's cabin was built in the area of the present-day downtown Marriott Hotel, where the pioneer had his farm. After he died, his wife had to pay the property tax on the land: 50 cents.

FIRST HOME, FUTURE SITE, ATLANTA HARDY IVY - 1836

13

Charner Humphries' Whitehall
Tavern was in business in 1835. It
stood at present-day Gordon and
Lee Streets, and was a major cross-
roads meeting place. Union troops
used it during the occupation of
Atlanta in 1864.

Col. Stephen H. Long was the
engineer for the Western & Atlantic
Railroad who selected the site for
the terminus which became Atlanta.
But he thought the area would
amount to nothing.

To Charles and Eleanor Latimer was born a daughter, Rebecca, who in 1922 would serve two days as the first female U.S. Senator. James Power established a Chattahoochee ferry (which Sherman later used) and gave his name to key roads. Hardy Pace built his home on a road east of Northside Drive (West Paces Ferry is named for him) near a later intersection that would bear the name of his son-in-law, Pickney H. Randall. Pace later founded Vinings and operated a tavern there. And Robert Smith built a home north of Decatur, later occupied by his great-grand-daughter Tullie; the home was moved a century and a quarter later to the Atlanta Historical Society's grounds.

Among those who reached out from the Decatur area was the Hardy Ivy family who —settling vacant land in the present Court-land-Ellis Street area—became future downtown Atlanta's first permanent white settlers.

Hardy Ivy's arrival triggered no mass emigration. Indeed, it would be months before any not-too-distant neighbors arrived. About three miles south of Ivy's farm Charner Humphries bought a lot in 1835 and erected a two-story tavern and store at the future Gordon and Lee Streets. The whitewashing of the tavern gave the road its name, "White Hall," and Humphries' place became a stage stop,

post office, locus of military drills and social center. Years after Humphries died, the tavern was a headquarters for Federal officers during Sherman's uninvited stay, and later was burned.

Final impetus for creating the Terminus came Dec. 21, 1836, weeks after a Macon railroad convention confirmed that "an excellent route for the (rail) road...can be obtained from Ross' Landing (Chatta-nooga) to some point on the Chattahoo-chee in DeKalb County." Gov. William Schley signed the bill creating the state-financed Western & Atlantic Railroad to tie middle Georgia lines to the North.

Though Decatur was never seriously considered as a site for the terminal of the W. & A. Railroad, its residents reflected mixed opinions over the coming of rails. One of its legislators, Dr. Chapman Powell, had wanted the railroad to come by Decatur, but James Calhoun opposed it, siding with fellow citizens who felt the rail-road would be a dirty nuisance.

"The terminus of that railroad," Calhoun predicted in 1836, "will never be any more than an eating house."

"True," Dr. Powell retorted, "and you will see the time when it will eat up Decatur."

The Terminus did not digest Decatur, but shadowed it as Atlanta, and Calhoun became its mayor.

Atlanta's seminal year came after other Georgia towns had begun to prosper—Athens, Augusta, Columbus, Macon, Milledgeville. Even Roswell took root in 1837, after low-country planter Roswell King visited that area and saw its abundant water as an ideal power source for a manufactory.

That same year, when Martin Van Buren was inaugurated president and had to contend with financial panic following canal speculation, the nation of 13 million (including 2 million slaves) already boasted major cities such as New York and Philadelphia; even New Orleans had 50,000 residents. But all of DeKalb County, including the future Atlanta, had 10,000 souls, 15 per cent of them slaves.

Mounting sectional division over the slave question began to turn more ugly. Nat Turner's fiery rebellion in Virginia in 1831 alarmed other slave-holding communities. And the question was inflamed in 1837 with the murder of abolitionist newspaper editor Elijah P. Lovejoy by a pro-slavery mob in Alton, Ill.

But the climactic eruption was almost 25 years off, and backwoods Georgia was more concerned in 1837 with the final forced displacement of its Cherokees. Their removal finally cleared the way for developing up-country settlements and the land-hungry railroads.

Gov. Schley's hope of hiring the firm of McNeil and Whistler as engineers for the Western & Atlantic Railroad bogged down over compensation. Whistler's name is minor in Georgia history; he became better known as the father of artist James Abbott McNeill Whistler.

Engineer J. J. Albert wanted $10,000 a year; he, too, was dropped for someone "more moderate in his (financial) views." Then J. Edgar Thomson, chief engineer of the Georgia Railroad, suggested Col. Stephen H. Long, a New Hampshire native and onetime math professor at West Point Military Academy and Western explorer.

Mindful of hard economic times, Gov. Schley whittled engineer Long's request for $9,000 to $5,000 annually. Long accepted in May, 1837, on condition he could remain in the army and be allowed one-third of the time off for personal affairs.

With an eye toward history, Long and his men began work on July 4, 1837, at Pittman's Ferry near Norcross, but soon abandoned the site because valleys, intervening creeks and gradients failed to coincide with Long's requirements. Long chose the locale of Standing Peachtree, reporting to Gov. Schley in November, 1837, that "the route leading from Montgomery's Ferry proved the more economical and favorable"—$18,000 per mile less, it turned out. When the railroad act of 1836 was amended the next year to confirm the new site, it was signed by the man who built Ft. Peachtree—Gov. Gilmer.

Construction, begun in 1838, was slow, impeded by lack of funds and a few

'The Center Of Creation'

1837-1850

Martha Lumpkin was a teenager when the town was named for her as Marthasville, its first official name (1843-45). Martha (1827-1917) was the daughter of Georgia Gov. Wilson Lumpkin, a preeminent booster of railroads.

Julia Carlisle was the daughter of a pioneer family who came to Atlanta in 1842, when it was still called Terminus. She is credited with being the first child born here—though Marietta was the site of the birth.

The first locomotive arrived in 1842: The "Florida" was pulled in by mules from Madison, 65 miles away, to make the 22-mile run from Terminus to Marietta.

Railroad engineer C. F. M. Garnett's two-story house in Terminus was near the plank depot. The structure served as his headquarters and later as a boarding house. It lasted into the 20th Century.

settlers who resisted the State's taking of land by the right of eminent domain. A clash among laborers in 1839 left two women dead and 34 men jailed. Grubby life in the railroad shanties could hardly support visitor Alexander Stephens' prediction of a "great inland city," for in 1839 the permanent residents included the Ivy family, the Humphries clan, a log house (now 10 Pryor St.) with a widow and her daughter, and pioneer Benjamin Thurman (on Magnolia Street). It was a wretched settlement, made even less promising when the Monroe Railroad's stock dropped to 10 cents on the dollar.

That railroad's grading contractor, John Thrasher, got the assignment to build what became the oldest man-made construction still extant in Atlanta: the Monroe Embankment, western base of the downtown railroad triangle. That work (in which Lochlin Johnson was Thrasher's partner) began in 1839 or 1840. Thrasher who was paid his $10,000 share partly in railroad stock, traded it off for goods to open the Terminus' first store, as well as a gold watch and a carriage.

The store seemed a better prospect than troublesome railroad work, for Thrasher broke the first strike when laborers demanded more pay. Thrasher dismissed them and promptly hired 25 blacks from a preacher, paying him $16 a month and board for their hire. Thus, slaves must be credited with some of the earliest building of Atlanta.

Hard times caught up with the Western & Atlantic. Soon after engineer Long left in 1840, declining an offer to buy half interest in 200 acres on Marietta Street, the W. & A. measured its progress: After four years of grading and surveying, $2.5 million had been spent and not one segment of rail laid.

A dispute erupted in 1842 when the W. & A. board moved the final terminus point 1,200 feet east for erection of a depot. Thrasher was livid: He had bought 100 acres close to the Embankment, but soon sold out for $4 an acre and, in disgust, moved to Griffin. (Three years later he returned, opened a cotton-buying business on Marietta Street, ultimately made and lost small fortunes, opened a railroad eating house in South Carolina, and died in 1899 in Dade City, Fla., where he owned an orange grove.)

As Thrasher first moved out, others

drifted in, huddling in makeshift homes near the plank depot built in 1842 and engineer C. F. M. Garnett's two-story house, which served as his headquarters and later as a boarding house. That same year 21-year-old Willis Carlisle and his pregnant 17-year-old wife arrived; in August she went by stagecoach to Marietta to bear their child, Julia, since the nearest doctor was there. Thus Julia just missed being the first baby born in Terminus; that honor fell in 1844 to Hardy Ivy's grandson, Socrates, but Julia's Oakland Cemetery tombstone describes her as Atlanta's first baby which, technically at least, she was.

Apart from an occasional preacher delivering outdoor sermons at the Monroe Embankment, Terminus was dormant. It was enlivened on Christmas Eve, 1842, when the engine Florida was brought the 65 miles from Madison on a wagon drawn by 16 mules to make the maiden 22-mile rail run to Marietta. Some 500 persons, mainly from Decatur and the surrounding country, came to celebrate the event, unaware that regular train service was still two years off. The time was so difficult for the W. & A. that there was a vain attempt to sell it for a million dollars. That news plus the brawling of gambling, hard-drinking railroad men hardly bode well for the town.

Despite this, the grubby hamlet secured official recognition on Dec. 23, 1843, when Gov. George W. Crawford signed a bill approving a commission form of government for the place then called Marthasville, named in honor of ex-Gov.

Lumpkin's daughter. Some had wanted to call the place "Mitchell," after the Pike County pioneer who had donated land; others suggested "Lumpkin." In retrospect, Marthasville was the best name, though later residents were grateful that *it* didn't last long.

When Marthasville became a legal entity, the town had several general stores run by Willis Carlisle, John Bailey, John Kile and others, a dozen or more dwellings, a rudimentary hotel (moved from Boltonville), the railroad boarding house, and four roads which converged at the present Five Points: Whitehall, Peachtree, Marietta and Decatur.

The several residents probably took no notice in February, 1844, when a 23-year-old army lieutenant passed through on a mail coach, bound for Marietta to take depositions of volunteer troops who had claims (for losses of equipment) against the Federal government. During his two months' stay in northwest Georgia, the lieutenant developed excellent knowledge of the terrain. He used it to advantage 20 years later when he returned during the Civil War, as Gen. William Tecumseh Sherman.

Marthasville residents certainly *did* note the attempt by the town's first five commissioners to levy a tax to open new streets. The citizens not only refused to pay the tax, saying existing streets were enough, but suggested their officials hitch up their own mules and clear the ground themselves.

The commissioners couldn't do

A Buck Is Shot, A Place Is Named

Soon after Henry Irby opened a tavern and grocery at the northwest intersection of present-day Roswell Road and West Paces Ferry, someone—possibly Irby—shot a buck nearby, and mounted its head on a post. The locality was known from then on—about 1840—as Buckhead.

A few months later a post office was established at Irby's tavern, and designated Irbyville, but it lasted little more than a year. It was reinstated and discontinued twice more, finally closing for good in 1873.

Irby died in 1879, and is buried in Sardis Methodist Churchyard on Power's Ferry Road near the Roswell Road intersection.

Henry Irby's 1840s tavern was situated approximately where Peachtree and Roswell Roads meet today, at the heart of Buckhead and very near a short street which bears his name.

Early in 1847 residents contributed funds to build Atlanta's first church (nondenominational) and school-house. The weatherboarded structure faced Peachtree Street in the triangle formed by Pryor, Peachtree and Houston Streets.

The Town's First Resort, Walton Springs, In 1840s

Atlanta's first resort was Walton Spring, on the low ground between the present YMCA and the Greyhound bus station.

The property was owned by one of Atlanta's first six councilmen, Anderson W. Walton; the street bears his name, and the waters gave Spring Street its name.

On the rising ground between the spring and Peachtree Street, Antonio Maquino sold drinks and knick-knacks at his wagonyard in the 1840s, and soon constructed a ferris wheel 40 feet in diameter, its power provided by two blacks.

State Owned One Slave, The Heroic Ransom

The only slave owned by the State of Georgia first belonged to pioneer James C. Montgomery.

Soon after the slave Ransom heroically saved a Chattahoochee River railroad bridge from burning, he was purchased in the 1840s by the State and "set as near free as the law would allow," Judge S. B. Hoyt recalled more than 40 years later. "The State took care of him to the time of his death."

John Edgar Thomson (right) was a native Pennsylvanian who suggested the coined word "Atlanta" as a substitute for "Marthasville," on the urging or railroad executive Richard Peters (far right). Thomson, who came south in 1834 as chief engineer of the Georgia Railroad, left Atlanta soon after renaming it, and was president of the Pennsylvania Railroad from 1852 until he died in 1874. Peters became a prominent land developer.

much, either, about the DeKalb Grand Jury's complaint that "vice and immorality seems (*sic*) to be prevailing...particularly on the line of the Rail Road..." But the Grand Jury did "take pleasure in saying that (the County's treasurer's) accounts are honestly and correctly kept...the only exception...is the style, which is not as neat and beautiful as we would desire..."

Despite the common unruly nature of Marthasville as a frontier town, other citizens moved in, lured by the promise of the railroad: Edwin Payne, cabinetmaker; Stephen Terry, possibly the first real estate entrepreneur; Ambrose B. Forsyth, who bought the first cotton sold in the hamlet; merchants James Loyd and brother-in-law James Collins, partners in a store; and Jonathan Norcross. The last five lent their names to streets and a town (though Loyd Street was later changed to Central Avenue and Collins to Courtland).

Norcross arrived in 1844 and established a sawmill, the town's first factory, its motive power supplied by an old blind horse. The mill lasted for about a year, but Norcross generously distributed many slabs which residents ued to construct their homes, giving the name "Slab Town" to the section around the Norcross mill. Soon after it closed, Norcross paid $200 for a lot at Peachtree and Marietta to open a general store. "Norcross Corner" became the site of the First National Bank.

In 1845 part of a triangular block bounded by Peachtree, Decatur, Pryor and Edgewood sold for $130; the property later occupied by the Olympia Building went for $200; a half-acre at the corner of Decatur and Central went to grocer John Kile for $150.

Marthasville's early population was primarily of Irish stock. But Jacob Haas and Henry Levi, German-born Jews, moved their Decatur dry goods store to Marthasville in 1845. (Jacob's younger brother Herman arrived in 1848, and his son Aaron later founded the real estate and

insurance firm which became Haas & Dodd.) Other Jewish citizens arrived before midcentury, Moses Sternberger, Adolph J. Brady and Aaron Alexander among them.

The first teacher is said to have been Martha Reed, who organized a small private school in a shanty; the first doctor was Joshua Gilbert, a horseback medico who kept no books and rarely presented a bill. Dr. Stephen T. Biggers also arrived in 1845. The first lawyer was Leonard C. Simpson (for whom a street is named), and William Whitaker arrived in 1845 to establish a shop making furniture and that other necessity: coffins.

The Georgia Railroad's first engine puffed into Marthasville on Sept. 14, 1845. News of its coming impelled hundreds to light campfires near the depot to await the arrival of the locomotive Kentucky, with engineer William F. Adair at the throttle. After an hour-long run from Decatur, the Kentucky reached Atlanta at 9 p.m. A passenger train, with William Orme as conductor, arrived the next day, completing the 12-hour ride from Augusta. The passengers on that initial run included George Washington Adair (later a major realtor); Judge John P. King, the Georgia Railroad's president, and Richard Peters, the line's superintendent.

Before bedding down, Judge King fell into a well. "It was only 10 feet deep and we soon pulled him out," said Peters, "but he was highly disgusted, and for years would not buy Atlanta real estate." (But Peters and Adair did.) Another man drowned in a well the night the first passenger train arrived, but wasn't discovered until the following morning.

Days thereafter the provincial name "Marthasville" began to disappear. Peters urged a more impressive one and J. Edgar Thomson, chief engineer of the Georgia Railroad, suggested "Atlanta" as the feminized version of Atlantic, so honoring the railroad which gave it birth. Within days

HOWELL'S MILL - PEACHTREE CREEK - 1860

Clark Howell established a grist-and sash-sawmill on the north bank of Peachtree Creek, downstream from the present concrete bridge on what became known as Howell Mill Road. Fire destroyed the mill (built in 1852) in the late 1870s. Members of the Howell family were associated with The Atlanta Constitution.

The Early Days Of Piety, Temperance and Mourning

Some women of early-day Atlanta bore charming and unusual names.

Benjamin Plaster's daughter was named Piety.

Lewis Peacock's daughter was called Temperance.

And John Johnson's first wife was named Permelia; his second, Mourning Britain.

Ironically, when Margaret Mitchell was writing *Gone With the Wind*, she considered the name Permelia for one of her heroines—but settled on Melanie. Ms. Mitchell's even wiser choice was that of Scarlett; the author had considered calling her Pansy.

Two pretty, unidentified women, photographed apparently in the 1840s, speak to us from the days of early Atlanta.

George Washington Adair, who became a major Atlanta realtor, was a passenger on the Georgia Railroad's first engine to puff into Marthasville, in September, 1845.

schedules of the Georgia Railroad referred to Atlanta, though some editors accused of being "addicts of classic mythology" assumed the name was misspelled and printed "Atalanta," recalling the goddess of fleetness and strength.

So the hamlet known variously as The Terminus, Whitehall, and Marthasville emerged late in 1845 as Atlanta. The legislature confirmed that name in December. The changes of name hinted at the creative restiveness that became a town characteristic.

When regular train service from Macon to Atlanta began in October, 1846, the steel triangle of rails which became the heart of downtown was completed, and there was another "railroad boom," as Norcross recalled 35 years later: "There were probably 12 new homes built on the strength of it...I believe the real growth of Atlanta began right then..."

Indeed it did: In 1846 Atlanta had about 50 houses and a few mercantile establishments. The railroads and citizens became interdependent, for the lines sought freight and passenger traffic, and the residents wanted trade. Farmers and planters came to Atlanta to replenish their livestock and animal drovers came to the railhead to ship their stock and purchase supplies.

Commerce and Atlanta's centrality as a transportation site stimulated new permanent arrivals and organized religious life. In the five years prior to 1850 the city developed other civilizing influences: newspapers and private schools. But growth also brought the problems of crime and political conflict.

The spurt of commerce was such that in 1847 Atlanta had nearly 2,500 inhabitants, 50 large stores and two hotels, though the woods were filled with shanties and the streets were a maze of stumps and roots. The people were friendly, said Dr. William N. White, an educator who arrived in 1847: They "bow and shake hands with everybody they meet as there are so many coming in all the time that they cannot remember with whom they are acquainted..."

Residents had the services of Dr. S. T. Biggers, "botanic physician"; Mrs. Wells' boarding house; George Washington Collier's store (and post office) at what is now Five Points; John Kile's tavern; Moses Formwalt's tin shop (where he also made stills); Addison Dulin's general store; the Georgia Railroad's banking agency run by agent John F. Mims; James McPherson's bookstore; Austin Leyden's foundry and machine shop, and two hotels established in 1846.

The first was the Atlanta Hotel, a two-story brick building with rambling galleries, situated across from the passenger depot; it was operated by Dr. Joseph Thompson until its wartime destruction in 1864. The second, Washington Hall, was erected by James Loyd. Residents could board in that rambling wooden structure for $12.50 a month, a reasonable price for the period when chickens were six cents a pair, butter was eight cents a pound, eggs seven cents a dozen, and good beef was two and a half cents a pound. Washington Hall was consumed in the Sherman-set fires of fall, 1864.

Atlanta's reputation as a city of churches was launched in 1847 when the first house of worship—a non-denominational church—was erected in a small weatherboard structure on Peachtree (in the triangle formed by it, Pryor and Houston Streets). Decatur Presbyterian Church's

Some Hard Advice To A Bride-to-Be: Obey, Stay Cheery

Just before James Clarke's daughter Mary was to wed up-and-coming merchant Sidney Root, her father penned her some marital advice in 1849:

"When your will and that of your husband should happen to conflict, whether you approve or disapprove, it is, under your marriage vows and the Holy Scriptures, your duty to obey.

"You must ever entertain for him affection and tenderness...but I would not have you make marked manifestations in the presence of third persons...

"All he will expect of you is that politeness and those attentions which affable, well-bred persons are wont to bestow...

"When he comes home from business you should ever meet him dressed in smiles...

"**Under your marriage** vow, you promised not only to LOVE, but to HONOR your husband... Be ever ready to show him distinguishing marks of preference and favor, and that he is the first object of your esteem... And should you ever be enabled to detect faults in his manners, or infirmities in his character, never suffer yourself to treat them with irony or indifference, or the least semblance of bitterness...

"If your views and opinions are permitted or suffered to thwart or counteract his, his character will lose much of its force and vigor; he will become feeble, vacillating and unsuccessful in all his endeavors, and losing all self reliance, he will become a weak and insignificant cipher in the world...

"**Should poverty** or pecuniary distress (Heaven grant that these trials may never visit you) be permitted to come upon your husband, it is then no time to upbraid him, or to visit him with railing and condemnation. It is then that he requires new signs of your confidence and attachment.

"With his spirit bruised and trodden down, forsaken by his friends and neglected by the world, his energies must sink, and he will be irretrievably lost unless, with angelic heroism you come forward to the rescue, and lay yourself out to cheer, comfort and console him..."

The first church erected by a single denomination (the Methodists) was Wesley Chapel, built in 1848 on the east side of Peachtree Street immediately south of the present Candler Building. The church survived the Civil War, but was demolished in 1871 to make room for the First Methodist Church; the latter remained until 1904 on the Candler Building site, and faced Houston Street.

Marthasville, 1845: Where the key roads cross is present-day Five Points. Kile's grocery was where the present William-Oliver Building stands; the Norcross Store occupied the present site of the First National Bank. The church and schoolhouse were Atlanta's first (depicted in this chapter on page 18).

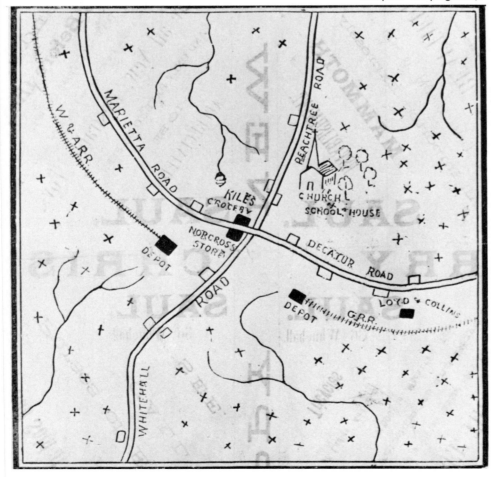

Capitol Square Land Was Part Of a Horse Trade

One of Atlanta's most historic plots of land is Land Lot 77: 200 acres owned by Samuel Mitchell of Pike County.

Five acres were deeded free by Mitchell so the first train depot could be built. Now dominating much of the area of the original acreage are the State Capitol, the Fulton County Courthouse and City Hall.

Land Lot 77 was first owned by Benjamin Beckman, who won it in a State lottery; his title is dated May 15, 1827. According to a granddaughter of Mitchell, Land Lot 77 passed to her grandfather in a curious way.

Beckman stopped at Mitchell's farm (near Zebulon), asked to spend the night, and became ill, thus prolonging his stay. At its end, Beckman—who had begun to fancy a horse Mitchell owned—sought to trade his own horse for it. Mitchell demurred, but when Beckman agreed to add some land he had won at a lottery, Mitchell accepted—and became the owner of Land Lot 77.

The value of Land Lot 77, which represented the difference in worth of the two horses, reportedly was fixed at $41 in a transfer of the deed. After Mitchell died in 1847 (before Atlanta was incorporated), the Beckman family challenged the title to the deed. After a long litigation, Mitchell's heirs retained ownership of Land Lot 77 for an additional $500 to be paid in cash or real estate.

Caroline, daughter of Mr. and Mrs. Jacob Haas, is believed to have been the first white girl born in Atlanta—on Nov. 14, 1848. She married a banker and insurance man also named Jacob Haas. The first white male born in Marthasville, was Billings Socrates Ivy (1844), grandson of pioneer Hardy Ivy.

George Washington Collier had a store (and operated the postoffice) in Atlanta in 1845 at Five Points. Collier became a major landholder.

Recipe for a Howling Time: Mix Kids and Some Pigs

One of the pranks of unruly youngsters in early-day Atlanta was truly a howl.

From a high embankment near the calaboose of the 1840s, the cutups would fill a hogshead with several pigs, fasten them inside, and roll the barrel from Whitehall down Alabama Street until it struck the foot of the embankment.

At impact the unfortunate porkers let loose such squealing and grunting that the noise always brought out crowds to determine the din at the jail.

Rev. John S. Wilson preached the first sermon there, and in June came the organization of the town's first Sunday school, the Atlanta Union Sabbath School.

In April, 1847, veteran land donor Samuel Mitchell gave property at Hunter and Piedmont to establish the Protestant Episcopal Church (later the Parish of St. Philip). Two months later Terrence Doonan conveyed to the Bishop of Charleston an acre of land for a Roman Catholic Church and Daniel McSheffery deeded an acre eight months later. A few years later the predecessor of the Church of the Immaculate Conception was built on the McSheffery acre.

Having organized Atlanta's second church, Wesley Chapel, in 1847, Methodists in 1848 paid $150 for a Peachtree Street lot (just south of the present Candler Building site) and dedicated Wesley Chapel, which featured rough wooden seats and a homemade tin chandelier. In the same year the Sandy Springs Methodist Episcopal Church was organized on Mt. Vernon Highway, then called Lawrencville Road, St. Philip's Episcopal Church was consecrated in May, 1848, in a $800 Washington Street edifice with vestry room and tower. Its bell was a gift of railroad pioneer J. Edgar Thomson. The First Baptist Church structure was dedicated in July, 1848, more than a year after Rev. David G. Daniell paid $150 for a lot at Forsyth and Walton.

When educator William N. White arrived in Atlanta in October, 1847, he noted that "there are but two Presbyterians besides myself in the place" and he hoped that by year's end "enough of our denomination may come forth to form a church." More than a year later they did: 19 Presbyterians banded in January, 1849, to organize the Presbyterian Church of Atlanta but not until 1852 did they secure a building, holding service meanwhile in the nondenominational church structure at Peachtree and Pryor.

The progress of educational facilities was less marked. The notion of public or "poor" schools was a subject of debate; the means of their support was cause for dispute. The concept of public schools had earned the legislature's interest (but no financial support), and the only progress in Atlanta's academe prior to 1850 was establishment of small private academies.

Mrs. Susan H. Smith opened the first female academy in January, 1848, charging 25 pupils $25 a year for instruction. A few months before, Dr. (Nedom) Angier's Academy (also called the Atlanta High School) opened to offer private instruction for students who could afford $3 to $8 per quarter per subject.

If operating an educational facility was risky in those uncertain times, running a newspaper was even more financially precarious. Apart from the problem of illiteracy, early papers lacked newsgathering resources, had no telegraphic communication (until 1849), found newsprint hard to get, had no mass of people to attract and, worse, found insufficient revenue (from readers or advertisers) to sustain them for long. Nonetheless, the impulse to com-

A wooden hotel, Washington Hall, was built late in 1846 by James Loyd. It faced the Georgia Railroad and Loyd Street (now Central Avenue), near Five Points. It burned in 1864.

FIRST MUNICIPAL ELECTION, ATLANTA, JAN. 1848

Kile's grocery (also a tavern) was the only polling place for Atlanta's first municipal election, in January, 1848. Moses Formwalt, a tinsmith whose shop was by the Collier grocery (see below), was chosen mayor over Jonathan Norcross.

George Washington Collier's grocery at Five Points faced Decatur Street; the building also housed the postoffice, facing Peachtree.

MARTHASVILLE, 1845

The Johnson-Thrasher store on Marietta Street near Five Points

Nancy's Creek Was Named For a Prolific Mother

Northwest Atlanta's Nancy Creek is believed to have been named for a settler's wife, though others have argued it was named after an Indian called Nance, who inhabited the area about 1800.

The Atlanta Constitution in 1883 held that the Creek was named for the widow of John L. Evins, who so honored her after they settled in the forested place about 1818.

In 1883 Mrs. John L. (Nancy) Evins was the mother of 11 children, and could boast of having 57 grandchildren and 93 great-grandchildren. She died that year, having lived in the original homestead—very near the present intersection of Peachtree-Dunwoody and House Roads —for about 65 years.

If Only Widow Doss Had Kept Her Land

Nobody ever denied that land increases in value in Atlanta. A prime example was the 202½ acres, known as Land Lot No. 78, drawn in the State lottery of 1825 by a widow, Mrs. Jane Doss of Jackson County.

The next year she sold it for $50 (less than 25 cents an acre), and its purchaser sold it 12 years later for $300 to Judge Reuben Cone. Seven years later Cone sold a half interest in the 202½ acres to Ammi Williams.

On those 202½ acres now stands the north half of the downtown business district. And you probably couldn't buy it.

municate would not be denied.

The pioneer paper was a four-page weekly, *The Luminary,* edited by Rev. Joseph S. Baker and partner Thomas W. Ison. It debuted July 14, 1846, was sold within six months, and sold again in 1848 when it was renamed the *The Tribune*— and died that year. *The Luminary* was the first to offer weather reports and forecasts: The editor stepped outside and made reports based on his thermometric readings.

A month after *The Luminary* bowed in, W. H. Royal and C. H. Yarbrough launched the weekly *Enterprise,* selling it next year to C. R. Hanleiter, who was forced to bury it months later. *The Democrat,* begun in 1847 by editor-publisher Dr. William H. Fonerdon, survived three months. Atlanta's fourth paper, *The Southern Miscellany,* was founded in Madison in 1842, and moved in 1847 to Atlanta with editor C. R. Hanleiter, who re-launched it in July, 1847. The weekly sought to survive at a subscription rate of $2 a year. Correspondents were warned that "All letters must come post-paid to insure attention."

The Southern Miscellany was suspended in 1849 when Hanleiter took over the telegraph office, and the paper and equipment were sold to Norcross, Benjamin F. Bomar, Ira O. McDaniel and Zachariah A. Rice (the first two would become mayors). They changed the name to *The Weekly Atlanta Intelligencer,* but within two years it changed hands again. *The Daily Examiner,* founded as a weekly in July, 1854, became a daily (Atlanta's first) the next month, and in 1857 was merged

with *The Intelligencer.* The latter became the only Atlanta paper to survive the Civil War.

The early newspapers, often only four pages, had to scratch hard for content. Apart from ads, they cribbed material from each other; published reader correspondence, poetry and essays, commented on events, lauded new commercial enterprises, and offered whatever material available about agriculture. An outsize crop was cause for comment; rail passengers were sought out for news; finally, the incorporation of Atlanta by the legislature —on Dec. 29, 1847—provided fresh political grist on the local scene.

As a signal of Atlanta's later reputation as a thrusting, upstart town, residents met days before its incorporation to urge removal of the state capital from Milledgeville to Atlanta. They were laughed off by legislators. In 1854 a statewide referendum on the capital question left it where it was; but in 1868 Atlanta won it. Aggressiveness had paid off: Twenty years after Atlanta's first effort to capture the capital, it was removed to a city just recovering from war's devastation.

In January, 1848, a month after incorporation, Atlanta held its first election for mayor and council members. In the excitement some 60 fights reportedly broke out as 215 residents attended the only polling place, Thomas Kile's grocery (site of the present William-Oliver Building at Five Points). The chief mayoral contenders: Moses Formwalt, tinsmith and "one of the boys," a popular maker of stills in his Decatur Street shop; and Jonathan Norcross, a temperance man who hated

First Church of the Immaculate Conception was erected by Roman Catholic residents in 1851 (the photo is of later vintage). It was at the southeast corner of Central Avenue and present-day Martin Luther King Drive, site of the church structure which replaced it in 1873. The latter burned in August, 1982.

Stone Mountain in 1848 was a recreational spot served by the railroad. Cloud's tower topped the mass of granite, and a hotel (at left) accommodated guests who trekked the mountainside. At one time, the nearby town was called New Gilbraltar.

Stone Mountain's Tower: The First Was In 1839

Construction of the first observation tower atop Stone Mountain was under way in 1838, the handiwork of Aaron Cloud, who hoped to raise it to 300 feet.

When erected in 1839, however, the tower was only 165 feet high, and had cost Cloud $5,000, "a unique and curious exploit," remarked one observer.

A storm blew it down, and another was erected.

The first cotton mill at Roswell, incorporated in 1839; 25 years later Gen. W. T. Sherman's troops destroyed it.

Jonathan Norcross was defeated in his bid to become Atlanta's first mayor, but was elected the fourth chief executive.

Dr. Benjamin Bomar became Atlanta's second mayor, succeeding Moses Formwalt. Bomar arrived in Atlanta from Dahlonega only 18 months before his election.

the kind of civic disorder that disturbed Formwalt less.

Formwalt won (Norcross became the fourth mayor), and the six elected councilmen were Dr. Benjamin Bomar, physician (and Formwalt's successor); cotton dealer Robert W. Bullard; merchants James Collins and Jonas S. Smith; lawyer Leonard Simpson, and Walton Spring owner Anderson Walton.

Atlanta's first trio of mayors appear undistinguished, but the brevity of their terms (one year) and the rude nature of the hustle-bustle town allowed little opportunity for them to achieve much in their parttime office.

After his year's service, Formwalt devoted his time to business, and in early 1852 also became a deputy sheriff. In May he was stabbed to death by a prisoner, and buried in an unmarked grave in Oakland Cemetery. His estate was appraised at $1751—of which $1500 was adjudged the value of four slaves. In 1916 Formwalt's remains were moved to another Oakland plot, and a granite marker erected to rescue Atlanta's first mayor from oblivion. A minor street also bears his name.

Dr. Bomar, the second mayor, had come from Dahlonega only 18 months before his election. He had stopped in Atlanta en route to Texas for his health, but remained. He died in 1868, the year Atlanta gained the capital. Wyllys Buell, a portrait painter, died in 1852—a few months after completing his term as the third mayor.

The first City Council dealt with organizational matters and minor civic details. Formwalt may have taken special satisfaction when his ex-contender, Norcross, was charged with draying without a license. William Mann was hailed before Council for not moving his scales off the sidewalk; Anderson Moody was fined $1 for shooting within the city limits; Antonio Maquino was fined $1.50 for keeping his store open on the Sabbath; and Ed Elliott was fined $1 for not removing a dead cow from the streets.

A more serious breach of the peace occurred in 1848 when Alexander Stephens, later vice president of the Confederacy, visited Atlanta during the Zachary Taylor-Lewis Cass presidential campaign. At a Taylor (Whig Party) rally, Stephens and Judge Francis H. Cone got into an altercation after the Judge called Stephens a traitor. Stephens struck him, Cone stabbed Stephens repeatedly, fled the angry mob, later surrendered and was fined.

For all their heat, political rallies of the 1840s did provide some amusement in a town that had few recreational outlets to siphon the pent-up steam of hard life.

The infamous Murrel's Row, hangout of thieves, gamblers, cutthroats and prostitutes, was the site of drunken brawls and staged cock fights. For calmer fare, Antonio Maquino offered drinks and a rudimentary ferris wheel at Walton Spring. Annual fairs by the Southern Central Agricultural Society began at Stone Mountain in 1846, and its big draw of 1849 was the appearance of that prince of humbuggers, P. T. Barnum, who displayed his wagon-show of freaks and animals including Tipo Sultan, the largest elephant in captivity. In the heart of town occasional fiddlers spun tunes *al fresco,* and below present-day Oakland Cemetery a great rainwater pond attracted swimmers *au naturel.* A major cooling innovation came in 1850 when Aaron Alexander opened the first soda fountain and brought in the first carload of ice.

Despite its salubrious climate, Atlanta fell victim to typhoid fever in 1848 and a siege of smallpox the next year, the latter mitigated by the heroic efforts of Dr. J. F. Alexander. Burials were outside the corporate limits—in land which now holds the Capital City Club and adjacent structures.

But Atlanta's annual show-off season, spring, was Nature's entertainment then as now. The woods blazed with showers of flox, lilies, trilliums, violets, dogwood, brilliant-hued honeysuckle, red woodbine, primrose and yellow jasmine. Such beauty melded with civic boosterism and caused a local newspaper to boast:

"Atlanta, the greatest spot in all the nation,

"The greatest place for legislation

"Or any other occupation—

"The very center of creation."

In 1849, "the very center..."? Hardly. But Atlantans crowed of the future in present terms. And then, having set the star of ambition in the heavens, strived to reach it.

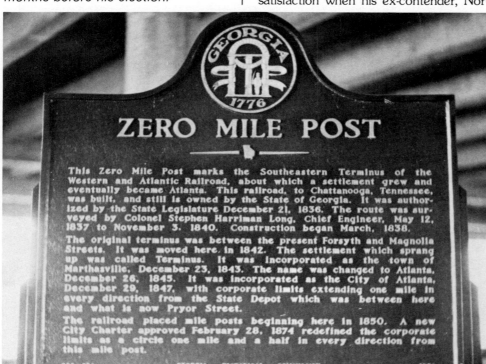

The marker is with Atlanta's oldest landmark, the Zero Mile Post, which dates from 1850. The three-foot stone Mile Post is near the entrance of the now-dormant Underground Atlanta section.

Hamilton & Hardeman,
Factors and Commission Merchants,
SAVANNAH, GEORGIA.

WILL give prompt attention to the sale of Cotton, Bacon, Flour, Wheat, Corn and Corn Meal, and the filling of orders for Bagging, Rope and Family Supplies. september 4 6m18

John B. DeSaussure,
FACTOR,
No. 10 Adger's South Wharf,
CHARLESTON, SOUTH-CAROLINA.
august 28 tf17

Hardeman & Hamilton,
Ware-House and Commission Merchants,
MACON, GEORGIA,

WILL give strict attention to the sale of Cotton and other Produce consigned to them, and will make liberal advances on the same, when in store or shipped by them.
september 4 6m18

General Advertisements

James McPherson & Co,
Wholesale and Retail Booksellers, and Dealers in Stationery, Music and Fancy Goods
Opposite the Macon & Western R. R. Depot,
ATLANTA, GEO.
november 20 29

New Store and New Goods!

THE subscriber has just opened a fine assortment of Goods, recently purchased in New York, consisting in part of
Gunny and Kentucky Bagging, Rope, Twine, Coffee, Salt, Crushed, Loaf and Brown Sugars, Molasses, Swedes Iron, Cast Steel, Nails, Train and Linseed Oil, Blankets, Homespuns, Ladies' and gentlemen's Saddles, Boots and Shoes,
Yarns, Kerseys, Sole Leather, Horse Collars, Riding and blind Bridles, Trace and Fifth Chains,
Powder, Lead, Shot, Spice, Pepper, Ginger, Indigo,
Madder, Copperass, Saleratus, Blue Stone, Saltpetre, Pearl Starch, Wool and Fur Hats. Caps,
A choice lot of Ready made Clothing,
Gentlemen's fine Cloaks, fine and common Trunks, and a limited but well selected stock of Dry Goods, all of which he will sell low for cash, or exchange for Country Produce, viz: Cotton, Corn, Meal, Flour, Wheat, &c. He solicits a call from ALL. A. DULIN,
Near the stand of J. Norcross.
Atlanta, Nov. 20, 1847. 29

Hat and Cap Store.
Belden & Co., (*Late G. A Kimberly.*)

WOULD invite the attention of the Merchants of Atlanta and adjoining counties to their large assortment of Hats, Caps, Straw and Fur Goods, &c. Our Hats are all made at our own Manufactory, 181 Water street, New York, and as to style and quality, cannot be beat. Those wishing to buy for their own use or to sell again, can get bargains for cash or good credit. Store on Mulberry street, sign of the big Hat.
Macon, Nov. 13, 1847. 6m28

New and Desirable Goods!
Just the kinds Wanted!
Every body Come and See—Come and See!

DON'T go near those Houses whose proprietors are too stingy to Advertise, [Good advice—EDITOR] or whose goods will not bear recommendation, and who have no pity on the Poor Printer. [Handsomely expressed—ED.] Come where you will find the best assortment in town—consisting of Buggy Springs, Axels, and all other kinds of Iron and Trimmings necessary for Buggies; Cutlery and Hardware of every description; Groceries, Dry Goods, and a great variety of other articles too numerous to mention, making the best assortment in town—all of which were selected with great care in the City of New York, and paid for in cash—except what was bought on credit! Come and take a look, if you don't buy. It will make you feel good to look at good, handsome and cheap articles. J. NORCROSS.
Atlanta, October 30, 1847.

Bacon and Lard, &c.

4,000 pounds Bacon Sides,
1,000 do. Shoulders,
700 pounds best Lard,
2,000 " Union White Lead, warranted No. 1,
for sale by A. DULIN.
november 20 39

A beautiful lot of Glass and Crockery ware, consisting of Flower Vases, Lamp shades, &c.
Syrups, Cordials and Wines of various kinds, of the best quality.
Cigars and Cigar cases and holders, Chewing and Smoking Tobacco, among which will be found Anderson's celebrated "fine cut;" Snuff, Pipes, &c.
FAMILY GROCERIES.—Loaf, powdered, crushed and brown Sugars; black and hyson Teas; Coffee, Chocolate, Mackerel, pickled Shad, dried Beef, smoked Herrings, Bologna Sausages Rice fancy wax, sperm and tallow Candles; butter water, sugar, soda and lemon Crackers, Starch, &c.
MEDICINES, etc.—Castor Oil and Spirits Turpentine, by the bottle or gallon; sweet oil, salts, cream tartar, calomel, julup, rheubarb, ipecacuana, quinine, liquid and powder, eye water, laudanum, paregoric, sugar of lead, camphor, Bateman's drops, Spencer's and other pills, balsam copavia, opium, opeldeldoc, lunar costic, British oil, assafoetida, balsam wild cherry, seidlitz and soda powders, roach and bedbug bane, mercerial ointment, spirits nitre, lump and calcined magnesia, No 6, ox vomit, blue stone, Spanish brown, blistering ointment, madder, indigo, brimstone, sulphur, gum tragic, salt petre, gum arabic, paints, oils and varnishes, copperas, soda, salaeratus, &c. Also, a few more of those identical Razor Strops and Cement, which he will sell as cheap as offered by the Razor-strop man himself.
He will keep constantly on hand throughout the summer, a large supply of ICE; also, Lemons, Oranges, Pineapples, Cocoanuts, etc., in their season.
Call at the Bazar before you purchase elsewhere!
JOSIAH E. MADDOX.
Madison, April 24. 51.

Shaw's Furniture Store.

THE subscriber is still at his old stand, and has on hand a variety of Furniture, which he will sell on the most accommodating terms. Call and see. His stock consists, in part, of
Mahogany Dressing Bureaus, fine, with marble tops,
Mahogany Dressing Bureaus, plain, with marble tops.
Mahogany Bedsteads,
" Wash Stands,
" Work Tables,
" Rocking Chairs,
" Cribs,
" Candle Stands,
Curled Maple Bedsteads,
" Rocking Chairs.
Walnut Bureaus, Walnut Washstands,
" Tables, " Bedsteads,
Stained Bedsteads, Painted Safes,
Painted Wardrobes, Washstands,
A fine lot of CHAIRS just received from New York, consisting of Bronzed Chairs,
Gilded "
Table "
Office "
Plain Rocking "
" for children,
Counter Stools, &c., &c.
Also, some pictures representing the Battles fought by "Old Rough and Ready."
Furniture repaired, painted and varnished with despatch. ALFRED SHAW.
Madison, August 14. 5m15

New Marble Yard.

THE undersigned respectfully informs the citizens of Georgia, that he has established a Marble Yard in this place, where he design, carrying on the business in all its branches, and will in a few days receive a large supply of the finest Marble found in the United States, from the Massachusetts, Vermont, Dover and other quarries; also, Georgia Marble, from the best quarries in the State. He will also keep constantly on hand a good supply of Italian and Egyptian Marble, all of which he will sell as low as the lowest. Carving and Engraving executed in the most approved styles at Charleston and Augusta prices. Long experience and a thorough knowledge of the business he thinks will enable him to please all. The public are invited to call and examine his Marble and work before purchasing. His shop is adjoining F. C. McKinley's store, near the Georgia Rail-road Depot.
Orders solicited and promptly executed.
june 12 J. T. NIX.

Getting UP in the World.

CHARLES WHITING takes this method to inform his friends and the public generally, that he has removed from the shop which he has occupied for several years past to one
Over John Robson & Co.'s Store,
where he may be found at all times, ever ready to execute the orders of his customers. He will regularly receive the reports of Fashions from the North and pledges himself that his garments shall FIT as well, and be MADE as strong as can be done in the State.
Now let there be "such a getting up stairs" as never was seen before.
January 2, 1847. 36

Administrator's Sale.

ON Wednesday, the 29th day of December next, will be sold at the residence of the late Alston H. Green, deceased, in DeKalb county, the personal property of said deceased, consisting of household and kitchen furniture, horses, mules, jacks and jinnies, cows, hogs and sheep, wagons, carts, plantation tools of various kinds, a large quantity of corn and fodder, wheat, oats and cotton, and various other articles too tedious to mention. Terms of sale: for all sums over five dollars purchasers will be required to give their notes with good personal security, due 12 months after date—all sums under five dollars, cash. The sale to continue from day to day, until all is sold. The improved lands and ferry will be rented at the same time.
WILLIAM EZZARD, Admr.
nov. 13 28

AGREEABLY to an order from the Court of Ordinary for Morgan county, will be sold on the first Tuesday in January next before the Court House door in the Town of Madison, Morgan county, within the usual hours of sale, the negroes belonging to the estate of Robert H. Fretwell, deceased, to wit: Betsey, a girl about twelve years old, and George, a boy about eight years old, sold for benefit of the creditors of said deceased. Terms cash.
THOS. B. BALDWIN, Admr.
november 20 29

BY authority of an order granted by the honorable Inferior Court of Morgan county, when sitting for ordinary purposes, will be sold before the Court House door in the town of Madison, in said county, on the first Tuesday in January next, a Negro Boy named Greene, about thirteen years of age, belonging to the estate of Abel Brown, deceased, and sold for the benefit of his heirs and creditors. Terms on the day.
AMOS BROWN, Administrator.
october 30 26

AGREEABLY to an order from the Inferior Court of Morgan county, when sitting for ordinary purposes, will be sold on the first Tuesday in January next, before the Court House door in the town of Rome, Floyd county, four Town Lots—numbers fifty-seven, fifty-eight, seventy-three and seventy-four in the plan of said town—each containing one-fourth acre, more or less. Sold as the property of James B. Lewis, late of Jasper county, deceased, for the purpose of a distribution among the legatees. Terms made known on the day. WM. H. BROOKS, Guardian.
october 30 26

WILL be sold at the residence of Samuel Stovall, late of Morgan county, deceased, on Friday, the 14th day of January, 1848, all the household and kitchen furniture, stock of horses, hogs, cattle, corn, fodder, oats, &c., and a variety of other articles too numerous to mention—all belonging to the estate of said deceased. Terms on the day.
SAM'L W. STOVALL, } Adm'rs.
GEORGE STOVALL, }
november 27 30

WILL be sold on the second Monday, the 19th day of January next, at the late residence of John E. Adams, in the town of Decatur, in the county of DeKalb, all the perishable property belonging to the estate of said deceased, consisting of household and kitchen furniture, and various other articles; also, at the same time and place, the interest of said deceased it (being one-half) in the mules, wagons and tin ware yet on hand, belonging to the late firm of J. E. & G. Adams. The entire interest in the mules and wagons will be sold, by consent of the surviving partner. Terms cash.
J. W. KIRKPATRICK, Adm'r.
november 27 30

BOOK & JOB PRINTING,
OF EVERY DESCRIPTION,
——SUCH AS——

Pamphlets,	Posters,
Circulars,	Hand Bills,
Catalogues,	Legal Blanks,
Bill Heads,	Business Cards,
Bank Checks,	Address Cards,
Blank Notes,	Visiting Cards,
Labels, &c.	&c. &c, &c.

Neatly and expeditiously executed at the office of the SOUTHERN MISCELLANY, Atlanta, Georgia.
Orders respectfully solicited.

For Sale,

MY Plantation, one mile South of Madison, containing three hundred acres, more or less, which is in good repair; also 40 head of Stock Hogs. If not sold privately before that time, I will sell the same at public outcry on the first Tuesday in December next.
I hereby forbid all persons giving any member of my family credit on my account.
DAVID BYER.
august 21 tf 16

Ads from the December 4, 1847, issue of The Southern Miscellany, one of Atlanta's first newspapers, tell something of city life.

27

The Prelude To Conflict
1850-1860

At midpoint of the 19th Century the nation of 31 states and 23 million persons was on the threshhold of great expansion and a decade away from the internal explosion of emotions spawned by the slavery question.

The War for Texan Independence had been won; the discovery of California gold in 1848 triggered feverish migratory waves west and precipitated a new era of Indian conflict; telegraph lines linked remote settlements with the populous East; fingers of iron extended the reach of locomotives; colleges were chartered; convening women urged their rights. In the year when 350,000 immigrants came to America, the Compromise of 1850—a patchwork pact to soothe sectional feelings—sought to reduce the rising tumult over slavery.

The decade of 1850 heaved with political events that baffled President Fillmore, exposed the inadequacy of President Franklin Pierce, and sorely tested the Democratic straddler, President James Buchanan. In 1858 a relatively obscure Illinois politician named Abraham Lincoln tested his political beliefs under the banner of the newly organized Republican Party as he debated the "Little Giant," Stephen Douglas.

The literate masses read the works of Washington Irving, James Fenimore Cooper, Nathaniel Hawthorne, Herman Melville and Henry David Thoreau. But these works were largely entertainment; the novel that ignited sectional feeling over slavery was Harriet Beecher Stowe's *Uncle*

City Hall, erected in 1854, stood on the site of the present Capitol. In the early years, City Hall (pictured apparently in the 1870s) served also as the Fulton County Courthouse.

Tom's Cabin (1852), an abolitionist work that stirred passions as much as Stephen Foster's gentle songs calmed them.

The excitement over slavery reached a peak in October, 1859, when abolitionist Ossawattamie (John) Brown raided Harper's Ferry, Va., to arm a slave insurrection. He was arrested by troops led by Col. Robert E. Lee, and hanged.

As the nation began to heave over the increasing shrillness of the slavery debate, Atlanta in the 1850s continued a modest march toward commercial and social development, not untouched by the slavery question nor heavily embroiled in it, for the area was not plantation country. Atlanta's progress was rooted in the railroads which attracted citizens and service industries, and ironically made it a target for destruction.

Soon after a tunnel was bored in the Chetoogeta Mountain between Dalton and Chattanooga, rail service opened in 1850 to the Tennessee line; until then the "fast passenger train" from Atlanta to Dalton—99 miles—required seven hours, if a rail didn't jump its timber bed. Atlanta's inadequate wooden passenger depot was replaced in 1854 with a spacious brick structure (alongside present-day Underground Atlanta); it served until Sherman destroyed it 10 years later. When it was erected, the Georgia Western Railroad Co. was chartered but the rail project languished and war prevented its launching. The Georgia Air Line Railroad—a link to Charlotte—was chartered in 1856 but also delayed.

While Atlanta in 1850 could boast 2,500 residents (493 of them slaves), the total would only triple in 10 years. But the first city directory in 1859 lauded Atlanta's size (two miles in diameter), the medical college, availability of granite, brick and lumber, its freedom from disease, its numerous water wells, churches, public buildings and hospitality. "Our people," crowed the directory, "show their democratic impulses by each allowing his neighbor to attend to his own business, and our ladies even are allowed to attend to their domestic and household affairs without being ruled out of respectable society."

The city's seeds as a financial center were sown in 1852 when the Atlanta Bank was chartered, but its issuance of paper money (common among banks) was criticized by Northern papers, and the Bank experienced several "runs." It met its obligations, but the major stockholder, weary of the assaults, closed it in 1855. The Bank of Fulton, chartered in 1856, prospered until it suspended on the eve of Sherman's occupation, and was never reorganized.

Others were launched with varying success: the Atlanta Building and Loan Association (1853), the Atlanta Insurance and Banking Co., the Georgia Railroad and Banking Co., the Bank of the State of Georgia Agency, the Augusta Insurance and Banking Co. among them. All located their offices around the intersection of Whitehall (now Peachtree) and Alabama. But for many decades thereafter, Atlantans had to look north—to more stable financial institutions—for financing major improvements. By 1859 17 insurance companies were represented in Atlanta—including Aetna Fire Insurance Co., Hartford Fire Insurance Co., Manhattan Life Insurance Co. and State Fire Insurance Co.

The presence of fire insurance firms resulted from the town's risky reputation. Though 19 substantial brick structures were built in 1858, the majority were of wood, and fire was a constant, ugly threat. The first of a series of volunteer fire companies was organized in 1850, and its manually operated engine, named "Blue Dick," was the town's pride. It was in action early when robbers, seeking to divert attention while they pilfered the money drawer at the Georgia Railroad freight depot, set ablaze A. W. Wheat's store, warehouse and stable. The second fire company was organized in 1856, and others followed; it was 1882 before Atlanta got a paid fire department, and—luckily—

Three early Atlanta mayors: William Markham (far left) was the sixth mayor, serving only a few weeks in 1853 when his predecessor, Dr. Thomas Gibbs, retired due to ill health late in his one-year term. William M. Butt (center) succeeded Markham, serving in 1854. Allison Nelson (above) was Atlanta's eighth mayor, but in his seventh month of service, July, 1855, he resigned following a dispute with City Council. Nelson died seven years later as a Confederate general.

The City's first official seal

Atlanta's first rail depot—the "car shed"—was built in 1853. The building, which stood adjacent to the present-day Underground Atlanta section, was destroyed by Union troops in 1864.

The Census of 1850: 8 Ministers, 5 Lawyers, 85 With No Occupation

When the census-taker had finished his Atlanta survey in late 1850, he showed a population totaling 2,569—of whom 493 were slaves and 18 were "free Negroes."

Included in the tally by occupation were six blacksmiths, 70 carpenters, eight clergymen, one dentist, one druggist, 10 grocers, five lawyers, 38 merchants, eight physicians, three printers and three tailors.

Eighty-five listed no occupation—a hint that Atlanta was home for some ne'er-do-wells.

Engineer Edward A. Vincent's map of 1853—for which he received $100—was the city's first, and shows the convergence of three railroads. The black, roughly oval symbol (upper left) denoted the railroad roundhouse; rectangle in the center indicates the depot.

1917 before a huge conflagration destroyed a significant segment of the city. The biggest blaze came in 1864, courtesy of Sherman's troops, but that was no accident.

Politics provided another kind of heat. In a sort of separatist movement, citizens pressed in 1853 for formation of a new county with Atlanta as its seat, and in December Dr. N. L. Angier's suggestion that it be named Fulton won legislative approval.

Whether the name honors Hamilton Fulton, the 1826 surveyor of canals and railroads, or Robert Fulton (credited with inventing the steamboat) was debated for years. Logic points to the latter since his name is linked with transportation, as is Atlanta's. Besides, Hamilton Fulton quit state service before 1828, leaving no heavy imprint on its history. In 1853 City Council borrowed $10,000 to build a City Hall, and on its completion in 1854 it served also as County Courthouse. It was erected on the site of the present state Capitol.

The multipurpose 50-by-70-foot brick City Hall, demolished in 1884 to make way for the Capitol, was used by the Atlanta Medical College for lectures, by the Second Baptist Church for services, by firemen for a ball, and by a social club for a speech commemorating St. Patrick's Day.

The City Hall/Courthouse was parttime home to some of Atlanta's most besieged citizens: its mayors. The turbulent decade provided a host of civic problems including lawlessness and the nagging difficulties of shaping a hamlet into a more refined political entity. Indeed, one chief executive quit in disgust after a conflict with the City Council.

After portrait artist Wyllys Buell's term as mayor ended in 1850, citizens elected that law-and-order man, Jonathan Norcross, backed by the Moral Party. Norcross was anathema to the opposing Free and Rowdy Party which had helped Formwalt beat Norcross in the first election. Following Norcross' election in a bitter contest against lawyer and former councilman Leonard Simpson, the Rowdies threatened Norcross with mayhem if he tried to sanitize the town.

One accused tough, tried before the mayor, attempted to stab Norcross, who defended himself with a cane-bottom chair, and the miscreant fled. A gambler who had defied arrest was collared by a citizen and clapped in the calaboose, but Rowdies pried loose some logs and freed him. The next day the town was in an uproar and there was talk of riot.

The Rowdies placed a small cannon at Five Points, loaded it with powder and gravel, and fired it at Norcross' store, leaving his porch untidy. Also left by the criminals was a note saying the mayor would either resign or see his store blown up.

Citizens promptly rallied to Norcross' call for a volunteer police force, and the Rowdies also organized. Within hours after the cannon incident, citizens were guarding the Norcross store. At midnight Alexander W. Mitchell led volunteers against the Rowdy Party's headquarters at the corner of Decatur and Ivy, and arrested several Rowdies as others fled.

The whole town turned out the next day for the trials of those arrested. Most offenders were remanded to jail, thus breaking the back of the rebellion, though the volunteer police continued to control the scene for weeks. Never again was Norcross molested, though there were mailed threats. The mood of the enemy camp, Murrell's Row, was ugly, though some habitues departed to a nearby area dubbed Snake Nation. Soon thereafter, citizens made a nighttime raid on the Snake Nation, whipped a bunch of the Rowdies, ordered others to leave, shipped their

A volunteer fire company, lined up in a lot which is now beneath Alabama Street, was photographed in 1856 near the original frame passenger depot. That's Pryor Street crossing the railroad. The fire engine was called "Blue Dick"; the ladder truck, "Old Reliable."

John H. Mecaslin was secretary of the Atlanta (Volunteer) Fire Company No. 1 about 1858, and was chief of the Atlanta Volunteer Fire Department in 1864. He became president of the Atlanta Gas Light Co. in 1897, and chairman of the board in 1904.

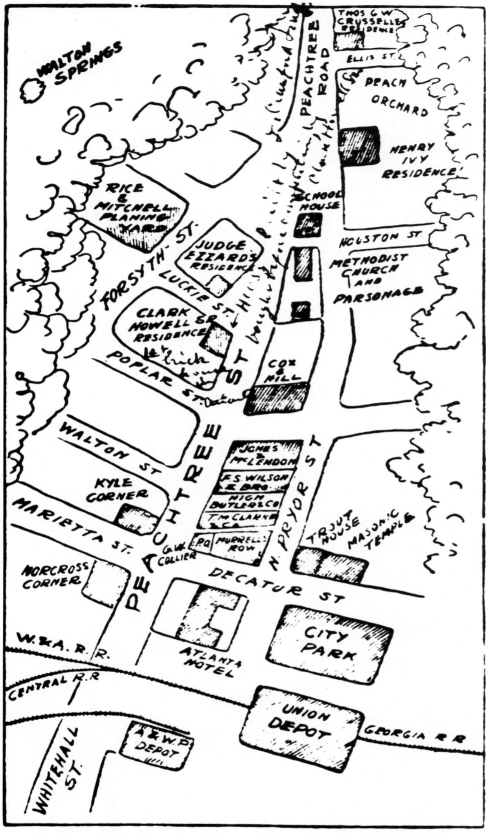

Downtown Atlanta in the 1850s was taking shape. Five Points was the ever-busy center (where Marietta, Peachtree and Decatur Streets still meet). Infamous Murrell's Row, hangout of the lower element, is shown at Decatur and North Pryor. Judge William Ezzard's residence stood on the site of the present Equitable Building. Walton Springs (upper left) was near the present-day Greyhound Bus station.

abandoned women to Decatur, and finally burned the Snake Nation (along Peters St.) and Slabtown shanties. The Snake Nation area later arose as a respectable residential area (Castleberry Hill), and then evolved into its present role as a business section.

The fifth mayor was the shadowy Dr. Thomas Gibbs, who arrived only two years before he was elected for his 1852 term, and left shortly after he was defeated for a second. During the one-year term of Gibbs' successor, John F. Mims, engineer Edward A. Vincent was authorized payment of $100 to create the city's first map. Mims' ill health forced his retirement late in his term, and William Markham was elected in November, 1853, to serve the remaining weeks. Following William M. Butt's term, Democrat Allison Nelson defeated Know Nothing Party candidate Ira O. McDaniel in a 425-415 contest in January, 1855. Cries of fraud were ignored.

Nelson, winner of the closest contest in Atlanta's mayoral history, gave up the office a scant six months later when the City Council reduced Nelson's fines of two men convicted of disturbing the peace. Angered over Council's failure to support his modest law-and-order instincts, Nelson resigned on the spot, moved to Texas, and died a Confederate general in 1862.

Councilman John Glen finished Nelson's aborted term, and lawyer William Ezzard was elected to succeed Glen in 1856, then re-elected, becoming the first mayor to serve two successive terms. Attorney Luther J. Glenn followed suit in January, 1858, winning re-election a year later. With some poetry, Luther Glenn said prophetically at his second inaugural: "Atlanta lies embosomed...diamond-like, in the very center of Georgia, yea, of the South, rough and unpolished as (Atlanta) may be, in the eyes of jealousy and prejudice, but destined...to becoming a bright and glittering jewel in the diadem of Southern cities..."

"Forward Atlanta" campaigns in the next century later did not boast better.

The city *was* "rough and unpolished," but hardly envied, despite improvements.

Until 1853 the noisome slaughterhouse was still within modest city limits, then was banished to the "suburbs." Only in April, 1855, did the first hospital open. Chief surgeon W. F. Westmoreland notified the public that "the usual fees...will be charged, with 15 cents per day for board..." At the same time the first medical society, the Brotherhood of Physicians, was formed, and the Atlanta Medical College was being organized. The *Atlanta Medical and Surgical Journal* published certain fees: A vaginal examination "with the finger" was $2-$5 (no reason given for the variance), or $5-$10 if done "with the speculum"; amputation at the hip joint ran $100-$200; natural labor was $10, with $15-$40 for a difficult one, and $25-$50 for delivery with instruments.

If the hospital had opened a few years

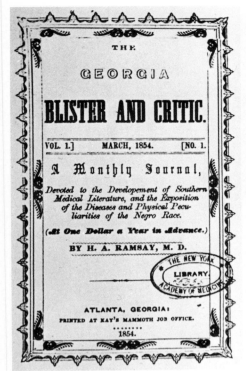

THE NEW YORK LIBRARY ACADEMY OF MEDICINE

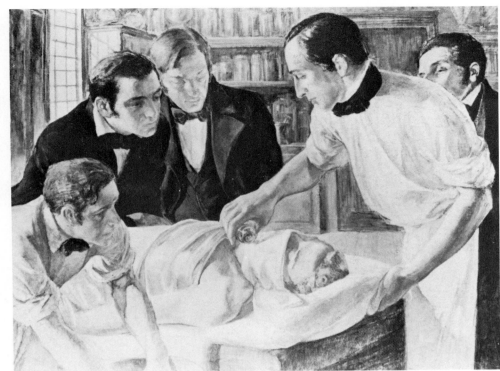

A medical journal, "The Georgia Blister and Critic," first appeared as a monthly journal in March, 1854. It was "Devoted to the Development of Southern Medical Literature and the Exposition of the Diseases and Physical Peculiarities of the Negro Race." The publication lasted a year.

Dr. Crawford Long, who lived briefly in Atlanta, is credited with being the first to use ether as an anesthetic during surgery. Dr. Long came to Atlanta in 1850 but remained only about a year before moving to Athens, Ga. He practised in Atlanta from his home which was at present-day Broad and Luckie.

Dr. P. P. d'Alvigny was a well known medico of Atlanta in the 1850s. It was he who slit the throat of the dead Dr. James Nissen in 1850, a promise the ailing Nissen had extracted for fear of being buried alive. D'Alvigny saved the Medical College from destruction by Union troops in 1864, when the building was used as a hospital, and some believe that d'Alvigny was the model for the character of "Dr. Meade" in "Gone With the Wind."

The Atlanta Medical College was chartered by the Legislature in 1854. The College, which initially used City Hall space for lectures, laid the cornerstone for the structure at left in 1855 (at Butler and Armstrong Streets). Dr. John G. Westmoreland was the prime mover and longtime guiding spirit in creation of the College.

Mr. and Mrs. Er Lawshe, pictured in the 1850s. He was a watchmaker and jeweler. Their spacious home, built in that decade, stood on the site of the present-day Peachtree Center.

A Scary Train Ride At 15 Miles Per Hour

For excitement in the 1850s, all you had to do was take a train ride from Marietta to Atlanta.

Dr. Henry C. Hornady, pastor of Atlanta's First Baptist Church from 1861 to 1867, recalled one such event:

"When we boarded the train at Marietta...the writer's nerves were not in first rate condition, he being somewhat dyspeptic, from too free indulgence in convention fare, and he could not avoid a cold shiver, when told that it was down grade to the Chattahoochee river, and when the engineer said he was behind time fifteen minutes, and he was bound to run into Atlanta on time, or run the thing off its wheels.

"I found myself clutching tightly the back of the seat in front, and preparing, as a prudent man should do, if there should come a sudden shock and crash which would tear things to splinters; nor was I reassured when holding my watch in full view I found that we were rushing along at the rate of fifteen miles an hour, and that the car was swaying from side to side like a ship in a billowy sea.

"Every nerve was wrought up to its utmost tension, and when we ran into the car-shed at Atlanta, and I found myself still together I breathed a sigh of relief, and immediately thanked God for escape from such dreadful peril."

earlier, a newcomer might have added his services to it. He was Dr. Crawford W. Long, first to use ether as an anesthetic during surgery. Dr. Long moved from Jefferson, Ga., in 1850, practicing from the home he erected on a $350 half-acre lot at Broad and Luckie. After a year, he apparently felt Atlanta lacked cultural opportunities for his two daughters, and moved to Athens.

The rudimentary nature of medicine at midcentury mandated a new cemetery. Before 1850 the only public burying ground lay along the side of west Peachtree Street, and included ground of today's Capital City Club. Unable to find reasonably priced land in the town's small confines, City Council that year bought a six-acre tract ($75 an acre) which became the nucleus of Oakland Cemetery (so named in 1876). In later years 85 acres were added.

Tradition holds that the first direct interment in Oakland was of James Nissen, a doctor who became ill while passing through in 1850. Having a mortal fear of burial alive, the ailing Nissen had asked Dr. Noel d'Alvigny a favor: In the event of death, Dr. d'Alvigny was to slit Nissen's jugular vein—just to make sure. It was done shortly after Nissen died on Sept. 22, 1850.

The first Jewish cemetery began as part of Oakland in 1860 when the City donated six corner lots to the Hebrew Benevolent Congregation. By about 1910 all of Oakland's lots were sold; thereafter it was possible to buy a plot only from its owner. More than 100,000 persons sleep in Oakland: Confederate soldiers, senators, governors, paupers, pioneers, millionaires and slaves as well as Pulitzer Prize-winner Margaret Mitchell, author of *Gone With the Wind,* and Martha Lumpkin, whose name was the first applied officially to Atlanta.

The cemetery was not, of course, the only civic advance of the 1850s. City Council authorized eight-foot-wide sidewalks, wells to aid firefighters, a 30-foot bridge (now part of Broad Street), street lamps and paving one or two streets, laying walking planks along others. Atlanta's first park, 1858, occupied the block between the railway station and Decatur Street. A jail was also built.

The need for a prison was obvious, for successive grand juries deplored rising lawlessness and one observed that crimes were "like the plagues of Egypt. When one (criminal) is removed from jail to be hanged ...there is another ready to step in..." But when the new jail, a 50-by-45 foot brick structure, opened in April, 1856, the inspecting grand jury criticized it: "The plan is defective, and the house wholly unfit for the safe keeping of prisoners..." Minor

The Er Lawshe home, shown about 1880, was used by the Union general, Prince Felix Salm-Salm, and his wife as their home during his brief posting as commander of the military district in 1865. She referred to it as a "little cottage." (The Prince died of wounds received in 1870 during the Franco-Prussian War.) The photograph shows members of the Lawshe family (the boy in front of the fence is astride a wooden velocipede) who occupied it until Lawshe's death in 1897. In 1912 the house gave way to business structures.

The John Neal residence (foreground) was built in 1859, and stood at 47 Washington Street. This view looks north along the west side of the street from south of Mitchell Street. The Neal house stood on grounds of the present City Hall, and was used by Gen. W. T. Sherman as his headquarters in the fall of 1864. The Neal home was used later as Girls' High School, and was demolished in 1929. Across Mitchell is shown the original Second Baptist Church; beyond it is the original Central Presbyterian Church.

The original First Presbyterian Church (dedicated in 1852, depicted in 1871) stood on Marietta Street on the site now occupied by the Federal Reserve Bank.

Banquet Toast Named Atlanta the 'Gate City'

Atlanta's designation as the "Gate City" originated as a banquet toast given in Charleston, S.C., in 1857, though the name of the person who coined the phrase is lost.

Following an odd ceremony when some water from the Mississippi River was conveyed through Atlanta for mingling with the Atlantic Ocean off Charleston, a banquet in the coastal city feted guests from Georgia and South Carolina.

As remembered by Atlanta Mayor William Ezzard, who was in Charleston at the time, the toast to Atlanta was: "The Gate City—the only tribute which she requires of those who pass through her boundaries is that they stop long enough to partake of the hospitality of her citizens."

Nedom L. Angier, who is credited with suggesting the name "Fulton" for the county, served as Atlanta's mayor in 1877 and 1878.

changes were made and the jail was destroyed in Sherman's torching of the city.

The town was rocked in the 1850s by several murders. When grocer Elijah Bird killed his brother-in-law, dentist Nathaniel Hilburn, Bird was sentenced to be "hung by the neck...until he is dead, dead, dead." But Bird was pardoned two years later by the legislature on condition he leave the state, and thereafter was killed by a plantation handyman who split his head with a hoe.

Six months after Hilburn's death, Atlanta's first mayor, Formwalt, was murdered by a prisoner. In 1853 John Humphries (son of the Whitehall tavern-keeper) killed Elisha Tiller, but was never tried, and later was involved with brother Asa in another killing. A slave named Frank, who got behind in his payments (for his freedom) to his blind master, W. H. Graham, so feared Graham's wrath that he killed him and was hanged. In 1855 Daniel Dougherty, founder of Atlanta's first bakery and operator of a tenpin alley, was stabbed to death on the street.

Buckhead's first homicide occurred on Christmas Day, 1856, during festivities including drinking and shooting at chickens for sport. Friends Henry Norton and Henry Irby scuffled over a raffle for a basket, and Irby's son, 14-year-old George, shot and killed Norton. The youngster was tried almost four years later, found guilty, and sentenced to two years imprisonment.

One of the period's more heinous crimes occurred in 1858 when John Cobb Jr., Gabriel Jones and R. J. Crockett murdered cotton merchant Samuel B. Landrum, who they suspected had $600 in his pocket. But Landrum had banked the money, and the trio got only $1.50. Cobb and Crockett were ultimately hanged, but Jones received a life sentence at Milledgeville. When convicts were released to fight against Sherman's march to the sea, Jones was among them. Later he fled the state; 25 years later Jones was reportedly living a reformed life in Philadelphia.

A similarly odd ending to murder was also seeded in the late 1850s. Prominent actor William A. Choice was served a bail process for a $10 debt by official Calvin Webb while both were at the bar in the Atlanta Hotel. Blows resulted but Mayor Glenn separated the two men. The next morning Choice killed Webb on the street and was sentenced to hang despite lawyer Ben Hill's defense plea of insanity. Just before the trapdoor dropped, Hill's influence won a legislative pardon for Choice, who remained briefly in an insane asylum, and later entered Confederate service as a sharpshooter. Almost 18 years after killing Webb, Choice died in a fall from the second story of a Rome, Ga., stable.

Apart from public safety, the most challenging local problem was general education. A true public school system was decades away. Though an inadequately financed "Poor School Fund" was overwhelmed by the need, some of Atlanta's well-to-do could afford a rudimentary education for their children.

In 1851 at least seven private academies opened, more than small Atlanta could sustain, even at rates charged by Prof. W. M. Janes: $4 per term for orthography, reading and writing; $6 for arithmetic, grammar and geography, and $8 for Latin, Greek and mathematics. Mrs. T. S. Ogilby's academy charged $10 a term for instruction in waxworks, fruit and flowers, and $12.50 for music and the use of a piano. Joel T. McGinty became principal of the Atlanta Male Academy in 1852 but died within a year.

The "Poor School Fund" helped support Atlanta's first attempt at public schools when the Holland Free School opened in 1853 but it lasted only five years, earning more grand jury praise than City Council support. Indeed there was great misunderstanding about the whole idea, necessity and support of public education, and lines were sharply drawn over qualifications of teachers, eligibility of "poor students" and source of funds. Under Gov. Joseph Brown's urging, the legislature in 1858 earmarked $100,000 annually from W. & A. earnings to educate those between 8 and 18, leaving with each county the power to find additional money. Some initial steps were taken but war halted progress.

Such uncertainties left the job of building moral behavior largely to the growing churches, which tried to grapple also with a problem cited by the grand jury in 1855: It denounced "as an intolerable grievance and evil of vast magnitude the herds of unruly and vicious boys who infest the streets...by day and night, especially on the Sabbath, to the great annoyance of...citizens...and recommend to the city authorities the adoption of stringent measures to abate the nuisance" which apparently parents could not mitigate.

The Roman Catholic Church in 1851, with Father J. F. O'Neill Jr. as pastor, built the Church of the Immaculate Conception, a wooden structure which stood until 1869, giving way to the building destroyed by fire in August, 1982. The initial $4,200 brick building of the Presbyterian Church was dedicated in July, 1852. Its bell

came partly from a contribution by John Silvey, the donation being made, it is said, on condition that no bell ringing would interrupt his sleep. Since Silvey bedded down in his home between the church and Spring Street by 7 p.m., the belfry was silent by dusk.

In 1850 the Peachtree Baptist Church was formed by 41 members who erected a log building at the present Briarcliff and LaVista Roads. War destroyed it and a frame structure replacement gave way to the present brick building completed in 1950. Trinity Methodist, which began as Mission Sunday School, was organized in 1853, led by Green B. Haygood; members secured a site opposite the first City Hall and the church, completed in 1854, remained there until 1874.

The Second Baptist Church was constituted in September, 1854; its 19 charter members erected a $14,000 church on their lot at Washington and Mitchell. Second Baptist merged in 1933 with Ponce de Leon Baptist to form Second Ponce de Leon Baptist at Peachtree and West Wesley. Original Second Baptist was the mother church of others, among them Church of Immanuel Baptist, Woodward Ave. Baptist, Baptist Tabernacle, Central Baptist, Jones Ave. Baptist, Temple Baptist and Capitol Ave. Baptist.

Other civilizing influences emerged in the 1850s. The first of five Masonic

Joseph E. Brown, chosen as Georgia's chief executive in 1857, served four consecutive terms as governor, and was also a U. S. senator who was prominent in Atlanta's civic affairs. He and Confederate President Jefferson Davis often clashed over military decisions. A statue of Brown and his wife is on the grounds of the State Capitol. Their son Joseph served as governor for two terms.

City Council of the 1850s: Keeping the Peace—and More

More than a century hence, those who read of Atlanta's history of the 1980s may find City Council actions quaint, if not funny. Whatever the readers' reaction, they will learn something of the city's life in the debates, petitions and actions of that governing body—much as we do when we read of Council activities of the 1850s. A sampling follows:

1852: Each councilman is to take his seat with his hat off when the Council is called to order. Fine of $1 for being 30 minutes tardy...Knives and forks purchased for the barbecue last year to be sold at auction as soon as possible... Rough seats made for the Council. Cost, $3...Slaves must have written permission to have spirits. No slave or other person of color could furnish liquor to another person of color. Penalty, 39 lashes on the bare back.

1854: Resolved, that Ransom, a slave belonging to the State of Georgia, be allowed to sell coffee, cakes, etc., in the passenger depot, for the accommodation of passengers...A bill was presented in favor of Er Lawshe (jeweler) for a clock and City Seal, amounting to $21. Ordered

paid...Marshal still reported chasing stray hogs...Council voted $500, and private citizens subscribed $385 for relief of sufferers of yellow fever in Savannah.

1856: Night watch accused of sleeping on duty, but excused...The petition of a Negro to open an ice cream saloon was refused as being unwise.

1858: E. W. Holland, having been fined $10 in each of two cases for allowing his slave to live on separate lots from him, appealed the mayor's decision to the full Council. The fines were increased to $20 in each case...An ordinance was passed prescribing a severe penalty for defacing tombstones in the cemetery (Oakland)... Edward Everett invited to come any time to deliver an oration on Washington. *(Author's note: Everett is best known for the four-hour oration he delivered in November, 1863, at the dedication of the National Cemetery at Gettysburg, Pa., but it Lincoln's speech—fewer than 200 words—which is better remembered, and recited.)*...Houses of ill fame declared a nuisance, and fine not exceeding $50 prescribed for violation of the ordinance ...The Council offered $25,000 and a 1,000 acre site provided the University of

the South—chartered earlier in the year —would be located in Atlanta. *(Author's note: It went to Sewanee, Tenn.)*...The marshal reported that the discrepancy in his accounts was caused from the fact that he had given away dog collars to the poor.

1859: Fish to be retailed nowhere in the city except in the Market House. Fine of $25 for violation...Many citizens petitioned the Council to require G. W. Collier to remove the scaffolding and embankments from around his new building at the corner of Decatur and Peachtree, "as he has had ample time to have completed the building twice over." ...Resolution adopted requiring better looking telegraph poles on Whitehall Street...An ordinance was passed imposing a $200 tax on free persons of color, to be paid within 10 days after coming to the city, if allowed to remain...A check for $15 was issued to Thomas M. Jones for taking to Walton County, for interment, the remains of John Cobb Jr., who was hanged for being a murderer...Petition that Alabama Street be changed to "Front Street" and houses numbered. Laid on the table.

This house, built by Stanley Root, was the Washington Street residence of former Gov. Joseph and Mrs. Brown, beginning in 1865 (photographed about 1880).

The house was designed by architect John Boutelle for himself, and built in 1852 at the southwest corner of present-day Courtland and Avenue and Ellis Street. The house was demolished in 1938.

Two sisters posed primly 120 years ago: Israella (left) and Rebecca Ella Solomons. The latter became Mrs. Julius M. Alexander (son Henry was one of the lawyers defending Leo Frank in his 1913 murder trial), and was the paternal grandmother of present-day architect Cecil Alexander.

Theatrical Attractions Included 'Blind Tom'

A few years after a Daniel Emmett minstrel tune was heard in an 1850 New York show, it had become the most widely heard Confederate anthem. The tune was *Dixie Land,* and Southern soldiers marched to its spirited cadences. But it was not the only music heard in early-day Atlanta.

Atlanta's one antebellum theatre was The Athenaeum, which could seat 700, and it was the scene of various entertainments including the Empire Minstrels, in 1857. Local groups such as the Evening Star Band—six players including a cellist, fiddlers, horn player and flutist—were favorites in the Fifties. And Atlanta's first city directory (1859) listed availability of the Fulton Brass and String Band.

But the most extraordinary figure on the Atlanta concert stage of the 1850s was "Blind Tom" Meefie, reportedly the son of slaves and the property of T. G. Bethune, a south Georgia plantation owner.

Tom, said to have been born blind in 1849, was regarded as an idiot—but with a vast musical talent first displayed at age four when he was able to play on the piano those tunes he had only just heard.

Tom first appeared in Atlanta in 1857, managed by the Bethunes, and five times in the 1860s.

"We never saw a more idiotic-looking Negro than Tom," observed the *Southern Confederacy* after an 1861 performance, "and his intellect is truly very feeble...He has a remarkably fine sense of hearing and the most extraordinary faculty of imitation...

"The most difficult and lengthy pieces are performed by him on his hearing them once...His fingers move with the rapidity of the wings of a hummingbird...and he never makes a mistake..."

At age 16, it was reported, he appeared in a concert simultaneously playing *Dixie* with one hand, *Yankee Doodle* with the other and sang *The Girl I Left Behind Me.* He is also credited with being the composer of a work representing the Battle of Manassas.

lodges chartered in that decade was Fulton #216, begun in 1857. By 1859 the fraternity's hall at Alabama and Loyd Streets was inadequate. E. E. Rawson agreed the Masons could house their activities in the second floor of his new building if they built the upper story. That Masonic Hall survived the war but fire destroyed it in May, 1866. The YMCA came to Atlanta in 1857 and while war forced it to disband, it later re-emerged. In 1858 the Hibernian Benevolent Society was formed principally to aid Irish immigrants; it developed into a mutual aid society but functioned primarily as a social group.

Though these amenities continued to attract newcomers, Atlanta's commercial energy gave the pulse to daily living. To the cotton warehouses, stores, railroad and banking entities and liquor shops were added a steam flouring mill, an iron foundry, machine shop, carriage shops, tanneries and other enterprises.

Charles Heinz came in 1854 to open a gun shop. It later manufactured rifles for the Confederate troops, and after the war John Berkele, Heinz' brother-in-law, became associated with the shop that bore their names. The four-story Trout House, a hotel, lasted from 1854 until Sherman's destruction. Shoemaker Christian Kontz, a linguist and member of the *Liederkranz* (musical club), developed a fine trade. Irish-

born Thomas Haverty signified his intention in court in 1852 to forego his allegiance to Queen Victoria, lived here briefly before working on the railroad in Tennessee, and then returned; among his five children James J. Haverty especially made marks on the city's business, religious and cultural life.

Joseph Winship, who had been involved in a tannery and a cotton gin, arrived in 1851 and set up a freight car factory; great-grandson Robert Winship Woodruff became the prime mover of The Coca-Cola Company, the city's greatest philanthropist, and is the soft drink company's most powerful executive. Thomas G. Healey arrived in 1852 and joined with Julius A. Hayden in the brick manufacturing business. After the Civil War, Healey and Maxwell R. Berry were partners in building many well-known structures including the Church of the Immaculate Conception and the U.S. Customs House (now the site of the Bank of the South, at Forsyth and Marietta). The older of Healey's two sons, William T., erected the Healey Building, while *his* two sons, William T., and Oliver M., built the William-Oliver Building in 1930.

Atlanta's oldest continuing corporate citizen was launched in 1856 when the legislature authorized the Atlanta Gas Light Company. The City Council-ap-

Two early-day mayors: William Ezzard (left), who served four terms—1856-57, 1860 and 1870—and Luther Glenn, who served in 1858 and 1859.

The home of Lemuel P. Grant, who donated the land for the park named for him, was built in 1858 on St. Paul's Avenue (photographed in 1938). It was used as a hospital in 1864. It was Grant who developed the line of fortifications around Atlanta in a vain attempt to protect it from Union troops.

proved proposal indicated that the coal-gas works would cost $50,000, with the City being required to take $20,000 of the gas company's stock, erect 50 street lamps and pay the Company $1,500 a year for keeping them all lit. The Council's approval of the proposal by William Helme, of Philadelphia, to erect the works, gave him the exclusive privilege of such a system for 50 years.

Atlanta's continued growth attracted more publications—primarily special-interest or party newspapers. Survival was painful. *The Atlanta Republican* is a case in point: It emerged as a temperance paper in 1851, was merged with *The Discipline* in 1855, went daily in 1858, became known as the *Gate City Guardian* and, later, as *The Southern Confederacy* after combining with a paper of that name. Another party journal, *The Whig Reveille,* appeared for four months in 1852, dying when its presidential hopeful, Gen. Winfield Scott, lost to Democrat Franklin Pierce.

A more substantial organ, *The Weekly Examiner,* began in July, 1854, and went daily the next month; but financial difficulties led the *Examiner* to merge with the veteran daily *Intelligencer,* the most durable of the early papers. But it, too, succumbed soon after *The Atlanta Constitution* emerged in 1868.

Specialized journals made brief splashes. *The Georgia Blister and Critic,* a medical monthly, published only for a year after its March, 1854, debut. The weekly *Literary and Temperance Crusader* (which moved from Penfield), lasted in Atlanta from 1859 until war came in 1861. *The Medical and Literary Weekly* also emerged in 1859.

The general journals in the 1850s devoted space to politics, agricultural fairs (Richard Peters won a $5 prize for showing his red heifer, Jenny Lind, and $3 for his bull DeKalb at the 1850 fair), circuses and sideshows and, by 1855, the attractions at the city's first regular theatre, The Athenaeum. Mr. and Mrs. W. H. Crisp made the theatre—on the second story of a building on Decatur Street—home for their acting troupe.

Cost of printing supplies and equipment and scarcity of paper undermined the best-intentioned editors. And news was in short supply. One editor warned he would soon have to advertise for "a dreadful accident maker, or make one" himself. Subscribers were loathe to pay: One collector reported that his 117 calls netted $3.12, added that he had thrashed several delinquents and admitted that occasionally he "got licked like thunder" himself. Ad revenue was chancy: When the president of the Georgia Temperance Society was asked how long he'd continue to run liquor advertising in his paper, he replied: "Just as long as it pays the printer's bill."

Among editors who quit in disgust over their lot was John Harney. He left town,

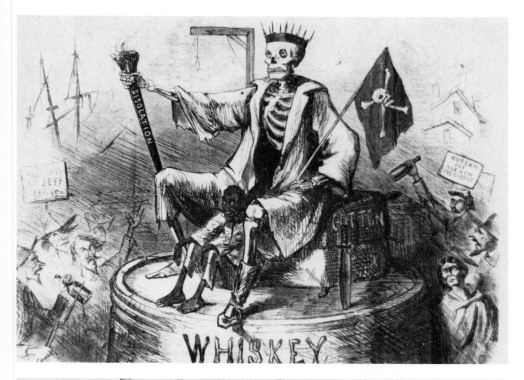

Propaganda War: The Savaging Of Jeff Davis

The pro-Union periodical *Harper's Weekly* carried on a propaganda campaign during the war to boost the morale of its Northern readers and demoralize Southerners who might see the publication.

One of its constants was the savaging of Confederate President Jefferson Davis, pictured persistently as a grim skeleton.

In the top cartoon, a crowned Davis sits atop a bale of cotton—his throne—which rests on a huge barrel of whisky. Between his bony knees, a slave; in his hand is a sceptre labeled "Desolation."

In a coach labeled "Rebellion" (left), a skeleton drives passenger Davis past a signpost labeled "To The Last Ditch."

Davis as grim reaper (lower left) harvests skulls, the toll of war.

Mocking Southern claims of victory, a Confederate newsboy scurries with news—but the point is that the message is not conquest, but death.

MAUD PRESTON PALENSKE
MEMORIAL LIBRARY
St. Joseph, Michigan 49085

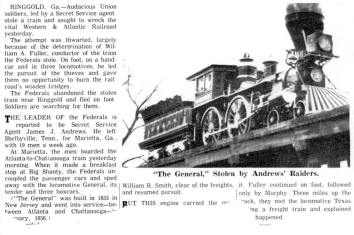

A Train Stolen on the W. & A!

RINGGOLD, Ga.—Audacious Union soldiers, led by a Secret Service agent stole a train and sought to wreck the vital Western & Atlantic Railroad yesterday.

The attempt was thwarted, largely because of the determination of William A. Fuller, conductor of the train the Federals stole. On foot, on a hand-car and in three locomotives, he led the pursuit of the thieves and gave them no opportunity to burn the rail road's wooden bridges.

The Federals abandoned the stolen train near Ringgold and fled on foot Soldiers are searching for them.

THE LEADER OF the Federals is reported to be Secret Service Agent James J. Andrews. He left Shelbyville, Tenn., for Marietta, Ga., with 19 men a week ago.

At Marietta, the men boarded the Atlanta-to-Chattanooga train yesterday morning. When it made a breakfast stop at Big Shanty, the Federals uncoupled the passenger cars and sped away with the locomotive General, its tender and three boxcars.

("The General" was built in 1855 in New Jersey and went into service—between Atlanta and Chattanooga—...nuary, 1856.)
...ended.

"The General," Stolen by Andrews' Raiders.

William R. Smith, clear of the freights, and resumed pursuit.

BUT THIS engine carried the m...

it. Fuller continued on foot, followed only by Murphy. Three miles up the track, they met the locomotive Texas ...ing a freight train and explained happened.
...

The theft of "The General" at Kennesaw was exciting news for Atlantans in April, 1862.

Big Shanty (near present Kennesaw) as it looked in 1862—when "The General" was stolen

James J. Andrews led the band which captured "The General." He was hanged in Atlanta two months later.

Capt. W. A. Fuller was "The General's" conductor—and led the chase to recapture the locomotive.

This was wartime Atlanta, showing the passenger depot at left, before the city's capture by Sherman. In the foreground is Whitehall Street, where army wagons (left) wait to cross the tracks. The Rock Depot of the Macon & Western Railroad is in the middle (to the right of the engine smoke).

Confederate Gen. Joseph Johnston had the task of stopping Gen. W. T. Sherman, but was relieved of command before Atlanta was assaulted.

The Battle of Lookout Mountain in late November, 1863, resulted in a Union victory, and set the stage for the Atlanta campaign, which began the following spring.

Gen. W. T. Sherman's capture of Atlanta won President Lincoln's thanks.

The W & A railroad machine shop and roundhouse in Atlanta, before the city was captured in September, 1864. The view is west, from about Broad Street, showing the Forsyth Street crossing (foreground).

Not Everybody Wanted to Fight

An unknown number of Southerners —including some in Atlanta—took an approved way out of military service by hiring substitutes.

Among them was the diarist and stationer S. P. Richards and his older brother Jabez. In September, 1862, they joined an exempted volunteer fire company since, as S. P. Richards noted in his diary, "It may be the means of preventing our being conscripted." But within weeks, he observed that the firemen weren't exempt and that officials were "taking up conscripts vigorously."

So he took a parttime job as a proofreader for the *Baptist Banner*, since printers were at the time exempt; but being uncertain of this protection, he hired a substitute. In the summer of 1863 Richards took other protection to avoid conscription by joining the Atlanta Press Guards, a home defense unit; but to do that he had to join the printing profession so he bought a share of the *Baptist Banner*. "Our company," he wrote, "does not expect or wish to do much duty; as one of the members remarked, our object is to have as little to do as possible."

Richards and his brother bought the *Soldier's Friend*, a religious publication, in August, 1863, to further establish their identity as printers, even though they believed they might be purchasing "an elephant."

Stationer Richards never was conscripted. During Sherman's occupation in the fall of 1864, he refugeed north, but returned to Atlanta almost a year later— to go into business again.

Ridiculing lagging recruitment efforts in the North, a "Harper's Weekly" cartoon suggested fathers could help by offering daughters as lures.

Atlanta merchant and diarist S. P. Richards was one of those who sought exemption from soldiering.

Continued from Page 42

"paying the highest market price"; the Dill & Rasberry picture gallery boasted that "all pictures taken by us are of artistic merit," and "no humbugging" in the use of "the largest Solar Camera"; W. W. Spalding assured patrons of the Trout House that his bar was "stocked with the choicest liquors and cigars"; two more banks opened, and railroad travelers paid $5.50 for the nine-hour run between Atlanta and Augusta, and $21 for the trip to New York.

Considerable energies were spent on speculating whom the South would favor in the November election for president. One wing of the Democrats backed Stephen Douglas; another, John Breckinridge. The old Whig and American parties were reconstituted as the Constitutional Union party, and backed by John Bell.

A week before the election Douglas arrived in Atlanta. After Alexander Stephens introduced him by endorsing Douglas' doctrine of territorial sovereignty, Douglas spoke for two hours, converting few listeners. The next day the Minute Men Association of Fulton County was formed to support states' rights, and defend homes and honor from a "black Republican" government.

Two days after Lincoln was elected (Douglas ran a poor third in Atlanta where Bell was favored), the Minute Men pledged to follow Georgia and any other state "in forming a Southern Confederacy." And two days after South Carolina seceded on Dec. 20, the Minute Men held a demonstration with speeches, the firing of 15 guns and

a torchlight procession in which Lincoln was burned in effigy.

As if signaling the awesome events to come, Nature rocked Atlanta on Jan. 3, 1861, with a 10-second earthquake. *The Intelligencer* hoped that its brevity would be "symbolical of the present political convulsion..." On Jan. 19 Georgia seceded, and the storm of disunion began quickly to gather.

A week after delegates in Montgomery, Ala., named Jefferson Davis president of the Confederate States of America (and Stephens, an opponent of secession, as vice president), Davis visited Atlanta where Mayor Jared I. Whitaker and other dignitaries feted him.

The visit stirred great enthusiasm and patriotic fervor, only slightly dampened when the city lost its bid to become the Confederate capital. To show its support, Atlanta in mid-February sent 18 regulars— its first—to Savannah to join state forces. When Stephens visited Atlanta March 12, a few days after Lincoln's inaugural, crowds applauded his assurance that Ft. Sumter would surrender in 10 days. While he believed peace would then prevail, preparedness for war, said Stephens, was the surest road to peace. That formula had become a cliché in history.

Ft. Sumter fell a month after Stephens' visit, but Lincoln took South Carolina's seizure as an act of war, not a signal for negotiation, and called for 75,000 volunteers. Atlanta, too, had begun to mass men: The Gate City Guard, 75 strong, left April 1 for Pensacola, Fla.; the

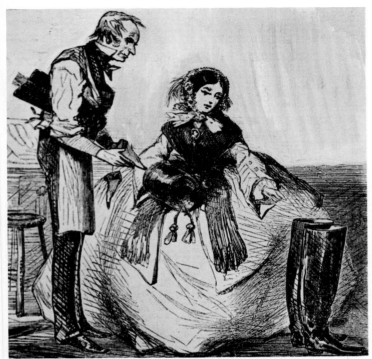

"Harper's Weekly" satirized young ladies and the wartime "Big Boot Mania." The caption had this one saying she preferred the cavalry boots made for "Col. Sabretash."

"Frank Leslie's Illustrated Newspaper" depicted Lincoln uncomfortably "supporting the dignity of my high office by force."

grand jury urged that militia units be organized and armed; the volunteer firemen of the city's four companies offered themselves for duty, and hundreds joined infantry units colorfully dubbed the Atlanta Grays, the Fulton Blues, the Jackson Guards, the Confederate Continentals and the Bartow Avengers.

Typical of the separatist movement was the April, 1861, decision by a convention of the Georgia Medical Association to secede from the American Medical Association.

Atlanta in 1861 was being turned into an arsenal, a conversion which, along with its centrality as a railhead, would spell its doom. W. & A. Railroad forges were appropriated by Gov. Brown to make gun barrels, and the firm of Peck and Day aided in manufacturing the famous "Georgia Pike," for which it received an order of 10,000. But not every firm or individual yielded to the State's demands. When the State wanted to buy Frank Rice's land (where the Candler Building now stands) for use by the Commisary Department and offered to pay in Confederate bonds, Rice balked: He wisely preferred gold. The State then confiscated the property, and erected a building that for almost 60 years after the war served as a school for black children.

The press became suspect. The grand jury called on "all proper authorities to exercise great vigilance (and) enforce the laws strictly against the circulation of all incendiary publications..." The watchfulness and criticism would mount against the newspapers, which had problems of their own: shortages of newsprint, lack of reliable news-gathering sources, high postage rates and the ban of reporters by some generals.

Atlantans moved in 1861 to strengthen the home front. Some elderly gentlemen formed the "Silver Grays" to protect the city and do relief work. Sixteen doctors promised free medical treatment to "destitute families" of soldiers. Property owner Larkin Davis offered eight of his Whitehall Street rooms rent free to such families as long as the war lasted. Amateur concerts raised funds for food and clothing, and J. F. Ezzard's store offered to donate material for soldiers' pants if ladies volunteered to do the sewing. Churches, schools and other civic organizations contributed material aid or staged fund-raising benefits.

The local celebration following news of Virginia's secession in April, 1861, was echoed three months later when Atlantans heard the outcome of the Battle of Bull Run. The seemingly easy Confederate victory hinted a short war, but joy turned to grief as casualty lists identified some of Atlanta's best citizens. The litany of sorrow rose as reports of other battles struck home: Phillippi, Big Bethel, Carthage, Manassas Junction, Wilson's Creek, Cheat Mountain and Ball's Bluff. There would be no short war, but in Georgia only its coastal islands were held by Union troops for more than two years.

The ever-effective Union blockade, however, was soon felt in Atlanta. Hard money such as silver coin disappeared, and shinplasters became substitutes. Newspapers condemned hoarders: the grand jury damned "those capitalists who are using their means to speculate and reap immense profits upon the necessaries of life" which were becoming scarce: salt, flour, bacon and leather goods. A grimness set in, scarcely relieved by *The Intelligencer's* punny attempts at humor: Observing that the Union army was to be uni-

"Harper's Weekly" cartoon appeared to be a thinly veiled attack on bearded Gen. U. S. Grant for his reported love of the bottle. The caption read: "No, it isn't regular drinking that hurts a man; it's this way you fellers 've got of drinking between drinks."

The first government vessel to be named "Atlanta" was this blockade runner used by the Confederacy in the Civil War.

The Confederate prison camp Andersonville, near Columbus, Ga., in August, 1864; in the foreground, a row of latrines.

formed in blue, the paper joked that, "It is a step in the right direction as blue does not run."

In the spring of 1862, two years before Sherman began the campaign climaxed by seizure of Atlanta, its citizens felt a taste of nearby action.

J. J. Andrews gathered 22 men in a Union scheme to cut the W. & A. Railroad between the city and Chattanooga. Having spent the night of April 11 in Marietta, the Andrews raiders boarded the unguarded locomotive General during its 20-minute stop at Big Shanty (now Kennesaw), as conductor William A. Fuller, engineer Jeff Cain and shop foreman Anthony Murphy breakfasted at the Lacy House.

As Andrews' raiders started north, Fuller, Cain and Murphy—first thinking the locomotive and three boxcars had been stolen by Confederate deserters—pursued in a handcar. Up the line the trio commandeered the locomotive Yonah, but at Kingston the Yonah was bogged down in freight yard congestion, and the pursuers boarded the William R. Smith, with Oliver R. Harbin at the throttle. Near Adairsville the raiders' removal of two rails halted the Smith; Fuller and Murphy ran two miles on foot (the consumptive Cain dropped out, exhausted), and flagged the locomotive Texas, Peter Bracken in charge. The Texas gave chase, running in reverse.

The General, set free of two boxcars, gave out of wood and water two miles above Ringgold; the raiders fled to the woods, but within days all had been captured by alerted militiamen and jailed in Chattanooga. In May, 1862, Andrews and seven raiders were sentenced to be

The handsome C. W. Motes struck an earnest pose in his Confederate uniform in 1862. After the war, he was well known as a fine studio photographer in Atlanta.

The map shows the line of Gen. Sherman's campaign—from Chattanooga to Atlanta—in 1864.

hanged; after Andrews escaped briefly and was recaptured, all were returned to Atlanta. Andrews was hanged June 7 (at the present intersection of Juniper and Third Streets); seven more raiders were hanged June 18 (near the present intersection of Memorial Drive and Park Ave.). Eight raiders escaped the Fulton County jail on Oct. 16, 1862, and made their way to Union lines; six others were exchanged as prisoners of war the following year. One of them—William Pittenger—later wrote *"The Great Locomotive Chase."*

In 1887 the bodies of Andrews and the seven others hanged were re-interred in the National Cemetery at Chattanooga, buried in a semi-circle at the focus of which is a granite pedestal, dedicated by Ohio, topped by a bronze reproduction of the General. (The six raiders paroled were later awarded the first Congressional Medals of Honor.)

In April, 1862—a year after Ft. Sumter's capture—the original flood of patriotism which brought thousands of men to the Confederate colors had waned. Many of those who had enlisted for a year declined to re-enlist, and many able-bodied men hired substitutes to take their places in the thinning Confederate ranks. Thus the Confederacy had to resort to conscription.

The enrolling officer for Atlanta posted a call in October, 1862, requiring all men between 18 and 35 to sign up, warning "delinquents and skulkers of their peril in attempting to evade the high...obligation... to their duty... Such vast and holy interests as you are now called upon to defend and pluck from danger must not be trifled with. The government expects that every man will do his duty..."

Atlanta itself was becoming increasingly a supply and hospital city. There were appeals for contributions to aid the poor

Behind conquering Union troops, many slaves moved off by torchlight to freedom. The sketch is by the famed Civil War artist A. R. Waud.

On the battlefield near Atlanta: "the last full measure of devotion"

men suffering winter in Virginia; a large general hospital was set up, and public and private buildings were converted into smaller clinics. Early in 1862 there were 3,000-4,000 sick soldiers convalescing in the city, their pain being somewhat relieved by distributions made by the Ladies Soldiers' Relief Society: It delivered an array of items ranging from shirts, drawers and pants to liquor, food, catsup, castor oil, honey and even spittoons.

The Atlanta Rolling Mills made heavy plate for gunboats, including the ironclad Merrimac; there were factories making pistols, buttons, belt buckles, saddlery, canteens, tents, Bowie knives, gun carriages, cartridges, swords, shirts, jackets, hats, pants and shoes. Churches were begged for their bells, to be converted into cannon, and Atlanta's ladies were asked to contribute milk and vegetables for sick soldiers.

Atlanta first became a military post in May, 1862, and fell under martial law three months later, the latter action creating considerable discontent. This was followed shortly by Gen. Braxton Bragg's appointment of James M. Calhoun, mayor since January, as "civil governor," an act which baffled His Honor since there was no law defining his duties. Made aware of Calhoun's unwanted elevation, Vice President Stephens indicated that Gen. Bragg had no more authority to name a civil governor than could any prostitute.

Calhoun may not have wanted to be mayor more than one term, either, but he served four years in a row, and was the chief executive who surrendered the city to Sherman's forces.

A modicum of civilized life remained, however increasingly strained. In 1862 the young could take lessons at Prof. Nott's Dancing Academy ("politeness and polished manners will be taught in a style that can nowhere else be attained to such perfection"). Barber Henry Young's Confederate Shop charged 25 cents for cutting hair; and the Athenaeum staged plays such

as *King Richard III* and *Romeo and Juliet.* But 1862 closed with the city suffering a siege of smallpox so severe that military authorities seized 155 acres of William Markham's land (between the present Grant and Ormewood Parks) to establish a hospital. Compulsory vaccination was ordered, and red flags fluttered from places where smallpox had struck.

It was a somber Christmas in many homes. Diarist S. P. Richards wrote that their "fine rooster...tasted quite as well as turkey." Another citizen recorded that at his family dinner "we...made the turkey squawk. He was worse cut up than Burnside at the Battle of Fredericksburg."

The same Richards, who chronicled so much valuable minutiae of the period, still hoped for an early end to the war. Lincoln's New Year's Day issuance of the Emancipation Proclamation drew Richards' bitter reaction: "This is the day for Abe Lincoln to issue his dreadful ukase which will set the sable sons of Africa all free and independent! In the face of the defeats which his grand armies have met with recently, the world will laugh to scorn such a Proclamation."

Though Lincoln's act had more propaganda than military value, the world did not laugh. And the armies, recuperating in winter quarters, were preparing for the year that proved decisive: 1863 was the turning point, when Confederate territory began to shrink.

In May, 1863, when Confederate Gen. T. J. ("Stonewall") Jackson was killed accidentally by his own men, Union troops took Jackson, Miss., thus firming up the line of control to captured New Orleans. In June Federal forces began pushing Confederates out of Tennessee; in early July twin blows struck Confederate hopes—the fall of Vicksburg, Miss., and the Battle of Gettysburg, where Gen. R. E. Lee's advance was checked. The "high water mark" of the Confederacy had been reached.

In early September, Knoxville fell to the Federals, and on Sept. 19-20 occurred the first major engagement on Georgia soil—the Battle of Chickamauga. Within days, Confederate troops exited Chattanooga, and the stage was set for Sherman's invasion of Georgia after winter's thaw. In November Lincoln gave a brief address at the dedication of the Gettysburg Cemetery, spelling out in memorable cadences the compelling purposes of the war as he saw them.

The fall of Vicksburg created deep concern in Atlanta. *The Intelligencer* pointed out the military consequences and added: "If Atlanta should fall, the backbone of the Confederacy would be, for a time at least, broken." Not even the guarded *Intelligencer* would admit that a corpse with a broken backbone was ultimately doomed, not just crippled "for a time at least."

The Union's arc of control—from the Mississippi Valley east to Chattanooga—

RAILROAD STATION ATLANTA 1860.

The railroad passenger depot at in Atlanta—before Union troops captured the city

stirred more than editorial speculation in Atlanta. Eleven days after Vicksburg's fall, Col. L. P. Grant, chief engineer of the Department of Georgia, and Col. M. H. Wright began mapping areas around Atlanta, particularly along the Chattahoochee, and by early August, 1863, defensive works were begun. Col. Grant that month began hiring blacks for $25 a month to work on Atlanta's forts.

A 10-mile line of 17 redoubts, linking rifle pits and almost encircling Atlanta, were well under way within three months. The radial distance of the line averaged little more than a mile from Five Points.

The effects of the ever-nearer fighting were strongly felt in Atlanta. Hundreds of injured troops poured into the city, as did the first men in blue—prisoners captured at Chickamauga. Confederate desertions also plagued the area. Citizens were forced to sell cheaply their carriage horses, on State orders; the animals were needed for the cavalry. The city, now further burdened with people refugeeing south, had become an army post, with various installations dotting the downtown.

When obtainable, certain items had soared in price. Coffee was $4 a pound; lead pencils, $1.50 each; playing cards, $5 a pack; flour, $75 a barrel; buttermilk, a dollar a gallon.

A new draft call was issued in July, hard on the heels of Mayor Calhoun's proclamation warning of the possibility of a Union raid. Only days before, citizens had been heartened by a visit of Gen. Nathan Bedford Forrest; he was presented a magnificent charger, its cost subscribed by admiring residents. New military units were formed, including the Independent State (Rail) Road Guards captained by

William A. Fuller, who led the chase of Andrews' raiders the year before. To help the Confederacy raise funds, the central government imposed a war tax on goods— two and one half per cent on gross sales. And to aid soldiers' families, the Fire Department hosted a ball.

The election of Mayor Calhoun to an unprecedented third term demonstrated a vote of confidence, but there was no zealous competition for the job, as Calhoun might have wished. The state's chief executive, Gov. Joseph Brown, defied precedent by being elected over two opponents to a fourth consecutive term.

Within days after their elections, two military decisions were made, setting in place the two key army protagonists into whose hands fell the fate of Atlanta. The Federal troops based at Chattanooga and Dalton at the turn of 1864 were placed under the command of Maj.-Gen. William T. Sherman; the conduct of the Confederate Army of Tennessee was placed under Gen. Joseph E. Johnston, following Bragg's request that he be relieved of its command.

Sherman's supply lines were longer than those of Johnston, who drew on materiel massed less than 100 miles south in Atlanta. But Sherman's 100,000 men were supported by 254 guns; only 60,000 Confederate troops and 187 guns at Dalton confronted him.

Sherman's objective was simply stated by Gen. U. S. Grant's directive: "Move against Johnston's army to break it up, and get into the interior of the enemy's country as far as you can, inflicting all the damage you can against their resources."

The prime "resource" was Atlanta—and 1864 was its year of destiny.

Marching to the Tunes Of Different Drummers

The onset of the Civil War stimulated the creation of musical groups to cheer the citizens, and spawned much sheet music.

Soon after the conflict began, three local bands were available for hire: the Young American Cornet Band, the Starlight Brass Band, and the Gate City Silver Band.

Bands played such new tunes as *Confederate's Grand March* and the *General Joseph E. Johnston Manassas Quick March*. Among the sentimental favorites were *Dear Mother, I've Come Home to Die* and *Farewell to the Star Spangled Banner*.

Even during Sherman's occupation of the city (September to mid-November, 1864) there were 17 concerts, plays and entertainments at The Athenaeum, with music supplied by the band of the 33rd Massachusetts Volunteers. Some proceeds went to Mrs. Rebecca Welch, an Atlantan who lost her husband and a son in the war, and had six other children to raise.

The Athenaeum burned in the Sherman-set fires of 1864, and it is said that when the general began his March to the Sea, his band played *The Miserere* from Verdi's *Il Trovatore*.

1864: Year Of Destiny

1864-1865

As Atlanta perfected its line of defenses early in 1864, few could foresee its fate nine months later. Yet the civic fabric was being strained and torn as the demands of war took their toll. Events 100 miles north preoccupied all conversations, and the visit of President Davis some weeks before and the February arrival of Gen. John Hunt Morgan, a recent escapee from an Ohio prison, offered little lasting cheer in the face of realities.

The Intelligencer bravely suggested that battles around "Chickamauga and Ringgold warn the enemy of what they may expect should they repeat the experiment of entering upon the soil of Georgia..." But its readers found that bravado weak in the face of reported demoralization in Johnston's ranks.

They were depressed further by reports of "Peace Societies" being formed in the state, and by Gen. Lee's plea for food for starving troops tortured by Virginia's brittle winter. Asked how the troops would be fed, President Davis reportedly observed, "I don't see why rats, if fat, are not as good as squirrels. Our men *did* eat mule meat at Vicksburg; but *it* would be an expensive luxury now."

As conditions worsened, criticism was turned inward and outward. Some papers scorned Gov. Brown's resistance to Davis' central authority. Others rapped Davis' conduct of the war, even proposing that Lee replace him as a dictator.

Shortages of meat, salt and bread plagued Atlanta, where boarding houses were condemned for charging $105 a week for room and board. "What makes it worse," said *The Intelligencer,* "is the miserable fare..." Nor did bread shortages stop the stills from steaming out liquor. The depreciation of Confederate currency caused further havoc, and speculation remained rife. "Too many Christians," said *The Intelligencer* in March, 1864, "pray for each other on Sunday and prey on each other through the week."

Continued on Page 57

Atlanta, 1864: The photograph is taken from Ellis Street, between Courtland and Clifford.

During a truce in the Battle of Kennesaw Mountain (June 27, 1864), Confederates (left) watch Federal troops recover their wounded from the burning timber.

Gen. W. T. Sherman's advance: view of the military college near Marietta (July, 1864)

ATLANTA, BEFORE THE FALL, 1864

This remarkable reconstruction of the downtown Atlanta area in 1864 was drawn by Wilbur Kurtz, based on the historical data. A grid has been applied so that the reader can identify certain key sites of 1864 and relate them to contemporary scenes. Street names used in the key (below) are the current ones. The view is toward the southeast.

B-4 *City Hall; now the site of the state Capitol.*
B-6 *Central Presbyterian Church (Washington Street)*
B-7 *Second Baptist Church (northwest corner of Washington and Mitchell Streets)*
C-8 *Roman Catholic Church of the Immaculate Conception (corner Central Avenue—formerly Loyd—and Martin Luther King Drive)*
D-7 *Central Avenue (formerly Loyd Street)*
E-2 *Washington Hall hotel (at Wall and Central)*
E-6, 7 *Area of the Underground Atlanta section*
F-3, 5 *City park*
F-7 *The railroad passenger depot (adjacent to Underground Atlanta)*
F-10, 11 *Railroad tracks*
F-12 *Office of The Atlanta Intelligencer newspaper (east side of Peachtree Street between Alabama Street and Plaza Park)*
GH-8 *Atlanta Hotel (at Pryor, Decatur and Wall Streets)*
G-10 *Georgia Railroad Bank Building (northeast corner of Peachtree and Wall Streets; now the Peters Building)*
H-8 *Five Points (then and now)*
H-17 *Broad Street Bridge (first bridge to span the railroad tracks)*
I-8 *Collier Building, which was at Five Points*
I-10 *Norcross Store, at today's Peachtree and Marietta; now the site of the First National Bank*
J-14 *Intersection of Marietta and Broad (then and now)*
L-13 *St. Luke's Episcopal Church (then at Walton and Forsyth, now the site of the Grant Building)*

Atlanta's Whitehall Street between the tracks and Alabama Street: next to F. Geutebruck's store is a firm that sold queensware and held auctions and "Negro sales."

Continued from Page 54

The strains on Atlanta's resources were exacerbated by the flight of refugees to the city's comparative safety. Even three newspapers—*The Chattanooga Rebel, The Knoxville Register* and *The Memphis Appeal*—found temporary homes and brought to seven the number of papers in the city. (*The Rebel,* whose best-known writer was Henry Watterson, later the "Marse Henry" of the Louisville, Ky. *Courier-Journal*—found other sanctuaries briefly in Griffin, Macon, Columbus and Selma, Ala.)

In the turmoil Atlanta also had to contend with other stresses: demands for food to supply a new prison camp to the south, known as Andersonville; soldiers' families still begging for aid; "idle and vicious boys strolling about...frequenting many places of vice," and the stench of the slaughterhouses, which was as alarming as the threat of disease due to poorly observed sanitary regulations. "It being said that disease is more terrible than an army with banners," observed the grand jury in April, "we should be ready...to fight the one while...we remove the cause of the other."

Despite all the ominous signs, Gen. Howell Cobb was applauded when he addressed a rally. There is no reason to despair, he said; noting the swelling Atlanta population, he added that refugees were in Atlanta "because they loved liberty and the South more than their homes and property..." It was odd construction to explain their flight and plight. Cobb concluded ominously: "This is their fate today; it may be yours tomorrow..."

Indeed it would be, for the Federal army

Passageway to Anywhere

Atlantans, proud of the city's transportation centrality, often observe that whether one was going to Heaven or Hell, one had to change planes in Atlanta.

But they weren't the first to suggest that.

A *London* (England) *Times* reporter in the Confederacy, Francis C. Lawley, remarked in 1861 that "no one goes anywhere without passing through Atlanta."

As one man kept a lookout, Atlanta women and children huddled in a bombproof shelter in a garden.

The center of Atlanta, 1864

Gen. Nathan Bedford Forrest: His cavalry raids kept Union troops off guard. After war's end, he was a founder of the Ku Klux Klan.

Col. Lemuel P. Grant supervised construction of Atlanta's forts. After the war, his land donation became Grant Park, present site of the Cyclorama.

Gen. W. T. Sherman's troops (Gen. O. O. Howard's 14th Corps) cross the Chattahoochee River, west of Atlanta, on July 12, 1864.

View is north on Washington Street from south of Mitchell: Neal house (left) was Sherman's headquarters in Atlanta: old Second Baptist Church is in the middle distance; beyond it, the Central Presbyterian Church.

The view is looking east on Alabama Street from Whitehall (early 1864).

Atlanta, 1864: The view is south from the corner of Broad and Marietta Streets.

was ready to move.

Its stirring was not lost on Atlanta, where a wave of religious fervor brought crowds to churches nightly in May. "Many persons," observed *The Intelligencer*, "are seeking the way to become Christians." Atlanta's Episcopalians had already strained their only church, St. Philip's, and a new congregation began services in the Protestant Methodist Church. Episcopalians erected a $12,000 frame building by April: St. Luke's (fronting Walton Street between Broad and Forsyth).

At Dalton, Confederate Gen. John Bell Hood was baptized by the Episcopal bishop who had gone to war, Gen. Leonidas Polk. (Less than two months after St. Luke's opened it doors, Polk, killed at the Battle of Pine Mountain, lay on its altar; by mid-August damage from Union shells rendered the Church unusable, and Sherman-set fires destroyed it in mid-November.)

In early May, as Sherman's troops moved on Johnston at Dalton, thus beginning the Georgia campaign, Atlantans from 16 to 60 were ordered to City Hall to be armed and equipped for local defense, even as *The Intelligencer* sought to reduce

growing fear that Atlanta was marked for Federal conquest. "On the streets, every minute, the ravens are croaking," the newspaper carped. "There is a knot of them on the corner shaking their heads, with long faces and restless eyes...But we have no fear of the results, for Gen. Johnston and his great and invincible satellites are working out the problem of battle and victory at the great chess board at the front."

Perhaps the journal was bouyed by a fine military display on Marietta Street on May 17; nonetheless, Mayor Calhoun on May 23 issued a fresh call for troops "in view of the dangers which threaten us." He warned that "All male citizens who are not willing to defend their homes and families are requested to leave the city at their earliest convenience, as their presence only embarrasses the authorities and tends to the demoralization of others."

At the same time an acre of freshly dug graves at Oakland was being filled with soldiers. It was, said diarist Richards, "the saddest sight I have seen. Not a blade of grass is left growing there."

Sadder still for Atlantans was the realization that the Federal advance had

Prices of Foodstuffs Soared in Spring, 1864

In the spring of 1864 prices of foodstuffs in Atlanta rose to extraordinary levels.

In March flour was $1.25 a pound; sugar, $10; butter, $8; beef, $3.50; coffee, $15.

Sweet potatoes cost $16 a bushel and syrup was $20 a gallon.

A few days later Confederate paper money was devalued by one-third, forcing costs up again.

The Intelligencer Snipes

The sometimes waspish *Atlanta Intelligencer,* a pungent newspaper of the period, rapped doctors in one pithy comment:

"The initial 'M.D.' after a physician's name signify 'Money Down.'"

A Federal troop wagon train in Atlanta, fall of 1864

A train piled high with citizen belongings prepares to leave Atlanta in the summer of 1864.

begun in earnest, Sherman using traditional flanking movements, Johnston defending the spine of railroad. Johnston gave up Dalton on May 12, and during the bitter stalemate battle at Resaca May 14-15—just 18 miles south of Dalton—Federal troops threatened the line of communications in the Confederate rear.

Johnston withdrew May 17 to three miles north of Adairsville and, hours later, to Cassville. Disagreement among his corps commanders forced Johnston to pull back near Allatoona, expecting Sherman to follow over the rough terrain. But Sherman remembered his Georgia reconnaissance of 1844, and rather than risk a suicidal assault, sent troops south of Kingston. Johnston met them at New Hope Church, five miles north of Dallas (Paulding County).

For four days beginning in the rainy afternoon of May 25, Johnston protected the roads to Atlanta, losing an estimated 900 to 2,100 troops, while the bitterest battle of the campaign cost Sherman 3,000 to 4,500 casualties. The battle site, said Sherman's men, was the "Hell Hole," and Atlantans heard the boom-booming of cannon 25 miles to the west.

Failing to dislodge Johnston, the frustrated Sherman returned to control the railroad, occupied Big Shanty, threw his line north and westward of Kennesaw Mountain, and occupied Pine Mountain's base. At its top, where he had gone with Gens. Johnston and W. J. Hardee to observe the Federal lines, Polk—the Episcopal Bishop of Louisiana—was killed by a direct hit from a cannon shot.

For two weeks, as rain turned fields and roads into mud bogs, elements of each army probed the other along Kennesaw Mountain, where Johnston's troops were in control. On June 22 Hood led an assault at the Kolb farm, southwest of Marietta; the one-legged general was defeated.

Sherman assaulted the Confederate center with almost 14,000 troops on June 27; at Cheatham's Hill Federals lost 1,580 men, with Confederate casualties about 200. At another point, the assault cost 600 Federals and about 300 Confederates. The assaults failed; the wounded overwhelmed doctors and aides who worked by torchlight.

Sherman resumed his typical flanking maneuvers; by threatening the communication line to Atlanta, he forced a Confederate withdrawal on July 2.

To all but the most sanguine, Atlanta's fall seemed certain; only the timing was unknown.

As Sherman readied his crossing of the Chattahoochee, Union troops burned two Roswell cotton mills and a woolen mill (flying a French flag to pretend neutrality) which employed 400 women making Confederate goods. Sherman ordered the hanging of any "wretch" who flew the French flag while laboring "in open hostility to our government," and the arrest of "all

people...connected with those factories, no matter what the clamor... Let them foot it, under guard, to Marietta whence I will send them by cars to the north...The poor women will make a howl. Let them take along their children and clothing..."

After calvarymen destroyed Sweetwater Factory several miles south, all its employees were sent—with those from the other mills—to Jeffersonville, Ind. Some moved to Indianapolis after the war; most returned to the Atlanta area.

On July 8 the first Federal unit made a virtually unopposed crossing of the Chattahoochee, midway between Power's Ferry and Johnson's Ferry, again forcing a Confederate withdrawal. Gen. Johnston established headquarters three miles west of Atlanta, in the six-room Dexter Niles house on a lot at present-day 1030 West Marietta Street. That same day, Confederate materiel and hospitals were ordered away from Atlanta, further alarming citizens; some were packing to leave, as others had done.

Sherman set up headquarters at Vinings, moving to Power's Ferry on July 17, as thousands of Union troops poured across the river at Pace's Ferry, over the rebuilt bridge at Roswell, and Power's Ferry.

At this point, the long-smouldering distrust among Gen. Johnston, President Davis and the latter's new aide, Gen. Bragg (whom Johnston had replaced seven months earlier), flared anew. Bragg arrived in Atlanta on July 13, and predicted its evacuation. On July 14, Hood—commanding a corps under Johnston—wrote Bragg, charging Johnston with incompetence. Bragg visited Johnston twice, reported him "more inclined to fight" and the army's morale as "good."

In an exchange of messages with Davis on July 16, Johnston complained that he was outnumbered two to one, and that his position was defensive: "My plan of operations must, therefore, depend upon that of the enemy." Davis was not reassured. The following evening Johnston received a wire notifying him Secretary of War James Seddon had relieved him of command "as you have failed to arrest the advance of the enemy...and express no confidence that you can defeat or repel him..." Seddon replaced him with Hood, whom he wired: "Be wary no less than bold." Hardee, the senior corps commander, was angered by Hood's promotion over him, threatened to resign, but stayed.

The change of command did not win wholesale approval in the Confederate ranks. Many soldiers were shocked by Johnston's removal, distrusting Hood, who was unpopular with officers. Gen. Pat Cleburne hinted the death warrant for the army had been signed; Gen. A. P. Stewart called Johnston's removal the *coup de grace* to the Confederacy. Diarist Richards observed hopefully that "Old Pegleg"

Continued on Page 65

Ephraim G. Ponder's white house on Marietta Road (near present-day North Avenue) was near

Confederate entrenchments, and became the target for Federal artillery.

The Ponder house, occupied by Confederate sharpshooters, shows heavy damage by Federal shells.

(Smaller brick structure—at left— was the kitchen.) The house was never re-occupied.

Odyssey of a Pioneer: Ephraim G. Ponder

Ponder Avenue, a short span which springs off Marietta Street near Northside Drive, is named for a pioneer whose 65 slaves included two who left imprints on history.

Ephraim G. Ponder bought his land in 1857, erected a fine, two-story stone house, and moved his much-younger wife of five years into it. Behind it he erected frame buildings for his slaves, most of them skilled mechanics whom others hired.

One of them was Festus Flipper, who operated a postwar shoe shop on Decatur Street. One Flipper son, Henry, became the first black graduate of the U.S. Military Academy at West Point, in 1877. Another, Joseph, became a bishop of the African Methodist Episcopal Church, and served also as chancellor of Morris Brown University here.

In 1861, four years after the Ponders moved into their home, Ephraim filed for divorce. He alleged that his wife Ellen had committed adultery shortly after their marriage, that she was a drunkard and had threatened him with a pistol. The divorce was granted 10 years later.

But Ephraim had already left Atlanta: His home had been shelled by Union troops as they sought to dislodge Confederate sharpshooters hiding in the mansion.

Influx of Blacks Triggers Rumors At the Newspapers

Even if blacks in Atlanta had wanted to fight among Confederate troops early in the war, they were not allowed to join.

As the war got under way and the black population enlarged, Atlantans became increasingly alarmed over weakening of control over slaves. "Our negroes are not kept under proper discipline as they were a few months ago," the *Southern Confederacy* warned in August, 1861.

The papers were filled with rumors of "abolition spies," rude behavior and thievery downtown. Black entertainments such as "balls" were "so frequent" as to be a "nuisance," said *The Intelligencer* in December, 1861. It urged that all black assemblages be suppressed. A black picnic, which drew 300 persons to Stone Mountain in August, 1862, worried the whites.

Editors were also annoyed at the "habit of negroes hiring their time and making contracts with white men for the performance of work and charging the most exorbitant prices... It is absolutely shameful to see the liberties that negroes are taking... Slaves should be treated as such..."

Former Confederate Fort K was situated at the present-day intersection of Peachtree Street and Ponce de Leon Avenue, in the area of today's Fox Theatre.

Confederate Fort F was situated in the area of present-day Marietta Road, in the vicinity of Northside Drive.

Confederate Fort E was in the area of today's Atlanta University campus, around present-day Martin Luther King Drive and Chestnut Street.

One of Atlanta's forts whose construction was supervised by Col. Lemuel C. Grant; he later donated land which became Grant Park.

The railroad roundhouse and machine shops, targets of Sherman's troops

As the Battle of Atlanta rages around the Hurt house in July, 1864, a Union soldier ignores onrushing Confederates as he gives water to the wounded Southern soldier he has suddenly discovered is his brother. The detail is from the Battle of Atlanta Cyclorama painting (below), on display in Grant Park.

In this section of the Cyclorama, showing the Troup Hurt house, the Confederates of Manigault's brigade have captured the Federal position (the Hurt house) and are attempting to hold it against the counter-assaulting Union troops.

Continued from Page 60

(Hood) is "said to be a fighting man..."

As Hood charged the army with its task, Sherman made clear his overall plan for assault: Gen. George Thomas' men were to move generally on Atlanta itself, while Gen. J. M. Schofield pressed on Decatur, and Gen. J. B. McPherson—with Gen. Kenner Garrard's cavalry—was to destroy the Georgia Railroad line between Decatur and Stone Mountain. The Union commander, headquartered briefly in an old brick house at the corner of Peachtree and Old Cross Keys Road, even gave detailed instructions how to heat railroad rails and twist them into useless spirals. They became known as "Sherman's Neckties."

The key Confederate line assigned to meet the Federal advance from the north and east placed entrenched troops behind Peachtree Creek. The line began two miles from the river, crossed north of Crestlawn Cemetery, Howell Mill Road, Peachtree Road at Spring; at the intersection of Highland Avenue and Zimmer Drive, it turned south, parallel to Highland Avenue and Moreland Avenues, until it reached the Georgia Railroad at the DeKalb-Fulton County line, where it extended south to the intersection of Glenwood and Flat Shoals Avenues.

Before July 20th Union troops had breached positions at points along Peachtree Creek, and the Federal line massed along the ridge of Collier Road. Sherman was staying at the J. O. Powell house on what became the Emory University campus.

The maneuvering and probes came to a climax when Hood launched a delayed attack (giving Thomas time to get ready) in the late afternoon of July 20. In the two-hour Battle of Peachtree Creek, some units dashed forward north of Piedmont Park, moved in Collier's woods along Peachtree Road, and others in the matted brush of Peachtree Road. One heavily contested point was where Collier Road crosses the Tanyard Branch; another, where Collier Road joins Howell Mill. By dusk the battle ended—an unsuccessful beginning for Hood's defense of Atlanta: Union casualties totaled 1,710; Confederate, 4,796.

On the same day Union troops met resistance along Briarcliff Road, Rock Springs Road, and Leggett's Hill (where Flat Shoals joins Moreland). But late the following day, after flags of truce allowed both armies to bury their dead, Union troops drove the Confederates from Leggetts' Hill.

On July 21 Hood moved to flank Sherman's left—at East Atlanta—and assaulted the Federal front simultaneously. The flanking march led by Hardee began from Spring and Peachtree and proceeded down Peachtree to Five Points, raising rumors that Hood was leaving the city. By daybreak of July 22, Hardee was not where

Confederate breastworks near the base of Stone Mountain in 1864.

Hood wanted him. Hardee later moved forward, but his 15-mile march lacked the surprise Hood planned. A pitched encounter ensued, and it enlarged to become the Battle of Atlanta, beginning at Clay and Memorial Drive. During it, Gen. McPherson was killed when he disregarded Confederate commands to surrender as he reconnoitered.

Leggetts' Hill became the center of the infernal battle, and the air was thick with shrapnel, the shouts of death and hand-to-hand combat. On the evening of the 22nd, Leggetts' Hill remained a Union stronghold. But north of the railroad Confederates briefly gained their major success of the day by breaking the Federal line at the Hurt house before being forced back.

On the same day Gen. Wheeler's dismounted cavalry drove Federals from entrenchments in and around Decatur's Courthouse Square.

As night sealed July 22, Hood had failed to dislodge the Federals; he sustained 7,000 casualties to 2,000 for Sherman. Hood withdrew to Atlanta's inner ring of forts.

Within the irregular circle of entrenchments, the town was in turmoil. Stores, warehouses and the post office were broken into by looters on rumors Hood was evacuating. With departing refugees clogging the roads, the town's last paper, *The Memphis Appeal,* also fled. With churches closed, people gathered at revivals. Mail piled up, incapable of delivery. Drunken soldiers infested the town, jeering at the lines of shadowy prisoners, and no woman felt safe on the streets.

Fires erupted from shells lobbed into the town. The first shelling victim, a little girl, was killed as she walked with her parents at Ivy and Ellis Streets. Trains continued to arrive empty and leave full. Many built bomb-proof cellars ("gopher holes"); one was big enough for 26 huddled

Quarreling, Card Playing Earned Punishment in 1863

The Atlanta City Code of 1863 laid down some stiff fines for those who, in the officials' view, "disturbed the peace." Some excerpts:

"1. No man slave or person of color shall walk with a cane...nor smoke a pipe or cigar in any street...(punishment) not exceeding 39 lashes...

"2. Any person or persons who shall keep a disorderly house or house of ill fame...shall pay a fine not exceeding $50 and shall be imprisoned in the Calaboose, not exceeding 30 days...

"**3. Any person who shall** hereafter suffer his or her hog or hogs to run at large in any street or public place in the City of Atlanta...shall...pay a fine of not exceeding $50...

"4. It shall be the duty of the marshal... to arrest...every slave who shall hire his or her time...to have and enjoy the privilege of laboring or carrying on business for himself or herself...

"5. No person shall work, or in any wise labor or cause any work to be done on the Sabbath day, except it be of necessity, in the City of Atlanta...

"6. Any (white) person...guilty of...quarreling...pay a fine of not exceeding $50...

"7. Any slave or person of color drunk, quarreling, fighting or playing cards for money...(punishment) not exceeding 39 lashes to be inflicted on the offender..."

Union Gen. James Birdseye McPherson, one of Gen. Sherman's closest and most beloved officers, was killed on July 22, 1864, while reconnoitering the Battle of Atlanta. Ft. McPherson, in south Atlanta, is named for this officer who died at 35. At the time of his death, McPherson was commander of the Army of Tennessee.

An upright cannon barrel topped by a ball, at the present intersection of McPherson Avenue and Monument Avenue, marks the precise site of Gen. McPherson's death.

residents. When scarce coffee was available, it sold for $20 a pound, sugar for $15, flour for $300 a barrel. A restaurant breakfast of ham and eggs with coffee cost $25. Butter, chicken and eggs virtually disappeared from private homes.

The Southern Confederacy, before moving to Columbus, still tried to echo the diminishing optimism of another paper, *The Intelligencer,* which went to Macon. *The Confederacy* said Atlanta was in "imminent danger" but "its capture...cannot be considered a foregone conclusion." Gov. Brown, meeting with the City Council, conceded that a crisis was at hand. From Virginia, Gen. Lee had written Davis: "We may lose Atlanta and the army, too. Hood is a bold fighter. I am doubtful as to other qualities necessary."

And in the midst of the turmoil residents shared some grim humor.

One man, sitting in the second story of his house, was knocked to the ground when a shell struck the building. His wife, who had escaped to safety, asked him: "Where is the left wing of the house?" And her husband replied: "Don't ask me. I couldn't bring it with me. It was all I could do to get here myself."

And a Federal soldier called to a Southerner in the trenches: "Well, Johnny how many of you are left?" And the Confederate replied: "Oh, about enough for another killing."

Killing on a larger scale soon erupted

again. By July 28th, Sherman had positioned major concentrations west of Atlanta to cut the two lines of railroads still open to Hood. The Confederate general moved to confront Sherman near Ezra Church, and the battle began about noon on Gordon Road (at the juncture of Anderson Ave.). Within three hours of fierce fighting, Hood's attempt to halt three army corps with three small divisions proved appallingly costly: Confederate casualties numbered 5,000; Union, 600.

The Confederate setback at Ezra Church was followed by shelling of Atlanta by siege guns, and a Federal drive begining August 4 to find the weak spots in Hood's defense of the railroads. The resultant clashes around Utoy Creek brought little Federal success—and a new phase, the increasingly heavy bombardment of Atlanta, was begun.

The Atlanta Intelligencer, safe in Macon, predicted early in August: "The Yankee forces will disappear from before Atlanta before the end of August." Its rationale for optimism wasn't given; indeed, the loss of Atlanta never seemed surer.

Desperate Hood, with 42,000 men left to face 85,000 Federals plus cavalry, soon sent Gen. Wheeler's 4,500 cavalrymen to cut Sherman's supply line to Chattanooga, hoping to effect a Federal withdrawal. A frontal attack on Sherman would have been suicidal, as Davis agreed.

Using 4½-inch siege guns brought from

Chattanooga, Sherman stepped up the bombardment. Among other buildings the Trout House was struck, as was Market Place, where shopping women were knocked to the ground. Churches were struck; a few soldiers, parents and children killed. Humorist Charles H. Smith, known as "Bill Arp," observed that "the shells fall as thick as Gov. Brown's proclamations." Citizens urged Hood to rescind his order that trains toot their whistles often to make Federals think reinforcements were arriving: The "tooting," they complained, also drew shellfire.

August 9, when the city suffered its heaviest bombardment, became, in memory, "that red day...when all the fires of hell, and all the thunders of the universe, seemed to be blazing and roaring over Atlanta."

Eleven Federal batteries and 10 Confederate units dueled. The latter included a huge cannon dragged to Peachtree and Ponce de Leon over a three-day period. In the inferno the city was struck by an estimated 5,000 shells. Streets filled with rubble of falling buildings which became blazing traps the volunteer fireman rarely contained. In the midst of the confusion 1,700 steers, captured in Wheeler's north Georgia raid, bellowed through the streets, destined for the army.

Atlantans smiled wryly when they heard of a soldier who was unhurt when the sack of corn on his back was struck by shrapnel: "That," wagged an onlooker, "goes against the grain."

The great wonder of the shelling was that perhaps only 20 citizens had been killed. Finally, on August 25, a relative silence fell: The bombing stopped as Sherman lifted the siege, not because of Hood's protests to him, but because he had developed other plans.

The bombardment imperiled thousands of noncombatants—innocent women and children—Hood protested. Sherman's reply was unequivocal: War, he said, was the science of barbarism, and one of its objects was to devastate enemy country. Further, Atlanta could not be regarded as a peaceable community since it was a key supply depot and manufacturing center. Sherman charged that Hood was responsible for the presence of women and children, and that he was cowardly in seeking shelter among the defenseless, then appealing for mercy.

When Sherman lifted the siege, the armies had been at virtual stalemate for almost four weeks. Union forces moved August 26 on Rough and Ready and Jonesboro, striking the A. & W. P. railroad at Red Oak and Fairburn to cut Hood's remaining rail line south—the Macon & Western (now Central of Georgia).

Hood responded and on August 31 the Battle of Jonesboro began. But hearing of a move on Rough and Ready, and thinking this an attempt by Sherman to assault Atlanta from the south, Hood withdrew

some units from Jonesboro, and one Confederate corps was nearly captured before retreating to Lovejoy's Station. Hood's reactions were poorly organized: Federal movements left Hardee's corps hemmed in at Jonesboro, another corps was between Jonesboro and Atlanta, and a third—supported by state militia—within the city. The overpowered Hood decided he must evacuate Atlanta or be cut to pieces.

Atlanta was in a state of virtual anarchy on September 1, troops moving with great dispatch, confused citizens seemingly unable to grasp the inevitable. By 5 p.m. Hood's evacuation was under way. By midnight most of the troops had gone, stripping gardens on the way. Some cavalrymen lingered to carry out Hood's orders: In five hours before dawn they blew up Hood's ammunition trains on the Georgia Railroad opposite Oakland Cemetery: seven locomotives and 81 loaded cars. The explosions rocked the area, shattered glass and sent fiery fragments spewing as awed hundreds watched the volcanic eruptions.

Then, silence. Some citizens waited in their damaged homes, pistols at the ready. The human fringes of war—stragglers, deserters, looters—plundered stores and homes in the city's center. A few who had supported the Confederacy now asked pro-Union residents to use their influence with Federal troops to protect their property. But in the early hours of September 2, no troops entered. There was little to do but wait. Sherman himself—26 miles away —was not certain, that morning, that the city lay open. But units under Gen. Slocum acted on his certain belief that Hood had left, and moved toward the city along the present Bankhead Avenue.

Mayor Calhoun, deciding the city had to be formally surrendered to save it further harm, met with members of the City Council and other leaders on horseback at

At Kennesaw Mountain Battlefield National Park stands the simple marker of a Union captain, Ohio's S. M. Neighbour, killed June 27, 1864.

A recent photo shows the lamp post, at the corner of Alabama and Whitehall, where barber Solomon Luckie was killed Aug. 10, 1864. Note the shell hole in the base.

Atlanta Mayor James M. Calhoun (right, on white horse) surrenders the city to an advance unit of Union troops, met on Marietta Road near present-day Northside Drive. The date: Sept. 2, 1864.

Stationer Richards Foresaw Postwar Riches in Slaves

Like some other Atlantans, stationer and diarist S. P. Richards believed in mid-1863 that war's end would create a kind of bonanza for slaveholders.

Noting that he had bought a 14-year-old girl, Ellen, "just at the right time," Richards added in his journal for May 2 that "she would sell now readily for $2,000."

He added:

"I must make out descriptive lists of my darkies...for future reference. It is said, and I think with truth, that when we come to a successful end to this war that Negroes will command very high prices, as there will be so much demand for labor to raise cotton, and a great many will have been taken away by the Yankees."

Richards was no prophet, but he did prosper after the war. He founded the S. P. Richards Paper Company. He died in 1910.

Marietta and Peachtree. And soon a group of them, unarmed and carrying a white flag, picked their way west through the rubble on Marietta. Beyond abandoned Fort Hood, where Curran Street originated at Marietta, the Calhoun contingent met Federal troops under Capt. H. M. Scott.

Calhoun was advised that Sherman was near Jonesboro, and that Gen. Slocum was nearby. Troops under Col. John Coburn came up and the officer advised Calhoun to write a surrender note to the nearest Federal officer, Gen. William T. Ward.

"Sir: The fortune of war," Calhoun penciled the note, "has placed Atlanta in your hands. As mayor of the city I ask protection to noncombatants and private property."

About 11 a.m. Calhoun's group returned to Atlanta, and by noon Marietta Street was filled with men in blue. Pro-Union residents greeted them enthusiastically; others expressed their distaste. A musical debate erupted with boys whistling *"Dixie"* and *"The Bonnie Blue Flag"* as Union bands countered with *"Yankee Doodle"* and *"The Battle Hymn of the Republic."*

The first troops to reach the center of the city, the 2nd Massachusetts Regiment, occupied City Hall and lofted the Union flag where it had not flown since early 1861. Some looting of stores—by Federals and a rabble of men, women and children—occurred in the midst of sporadic shooting that afternoon and Saturday, as soldiers looked especially for liquor. The following day, 1,800 Confederate prisoners taken at Jonesboro were marched through Atlanta to the loud cheers of Union troops.

The fall of Atlanta Sept. 2 climaxed the fighting war for its citizens, but not the agony. As citizens began to deal with the impact of Union control—which meant evacuation for many, loss of their property, personal deprivation and ruin—Lincoln

was joyous. The conquest spelled not only military victory but greatly advanced his hope of re-election among Northerners weary of war.

The first phase of the war was over for weary Atlanta; the second phase—occupation and destruction—was about to begin. The fighting war would endure elsewhere for more than seven months, and after Sherman left Atlanta in mid-November for his historic "March to the Sea," some Atlantans began to return to their ruined city. It was not yet 17 years an incorporated town when devastation came, but in that period something indefinable had been born among its pioneers and newcomers—a spirit exemplified in a motto adopted later: *"Resurgens."*

But before Atlanta could begin to rebuild, it had to face new and terrible realities: destruction and the harsh years of Reconstruction.

The fall of Atlanta triggered Southern recriminations, reassurances and predictions among Confederate newspapers and leaders. "President Davis (is) the guilty cause of our failures," charged *The Intelligencer*. The *Richmond (Va.) Whig* blamed Hood as young and inexperienced. The *Augusta (Ga.) Chronicle* called Atlanta's loss "a great disaster," but "not irreparable"; the paper exhorted the people to fight on. The *Richmond (Va.) Dispatch* said the fall "in itself is no misfortune whatsoever," but conceded the loss would strengthen Northern resolve. Said Gen. Robert E. Lee: "The fall of Atlanta is a blow to us, which is not very grievous and which I hope we will soon recover from."

But these were distant voices, eyeing reality in the prism of hope. In Atlanta, matters were "very grievous" indeed, and Hood's pleas to Davis, forewarning calamity if no troops came forth to prevent Sherman from overrunning Georgia, earned only this reply: "No...resource remains."

Bivouacked at Lovejoy's Station, Hood could only watch helplessly as Sherman ordered Gen. Thomas to occupy the city, Gen. O. O. Howard to hold East Point, and Gen. Schofield to control Decatur. Then Sherman issued the order on Sept. 4, three days before he himself arrived in Atlanta, that was the most painful for residents: "The city of Atlanta being exclusively required for warlike purposes, will be at once vacated by all except the armies of the United States, and such civilians as may be retained."

The following day another order required civilian families to leave "within five days" and "go south." They were to register at City Hall Sept. 12, and be allowed to take clothes, a limited amount of furniture, and a small amount of food. They were given until Sept. 20 to depart, those going north being promised food and transportation, those going south being promised transport as far as Rough and Ready. They were allowed to take "servants, white and black" so long as such servants were not coerced.

Hood protested these orders, writing Sherman that they surpassed in "ingenious cruelty, all acts ever brought to my attention in the dark history of war…" Sherman reminded Hood of the latter's own dispossessions and "atrocities" and added: "I say it is a kindness to these families…to remove them now…from scenes that women and children should not be exposed to… In the name of common sense, I ask you not to appeal to a just God in such a sacrilegious manner… Talk thus (of atrocities) to the Marines, but not to me, who have seen such things…"

Sherman moved Sept. 7 into one of the finest homes, the John Neal house at Washington and Mitchell. The columned house had been used for the Female Academy. (After the war it was briefly the home of Oglethorpe College, then for 50 years was the Atlanta Girls High School. In 1928 the Neal house was torn down to make way for Atlanta's present City Hall.) Gen. Thomas had headquarters in the 1859 Herring-Leyden house, which stood on land now occupied by Davison's. The home was demolished in 1913, having been used as a boarding house in its final days.

As those two Federal officers made themselves comfortable, registration began for the evacuation and continued through Sept. 20, whereupon the sorrowful exodus began. The flight of 446 families—totaling 705 adults, 860 children and 79 servants—brought to towns deeper south

(for most went there) the same problems of overcrowding, lack of food and shelter faced earlier by Atlanta as a refugee center.

In the meantime, following a speech by President Davis at Palmetto, Hood with 40,000 men moved southwest of Atlanta to begin the northward thrust to force Sherman's withdrawal. Some Federal troops pursued Hood, but he did little lasting damage, and soon crossed through Alabama, into middle Tennessee—where he was defeated before Franklin and Nashville, Tenn., late in November and mid-December.

The remnants of Hood's army were again defeated Jan. 3, 1865, at Tupelo, Miss. A few veterans of his army found their way to their old commander, Gen. Johnston, but they finally surrendered to Sherman following battles in North Carolina in early 1865.

Sherman's future intent was obvious: Armies must move. To remain static in wasted Atlanta—which no Confederate troops threatened—was pointless. During October, when Sherman was north of the city still pressing on Hood, the Federal commander was already formulating Atlanta's fate and his next march.

As if in preparation for the coming plunder of Georgia, Federal units in Atlanta raided nearby farms, sending out empty wagons which returned full of produce and livestock. The soldiers, justifying this action because Hood temporarily

Continued on Page 78

Many Decades Ahead Of Modern Medicine

Long before the Food and Drug Administration or the American Medical Association were on the scene, medical quackery was rife.

Dr. F. C. Ford in May, 1864, offered an ad in *The Atlanta Intelligencer* to call attention to his own skills. It read:

"I have been in the practice of medicine for several years, and have made a discovery of a complete cure for cancers, old ulcers, polypus, fistulas, etc.

"I can be found at all times six miles northwest of Atlanta, on the Pace & Howell's Ferry Road."

As a fanciful Northern artist saw it, this shows Federal troops entering Atlanta.

69

Five Points, as it appeared to an artist in September, 1864, following the entry of Federal troops. the Athenaeum (theatre) and Trout house (a hotel—at right) were on Decatur Street.

Federal troops man emplacements by the City Hall and Courthouse, Atlanta, in the fall of 1864. City Hall survived Sherman's destruction of the city, and was replaced 25 years later with the state Capitol.

This was a Northern artist's view of the City Hall area in the fall of 1864, after Atlanta's capture. City Hall (now the Capitol site) was at right; tents are those of the Second Massachusetts Volunteers.

A puffing train stands by the stone depot adjacent to The Atlanta Intelligencer newspaper office (right), which was on Whitehall between old Alabama Street and present-day Plaza Park. Across the tracks sat the Atlanta Hotel, then at Pryor, Wall and Decatur Streets. The time: fall, 1864.

The Neal house on Washington Street—Gen. W. T. Sherman's Atlanta headquarters—pictured years after he'd left

Tents mark the camp of the Second Massachusetts Volunteers on City Hall (now Capitol) grounds in the fall of 1864.

In the fall of 1864 Union troops used the Windsor Smith home (Whitehall opposite present Hood Street); it had been Gen. John B. Hood's headquarters.

After the rails were pulled free, they were heated. Many were then twisted around trees into shapes known as "Sherman's Neckties." City Hall of 1864 is upper left.

Federal troops finish destruction of Atlanta's buildings damaged in their bombardment of the city weeks before.

Some Atlantans who fled after Sherman's evacuation order lived in temporary camps, where a courier on horseback would sometimes bring welcome news and mail.

Sherman's destruction of the railroad track area of Atlanta in November, 1864

Continued from Page 69

cut supply lines, live "like epicures," one wrote home. The raiders left burned farm structures and terrified residents who sought to hide foodstuffs.

Sherman regathered his troops in Atlanta, and by his return on Nov. 14 the 62,000 were arranged in two massive wings supported by droves of cattle. The army would live off the countryside, collecting forage as it pressed on Savannah.

Sherman set the night of Nov. 14 for the wasting of Atlanta. Troops leveled railroad facilities and fires destroyed many structures in the heart of the city but, Sherman said "not...parts of Atlanta where the Courthouse was, or the great mass of dwelling homes."

The Atlanta Medical College (Butler Street) was saved by Dr. P. P. Noel d'Alvigny who intervened with Federal officers, saying it was filled with wounded men. Local Masons intervened with fraternal members in the Union army to spare the Masonic Hall (on Decatur Street). Father Thomas O'Reilly, pastor of the Church of Immaculate Conception, is credited with saving his own institution (at M. L. King and Central), City Hall, and the nearby Presbyterian, Second Baptist, Trinity Methodist, and St. Philip's Episcopal churches. As a result, many nearby homes were spared the flames. (During the occupation, St. Philip's was desecrated by use as a bowling alley, commisary, dance hall and stable.)

Atlanta was thus rendered useless as a military center, and almost uninhabitable. Surveying the damage days later, Confederate Gen. W. P. Howard noted that while a lot of bricks remained for rebuilding, the rolling stock of the railroads was ruined as were the depots, machinery shops, foundries, rolling mills and arsenals. Howard said 4,000 to 5,000 houses were destroyed within a 1½-mile radius from the city center, leaving a few hundred, more or less, intact. "The suburbs"—the area beyond the radius—"present...one vast, naked, ruined, deserted camp." The city was filled with thousands of dogs and cats, ownerless and almost wild.

Bushwhackers, robbers and deserters, said Howard, had been engaged in the "dirty work" of pilfering every manner of goods. "This exportation of stolen property had been going on ever since the place was abandoned" by Union troops. "Many of the finest houses, mysteriously left unburned, are filled with the finest furniture, carpets, pianos, mirrors, etc., and occupied by parties who six months ago lived in humble style." There were, on Dec. 1, about 100 families living in Atlanta, half of whom had remained in the city during the occupation.

From 2,000 to 3,000 carcasses of dead animals remained in the city limits, Howard noted. He added that "The crowning act of...wickedness and villainy was committed by our ungodly foe in removing the dead from the vaults in the (Oakland) cemetery, and robbing the coffins of the silver name plates and tippings, and depositing their own dead in the vaults."

Atlanta was not meant to recover, but early in December a small detachment of Confederate troops occupied the town and raised the Southern flag from City Hall. Within days citizens began to return and, said a newspaper, "the general watchword is repair and rebuild." Quickly there was a bar on Decatur, a grocery on Peachtree, the reopening of the post office, a barbershop, a salt factory.

The Intelligencer returned from exile in Macon, and described the awesome scene: "A city destroyed by fire! Two-thirds at least devoured by flames. Doomed to utter desolation, one-third of Atlanta lives...the nucleus, the cornerstone...upon which the city will again be restored...We can only liken Atlanta to Moscow after her own citizens had fired it..."

The paper found its old hopeful voice again: "The energy for which her citizens have been distinguished has already begun to manifest itself...Let us now look to the future...Her citizens must put their shoulders to the wheel...Efforts like these will soon restore her to her former greatness."

"Former greatness"? *The Intelligencer* underestimated.

On Dec. 7—only three weeks after Sherman left—Atlanta elected James Calhoun to his fourth consecutive term. He had served since early 1862, and was the only chief executive ever to surrender the city. Now the mantle was his again.

On Christmas Day, in the First Baptist Church, Dr. Henry C. Hornady preached the first sermon since Atlanta's fall. His message combined hope and prophecy.

Mayor Calhoun surveyed the devastated city, aware that its only promise lay in the energy of good men and women, and the hopes and dreams of those who began to rebuild from the ashes.

They first concentrated on base survival. The war was still on, waged in the interior of Georgia and elsewhere. Their political future was uncertain, and not much help could be expected from public institutions: When Mayor Calhoun was inaugurated in January, 1865, the City treasury had but $1.64.

Atlanta in Turmoil

Soon after Ft. Sumter was seized, Atlantans began to lose control over civic decency.

Transient soldiers, sick troops, refugees, deserters—all created turmoil: Crime, speculation, inflated prices and prostitution were rife.

A local journalist in April, 1862, called the city "headquarters for itinerant speculators in gold, bank notes, Confederate currency, meat and bread." Another said Atlanta was "the very den of sharpers and extortioners..."

In 1862 soldiers threatened to rob Confederate freight cars of food. When George Adair sold his interest in the *Southern Confederacy* in 1863 for $200,000, he bought gold pieces and had his wife sew them into her skirt for safekeeping—"just far enough apart to keep the gold pieces from rattling."

One newspaper's editors announced that they had nothing in their homes or at the office worth stealing. Thievery in stores and hotel rooms was not uncommon. And, said *The Intelligencer* in January, 1864, there was at least one killing almost every week.

Prostitutes acted so openly in The Athenaeum that in April, 1862, *The Intelligencer* suggested a "place in the gallery be set apart for such creatures, if they are allowed to visit the theater at all."

Burning of the railroad roundhouse in Atlanta by Federal troops in November, 1864, just before Sherman launched his "March to the Sea."

'All Is Dark And Gloomy'

1865-1870

Sherman, who knew war is hell but never said precisely that, had cruelly devastated a large part of Atlanta, humbling it, firing it into wasteland, making such ravage that there were no birds when spring came. But an even greater debilitation of the spirit followed.

The turmoil of that period known as Reconstruction chained Atlantans to the most terrible confusion for more than five years, and strained their economic, social and cultural fabric for decades. Their energies for rebuilding shattered lives and livelihoods were drained in the postwar period by contradictory military regulations, fierce political firestorms exacerbating racial tensions, and the frustrations of simple survival in a land torn by economic chaos.

Atlantans' determination in the face of awesome odds during these years later was symbolized in the City seal: a phoenix, recalling the mythical bird which rose from its own ashes, amid the word *"Resurgens."* Atlanta would rise again, but for years the ascent was perilous—and remarkable. The city became the triumph of a people.

"We are a powerless people," resident Thomas Maguire confided to his journal, "but by no means a conquered people... We are back in the Union but how I do not know and do not much care. I look for nothing but hard times for the balance of my life... All is dark and gloomy..."

Maguire's pessimism was justified. As Atlantans returned to the havoc wrought upon their city, they found food and fuel scarce. Suffering in the winter of 1864-65 was dreadful. People scoured battlefields for spent bullets which they sold for lead to buy food. Persimmon seeds were pierced to become buttons; old clothes were raveled and rewoven; corn-shuck hats and wooden-sole shoes were fashioned; diced meat was used for lard.

Gentlemen of the leisure class learned to mix mortar and lay brick; their women, deprived of servants, renewed the tasks of kitchen and garden. Hundreds of wooden shanties sprouted. Beggars infested the town, many showing their war wounds. On the outskirts destitute families fought for the edible scraps of survival. Crime was rife: Horses were stolen, and bricks spirited away wholesale. The return of hapless soldiers added strains. Confederate money was worthless, the railroads were in ruin, and the Ku Klux Klan was beginning to flex its feared muscle.

Blow after blow wracked the town. Those who found hope in the gentle lines of President Lincoln's second inaugural— "with malice toward none, with charity for all"—were thunderstruck in mid-April, 1865, when they learned of his assassination a few days after Gen. Lee's surrender at Appomattox Court House, Va. Worse was to come, as Radical Republicans in Congress laid plans to keep Atlanta—and the South—in bondage, first by military

Life had begun to stir in Atlanta when this 1865 photograph was made of Peachtree Street, looking north from the railroad tracks. Signs of wartime devastation were still evident in the wrecked building (right) next to the fire-scarred billiard parlor and saloon.

rule, then political advantage.

But guided by Mayor Calhoun, public meetings pledged obedience to the laws, condemned Lincoln's assassination, declared confidence in President Andrew Johnson, and generally expressed the intent to identify with the old Union of states. In July the City Council repealed "all ordinances (which made) Negroes guilty of crimes different from white persons," a concession unthinkable a few years before. There was to be equal treatment of the law. But *The Intelligencer* complained that many former slaves survived "in persistent idleness. Life to them—and more especially a life of freedom—is a curse. Nothing short of the strong arm of the law can ameliorate their condition..."

Stationer S. P. Richards, the well known Atlanta diarist who had gone to New York following Sherman's evacuation order, returned several months later, finding "a dirty, dusty ruin...but busy life is resuming ...in the desolate streets (and)...stores of all kinds are springing up as if by magic in every part of the burnt district..."

It was true. Early in 1865 merchants began to return with stocks, opening stores in wooden shanties. A private school opened in the basement of the Second Baptist Church. William H. Crisp's thespic companies staged plays including the dark *"Macbeth"*; more popular amusement was found in the future area of Underground Atlanta where Humbug Square attracted sideshows, medicine men, carnivals, itinerant salesmen and impromptu banjo pluckers ready to cadge some scarce coin.

In the fall the Georgia National Bank opened, as did the Atlanta National, which first conducted business in Gen. Alfred Austell's home. The post office reopened, the Atlanta Medical College resumed lectures in the fall, and those hardy spokesmen, newspaper editors, regained some vigor and started anew.

To compete with *The Intelligencer, The Daily New Era* was launched, then sold within a year to Dr. Samuel Bard, a journalist and onetime Democrat who converted to Republicanism. Five years later he sold it to a stock company backed by Gov. Rufus Bullock; they bought the paper to stop its criticism of the Chief Executive. It lasted only two more years, suffering the same fate as a literary periodical begun in 1865, *Scott's Monthly Magazine.* Its originator, Rev. W. J. Scott (former Wesley Chapel Methodist Church pastor), gave it up after four years.

More hardy than the periodicals was the Atlanta National Bank. During a series of moves to ever-better quarters, the Bank merged with the Lowry National Bank in 1924, and that combination merged in 1929 with the Fourth National to become the First National Bank, still resident on the old Norcross Corner.

Education for black children made a modest start about the same time as the Bank. Ex-slaves James Tate and Grandison B. Daniels established a school in a small church (near today's Georgia State University). The Rev. and Mrs. Frederick Ayer were sent by the American Missionary Association in November, 1865. Soon thereafter, sisters Rosa and Lucy Kinney joined them. For $130 they bought a freight car in Chattanooga, moved it to Walton Spring and partitioned it into two classrooms. Ayer and Lucy Kinney taught at the first school, Mrs. Ayer and Rosa Kinney at the "Car-Box" school.

The Georgia Railroad roundhouse, pictured in ruins in the summer of 1865, was south of the tracks between the present-day Washington Street bridge and today's Piedmont Avenue. The view is to the west; the cupola (upper left) topped Fire Engine House #2, which faced Washington Street.

ATLANTA'S 1869 AIR AGE PREVIEW

More than 5,000 Atlantans jammed the Marietta-Walton Street area on December 10, 1869, to witness the city's first glimpse of the air age.

Dr. Albert Hape and Prof. Samuel A. King went aloft in a balloon about 2:30 and floated over north Fulton and DeKalb Counties. Some witnesses there speculated that revenue agents had found a new way to discover stills; one gent thought the balloon carried Gov. Rufus Bullock out of the state—with public funds. When Prof. King played several pieces on a bugle while passing over a religious meeting, one woman thought she heard Gabriel blowing his trumpet to signal Judgment Day.

The balloon landed six miles north of Alpharetta about sundown after striking a treetop.

Hape, a dentist, died 14 years later—of heart failure. Several years after the balloon ascensions, Hape's older brother Samuel, also a dentist, founded Hapeville —a few miles from present-day Hartsfield International Airport.

Jeweler and watchmaker Er Lawshe (right) was photographed at the door of his new store, 47 Whitehall Street, in May, 1865. The store is said to have been the first building erected after the fall of Atlanta.

Thus were laid the beginnings of the Atlanta University Center.

War's end had brought the return of Federal troops. On May 3, 1865, Confederate soldiers surrendered in Atlanta to Col. B. G. Eggleston, who promptly issued an order prohibiting the sale of liquor to any soldier. Atlanta had become a military post again.

Within two weeks after Eggleston's order, the fleeing President Davis was captured at Irwinville, Ga. Gov. Brown, though deprived of authority, called for the legislature to meet in Milledgeville on May 22, but Federal authorities quickly arrested him as well as former Confederate Vice President Stephens, Howell Cobb, Benjamin Hill and other leaders.

After meeting with President Johnson, Brown resigned as governor, an academic act since on June 17—12 days before—the President named University of Georgia graduate James Johnson, a Columbus lawyer who had opposed secession, to be Provisional Governor of Georgia. In mid-July Gov. Johnson called an October election for delegates to a constitutional convention, wherein citizens could vote if they took an oath to the Union.

Gov. Johnson's authority was backed by Federal troops who obtained a new Atlanta commander in July: Gen. Felix Salm-Salm, a Prussian prince. Salm-Salm, the only titled individual ever in authority in Atlanta, and his wife (who was particularly well liked), lived in the Er Lawshe residence at Peachtree and Cain Streets. They left after a few months, and five years later the prince was killed in the Franco-Prussian War.

In the election of late 1865, Charles J. Jenkins was chosen governor, and signaled

the promise of some semblance of political order. The election came a year after Sherman had left Atlanta a smoking ruin. But a correspondent for Northern newspapers wrote hopefully of the place after his brief visit:

"From all this ruin and devastation a new city is springing up with marvelous rapidity. The narrow and irregular and numerous streets are alive from morning until night with drays and carts and hand-barrows and wagons—with hauling teams and shouting men—with loads of lumber and loads of brick and loads of sand—with piles of furniture and hundreds of packed boxes...with a never-ending throng of pushing and crowding and scrambling and eager and excited and enterprising men, all bent on building and trading and swift fortune making. Chicago in her busiest days could scarcely show such a sight as here...Men rush about the streets with but little regard for comfort or pleasure, and yet find the days all too short and too few for the work in hand...Atlanta seems to be the center from which this new life radiates; it is the great Exchange, where you will find everybody if you only wait and watch. The very genius of the West, holding in one hand all its energies and in the other all its extravagances, is there; not sitting in the supreme ease of settled pause but standing in the nervous tension of expected movement..."

But a destructive tension also loomed: Reconstruction and the first shock waves of it would last for 10 years, until Federal troops were finally withdrawn in December, 1876.

In that 10 years Atlanta—and Georgia—would undergo a painful political evolution which left marks still sensed.

For four years Atlanta was impacted, then decimated, by war. With the death of the Confederacy in April, 1865, the ravaged community was preoccupied first with civic survival—the rebuilding of public institutions and private enterprise. During the next six years Atlanta was under on-again, off-again military control. Civil restoration started in 1865 but did not last. Instead, political partisans launched a five year contest to control the state from Washington.

There, Radical Republicans sought to punish the South despite President Johnson's more lenient requirements. He held the theory that the Southern states, *per se,* had never exited the Union, but that their attempted secession put them in a sort of political limbo. In that, he shared Lincoln's view: that war had been waged not against the states but powerful individuals who were in violation of Federal law.

Southern states agreed to the 13th Amendment: In exchange for the abolition of slavery, Confederate war debts were repudiated, and in April, 1866, the President declared peace restored. But his opponents, Radical Republicans in Congress led by Charles Sumner and Thaddeus Stevens, demanded an investigation to determine whether the Southern states were entitled to congressional representation.

The Radicals pressed for a civil rights bill to make citizens of the freedmen, a bill that disfranchised all citizens who had held Confederate offices and fought for the South, and readjusted congressional representation in proportion to citizens who were eligible to vote.

Congress passed the bill over Johnson's veto, and despite the South's vehement anger over it, the national elections that fall were carried by Radicals in both houses of Congress, thus dooming Johnson's milder plans for reconstruction. Before many months this confrontation would lead to a near successful attempt to impeach him.

The urban flocking of thousands of new freedmen revived old fears of slave revolts, and nourished new ones: black political power and competition for labor. Most Southern state legislatures in 1866 enacted Black Codes which confirmed blacks as free men but restricted their speech, freedom of movement, conditions of employment and the like—thus returning them to a kind of bondage, continuing to deny them social and political equality. The Black Codes nullified the hopeful work of the Freedman's Bureau but in 1866 Congress passed a civil rights act invalidating the Black Codes, and later the 14th Amendment guaranteeing all citizens equal protection of the laws.

When Georgia refused to ratify the 14th Amendment, Radical Republicans wiped out civil governments established under Johnson's administration. By mid-1867, Atlanta was ruled by troops again.

The Reconstruction Act of March,

1867 (and its supplements), created enormous turmoil in the South. It included enfranchisement of blacks, but excluded from voting many respected and capable white citizens. It required new state constitutions as well as approval of the 14th Amendment, rejected earlier by all Southern legislatures. The Act called for resumption of military rule—which would be withdrawn only after states were readmitted to the Union.

Thus, military rule in Atlanta, withdrawn late in 1865, returned early in 1867, and Federal troops were not finally withdrawn until the end of Reconstruction, after the national election of 1876. Some Atlantans, including ex-Gov. Brown, stated their abhorrence to the Reconstruction Act of 1867, but publicly counseled cooperation. The fiery Benjamin Hill violently opposed the Act in public, gaining popularity among those who could not stomach black enfranchisement.

"It was an amazing piece of statesmenship to disfranchise our intelligence and make the hereditary slaves of two centuries rulers of our political destiny," I. W. Avery summed up the general view. The Act "degraded, alarmed and exasperated our people. We had the whole argument of

Kimball's Opera House, at the corner of Marietta and Forsyth, was used for years as the temporary state Capitol after Atlanta had been designated the capital in 1868. The view is to the west; just beyond the building (at right) is the present location of the Atlanta Journal-Constitution building.

FULTON COUNTY GOLD

There was considerable excitement in Atlanta in December, 1866, following newspaper reports that gold had been discovered "on Nancy Creek and near the Chattahoochee River."

The area became the present-day section of Mount Paran and Randall Mill Roads and Harris Trail.

Soon after the reports, Pinkney H. Randall bought the land, and established a grist mill on Nancy Creek just below present-day Randall Ridge.

The mill produced more revenue than the reported veins of gold—which apparently didn't warrant serious mining efforts.

WM. RICH & CO.,

HAVE just received the largest stock of goods lately broght to this mark comprising a complete assorted stock of

Staple and Fancy
DRY GOODS!

A large and well selected stock of

Fall and Winter
CLOTHING!

Together with an elegant stock of

Gents' Furnishing Goods,

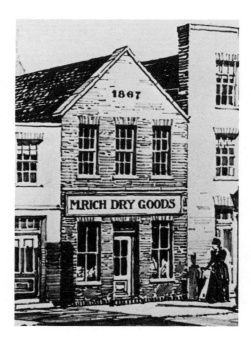

William Rich was a thriving merchant, as his newspaper ad suggests, before he loaned younger brother Morris the funds to set up a modest store (below) in May, 1867, on Whitehall Street.

the case on our side. They had the might... Our people were angered to white heat..." They vented their anger in a series of loud public meetings that changed nothing.

Under the Act, Gen. John Pope came to Atlanta to command the military district and, to his surprise, was welcomed. At one dinner, the chairman of the affair toasted the General: "Our Pope—may he be as infallible as the law has made him powerful." But Pope was soon surrounded by unprincipled politicians and opportunistic carpetbaggers who used him to their advantage, and created havoc. His appointments to vacancies in elective offices were ridiculed by the newspapers, and Pope's order forbidding City printing contracts from going to any paper that spoke against reconstruction raised a howl. Pope's order giving blacks the right to jury service brought Judge Augustus Reece's refusal—and his removal by Pope. Citizen hostility increased.

Some remembered Pope's aggressive wartime boast on taking a new command: "My headquarters will be in the saddle." To which Gen. Robert E. Lee was supposed to have remarked that Pope's headquarters were where his hindquarters ought to be.

Many white conservatives opposed

the constitutional convention, as ordered by the Act of 1867, but it was held. To assure black political strength, Gen. Pope registered men by different names, and even brought in blacks from South Carolina to register. By the time of the balloting, 93,000 blacks were registered and 95,000 whites, but many of the latter abstained from voting.

Of the 166 delegates selected for the convention to write a new constitution, 37 were black; most delegates were conservative, once-wealthy men who viewed opposition to Republicanism as fruitless, and thus earned the name "scalawags." The resultant constitution had laudable reform elements, but many of the "scalawags" and "carpetbaggers"—Northern opportunists—took advantage of the doors opened to the treasury.

Weeks before the three-month convention ended in March, 1868, President Johnson paid heed to Atlantans' complaints about Gen. Pope, and replaced him with Gen. George Meade. When Gov. Jenkins refused to pay the $40,000 in convention expenses, Meade removed Jenkins—but not before the latter fled to New York with $400,000 of State money, depositing it in a New York bank to keep it from the military. Meade replaced Gov. Jenkins with Gen. Thomas Ruger.

The Radical Republicans chose former New Yorker Rufus Bullock, president of the Macon & Augusta Railroad, as their gubernatorial nominee. And when Meade declared two judges ineligible to oppose Bullock, Democrats backed Gen. John B. Gordon. Federal troops surrounded the courthouse polls, and Bullock was elected, partly because of his statewide black vote (even the Klansmen kept some from voting), and because many whites abstained. In the election of 1868, the new constitution was approved and Atlanta was chosen as the state's new capital, a prize it had sought for 20 years. In June, Georgia was allowed congressional representation if it approved the 14th Amendment.

On July 22, 1868—fourth anniversary of the Battle of Atlanta—Bullock took the oath in City Hall to the scattered applause of assembled legislators and an onlooker's satirical shout, "Go it, niggers!" The Republican-dominated legislature, with Georgia's first blacks in both houses, adopted the 14th Amendment. Within days, some 20,000 Democrats sweated for five hours under an Alabama Street bush arbor as they heard fiery, condemnatory speeches. The famed "Bush Arbor" meeting triggered a campaign to end carpetbagger and Republican rule in Georgia.

Those were exciting days. Two months after the 14th Amendment was ratified, Democrat and Republican legislators banded to eject all the black legislators as ineligible under Georgia's constitution. As their fate was being debated, one of them, G. H. Clower, said to the body: "Whenever

you cast your votes against us, dis nigger will take his hat and walk straight out but, like Christ, I shall come again..." Clower was right: The following year the State Supreme Court overturned the expulsion decision.

More ill will was created when Congress refused to seat the Georgia's two new senators, Joshua Hill and Dr. Homer V. Miller, until eight months after their election.

In August, military rule ended again, and Meade departed, leaving behind a memory of one decent deed: It's said that he helped raise $5,000 toward renovation of St. Philip's Episcopal Church. The garrison at McPherson Barracks remained, however, and some soldiers' pranks resulted in altercations with the police later that year. There were other confrontations with the military: Public hostility grew over the latter's treatment and trial of some innocent whites and blacks arrested in connection with a Columbus murder. In January, 1870, 24 white legislators were excluded from service by a Federal military commission, and 31 blacks seated.

Another Federal reconstruction bill (advanced by Sumner) developed in December, 1868, and when the Georgia legislature refused to ratify the 15th Amendment, Bullock spent part of 1869 in Washington on an expensive wining-and-dining junket to urge congressmen to resume military rule. His efforts were described by one observer as "about the boldest piece of lobbying ever witnessed in Congress." Bullock warned that troops were needed to maintain order, and sought a reorganization of the Georgia legislature under the test oath which would exclude some white legislators and reinstate expelled blacks. The Congressional Act of 1869 gave Bullock the ammunition he

needed.

Georgia was remanded by Federal authority to military rule, with the additional requirement that the 15th Amendment be ratified as a condition of the State's readmission to the Union. After Gen. Alfred H. Terry was named military commander, a number of Atlanta citizens dated their letters "Terry-tory of Georgia."

The irony of the two amendments did not escape notice: The validity of the 14th Amendment rested partially on Georgia's ratification as a state, but it was declared *not* a state, though the ratification was validated. The state was not allowed to be a state, but its ratification of the 15th Amendment was sought. Thus, the act of a state—ratification—was required before it could become a state.

Like Gen. Pope, Bullock had winked at

Three strong men prominent in Atlanta's life soon after the war ended: Gen. George Gordon Meade (left) was Union commander of the military post for a short time. Hannibal I. Kimball (center) was an energetic entrepreneur who survived reports of scandal in the use of state goverment funds; and Rufus Bullock (right) was the Republican governor (1868-1871) hated by most citizens for his abuses of power in the Reconstruction era.

The Georgia Railroad freight depot (photographed in 1898) stood at the foot of old Alabama Street, facing the contemporary Underground Atlanta section. Part of the depot still remains.

CONSTITUTION.

ATLANTA, GA., THURSDAY MORNING, JUNE 18, 1868. NUMBER 3

[GEOR]GIA LEGISLATURE.

SENATE.

[...]ict—Chatham, Bryant and Efing-
[...]y, negro.
[...]rict—Liberty, Tatnall and McIn-
[...]ell, negro.
[...]ict—Wayne, Pierce and Appling—
[...], Dem.
[...]strict—Glynn, Camden and Charl-
[...]leman, Rad.
[...]rict—Coffee, Ware and Cliach—A.

[...]ict—Echols, Lowndes and Berrien—

[...]istrict—Brooks, Thomas and Col-
[...]mith, Ind.
[...]trict—Decatur, Mitchell and Miller—
[...], Ind.
[...]ict—Early, Calhoun, and Baker—R.
[...]em.
[...]rict—Dougherty, Lee and Worth—

[...]District—Clay, Randolph and Ter-
[...], Dem.
[...]strict—Stewart, Webster and Quit-
[...] Dem.
[...] District—Sumter, Schley and Ma-
[...]Rad.
[...] District—Dooly, Wilcox and Pu-
[...], Dem.
[...]District—Montgomery, Telfair and
[...]thur, Dem.
[...] District—Laurens, Emanuel and
[...]cks, Dem.
[...]h District—Bullock, Scriven and
[...]. Hungerford, Dem.
[...] District—Richmond, Glasscock and
[...]nley, Rad.
[...] District—Taliaferro, Warren and
[...]ns, Rad.
[...] District—Baldwin, Hancock and
[...] Wallace, negro Rad.
[...]st District—Twiggs, Wilkinson and
[...]in, Ind.
[...]ond District—Bibb, Monroe and
[...] Rad.
[...]ird District—Houston, Crawford and
[...]erson, Dem.
[...]urth District—Marion, Muscogee and
[...]ee—Hinton, Dem.
[...]th District—Harris, Upson and Tal-
[...] Rad.
[...]xth District—Spalding, Fayette and
[...]ally, Dem.
[...]venth District—Clark, Walton and
[...]rris, Rad.
[...]ghth District—Jasper, Putnam and
[...]dan, Rad.
[...]nth District—Wilkes, Lincoln and
[...]herman, Rad.
[...]District—Oglethorpe, Madison and
[...]Shorter, Rad.
[...]t District—Twiggs, Wilkinson and
[...] Bowers, Rad,
[...]ond District—White, Lumpkin and
[...]ndrum, Dem.
[...]d District—Hall, Banks and Jack-
[...]r, Rad.
[...]th District—Gwinnett, DeKalb and
[...]ller, Dem.
[...] District—Clayton, Fulton and
[...] Dem.
[...]h District—Meriwether, Coweta and
[...]nith, Rad.
[...]enth District—Troup, Heard and
[...]rill, Rad.
[...]th District—Haralson, Polk and
[...]ead, Dem.
[...]th District—Cherokee, Milton and
[...]lcombe, Dem.
[...]istrict—Union, Towns and Rabun—
[...], Dem.
[...]District—Fannin, Gilmer and Pick-
[...]ckey, Dem.
[...]d District—Bartow, Floyd and
[...]Burns, Dem.
[...] District—Murray, Whitfield and
[...]n, Dem.
[...]h District—Walker, Dade and Ca-
[...]chen, Dem.

HOUSE.

[...]Reddish, Dem.
[...]uston, Dem.
[...]er, negro Rad., and Franks and
[...] white Rads.
[...]kness, Dem.
[...] M. Ford and M. J. Crawford, Dems.
[...]W. George, Dem.
[...]A. Lane, Ind.
[...]lcom Claborn, John Warren, ne-
[...]Madden, Rad.
[...]O'Neil, negro Rad.
[...]ll, Rad.
[...]all, Dem.
[...]aulk, Dem.
[...]Moon, negro, Rice, Rad.
[...]eppe, Dem.
[...]—C. C. Cleghorn, Dem.
[...]t. Davis and Alf. Richardson, ne-

[...]bee—McDonald, Dem.
[...]ipseed, Dem.
[...]rson and Gober, Dems.
[...]Osgood and Porter, white Radicals:

MUNICIPAL GOVERNMENT.

J. E. WILLIAMS .... Mayor.
S. B. LOVE .... Clerk of Council.
J. T. GLENN .... City Attorney.
R. M. FARRAR .... City Treasurer.
E. J. ROACH .... City Physician.
JAS. F. COOPER .... City Engineer.
GEO. STEWART .... Street Overseer.
JO. S. SMITH .... City Tax Receiver and Collector.
PAT. FITZGIBBON .... Hall Keeper.

BOARD OF COUNCILMEN.

First Ward—Richard Peters and M. T. Castleberry.
Second Ward—E. E. Rawson and A. W. Mitchell.
Third Ward—W. C. Anderson, and one vacancy.
Fourth Ward—J. E. Gullatt and W. B. Cox.
Fifth Ward—J. A. Hayden and R. W. Holland.

POLICE DEPARTMENT.

L. P. THOMAS .... Chief Marshal.
E. C. MURPHY .... Deputy Marshal.
J. L. JOHNSON .... First Lieut. of Police.
T. C. MURPHY .... Second Lieut. of Police.

POLICEMEN.

F. J. Bomar, D. Rogan, J. Cook, E. A. Center, F. T. Kicklighter, J. A. Hinton, E. D. Hall, J. L. Crenshaw, G. W. Bowen, A. Jarrard, O. P. Woodliff, Jasper Groves, J. S. Holland, R. O. Haynes, D. Queen, J. A. Lang, Green Holland, H. W. Wooding, H. J. Holtzclaw, J. F. Barnes, T. G. McHan, J. A. Lanier, Jack Smith, J. McGee, J. M. Cook.

CLERK OF 1ST MARKET.—Theophilus Harris.
CLERK OF 2D MARKET.—F. T. Ryan.
SEXTON.—G. A. Pilgrim.
CITY ASSESSORS.—H. C. Holcombe, C. P. Cassin, and B. D. Cheshire.
ASSESSORS OF LAND TAKEN FOR OPENING STREETS.—Levi C. Wells and Frank P. Rice.
KEEPER POWDER MAGAZINE.—W. W. Davis.
SUPERINTENDENT ALMSHOUSE.—W. Y. Langford.

STANDING COMMITTEES OF THE CITY COUNCIL.

Finance—Peters, Mitchell, Rawson.
Ordinance—Mitchell, Hayden, Peters.
Streets and Sidewalks—Gullatt, Rawson, Hayden.
Wells, Pumps and Cisterns—Cox, Anderson, Castleberry.
Lamps and Gas—Hayden, Peters.
Relief—Castleberry, Rawson, Gullatt, Hayden.
Market—Hayden, Castleberry, Holland.
Fire Department—Gullat, Cox.
Police—Rawson, Cox, Anderson.
Cemetery—Mitchell, Rawson.
Public Buildings and Grounds—Anderson, Peters.
Tax—Holland, Rawson, Cox.
On Printing—Holland, Castleberry.
Salaries—Cox, Mitchell, Holland.

FULTON COUNTY OFFICIALS.

B. N. WILLIFORD .... Sheriff.
W. L. HUBBARD .... Deputy Sheriff.
DANIEL PITTMAN .... Ordinary.
W. R. VENABLE .... Clerk Superior Court.
C. M. PAYNE .... County Treasurer.
JNO. M. HARWELL .... Tax Collector.
SAMUEL GRUBB .... Tax Receiver.
T. A. KENNEDY .... County Surveyor.
WM. KILE .... Coroner.

JUDGES OF THE INFERIOR COURT.

E. M. Taliaferro, C. C. Green and Wm. Watkins.
J. W. Manning, Clerk.

Atlanta Fire Department.

THOMAS HANEY .... Chief
ELISHA BUICE .... 1st Assistant
JESSE SMITH .... 2d Assistant
B. F. MOORE .... Secretary
JAMES E. GULLATT .... Treasurer

ATLANTA ENGINE COMPANY NO. 1.

J. H. MECASLIN .... President
T. C. MURPHY .... Foreman
L. ALEXANDER .... Secretary
H. MUHLENBRINK .... Treasurer
JACOB EMMEL .... First Director
GEORGE RAAB .... Second Director
HENRY HANEY .... Third Director
M. L. COLLIER .... Engineer
J. K. WEAVER .... First Assistant Engineer
WM. KROGG .... Second Assistant Engineer
JOEL OSBORN .... Third Assistant Engineer
J. S. GERMANY, JERRY LYNCH, ... Axemen
SAMUEL WILSON, Delegate to Fire Department

MECHANIC ENGINE COMPANY NO 2.

J. E. GULLATT .... President
J. G. KELLEY .... Vice President
W. D. LUCKIE, Jr. .... Secretary
O. H. JONES .... Treasurer
JOEL KELSEY, Jr. .... First Director
HENRY GULLATT .... Second Director
JAS. M. TOY .... Chief Engineer
W. G. MIDDLETON .... First Assistant Engineer
FRED KROG, Jr. .... Second Assistant Engineer
W. J. MIDDLETON .... Third Assistant Engineer
G. P. CAMPBELL, W. F. WOODS, ... Pipemen
J. M. BUICE, JOSEPH WILEY, ... Axemen
CARL HARMSEN, Delegate to Fire Department

For the Constitution.]

A Prophet Foretelling His Own Infamy.

NUMBER III.

GOV. BROWN AND HIS SPECIAL MESSAGE OF 1860.

The Governor, in order to array the "poor white laborers," as he called them, on the side of his favorite doctrine of secession, made an artful appeal to their prejudices against negro equality. Hear him:

"Among us the poor white laborer is respected as an equal. His family is treated with kindness, consideration and respect. He does not belong to the menial class. The negro is, in no sense of the term, his equal. He feels and knows this. He belongs to the only true aristocracy. The race of *white men*."

"These men know that in the event of the abolition of slavery they would be greater sufferers than the rich, who would be able to protect themselves. They will, therefore, never permit the slaves of the South to be set free among them, come in competition with their labor, associate with them and their children as equals—be allowed to testify in our courts against them—sit on juries with them, *march to the ballot box by their sides*, and participate in the choice of their rulers; claim social equality with them, and ask the hands of their children in marriage. That the ultimate design of the Black Republican party is to bring about this state of things in the Southern States, and that its triumph, if submitted to by us, will at no very distant period, lead to the consummation of these results, is, I think, quite evident to the mind of every cool, dispassionate thinker, who has examined the question in the light of all the surrounding circumstances."

That was the argument addressed by Gov. Brown in 1860, to the "poor white laborer." Where does he stand in 1868? Is he on the side of "the race of *white men*?" or has he abandoned them, and gone into the ranks of the negroes, "and marched to the ballot-box by their side, and participated with them in the choice of rulers?"

What if some one in 1860, after the delivery of that special message, had told the Governor that "at no distant period," he would "march to the ballot-box by the side of negroes, and participate with them in the choice of rulers," would he not have replied, "What—is thy servant a *dog* that he should do this thing?" Well, he has done it, and what he was when he done it I shall not say. In 1860 the Governor felt great solicitude for "the poor white laborer." He could not tolerate the thought that they "would permit the slaves of the South to be set free among them—come in competition with their labor—be allowed to testify in our Courts against them—sit on juries with them, march to the ballot-box by their sides, and participate in the choice of rulers"

Such things would be degrading to the race of white men, and especially "the poor white laborer." [...]

public service. We disagree with any such aristocratic theory, and with the ideas and practices which it engenders. Gen. Grant himself is the recipient of pay and emoluments inconsistent with the practice or propriety of our republican system. His income from these sources alone is over $22,000 per annum. He received a gift of $100,000 in bonds from New York; a splendid house, entirely furnished, from Philadelphia; and other valuable presents, which make his private fortune very considerable. This sudden change from poverty and obscurity has had an effect upon the beneficiary for it it is a subject of common remark and of deserved censure, that his children are habitually attended by soldiers of the United States army, just as they were body servants or equerries in waiting. At all his evening receptions a detail from the troops stationed in this city was ordered to attend, where they officiated in the double character of police and lacqueys, just as is done in the rotton old monarchies of Europe.

This military regime which Congress has strengthened and encouraged in every possible way, has become rather obtrusive for our notions of free government, and these significant indications foreshadow what would come to pass if Gen. Grant and his surroundings could attain that goal of ambition to which their efforts are now so earnestly directed, but in which they are doomed to the most utter disappointment. The country has paid dearly enough for seven years' rule of Radicalism without extending it through four years more of mean and vulgar military despotism.

From the Savannah Republican.]

The Officers of the Army.

Grant wrote to the House Committee on Military Affairs, recommending a removal of thirty three and one-third per cent. in pay of army officers.

Forney writes to the Philadelphia papers "that the Republicans in Washington had to contend against returned rebels and the officers and men of the regular army stationed here."

In Washington, the other day,
The officers, the papers say,
Went wholly, solely Democratic
The officers of the army.
Grant looked quite sad,
Wade raging mad,
Forney as bad,
And each one had
A twinge infernally rheumatic.

A meeting then and there took place,
This army treason to erase,
So ominously Democratic
In officers of the army.
Wade, "'Tis outrageous,"
Grant, "Raise their wages,"
Forney, "Blood and ages!"
"Why, Grant a sage is!
Yes! raise their wages, that's ecstatic!"
For the officers of the army.

"*But what about the men*," said Wade,
They must be had, and bought, and paid,
To kill this viper Democratic,
As well as officers of the army.
Grant shook his head,
"They can be led
By nose instead;
Machines are dead,
And men well drilled—phlegmatic,"
Not so the officers of the army.

Then Grant without a single word,
Wrote off to raise the pay one-third,
A bait to catch the Democratic
Of the officers of the army.
Grant smoked and thought—
Wade screeched out, "Caught!"
The dead duck bought!
Then rose the lot,
With White House visions quite beatic,
And the officers of the army.

PAUL PRY.

The Rebound.

How "Match Him" Grant's Hebrew Order is Recoiling on the Writer.

The following important protest against the election of General Grant [...]

Part of the front page of the third issue of The Atlanta Constitution, June 18, 1868. In a major story (upper right), a correspondent blasts former Gov. Joseph Brown for changing his views on blacks as laborers.

inhabitant...between 16 and 21...and any disabled and indigent soldier...under 30." No provision was made for blacks. It did not matter: Prevailing poverty made collection of sufficient taxes impossible, and a statewide public school system did not emerge until 1873.

Tuition schools continued to fill the gap: The Atlanta High School resumed classes early in 1867, and a primary school for blacks opened in Clark Chapel in 1869 under the guidance of Rev. and Mrs. James W. Lee. In 1870 the Freedman's Aid Society of the Methodist Episcopal Church took it under its wing. With contributions nationwide, it was chartered as Clark University in 1877; the cornerstone of its first brick building, Chrisman Hall, was laid in February, 1880. The building was largely the gift of Mrs. Eliza Chrisman of Topeka, Kans. Clark was named for D. W. Clark; he and Gilbert Haven were the bishops most aggressive in helping it grow initially.

Banker-philanthropist George Peabody's $1 million donation to encourage Southern education inspired Georgia educators to meet in Atlanta in August, 1867, and organize the Georgia Teachers Association. It favored "educating the blacks with equal privileges with the whites," though in separate schools. Decades later GTA became the Georgia Education Assn., and years after the Supreme Court's 1954 desegregation decision, it merged with a black educators group, and is today known as the Georgia Teachers Education Assn.

With all its modest progress toward community stability in the postwar years, Atlanta had to contend with problems. A smallpox epidemic raged throughout 1866. There was a constant search for funds to aid the destitute, their ranks swollen by the urban influx of ex-slaves, and resultant racial tensions derived, in part, from the competition for jobs. Blazes taxed the volunteer firemen despite the arrival in 1866 of the first steam fire engine and the completion that year of the cistern at Central and Alabama. Amid the struggle for survival, lawlessness was rife.

Highway robbery, burglaries and murder were not uncommon. Early in 1867 the Grand Jury called for a force of "secret detectives" to patrol leading avenues to lessen "the present alarming state of affairs." The army post on Peters Street (later Ft. McPherson) contributed to crime: In 1868 a teacher noted that "the garrison is a great temptation (for her scholars); the soldiers are lions looking for poor sheep to devour... Last week two young girls of my school succumbed to the temptation..."

By late 1866 the State prison system was woefully inadequate, and the legislature approved "farming out" some convicts. Convict labor was first leased in May, 1868, when 100 blacks were hired by the Georgia & Alabama Railroad for a year for $2,500. The Atlanta railroad-building firm of Grant,

Alexander & Co. leased the entire penitentiary population in June, 1869, and by the first of the year was working 393 convicts —paying the State nothing, but relieving it of prisoner upkeep.

The convict-lease system was perceived initially as a boon to the State: producing income rather than draining it. Within a few years, however, abuses crept into the system which placed convict labor in competition with "honest labor," and the system was ended in 1909. Thereafter, convicts could be employed only on public works by county and State authorities.

The first five postwar years, the most trying period in Atlanta's history except for its destruction, signaled the city's intent that it meant not only to survive but to prosper.

Samuel M. Inman (left) was one of Atlanta's best merchants and citizens; the city's first suburb is named for him. Gov. Charles J. Jenkins (right) served from 1865 to 1868, defying Radical Republican designs as best he could. Gen. Meade replaced him with a puppet governor (Gen. T. H. Ruger) until Rufus Bullock was chosen in mid-1868. Bullock is Georgia's only Republican governor.

First home of the Atlanta National Bank, founded in 1865 by Gen.

Alfred Austell, who became its first president.

Atlanta Resurgens
1870-1880

The observer of Atlanta in 1870 could hardly label it a vignette of the old plantation South. Commerce, not solely in cotton, was its motive force. The railroads had fixed it as a transportation and distribution center, and brought newcomers who staked their fortunes in a thriving, energetic town. A visiting journalist wrote that, "One receives at every step a lively impression of...great power..."

Stores burst with goods from everywhere; traveling salesmen crowded hotels where they demonstrated new notions and devices; drummers drove merchandise-laden rigs to sell wares to rural areas where country stores sprouted.

Atlanta in the 1870s hummed with the noise of legislators, the construction of commercial buildings, horse cars, factories. Morehouse College's antecedent moved to the city, a public school system began, and baseball took lasting hold. A new railroad line was launched, the telephone arrived, the waterworks were opened. Editor Henry Grady urged his vision of an industrialized "New South," and Atlanta promoted herself to the nation with the first of a series of expositions. Atlanta's nemesis, Gen. Sherman, came by invitation to one in the Seventies, and even invested in a fair sponsored by the city he had burned only 15 years before.

In 1871 Atlanta had 50 liquor saloons, 28 butchers, 150 hacks and drays, 17 insurance agents, eight wagon-yards, nine printing offices, 391 merchants (not including saloon-keepers), 46 lawyers, 76 physicians, 15 contractors, 15 barbers, six milliners, six photographers, four livery stables, seven mills, five non-railroad foundries, 11 blacksmiths, five bakeries, two breweries, two marble yards, three theaters, five hotels, three warehouses,

This stereopticon view shows the center of Atlanta, 1875, as one looks from the northwest to the southeast. The photograph was taken probably from the roof of the temporary Capitol at Marietta and Forsyth Streets. The Roman Catholic Church of the Immaculate Conception (upper right)—at present-day Central Avenue and Martin Luther King Drive—was the *only complete building of the Seventies standing until fire gutted it in August, 1982. The rear of the National Hotel (lower left) was at the site of the present First National Bank tower. Some of the bottom floors of the building which abut the railroad tracks beyond the James Bank Block (three story building at right) still exist in the Underground Atlanta section.*

eight banks, 10 dentists, six real-estate agents, three book binderies, four bookstores, five boot-and-shoe stores, four carriage-makers, four crockery stores, five wholesale tobacconists, four cigar-makers, four wholesale clothing stores, two coal yards, seven dressmakers, eight drugstores, six furniture retailers, four hardware stores, three hat shops, 20 boot-and-shoemakers, two broom factories, 10 jewelers and watchmakers, 11 lumber yards, three tobacco factories, a gunsmith, skating rink, bowling "saloon," and factories turning out candy, soap, crackers, hoopskirts, furniture and ice.

Claimed one resident, Dr. John S. Wilson, in 1871: "Notwithstanding the denunciation that has been heaped on Atlanta as a sink of moral pollution and a seething hot-bed of political corruption, ...the moral and social condition...compares favorably with most cities, old or new, North or South...We have a large number of the best, most refined, and intellectual, as well as the most progressive and enterprising men and women to be found in the North or in the South...Though there are many men of wealth here, there are but few men or women of elegant leisure, with nothing to do except pass away time in fashionable follies and fripperies. Our people are emphatically a business people, who come here to *work*; and therefore the devil does not find many workshops here in the form of idle brains...

"So intense are the business pursuits of most men here that they cannot find time to loaf on the corners, get drunk in the daytime, and indulge in other disreputable acts. As to our women (bless them) they, as a general rule, find ample occupation in the domestic duties they have so gracefully assumed, and in works of charity and be-

nevolence, leaving them but little time for fashionable calls, balls, parties, theatres, etc...

"Industrious men...are welcomed from every section of the country...True, our citizens have no great love for mere political adventurers of the 'carpetbag' class; but even these are tolerated without resort to violence..."

The welcome mat was indeed out, and newcomers responded. By 1880 the population had jumped to 37,000 from 21,000 in 1870, and the Chamber of Commerce, re-

Continued on Page 98

Old Alabama Street (running from lower right to upper left) is shown at the crossing of Pryor Street, in 1875. Old Alabama was the main artery of the Underground Atlanta section.

The horse trough was at Walton and Marietta Streets; in the center (left), the first Grant Building. The photo was taken in 1871.

93

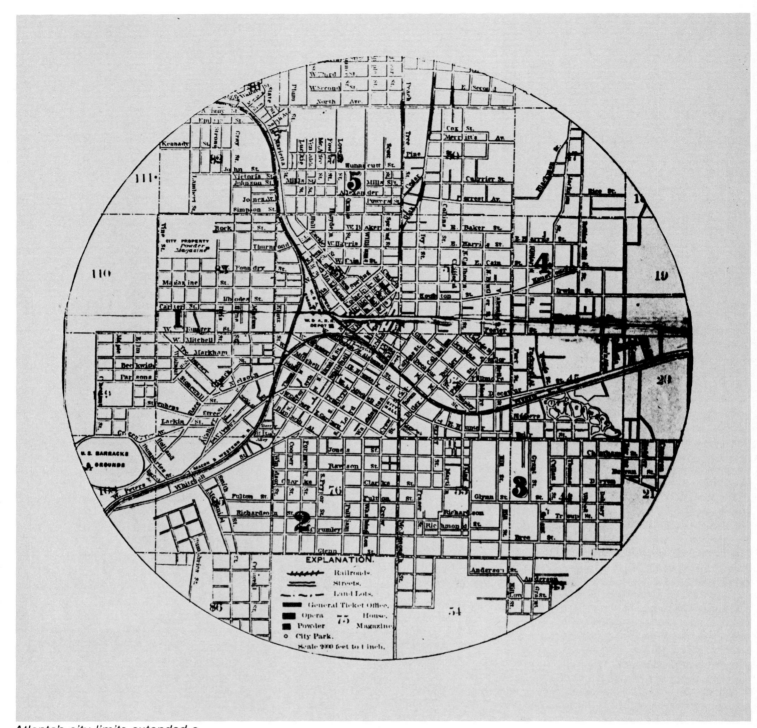

Atlanta's city limits extended a radius of little more than a mile from the center, according to this 1870 map. The northern arc touched present-day Fourth Street. The Underground Atlanta section is near the triangular loop made in the city's heart by the converging railroad tracks. The U. S. Barracks and Grounds lay along the tracks to the southwest near West Peters Street (left). The city cemetery (Oakland) lay adjacent to the Georgia Railroad tracks (right).

First Phone Message:

The first telephone chat over the Atlanta system in 1877 was hardly as historic as Alexander Graham Bell's first words heard by his assistant. But the gist of the conversation in Atlanta is worth noting.

The first telephone installation connected W. & A. Railroad passenger agent B. W. Wrenn's office with that of the train dispatcher in the Union depot.

The installer turned the crank to ring the phone. Wrenn picked up the device which then served as a receiver, and cupped it to his ear.

Brief, Hungry Request

"Who's there?" Wrenn asked.

"Kontz," came the reply. "Anton Kontz. That's Wrenn, ain't it?"

"Yes, I'm hungry. Send word to Henry Durand to get me a good dinner."

Not as classical an utterance as that which Samuel F. B. Morse sent in the first telegraph message in 1844: "What hath God wrought."

On the other hand, Bell's first telephonic message to his assistant in 1876 was, "Mr. Watson, come here; I want you."

Wall Street in the 1870s: In the center (background) is the temporary state Capitol—Kimball's Opera House—which stood at Marietta and Forsyth Streets.

Ladies Erect a Monument

In October, 1870, the Ladies Memorial Association saw first fruit of one of their projects: the laying of the cornerstone of an Oakland Cemetery monument inscribed "Our Confederate Dead."

The 65-foot monument of Stone Mountain granite was finished in 1874, and was unveiled that April on Confederate Memorial Day, as 15,000 people watched.

This was old Hunter Street (now Martin Luther King Drive), as one looked east from just west of Pryor, in 1875: The Roman Catholic Church of the Immaculate Conception (center of photo) was completed in 1873. The corner indicated by a picket fence (just past the store with the shed roof, at right) is the present site of the Fulton County Court House.

This was Peachtree Street (1875), as one looked south from a point near present-day Auburn Avenue (old Wheat Street). The Norcross Building at Five Points was at the center, right; it is now the site of the First National Bank. The James Bank Block (center, background) was beyond the railroad tracks. The structures on the left were on ground which is now part of Central City Park.

The first Kimball House, built in 1870, burned in 1883—and was replaced in 1885 by its namesake, a hotel which lasted 70 years. The first depot was to the right.

As one looked west from Mitchell Street toward Washington Street in 1875, the view included the Second Baptist Church (left), the tower of the Church of the Immaculate Conception (center), the Central Presbyterian Church (with spire) and (at right) the City Hall and Courthouse (where the state Capitol now stands).

The horse and buggy were the principal means of inner city transportation before the trolleys came, as evidenced in this scene of bustling Wall Street.

Shortly after the Civil War, a wooden structure served as the railroad station until this iron shed replaced it in 1871. The structure shown (between Pryor Street and Central Avenue) was demolished in 1930.

In the early 1870s, Ponce de Leon Springs (on the site of the present-day Sears, Roebuck store) was a popular watering spa—and out in the countryside. In 1874, the Atlanta Street Railway (a Richard Peters enterprise) extended its line to the Springs—and away they went!

Continued from Page 93

organized in August, 1871, was becoming a potent force.

A Northern journalist in 1873 found residential areas with "a smart, new air" with "many fine houses" whose "Northern architecture and trim gardens afford a pleasant surprise after the tumble-down, unpainted towns of which there are so many in the South. Atlanta is a new, vigorous, awkwardly alert city in which there is little that is distinctly Southern."

An enterprising merchant of that period echoed the appraisal in a clever ad titled "The Seven Wonders of Atlanta." It boasted:

"1. The free mail delivery
"2. The mineral spring
"3. Uniformed police
"4. The magnificent fire department
"5. The new Iron Bridge (Broad Street)
"6. The beauty of the ladies.
"7. The greatest of all—how Ladies Underwear can be sold so cheap at No. 45 Marietta Street..."

Newspapers crowed over every improvement. In 1878 *The Constitution* said "Atlanta moves on with wonderful speed. Every street has its new buildings. Most of them are very good indeed—some of them are elegant...Our people are learning to build slowly and well. The hurry of the recuperating days of 1866 is passing away before the solid prosperity and assured importance of Atlanta...The sound of the trowel has been an unceasing music in our ears...There are no houses begging for tenants..." The paper was certain that Alexander H. Stephens' 1875 prediction—that Atlanta would have 100,000 residents by 1885—would come true.

Before 1880 dawned, Atlanta had shed the long-ago look of a "sleepy cotton market," reported a visiting journalist. Atlanta, he added, "has waxed great and powerful, and withal attractive." At colorful streetside auctions, "You may buy worn-out stoves and tables, bacon, muddy croquet sets, rubber hose of one kind and cotton hose of another, canary birds, hat racks, baby carriages, old fruit jars, clothing, bath tubs, straw sunbonnets, squirrel cages, carpets, books, bedclothes made 'befoah de wah,' sweet oil, saws, crockery, iron garden sets, ice cream freezers, saddles, window sashes—everything...from a pair of snuffers to a horse and wagon, alive and harnessed."

Local boosters and newspapers notwith-

standing, in the early 1870s Atlanta was called "Mud City" by *The Columbus* (Ga.) *Sun,* and with good reason: Getting *to* Atlanta was easier than getting around *in* Atlanta. The unpaved streets and lack of sidewalks made the town difficult to negotiate; after heavy rains, carriages stuck in the mud were common. But in 1871 a remedy loomed when the idea of a horse-drawn streetcar line finally matured as a two-mile system which began at Whitehall and the railroad tracks and ran along Peters Street to the so-called Yankee Barracks, as later Ft. McPherson was first dubbed.

Two leading citizens—railroad boosters Richard Peters and George W. Adair—purchased the charter of the dormant streetcar company and organized the Atlanta Street Railway Company. It ran by Peters' house and terminated near the Adair residence.

The system was popular, and the Company during the next three years opened other lines: from Marietta Street to near North Avenue, out Decatur Street to Oakland Cemetery and later Boulevard, and a third out Peachtree to Pine. In 1874 its stables with 17 mules, offices and 17 cars were on lots around Exchange Place and the present Hurt Building site. To calm female passengers, the Company promised that its "drivers...are mostly married men...so careful of their duties that ladies by themselves could ride in perfect safety at any hour..."

The first streetcar company's success stimulated competition: The Gate City Street Railroad Company (with Laurent DeGive as a key figure) was formed in 1879, but five years passed before it built its first line, from Pryor out Auburn to Angier. It later opened branches out Boulevard and to Piedmont Park.

The intra-city transportation system boosted commercial expansion. That energetic promotor Hannibal Kimball in 1870 built "the finest hotel south of New York" on the old Atlanta Hotel site. The Kimball House was so splendid that its arrival "marks (Atlanta's) city maturity," enthused *The Constitution.* The paper raved about the yellow-and-brown six-story structure with its mansard roof, iron framework, gas chandeliers, heating equipment, steam elevators and appointments. "There is not a cheap thing about it...It will cost Mr. Kimball over $600,000 when it is done...a splendid monument to his energy and enterprise." Before the hotel was completed, Kimball faced financial problems and lost control. But the city had a wondrous hotel until fire destroyed it 13 years later. Kimball himself left Atlanta in 1872 as the Legislature investigated him and the Bullock regime.

Five years after the debut of the Kimball House, William Markham completed his hotel on Loyd Street (now Central Ave.) at the foot of Wall Street. The 107-room Markham—with running water and "the

En route to Ponce de Leon Springs, the horse-drawn Atlanta Street Railway car crossed the low ground (at today's Penn Avenue) on a wooden trestle 40 feet high. This is an 1874 photo of the bridge over Clear Creek (now Penn Avenue).

An 1870s outing at Ponce de Leon Springs was just the ticket for a Sunday afternoon. There was target shooting, the refreshing mineral water by the glass, picnicking and just plain loafing.

Stately Trinity Methodist Church stood at Whitehall and Peters Street; at left can be seen the onion-like dome of the Hebrew Benevolent Congregation's synagogue.

Advice to the Public:
Let the Firemen Alone

In the 1870s, as now, a fire would bring out crowds, but more than a 100 years ago bystanders too often were free with advice to firefighters.

That prompted *The Daily Herald* to publish this in March, 1875:

"Our most recent excellent chief of the Fire Department, Mr. Jake Emmel, is one of the most efficient and prompt officials that the department has ever had. But he is very seriously retarded in his management of fires by the number of outsiders who rush up during a blaze and assume more authority than is proper or necessary by excitedly yelling and giving orders, and pressing suggestions upon the chief and firement, thereby tending to produce confusion and discord in the work.

"At the fire on Tuesday night this was remarked by a number of persons who witnessed the performances of some over-nervous people. Let the firemen alone, and do not embarrass the chief by suggestions and retarding operations by getting in the way of the workers. They are supposed to understand their business, and this part of the city government is entrusted to them."

best system of sewerage in the city," said *The Constitution*—is "the best hotel for the money in the Union." It lasted for 20 years until fire destroyed it, too.

The debuts of the two major hotels bracketed the initial period of financial gloom which swept the nation late in 1873: A financial panic occurred early in President Grant's second term. There had been corruption in government, excessive railroad building, speculation and inflated credit. The resultant upheaval crippled commercial enterprises and brought building operations to near immobility as real estate prices dropped and business stagnated. In Atlanta, the effects included runs on the banks, but not one collapsed.

Prior to the panic, Atlanta witnessed improvement and new enterprises. A new railroad depot was finished in 1871, soon after DeGive's Opera House opened and began staging popular plays. Brothers Julius and Gabriel Regenstein opened a modest millinery and dry goods store at 74 Whitehall in 1872, and became the first to employ a woman salesperson—Mrs. Martha Owens, a soldier's widow who stayed with the store until her death. Julius Regenstein headed the firm until his death in 1914, when three sons—Meyer, Louis

and Joseph—took over. The store over the years shifted locations, lately settling in Buckhead.

Two new banks emerged before the Panic of '73: The Citizens' Bank of Georgia opened on the ground floor of the Kimball House in 1873 but failed eight years later, costing depositors $350,000. The Bank of the State of Georgia opened in the spring of 1873, operated for years from the original Healey Building, and was liquidated in 1917, having been known as the Coker Banking Co. since 1895, and long since located on Central Ave. below Alabama Street.

Other banks emerged after the Panic of '73: The Atlanta Savings Bank opened in 1875. It became the Gate City National Bank in 1879, and died in 1893. The Merchant's Bank of Atlanta appeared in 1876 as successor to the State National Bank of Georgia.

As banks emerged and died, so did newspapers. The hardy *Atlanta Intelligencer*, the only paper to survive the war, died in 1871, having lost ground to the rising three-year-old *Constitution*, which bought most of its mechanical equipment. But a new paper competed for four years: In 1872 Alexander St. Clair Abrams

The synagogue of the Hebrew Benevolent Congregation, first Jewish house of worship in Atlanta; it stood at the corner of Forsyth and Garnett Streets. It was dedicated in August, 1877.

George Muse Corner Lot: Its Value Kept Climbing

To assess the increasing value of real estate in Atlanta, one can use a prime downtown corner as an example.

On it today sits Muse's, a top-quality clothing store, at Peachtree and Walton Streets.

In 1862 its owner, Ammi Williams, sold it for $6,000. In March, 1872, the purchaser sold it to Richard Peters and George W. Adair for $15,000.

Two months later Peters and Adair sold the lot to Calvin W. Hunnicutt for $16,000. For more than a generation, the Hunnicutt and Bellingrath firm (gas and plumbing fixtures) occupied the site.

In November, 1917, Asa G. Candler, Inc., paid the C. W. Hunnicutt estate $420,000 property.

What's the value of the lot today—65 years later?

launched the lively *Atlanta Daily Herald,* named for a New York paper he served as editorialist. With less than $200, his wife's one-third interest in the building once occupied by the *Daily New Era,* and Gen. John B. Gordon's aid, Abrams developed the sensationalist *Herald* as an intense rival to its street-side neighbor, the *Constitution.*

As the *Herald's* editor, Grady enunciated his vision of the "New South" in 1874. He insisted that prosperity required factories as well as farms, and urged businessmen into new ventures. He even supported the tarnished but energetic Kimball as president of a new cotton mill, The Atlanta Cotton Factory. It opened in 1875 at Magnolia and Marietta, with E. E. Rawson as secretary-treasurer.

Other papers of the period were less fortunate than the *Herald.* Alston and Grady launched the *Atlanta Courier,* but it collapsed in three weeks. *The Atlanta Times* published briefly; its name was revived for a short-lived newspaper in 1964-65. *The Atlanta Telegram* lasted but weeks, as did *The Atlanta Tribune. The Atlanta Post* emerged in 1878, but went under in 1881.

The Constitution in 1876 hired Grady, who promptly offered his friend Joel Chandler Harris $25 a week as editorial paragrapher. Humorist Harris, who had worked on other papers, once had registered at the Kimball House as "J. C. Harris, one wife, two bowlegged children and a bilious nurse." His anecdotes so amused his fellow roomers that the hotel charged him nothing for his brief stay. Harris thus began a 23-year career with the *Constitution,* spinning his delightful "Uncle Remus" tales, some of them written at his home, "Wren's Nest," where Andrew Carnegie and President Theodore Roosevelt visited to do him honor.

Grady became the quintessential Atlanta booster during his 13 years at the *Constitution,* until his death in 1889. He prodded entrepreneurs, supported civic enterprises, and even promoted baseball —his passion—so fervently that he was named first president of the Southern Baseball League. His editorials and speeches were widely acclaimed, and his love of the region won him the sobriquet as "spokesman of the New South."

The *Constitution* became so dominant that only one other newspaper seriously contested it for decades: *The Atlanta Journal,* born in 1883. In 1950 they merged under the leadership of the James Cox

D. F. Hammond, Atlanta's mayor in 1871

101

Three Atlanta mayors of the early 1870s: John H. James (top), whose first home, on Peachtree, became the residence of the governor, served in 1872; C. C. Hammock (middle) served in 1873, 1875 and 1876; H. B. Spencer was mayor in 1874.

family, whose leader—a former Ohio governor—had sought the presidency in 1920 with Franklin D. Roosevelt as running mate.

The newspapers had an increasingly large and lively community to tap for material, especially the city's politics and civic and commercial gains.

In the Seventies Atlanta's mayors ranged from medicos to merchants: William Ezzard, the only prewar mayor to serve later, held the post in 1870; Judge Dennis F. Hammond in 1871 was the first chief executive to serve with two black City Councilmen: tailor William Finch and carpenter George Graham. (Only 96 years later did a black again sit on the City Council.) Banker John James served in 1872. Judge Cicero Hammock was mayor in 1873 when Atlanta obtained a new City charter, a reform document which protected the people from municipal bankruptcy and burdensome taxation, as well as providing improved administration of the laws. Lawyer Samuel B. Spencer was mayor in 1874, and Hammock was returned in 1875 as the first to serve a two-year term under the new charter. Dr. Nedom L. Angier was elected for 1877-78, followed by lawyer W. L. Calhoun, son of Atlanta's wartime mayor, for 1879-80.

In the Seventies Atlanta inaugurated a downtown garbage service and free mail delivery (with five carriers in 1873). The City paid $50,000 for the northwest corner lot of Marietta and Forsyth (present site of the Bank of the South) so the Federal government would build a customs house and post office. The waterworks opened in 1875 (pumping from a Lakewood Park reservoir), and the first telephones were installed in 1877.

The first phone line connected the passenger agent's office of the W. & A. Railroad and Union Station, a short stretch. By 1879 the National Bell Telephone Co. had an exchange in the Kimball House, and 55 subscribers. Later known as the Atlanta Telephone Exchange, the company was purchased by Southern Bell Telephone and Telegraph Co. in 1881. By then there were 315 subscribers, 80 per cent of them businesses. Women operators were hired in 1888 when it was decided that the language of the first operators, who were young men, was a bit rough.

Along with commercial expansion, political stability in Atlanta improved in the Seventies, though the decade began in turmoil with Democrats seeking to unseat the Radical Republican administration of Gov. Rufus Bullock.

The key question when the Legislature opened in January, 1870, was the eligibility of members. Neither Democrats nor conservative Republicans opposed to Bullock could block his organizing a majority in both houses by purging some conservative whites and reseating blacks. The Republican Legislature promptly ratified the 14th

Continued on Page 105

Rev. William M. Finch was one of the first two blacks to become City Council members; both were elected to serve in 1870. After their one-year terms, blacks were not elected to the City Council for more than 90 years.

Jackson McHenry, a prominent black businessman and politician, was a captain of the Governor's Volunteers.

Bullock's regime were fraudulent, null and void. In February, 1874, Kimball returned, denying any illegality. His challenge went unmet, and soon Bullock and Kimball were numbered among Atlanta's leading businessmen.

The Reconstruction era ended when the last of Federal troops were withdrawn after the gubernatorial election of 1876. Ratification in 1877 of a new state Constitution confirmed Atlanta as the permanent capital. Georgia regained control of its political destiny with Smith's reelection in October, 1872.

The election (by the Legislature) of popular Gen. John B. Gordon to the U.S. Senate also signified a new phase of politics as he bested two who had long political service. Gordon devoted much energy to promoting intersectional harmony. When pioneer Jonathan Norcross lost to Democrat A. H. Colquitt in the gubernatorial contest of 1876, the Republican Party became an also-ran in Georgia for a century.

As Georgia reshaped its political independence in the Seventies, it finally established free public education. The Legislature endorsed it, City Council passed an ordinance establishing it, and voters approved in December, 1870. The first schools were readied in 1871; of 85 teacher applicants examined, 29 were chosen. Ivy Street School, Boys' High School, Girls' High and Crew and Walker Street schools opened early in 1872, but they could accommodate only 1,000 of the 2,100 pupils who sought entry. By year's end two more temporary schools were established, and a third was underway.

Boys' High became a nomad over the years, at one time sharing the Girls' High quarters in the Neal House (Sherman's headquarters and present site of City Hall), and ultimately moved to a Parkway and Tenth plant, where it was combined with Tech High (founded in 1909). Both schools are now gone, and the Henry Grady School occupies the plant. Girls' High remained in the handsome Neal house until 1926, then occupied a brick building on Rosalia Street near Grant Park; it later was replaced with co-ed Franklin D. Roosevelt High.

In 1872 financially depressed Oglethorpe University had become moribund, but in the Seventies other private institutions were added to Atlanta's growing educational prominence. Anita and Lola Washington, great-nieces of a half-brother of George Washington, launched Washington Seminary in 1878 in the Peachtree Street home of their aunt, Mrs. W. S. Walker, a general's wife. Washington Seminary, a "home and day school for girls," relocated to various sites as it grew.

The Symphony Emerges

Early in the Reconstruction period, Atlanta's Beethoven Society formed an orchestral group, but attempts to establish a symphony failed.

The formation, years later, of the Atlanta Symphony Orchestra Association, the Atlanta Musical Association, the Atlanta Music Festival Association and the Atlanta Choral Club all created a climate of desire for an orchestra.

An Atlanta Symphony Orchestra dates from 1920, and for a decade its conductor Enrico Leide further elevated Atlanta's musical awareness. But the orchestra did not survive the 1930s. In the Twenties, the Atlanta Music Club, incorporated in 1921, booked some of the world's great performers. The present orchestra is a relative of a Music Club project.

Chicago music educator Henry Sopkin came to Atlanta in the early 1940s to direct a public school music festival, and the Music Club offered him the chance to form the Atlanta Youth Symphony Orchestra. It gave its first concert in 1945, and was renamed the Atlanta Symphony Orchestra in 1947. By 1950 the American Symphony Orchestra League called it "a major orchestra." Since 1967 it has been led by Robert Shaw.

This view of Pryor Street, looking south from present-day Edgewood, was photographed in 1875. The six-story structure just past Decatur Street (on the right, with the portico across the sidewalk) was the first Kimball House. Across the street from the Kimball was the Republic Block; just beyond it, on the left, can be seen the arched front of Union Station, completed in 1871 (and demolished in 1930). A. C. & B. F. Wyly (sign at left) were wholesale grocers.

107

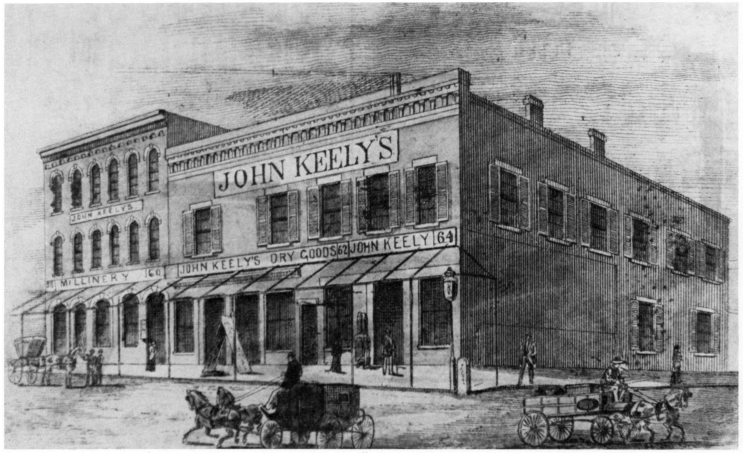

One of Atlanta's prominent stores of the Seventies was John Keely's Wholesale and Retail Dry Goods and Millinery establishment. It was at the northeast corner of Whitehall and Hunter Streets. Below, John Keely.

In 1879 Dr. Thomas S. Powell founded the Southern Medical College, and established the Ivy Street Hospital in connection with it in 1882. The Hospital, Atlanta's first to receive emergency cases, lasted 10 years, until Grady Hospital was established. In 1887 Dr. Powell established a dental department, which became Southern Dental College in 1892 (later the Atlanta Dental College). Rivalry between Dr. Powell's Southern Medical College and the older Atlanta Medical College led to their merger in 1898 as the Atlanta College of Physicians and Surgeons. Later it was incorporated into the medical department of Emory University.

Black education received a boost in 1879 when the Augusta (Ga.) Institute, founded in 1867, moved to Atlanta. It was renamed the Atlanta Baptist Seminary, and first classes were in the Friendship Baptist Church. By 1880 the Seminary was in a new brick building at West Hunter and Elliott; it moved to a tract at West Fair and Chestnut in 1889. It was renamed the Atlanta Baptist College in 1897, and Morehouse College in 1913, for Dr. Henry Morehouse, corresonding secretary of the American Baptist Home Mission Board. The first black president of the College, Dr. John Hope, served from 1906 until his resignation 25 years later.

Religious institutions continued to expand. St. Stephens' (Episcopal) Church was organized in July, 1870, and in 1872 was renamed St. Luke's. Its first sanctuary was built at Spring and Walton in 1875. In 1881 it became St. Luke's Cathedral, and in 1883 moved to Pryor and Houston. In 1906

the present St. Luke's was opened at 435 Peachtree. St. Philip's became the official Cathedral church that year.

The cornerstone was laid for the new First Methodist Church, successor to outgrown Wesley Chapel, at the present site of the Candler Building in September, 1870. Its 170-foot spire was a landmark for years. The same year, to serve West End, the Fourth Baptist church was constructed (as James Chapel, thanks to the munificence of John H. James) where Whitehall met the M. & W. Railroad (now Central of Georgia). In November that same year Rock Springs Presbyterian Church was organized at Piedmont and Montgomery Ferry Roads.

Trinity Methodist, organized in 1853, moved into a new structure at Whitehall and Trinity in 1872; after that was sold in 1911, the church occupied a new sanctuary at Washington and Trinity. And in 1879 the First Presbyterian Church, which had dedicated its first structure on Marietta Street in 1852, occupied a new Gothic building on the same site; it served until 1915 when the congregation moved to its present location, Peachtree at 16th Street. The Church's original site is occupied by the Federal Reserve Bank.

Atlanta's progress in the Seventies drew approving comment from newspapers and periodicals that sent reporters to describe the once-devastated town. But to make another kind of public statement, Atlanta turned to a device that created self-satisfaction, revenue and wide notice: expositions. There had been fairs in Atlanta as early as 1850, but the one in 1870 had a broader self-promotional purpose. It was the forerunner of three major expositions the city would support between 1881 and 1895.

Oglethorpe Park, a woodland retreat just northwest of the city on the W. & A. Railroad, became the fairground (later the site of Exposition Cotton Mills). The Park featured a race course and lake. (The rowing, said one observer, "would be a very beneficial exercise for our feeble young ladies who are suffering from narrow chests and crooked spines.")

A prime promoter of the fair was that ace entrepreneur Hannibal Kimball. The October, 1870, event proved highly popular, with some 20,000 people showing up on a peak day. Though it was primarily an agricultural fair, it also featured fiddling contests, competitions for the finest horses, best handiwork and most artistic paintings, as well as the first trap-pigeon-shooting event and a tournament. That last event, wherein riders sought to capture on their lances the greatest number of rings hanging from a post, ended in tragedy: Michael E. Kenny, proprietor of the Chicago Ale Depot, was killed when his horse leaped a railing. Kenny's Alley bore his name.

Nonetheless, the fair helped encourage the fine art of recreation, and Atlanta needed respite from daily drudgery.

The fun-minded could use the skating rink (at Forsyth and the railroad) in 1870 (though it declined in popularity after Sallie Solomon received fatal injuries while skating). Ponce de Leon Springs (across from the Sears, Roebuck Building on Ponce de Leon) proved a delightful spa for picnickers and those who quaffed its healthy waters (gallons of it were also delivered to homes). An elegant saloon named Big Bonanza provided more spiritous refreshment. Baseball was still the rage, and a team called the Osceolas appeared in 1872 but vanished the same season after losing a 1-0 game to a Rome, Ga., club.

In the same year the "walking craze" hit as competitors vied to see who could pace the longest. Atlanta had its own Mardi Gras—complete with parades, "King Rex" and a ball at DeGive's—as early as 1873. There were army band concerts at the Yankee Barracks, and actor Edwin Booth —brother of Lincoln's assassin—played in a series of dramas at DeGive's in 1876. The City Council met early one day so its members could see Booth that evening; he was a rousing success.

For the literary, Atlanta offered added lures. A literary weekly, *The Sunny South,*

Continued on Page 117

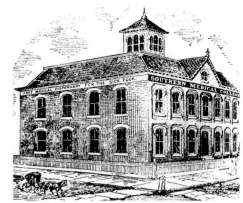

The Southern Medical College, founded 1879, was known also as a "medical dispensary for the sick poor."

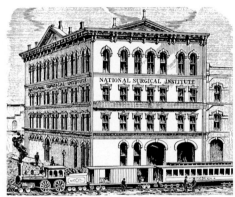

National Surgical Institute, as it appeared in 1872

McBride's crockery store was at the corner of Pryor and Decatur Streets.

The first Healey Building, erected in 1877 at the northwest corner of Marietta and Peachtree Streets, was demolished in 1930. Atlanta's papers of 1877 called it "quite modern looking."

SCHAUB & PERKINS,

SOUTHERN PORTRAIT GALLERY

—AND—

PHOTOGRAPHIC COPYING HOUSE

NO. 28 WHITEHALL STREET,
(Connally Building)

—☜ PHOTOGRAPHS ☞—

OF ALL STYLES

MADE IN THE MOST FINISHED MANNER.

SPECIAL ATTENTION GIVEN TO PORTRAITS

OF ALL SIZES

COPIED FROM SMALL PICTURES OF ANY KIND,
EITHER PLAIN OR ARTISTICALLY PAINTED,
IN OIL OR PASTEL, INK OR CRAYON.

——ALSO——

THE EXQUISITE PEARL CAMEO PHOTOGRAPH AND PORCELAIN IVORYTYPE.

☞ All are invited to call at our splendid Gallery and see specimens of these beautiful styles of portraiture.

☞ Mr. J. W. PERKINS, formerly of Augusta, will be happy to meet here his many friends and former patrons in different parts of the State.

Our new sky-light is so arranged that we can do as good work in cloudy as clear weather.

Park Medical Institute,

Marietta Street, Cor. of Peachtree Street

IN NATIONAL HOTEL BUILDING, ENTRANCE MARIETTA STREET,

ATLANTA, GEORGIA.

Diseases of all kinds, including surgical cases and the most inveterate Chronic, or old standing diseases, in both sexes, treated upon Scientific Eclectic Medical Principles, using the best and most efficient remedies of all schools of practice, and the latest appliances and improvements known to the Medical World—bringing to bear, also, the individual discoveries and improvements made by Dr. W. T. Park, who has an experience of 25 years in an extensive practice, and who has acquired an established medical reputation and a national fame

Advice and Medicines furnished in the Institute, or forwarded by Express or Mail, (Express preferred), to any address on reception of a full statement of the case. Patients from a distance requiring personal attention, provided with board, lodging and treatment at the Institute, hotels, boarding houses, or at private residences in the city, as they may select, at reasonable rates, paid in advance per week. Call at office, or address

W. T. PARK, M.D.,
Or **J. H. GOSS, M.D.,**
Physicians and Surgeons in Charge.

Post Office Box 158, Atlanta, Ga.

OPIUM ANTIDOTE.

A PAINLESS and PERMANENT CURE for

The Opium and Morphine Habit,

Guaranteed by Dr. W. T. Park.

Address as above directed.

The Entrepreneurs Enliven the City

The postwar bursts of entrepreneurial energy were reflected in advertisements of the 1870s.

Atlantans, emerging from the devastation of political Reconstruction, were eager for new products, new services, new cures. The city increasingly attracted opportunists from other sections, visionaries who saw reviving Atlanta as a place with potential.

On these two pages are ads selected from the Atlanta city directory of 1876.

In that edition, The Atlanta Constitution offered a yearly subscription for $10.60; Freeman's Billiard Hall proclaimed itself "The Finest in the South"; John Hoffman's Barber Shop assured would-be patrons, "Everything Clean and Neat"; and an establishment called Two Orphans, operated by Reed & Shane, promised "None but pure and unadulterated liquors dispensed."

CHICAGO ALE DEPOT,

——AND——

Wholesale Wine and Liquor House,

NO. 44 SOUTH PRYOR ST., ATLANTA, GEORGIA,

AGENTS FOR THE CELEBRATED

RUSSELL AND OLD WICKLIFFE WHISKIES,

CHOICE WINES AND LIQUORS,

PUT UP FOR FAMILIES AND MEDICINAL USE,

English and Scotch Ales and Porter

BY THE CASK OR BOTTLE.

O. C. CARROLL,

PROPRIETOR.

1876—SOMETHING NEW—1876

No Residence or Hotel Complete Without Them.

 GEORGE L. DAVIS

Electrical Engineer,

PUTS UP HOTEL, HOUSE, BURGLAR AND
THERMOMATIC FIRE ALARM

Annunciators!

All kinds of ELECTRICAL BELL HANGING. Work as cheap as in the North or elsewhere, where these systems are in exclusive use. Wires concealed and no defacing walls or plastering in putting them up. Also,

GAS LIGHTING BY ELECTRICITY.

Electrical Clocks, Watchman's Time Recorder, School, Philosophical, Experimental and Medical Electro-Machinery; in fact, all kinds Electrical work, put up, repaired, and kept in order.

AMATEUR & PRIVATE TELEGRAPHS

Constructed so as to be operated with the Gray's, Dial or other Printing instruments, the Morse or other telegraph systems. Personal and written instructions FREE, as to manipulating and keeping the same in order.

 **Lightning Rods.**

Resistance calculated, *located,* removed and repaired in old rods. New rods put up. My work is not experimental, but the result of many years of practical experience.

When requested I will be pleased to make estimates, free of charge, as to costs, etc., for parties contemplating any or all of the above work.

☞ Call on or address me at HUNNICUTT & BELLINGRATHS, No. 12 Marietta St.

REFERENCES—Messrs. Hunnicutt & Bellingrath, Col. Wm. Markham and Col. James E. Owens, Proprietor Markham House.

HYGIENIC INSTITUTE.

GRAND

IF YOU would enjoy the most delightful luxury; if you would be speedily, cheaply, pleasantly and permanently cured of all Inflammatory, Nervous, Constitutional, and Blood Disorders; if you have Rheumatism, Scrofula, Dyspepsia, Bronchitis, Catarrh, Diarrhœa, Dysentery, Piles, Neuralgia, Paralysis, Disease of the Kidneys, Genitals or Skin, Chill and Fever, or other Malarial Affections; if you would be purified from all Poisons, whether from Drugs or Disease; if you would have Beauty, Health, and Long Life, GO TO the

Hygienic Institute,

and use NATURE'S GREAT REMEDIES, the

TURKish

TURKISH BATH;

the "**Water-Cure Processes,**" the "**Movement-Cure,**" ELECTRICITY AND OTHER HYGIENIC AGENTS.

SUCCESS WONDERFUL!

CURING ALL CURABLE CASES.

If not able to go and take board, send full account of your case, and get directions for TREATMENT AT HOME. Terms reasonable. Location, corner Loyd and Wall Streets, opposite Passenger Depot, ATLANTA, GEORGIA.

BATH!

JNO. STAINBACK WILSON,
PHYSICIAN-IN-CHARGE.

Southern Shirt Manufactory

ED. F. SHROPSHIRE & CO.

—— MANUFACTURERS AND DEALERS IN ——

White and Colored Shirts!

COLLARS, BOSOMS and DRAWERS

 21--23 East Alabama St., **Atlanta, Georgia.**

 We will take your measure, make to order and guarantee a good fit, at lower figures than inferior work is sold at.

111

Chrisman Hall was erected in 1877, and became part of the Clark College complex on the Atlanta University campus. Chrisman Hall, whose architecture was influenced by the Italianate style, burned in 1934.

Barrels line the sidewalks outside the establishment of A. C. & B.F. Wyly, wholesale grocers and commission merchants, in this photo made about 1875. The building was at the corner of Pryor and Decatur Streets. The photograph was by Smith & Motes; the latter is depicted earlier in this history, dressed in his Confederate uniform.

Fulton County prison, about 1875

A cotton press of about 1875: This was the "white gold" on which the Southern economy rested before the Civil War and for some years thereafter—until depressions forced prices to fall precipitously.

In September, 1877, President Rutherford B. Hayes came to Atlanta and drew a crowd when he spoke from the balcony of the Markham House, which faced Wall Street and present-day Central Avenue. A corner of the railroad passenger depot is seen at right. The Markham House, a major hotel for more than 20 years, opened in 1875 and was destroyed by fire in 1896.

Long before there was a public library, the Young Men's Library Association offered services to members in a Marietta Street building, the interior of which was sketched in the 1870s.

If you look carefully at this posed photograph of September 23, 1876, you can identify 10 persons at Dr. A. J. Bell's residence at the corner of Alexander and Luckie Streets. Note the gas lamp (left, foreground) and the protective framing around the young trees.

Bernard Mallon was the first superintendent of the Atlanta Public School system, serving from 1871 to 1879.

Major William Franklin Slaton served as the second superintendent of the Atlanta Public School system, 1879-1907.

The sturdy home of the William Ezzard family from 1850-1879 was occupied from 1879-1899 by Dr. James P. Alexander. It rested on the northwest corner of Peachtree and Luckie Streets, but was demolished in 1902 to make way for the Piedmont Hotel. The site is now occupied by the Equitable Building.

William A. Kuhns was a prominent photographer in Atlanta's early years; some of his work is seen in this book.

Hexagon Hall, one of Atlanta's unique residences, was originally the home of Col. John M. C. Reed, who died in 1880. Subsequently, it was the home of his son-in-law Samuel B. Turman and his family. The house stood on a large tract of land in the angle formed by McDonough Road, which it faced, Jonesboro Road and Lakewood Avenue.

Continued from Page 109

was launched in 1874, but was sold by 1893 to *The Atlanta Constitution,* where it appeared as a supplement. In 1907 it was incorporated into the *Uncle Remus Magazine,* which folded in 1913. The Catholic Library Association was organized in 1877. The Atlanta Pioneer and Historic Society was organized in 1871 to preserve the young town's history, but its founders apparently never met again, and only 30 years later was a similar entity organized.

The first incumbent President to visit Atlanta, Rutherford B. Hayes, came in 1877 to help cement warmer feelings between North and South. He toured the city (where he had fought 13 years before as a Union officer), then appeared before crowds, bands, fluttering flags and speech-makers who welcomed him at the Markham Hotel. Later the same day, following a reception attended by 1,000 at the Executive Mansion, President and Mrs. Hayes were northbound again.

The visitor who really excited Atlanta had been in town twice before: once ignored, once damned. On his third visit, in 1879, Gen. William T. Sherman returned to the place he had torched 15 years before. In the waiting, good-humored crowd there was ample raillery. One man shouted as the Sherman train arrived, "Ring the fire bells! The town will be gone in 40 minutes!" Sherman, two daughters and aides toured the city, admiring Atlanta's restoration. He was honored with a ball at the Yankee Barracks, a grand military review, receptions and a visit with Gov. Colquitt. Within 24 hours the party was gone—but Sherman would return.

Evidence of Atlanta's seamier life was capsuled in the police chief's report covering 1874. Capt. Thomas Jones, commanding 46 men, reported that the city "is no longer the rendezvous of thieves and criminals," though 3,605 arrests were made, and he asked for more officers. He endorsed the chain gang, deplored confinement of "youths with more hardened criminals" in Atlanta's new jail, asked for salary increases, and confessed that "No means (have) been discovered to abate the social evil"—*i.e.,* prostitution. It sounded like a police report of a century later.

Stray animals also preoccupied the police, causing City Council to pass the 1875 "cow ordinance" requiring owners to keep their animals penned at night or be fined $2 per captured cow. The ordinance asked the public to round up the heifers, but the police mainly handled the nuisance, as one amusing police report of 1875 showed:

"Officer Monaghan found Judge Hopkins' cow asleep on the sidewalk, and he forthwith began to drive her in. Monaghan had a hard time of it, and it several times happened that the thing got reversed, and he discovered that the cow was driving *him.* It was upon these occasions that officer Monaghan developed

The three men are unidentified, but they were obviously performers—the two in togas (above, left and right) obviously in some drama, and the lecturer (below) offering a stern lesson in morality as he strikes a Napoleonic pose.

that agility, for which he is so distinguished, and made for the nearest tree. After much time had been spent in alternately advancing and retreating, reinforcements arrived, and the cow was safely driven up."

Atlanta was an oversize country town in the 1870s, but in the last two decades of the century there were extraordinary bursts of commercial and residential development as war scars diminished and the city reached for a kind of cosmopolitanism.

In three expositions Atlanta confirmed to the world its progress; new colleges were launched; fine Victorian homes dotted the suburbs reached by expanding trolleys; electricity powered new enterprises; a wide range of nationally known personalities appealed to those hungry for amusements, culture and political guidance. Much of all that energy would develop new institutions and products—including a "headache cure" introduced without special fanfare in 1886.

That nostrum would later make millionaires whose enterprise and philosophy did so much to improve the face and character of the city. The original "headache cure" was a syrup whose name became the world's most famous trademark: Coca-Cola. Profits from that original 5 cent drink helped cure a lot of Atlanta's civic headaches, too.

It looked like they were tearing up old Alabama Street again: The view in 1877 is west from Pryor Street. The stone building at the center is the Atlanta National Bank, founded in 1865. In the distance was the site of today's Rich's department store.

One of Kuhns' photographs: This is Peachtree Street, 1872, as one looked north from the railroad crossing. The horsecar was heading south on Whitehall. The sign at right is for C. C. Hammock's Real Estate Office; Hammock served as mayor in 1873, 1875 and 1876.

On the foundations of the renewed enterprise of the 1870s, Atlanta in the next 20 years sealed the door on Reconstruction and launched a series of remarkable commercial, cultural, educational and social advances that set the city's progressive tone for a century. The Seventies were an uneven overture; the Eighties and Nineties hummed with the rousing music of a lusty town eager for its place in the sectional sun, at least.

Spurts in population paced the progress: The hamlet of 22,00 in 1870 became a town of 37,000 in 1880, and a city of almost 90,000 by 1900. And what a new city began to emerge!

Editor Henry Grady, addressing the New England Club in New York City on December 21, 1886, painted the spirit of Atlanta's renewed vigor: "We have caught the sunshine in the bricks and mortar of our homes..."

The town born only 40 years before as a rail terminus developed its intra-urban transport system: Streetcars were first mule-drawn, then steam-powered and finally electrified, opening subdivisions and suburbs to accommodate residents spilling into new homes built over once-ravaged vales. Office buildings exceeded the height of church spires. The city climbed above its hazardous railroad tracks; some treacherously muddy streets were paved just prior to the Age of the Automobile. City officials established library and fire services, and

New Visions, New Ventures
1880-1900

Transportation continued to shape Atlanta as electric-powered trolleys opened up the city. This one ran from Fair Street to Grant Park.

119

The onetime Peachtree Street home of banker John H. James served as the Governor's mansion for 50 years until 1921, when a residence in Ansley Park was occupied for that purpose. The pictured home was near present-day Davison's.

extended water and sewage facilities. Electric lights replaced sputtering oil-and-gas fixtures. Public schools expanded.

By 1900 the Georgia Institute of Technology, Agnes Scott College, Morris Brown College, Spelman College and the antecedent of Emory Medical College were established. Private and professional clubs —such as the Atlanta Bar Association, the Benevolent and Protective Order of Elks, the Capital City Club, the Piedmont Driving Club, the Salvation Army, the Atlanta Athletic Club, the United Daughters of the Confederacy, the Women's Club and the Burns Club—took root, as did new churches.

With prosperity and better transportation, Atlantans pursued leisure at growing theaters, football and baseball games, golf, fairs, the parks and the zoo.

By 1900 a host of firms, spawned in and after 1880, were prospering. They include some of present-day Atlanta's best known enterprises: St. Joseph's Hospital, Southern Railway, Davison's, Randall Brothers, *The Atlanta Journal,* Miller's Book Store, King Hardware, The Coca-Cola Company, Haverty's, Robinson-Humphrey Company, Trust Company Bank, Life of Georgia, Grady Memorial Hospital, Georgia Power Company, H. M. Patterson's Funeral Home, Citizens &

Southern National Bank, Atlanta Title Company, King and Spalding, Westview Cemetery, Maier & Berkele, Equifax, Troutman, and Sanders, Lockerman and Ashmore. Most of these bear their original names.

The city's new dynamism attracted visiting personalities who came to be seen and heard: Presidents Grover Cleveland and William McKinley, Vice President Adlai Stevenson, suffragist Susan B. Anthony, explorer Henry M. Stanley, Socialist Eugene V. Debs, Gen. Winfield Scott, orator William Jennings Bryan, actress Anna Held, Rear Admiral William S. Schley and poet James Whitcomb Riley. Woodrow Wilson came to Atlanta in the Eighties, practiced law for a time and then left, certainly unaware he would become President.

To promote its growing eminence Atlanta hosted three major self-boosting expositions: in 1881, 1887 and 1895—the last attracting such luminaries as conductor-composer John Phillip Sousa, educator Booker T. Washington and thousands of visitors among whom were some who elected to cast their futures with the city, such as Ivan Allen and H. G. Hastings.

There was another attraction: the State Capitol, dedicated in 1889 after five years' construction. That made Atlanta a battle-

The second Kimball House was erected in 1885, two years after Hannibal I. Kimball's first hotel was destroyed by fire. The second Kimball—close by Five Points—was torn down in 1959.

Ruins of the first Kimball House, which faced the railroad tracks. It burned in 1883, having survived from 1870 as one of Atlanta's finest hotels. It was Atlanta's largest building of the 1870s.

Artesian well at Five Points soon
gave way after this 1892 photograph;
the laying of electric trolley lines
spelled progress.

Laying trolley tracks at Marietta and
Broad brought the same sort of
interruption of traffic that MARTA
construction brings today.

ground among politicians. The business of Atlanta was commerce but the business of most Georgians was agriculture, and rural and urban politics competed for their different, sometimes opposing, interests.

The nationwide financial panics of 1873 and 1893 were particularly stressful to farmers: Their crops declined in value while they remained in debt to suppliers. Thus the rural residents responded to the appeal of Populism, which urged controls on money-lenders and businessmen, and for easier credit and wider circulation of money.

Other Georgians insisted that the state's salvation lay in industrial expansion, warning that the South would suffer economic slavery so long as it relied solely on the North for manufactured goods. Both segments of Georgians were correct, of course, for what was needed was a balance. It was an age of robber barons, an era when labor felt deprived of its just rewards, and most wealth was controlled tightly by a few; legal restraints were needed to protect the weak, and industrialization was perceived as a vehicle to correct the imbalances, and convey the South to new strength.

Henry W. Grady, editor of *The Atlanta Constitution*, was the most aggressive promoter and eloquent spokesman for the industrialization of the "New South," a principle he enunciated before joining the paper. He pointedly told of the Georgia farmer who was buried in the clothes and a coffin of Northern manufacture; even the coffin nails, the shovel to dig the grave and the marble marker came from the North. All Georgia provided was a hole in the ground—though the raw materials for all the farmer's needs existed in Georgia.

Four years after Grady joined *The Constitution,* he borrowed $20,000 from Wall Street capitalist Cyrus Field and bought a one-fourth interest in the paper. His position gave Grady a powerful platform and he aligned himself with key businessmen and politicians, notably three conservative Democrats: ex-Gov. Brown, Gen. (senator and later governor) John B. Gordon, and Gov. A. H. Colquitt. Indeed, Grady did not shy from political involvement as later journalists were required: He was the manager for Gordon's successful gubernatorial campaign of 1886.

The editor, an extraordinary figure much loved in the North and South for his conciliatory views, supported numerous civic causes and educational advances. He was a prime mover in bringing the Piedmont Chautauqua circuit to Lithia Springs; the educational programs, concerts and lectures of Chautauqua were rousing suc-

Atlanta never looked busier at Five Points where, at one time, the trolleys turned around to continue their runs.

123

Electrified trolleys brought Atlantans into the city, and back to the new suburbs. The name, Atlanta Rapid Transit Co., is similar to that of present-day MARTA.

This was old Alabama Street, which lies dormant beneath the present-day Alabama. Old Alabama became the heart of the revived Underground Atlanta section. In this 1895 photo, the view is west toward Whitehall Street from east of Pryor. Keeping order amid the mule-drawn wagons is one of "Atlanta's finest," a chunky policeman. When viaducts over these streets were completed in 1929, this part of Atlanta went underground, and lay dormant until the tourist attraction revived the area for a few years.

cesses. Grady spoke heartily for the establishment of Georgia Tech, was a key mover in organizing the Piedmont Driving Club, and deserves much credit for the large expositions which Atlanta hosted in 1881 and 1887.

He was also an avid sports fan who promoted baseball and, as his paper's managing editor, alarmed editor Evan Howell by running up large expenses for telegraphic reports of the games. "If you don't stop it, I'm going to charge it up to you," threatened Howell. Said Grady: "That's all right. Charge it. But I'm going to have the baseball news just the same." So strongly was Grady's backing that in 1884 he became first president of the Southern Baseball League.

In late 1889, during a Boston speech wherein he urged mutual sectional understanding and respect, Grady caught cold; it worsened during his pilgrimage to Plymouth Rock. A few days after his return to Atlanta, he died on December 23, at age 39. A public subscription was launched immediately to erect Grady's statue. Unveiled in 1891, it remains at the intersection of Marietta and Forsyth, across from the building now housing *The Constitution*. His name was applied to a hotel, a high school, the city's huge charity hospital and a World War II naval vessel.

The first of the two fairs Grady espoused to herald the city's growth and potential was the International Cotton Exposition from Oct. 5 to Dec. 31, 1881. The idea emerged from *The Constitution's* reprint of a Boston economist-inventor's letter in the *New York Herald*. Edward Atkinson's letter urged a Southern convention of those interested in cotton production and the use of waste incident to the methods used in gathering the crop. Grady became an evangelist for the idea of an exposition, and Atkinson's Atlanta friend, H. I. Kimball, president of the Atlanta Cotton Factory, joined in.

Following a presentation by Atkinson in Atlanta, planning was led by Colquitt, Brown, Samuel M. Inman, John Ryckman, Howell and others. Local leaders visited cities whose merchants were interested, and a site was selected along the W. & A. tracks three miles from the city's center. Kimball was named director-general, and within 150 days the principal construction work and the 19-acre grounds were ready. (The site later became the home of the Exposition Cotton Mills, a division of J. P. Stevens Co.)

It was an extraordinary show, with 1,113 exhibits including those from seven countries. Dignitaries from various states were among the 300,000 who attended the events, listened to the bands and speechmakers, and reveled in the parades. Even the legislatures of Kentucky and South Carolina adjourned so members could view the improved textile machinery. A

The temporary state Capitol was the leased Kimball's Opera House, at the southwest corner of Marietta and Forsyth Streets (photographed about 1880). It served the Legislature for almost 20 years until the new Capitol was opened in 1889. At left is Concordia Hall. About 11 years after this photo was made, the Henry W. Grady statue was dedicated at its present site on Marietta—just to the right in the picture.

The U. S. Post Office and Custom House—shown in the 1890s (left center)—was purchased to serve as City Hall. The view is to the north on Forsyth Street. The top of the Henry Grady statue can be seen in the foreground (center). Now on the site of the onetime Post Office is the Bank of the South Building. The Healey Building (just up from Marietta on Forsyth, at right) was on the site of the present Grant Building.

The view looking north on Forsyth Street in 1882: The street crossing it in the foreground is Walton. At lower right, the present site of the Standard Federal Building. Tower in the upper right was that of the First Methodist Church, now the site of the Candler Building. The church with the spire (center of photo) was the First Baptist, present site of the old post office.

The Fulton County Court House stood where its successor was erected. This photo shows the old Court House in 1890, nine years after it was opened. It was demolished in 1911. At left, present-day Martin Luther King Drive; at right, Pryor Street.

remarkable demonstration was staged during the Exposition: Shortly after one sunrise, enough cotton was picked to be ginned on the grounds and woven into cloth for two suits worn that evening by Gov. Colquitt and Connecticut Gov. Bigelow.

The most unusual guest, making his fourth visit to Atlanta, was Gen. W. T. Sherman, a substantial subscriber to the Exposition. Speaking to Mexican War veterans, Sherman observed, "I have come today to look upon these buildings where once we had battlefields. I delight more to look upon them than to look upon the scenes enacted here 16 (sic) years ago. I say that every noble man and kindly woman over this broad land takes as much interest in your prosperity and in this Exposition as do those sitting in this presence, and that we are now in a position to say, every one of us, great and small, Thank God we are American citizens."

Sherman's remarks came on the 17th—not the 16th—anniversary of his departure from the city he burned.

Six years later the Piedmont Exposition was developed as a 12-day fair in Piedmont Park, on grounds leased to the Exposition by the Gentlemen's Driving Club (later Piedmont Driving Club), which had purchased the almost 200 acre site. The Fulton County chain gang was used to help clear the land of crops, and again Grady kept up an editorial drumfire of support. The Piedmont Exposition began Oct. 10, 1887 (two days after the Driving Club opened) and rural patrons poured into the gaily decorated city by train so that 20,000 attended on opening day. "The people were in good humor, the sky was like sapphire," noted wholesale grocer James R. Wylie, "and the earth smiled" on the parades, the speeches, the balloon ascension, the music, the races and the displays.

A week later President Grover Cleveland and his recent bride, Frances Folsom, arrived to booming cannon as crowds packed the Union Depot area in inclement weather. Festivities for the President (at

"Humbug Square" Became Pitchmen's Heaven

As the city began to recover from its destruction, there developed a central lot—bounded by the railroad, Whitehall, Alabama and Pryor Streets—that became a locus for pitchmen.

It earned the name "Humbug Square," and became the busiest vacant lot in town. Carnivals, medicine shows, snake-oil hustlers, auctioneers and fakers attracted crowds by day and by the night-time glow of pine knot torches.

"Humbug Square" was in the area more recently occupied by the Underground Atlanta development. that area proved equally busy—by day and night—during its life of a few years.

127

The lead article in the March 5, 1883, issue of The Atlanta Post-Appeal reported on the death—two days before—of Gov. Alexander H. Stephens. The former Confederate vice-president had predicted in 1839 a great future for the railroad terminus which became Atlanta. At right, the Stephens funeral procession on Marietta Street.

A Nation's Loss

Governor Alexander Hamilton Stephens, ex-Vice-President Confederate States, is No More.

The Last Hours of the Great Statesman— Disposition of the Remains—Graphic Details, Supplemented by

An Interesting Sketch of His Private and Public Life and Services, by His Friend and Earliest Biographer, Rev. Henry W. Cleveland, of Atlanta.

The evening shades gathered over Atlanta in sadness on Saturday, March 3d, 1883.

There was a hushed calmness that seemed to pervade everywhere, which was only disturbed by the soft inquiries of anxious people passing to and fro along the streets as to the condition of Georgia's illustrious Great Commoner, Alexander Hamilton Stephens.

That he was approaching death rapidly seemed to gain credence as if by intuition. There was that fond lingering hope that this "spell" might prove to be as so many that have preceded it—only temporary, and one from which the great patient sufferer would soon recover. Precedent seemed to have established the impression in the minds of even those closest to the Governor that he would soon rally and be "as well as ever." There were only a few who seemed to know that the final dissolution was near at hand. Even Gov. Stephens' private secretary, Colonel Seidell, believed up to the very last moments that his illustrious patron would be "all right in a few days."

the Driving Club and Capital City Club) allowed Atlanta's elite to put their best feet forward and by the following night the Chief Executive was gone. Booming cannons at ends of the Exposition grounds climaxed its closing. The fair made a profit of $9,746.

In 1904 the City agreed to pay $98,000 for Piedmont Park, and later sold the Driving Club certain rights in the Park adjacent to the Club's grounds for $5,000. So the 185 acres of Piedmont Park fell into the city's hands for $93,000. The Park then included vast grading, the lake, improvements, large buildings, sewerage and a race track—later an area for baseball and softball.

Four years after Grady's death, *Constitution* business manager and then-mayor William A. Hemphill suggested a another fair. Samuel Inman promptly presided over a meeting of 300 businessmen who launched the greatest of Atlanta's fairs: The International Cotton States Exposition of 1985. The City appropriated $75,000 for the fair to be held in Piedmont Park (after Lakewood was rejected); citizens chipped in $134,000, and Fulton County did $150,000 worth of work in the Park—but the event outdistanced such modest financial underwriting.

Ultimately it cost nearly $3 million, but it achieved its purposes—two of which were to exhibit the resources of cotton states and stimulate trade with Spanish-American nations. This time Charles Collier became director-general. Key figures read like a "Who's Who" of the Nineties, and one of the most effective units was the Women's Department, with Mrs. Joseph Thompson as president of the Board of Women Managers. The ladies were coming out of the kitchen.

Laywer Jack J. Spalding drew a bill to submit to the Federal House Committee on Appropriations to seek funds. Rep. J. G. Cannon, chairman, asked: "Do you mean to say that the whole nation should spend its money for something that benefits only a few states?" With that, he was told that "This exposition is for the benefit of all those who grow cotton and all those who wear cotton." Added testimony before the Committee came from three prominent blacks—educator Booker T. Washington and Bishops Gaines of Georgia and Grant of Texas. Congress voted $200,000—with support from Rep. William Cogswell, the man who, as a colonel, had led the first Union troops into Atlanta on its surrender 30 years before.

Grant Wilkins and James R. Wylie supervised transformation of Piedmont Park into a fairyland within eight months. It was a mind-boggling conglomeration of buildings surrounding a lake and a midway. Various structures were named for states wherein they exhibited their wares. In addition there were the Fire Building, with the latest apparatus; the Fine Arts Building; the 65,000-square foot Government Building; a U.S. Army encampment; the Agricultural Building topped by a 180-foot pyramidal tower; a Mexican Village with musicians, peons, matadors and toreadors—but bullfights were forbidden; the Negro Building (erected by a black contractor); Machinery and Minerals and Forestry Buildings (atop the last was a roof garden where diners listened to Gilmore's Band); the Southern Railway Building with a small-scale depot; Transportation Building; Electricity Building; a Japanese Village with a teahouse; the Women's Building; Manufacturers' Building and others.

Buffalo Bill and his Wild West Show entertained thousands seated in grandstands; an 1849 Mining Camp featured a grisly graveyard; in Lake Clara Meer erupted a spectacular electric fountain. Along the popular Midway Heights was a maze of attractions including Rocky Mountain Ponies, Monkey Paradise, the Ostrich Farm, Indian Village, Chinese Village, Water Chutes, the Ferris Wheel, Deep Sea Diving, Gold Mine, Moorish Palace, the

Gov. Alfred H. Colquitt (above) was one of the "Bourbon Triumvirate," along with former Gov. Joseph Brown and Gen. John B. Gordon. They dominated Georgia politics from 1872 to 1890. Colquitt served as governor for six years following his initial election in 1876.

Capt. James W. English was a banker who served Atlanta as mayor in 1881-1882. He lived in his 40 Cone Street home, one of the first to have electric lights and a phone, from 1880 until his death in 1925.

Lumberman George V. Gress (above) and Thomas J. Jones bought some animals at the auction of a defunct circus and gave them to the City to start a zoo in 1889. Gress later bought and donated the Cyclorama to the City.

Mystic Maze, and the Streets of Cairo including a camel and hootchie-kootchie dancers.

President Cleveland in Washington pushed a button on Sept. 18 to start the Exposition machinery, and 25,000 people surged through the gates on opening day as military parades led the way and a band played Victor Herbert's new *Salute to Atlanta*.

By the time the Exposition closed 3½ months later, some 800,000 people had attended. President Cleveland made his second Atlanta visit; Civil War veterans held reunions; crowds gawked at the Liberty Bell, on brief loan from Philadelphia; governors spoke; awards were presented; Henry Grady was paid tribute; soldiers drilled; Walter Damrosch and his Opera Company performed, as did John Philip Sousa and his famous band, which premiered a march he had written for the event, *King Cotton*. Sousa came despite the Exposition's cancellation of his contract when it ran into financial difficulty, but he convinced the directors to keep the pact. There was a slight disagreement when the Exposition transportation department charged Sousa $3 for carrying his large instruments to the bandstand.

Despite the crowds, the Exposition could not meet its nearly $3 million tab, and Samuel Inman, chairman of the finance committee, offered to advance $50,000 if the other directors would match the sum to meet obligations. It was promptly done, and bankruptcy avoided. The Exposition proved to be the greatest boost Atlanta had since its birth, and for many decades thereafter.

One feature did not catch fire: the "Living Pictures," which offered animated life-size figures projected on a screen. The focus was often wrong and the spotty film broke. After a few dull days, the tiny theater was destroyed by fire. Only years later did motion pictures became the rage in Atlanta.

Apart from the Exposition's promotional and economic impact, it also provided a platform for a speech of significance—that of Booker T. Washington. In it the pragmatist accepted political disfranchisement in exchange for educational and employment opportunity—thus tacitly admitting the "separate but equal" doctrine which, the following year, became fixed into law. It was finally overturned by the U.S. Supreme Court almost 60 years later.

By the advent of the 1895 Exposition Atlanta had other civic improvements to boast about.

The City had established a uniformed police department in 1873, and in early 1882 organized a 26-man paid fire department under Chief Matt Ryan. The volunteer fire organizations disbanded in May, following a parade and a banquet for 200. In 1882 Chief Ryan reported 129 blazes; later, two major ones destroyed landmarks: the Kimball House, in 1883 (but soon rebuilt), and the Markham Hotel in 1896. The city's most destructive fire struck in 1917.

Though the city's first water system was inaugurated in 1875, in 1885 Atlanta had only 17 miles of sewers and they were inadequate; that year 9,000 outdoor privies, serviced by 12 night-soil wagons, outnumbered flush toilets three to one. Over the decades the sewer lines were greatly expanded and treatment plants installed.

To help relieve the inadequate water supply begun with the waterworks on the South River in 1875, City Council

The entranceway to Oglethorpe Park, sketched about 1880. The Park was along the W. & A. Railroad tracks, three miles from the city's center. The International Cotton Exposition in the fall of 1881 showed it off to best advantage.

A FAMILIAR PLAINT

A complaint of 1886 has a contemporary ring.

On September 16, an angry citizen of Pea Ridge wrote the editor of an Atlanta newspaper:

"Mr. Editor: I wish you would tell us what's the matter with the Post Office at Decatur. We can't get our mail half the time. Surely it don't take a month for the weekly (Atlanta) *Journal* to come from Atlanta to Decatur... I heard a man say he received a *Journal* on September 11 that was printed on August 12..."

approved drilling an artesian well at Five Points in 1884. The well's steam-powered pump delivered 200,000 gallons daily, delivered along key downtown streets by mains to public taps where the thirsty could use a chain-secured cup. The artesian well passed into history in 1894 when City Council declared the water impure. Atlanta's water source became the Chattahoochee in 1893, following bond issues in 1890 and 1891 to construct a new waterworks.

By the end of 1893 the system was complete, brought in for $809,000. A City Council committee reported that the "only ...failure in the Water Department...is the failure of the employees...to please the consumers... This state of affairs is...the condition everywhere that water bills are paid. There is no remedy...the employees ...will never please the general public but will continue to try..."

After all, artesian well water, however inconvenient and impure, was free.

Until some streets were lit by Atlanta's oldest corporate citizen, Atlanta Gas Light (founded 1856), only oil lamps—filled at property owners' expense—were seen. Electric lights were reportedly first shown in a Markham House tent in October, 1880. And Major James W. English's Cone Street home was one of the first to have the

new illumination. The first franchise for electrical lighting went to Brush Electric Co., in 1882, but it was soon outdistanced by a firm founded the following year: Georgia Electric Light Co., a predecessor of Georgia Power Co.

The modest debut of electric street lamps came in 1885 when downtown was illuminated by 22 of them—along with 407 gas and 136 gasoline fixtures. While there was City Council dismay at the cost of electrifying the streets, only four years later electricity had replaced all the other lamps. The next year—1890—Henry M. Atkinson acquired controlling interest in the Georgia Electric Light Co., greatly expanded its services—and got embroiled in a commercial battle with one of the Company's major users, the streetcar operators.

It was the streetcar which helped settle residential patterns, allowing persons to work some distances from their center city jobs.

Mule-driven streetcars became passe by 1894. An expansion of the system—actually, companies ran lines independent of each other—came in 1882 when Jesse Rankin was named president of the Metropolitan Street Railway Company. It operated two lines feeding the Grant Park area, just starting to develop following Col. L. P. Grant's gift of 100 acres of land as a

A general view of the design of the International Cotton Exposition of 1881 at Oglethorpe Park. It later became the site of the Exposition Cotton Mills.

Grandstands afforded spectators a high view of the race track at Oglethorpe Park.

The Inimitable Grady

Soon after he joined *The Atlanta Constitution* in 1876 until his death 13 years later, Henry Woodfin Grady, criminal lawyer-turned-journalist, was rightly perceived as the spokesman for the "New South."

He was a civic promoter, a political strategist and an eloquent platform speaker who brilliantly captivated Northerners and Southerners alike as he envisioned a great future for his region while loving the memory of the old South.

Just before Christmas, 1886, Grady spoke to the New England Society in New York City, his remarks being preceded by those of Gen. William T. Sherman.

The General contended that the war had been forced upon North and South "by men influenced by a bad ambition; not by the men who owned ...slaves but by politicians who used that as a pretext, and forced you and your fathers and me, and others who sit near me, to take up arms and settle the controversy once and forever."

Grady then reiterated the summary of events issued by Georgia Sen. Benjamin H. Hill in 1866: "There was a South of slavery and secession; that South is dead. There is a South of union and freedom; that South, thank God, is living, breathing, growing every hour."

And then Grady paid a startling tribute which triggered applause: "From the union of...colonial puritans and cavaliers...slow perfecting through a century, came he who stands as the first typical American, the first who comprehended within himself all the

About 1880 photographer C. W. Motes made this shot of an amateur baseball team in Atlanta. On the far right stands the lover of baseball, Henry W. Grady, managing editor of The Atlanta Constitution and in 1884 first president of the Southern Baseball League.

The Atlanta Constitution Building in 1890: It was at the corner of Forsyth and Alabama Streets, across from present-day Rich's.

132

a Negro 15 cents to take him up bodily and carry him over the mud... Peters Street... (is) a disgrace... Dozens of small streets are almost impassable... Beyond Spring Street there is not a piece of paving on Marietta Street... Between Collins and Calhoun (Piedmont) the people have abandoned the sidewalk and walk in a gully three feet deep..."

Urged by Mayor English, the Council acted—but only modestly, allowing $25,000 for street work in 1881. Even by the end of 1885 there were fewer than 13 miles of paved streets. Nonetheless, the street railways, wagons, rigs and pedestrian traffic led to a traffic ordinance in 1885: Council prohibited driving any carriage, dray or other vehicle over or across any public bridge at a speed greater than a walk. And conditions of the streets made a walk slow indeed.

The extending streets, however, were being framed by residences at the town's center as well as in the newly developed suburbs. Along a placid stretch of Peachtree from the site of the present Georgia-Pacific Building to the Hyatt Regency sat some of Atlanta's most desirable homes, green lawns separating their doors from the cobblestone streets alive with the sounds of pedestrians and clattering horses. As parallel streets also began to fill with homes, so did outlying avenues: Boulevard, Ponce de Leon, Highland, Virginia, Bleckley (now 10th), in West End, Grant Park and along West Peachtree.

"Even the shrewdest speculators are scarcely able to keep track of the growth of the city and its suburbs," *The Constitution* crowed in 1890. "The old breastworks are being leveled for front yards, and the rifle pits are being enlarged for the basements of workingmen's homes..."

Kimball (again!) is credited with inspiring the city's first subdivision. In 1884 he, realtor George W. Adair and landowner Richard Peters combined to develop 180 acres of land bounded by present-day 8th Street, North Ave., W. Peachtree and Atlantic Drive. Peters had owned the land (and 22 adjacent acres) since 1849. Now he headed a stock company to build a subdivision; subscribers paid $300,000 into it. Of that total Peters received $180,000 for the 180 acres which, 35 years before, had cost him less than $900. Peters Park was laid out in 1884; Georgia Tech today occupies part of the original area.

Baltimore Block, Atlanta's first apartment project, was the precursor of the contemporary condominium. Its development began in 1885 when a Baltimore company headed by Jacob Rosenthal bought the present site for $22,000. The 14 units sold for $4,000 each plus annual rental of $110; lessees also paid property taxes and maintenance costs. But in a few years Baltimore Block lost is original lustre; after the Depression took its toll, there began a spate of renovations in 1932, but the Vic-

On the left, the National Hotel; on the right, a restaurant; in the distance, the artesian well at Five Points: This was Peachtree Street at the railroad tracks in 1887.

torian structures suffered other setbacks.

The major survivor of pre-1900 suburban developments is Inman Park, a 100-acre Joel Hurt development. Many of its Victorian homes dating from 1889 remain as gems of renovation. Among their early residents were the families of Asa, Charles and Warren Candler, Ernest Woodruff, Joseph Maddox, Joel Hurt, Samuel C. Dobbs, Fitzhugh Knox, Aaron Haas and John R. Wilkinson.

As downtown land grew dear and electric elevators were developed, multistory office buildings emerged prior to 1900: the Moore & Marsh structure, the eight-story Equitable Building (later Trust Co. of Georgia headquarters and the city's first modern office building), the Aragon and Marion Hotels, the Flatiron Building and the Grant Building among them.

Such structures and their smaller neighbors guaranteed the extraordinary spurt of

Continued on Page 142

Looking out Marietta Street from Five Points, about 1900.

137

A dandy looking group—the personnel of the Lowry Bank— posed in front of their building at the southwest corner of Alabama and old Loyd (now Central) in 1890. The Lowry Bank was an antecedent of today's First National Bank.

Two Phones: $104 a Year

In December, 1884, the Atlanta phone system could boast of 566 subscribers, according to S. P. Richards.

"The cost," he noted, "is $104 per year" —for his home and store phones. "It is very convenient. I do not know whether it will *pay* or not but we must in a measure keep up with the times."

Two Atlanta women of the Victorian Era posed in their finest for a studio photographer who had an eye for detail and composition. The names of the two are unknown.

Mary Ella Smith (circa 1880) was the wife of William B. Smith, and mother of Tullie. The Tullie Smith home was moved to the grounds of the Atlanta Historical Society.

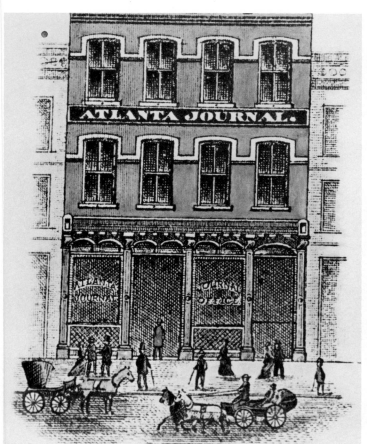

First home of The Atlanta Journal, at 14 Alabama Street. The newspaper was founded in 1883, 15 years after The Atlanta Constitution was born.

Rich's, begun in a modest wooden building in May, 1867, had become a strong Whitehall Street institution within a few decades.

When founded in 1880, it was known at St. Joseph's Infirmary; now it's St. Joseph's Hospital, Atlanta's oldest such institution. It began on present-day Courtland, moved to Ivy Street, and now occupies expanded quarters on the northside. The sketch is from 1890.

THE $2,300 INVESTMENT

Where Coca-Cola was born in 1886: John Pemberton occupied this antebellum home, which he used also as a laboratory. It was 107 Marietta Street, on the northeast side between Spring and Bartow, near the present Omni Hotel.

John S. Pemberton was the pharmacist who invented the formula for Coca-Cola, and first marketed it in 1886. But he soon sold his interest in it and died, never seeing any of the huge profits it earned.

Frank Robinson was the Pemberton partner and early associate in the company which developed Coca-Cola, and the man whose penmanship scripted the elegant trademark name.

Asa Candler was the visionary entrepreneur who paid $2,300 to own Coca-Cola in 1891; he marketed it ingeniously. He was later a mayor and prime philanthropist before selling the company in 1919.

Warren A. Candler, Asa's brother, was a Methodist Church bishop, and served also as president of Emory. It was to Warren that Asa confided that Coca-Cola had helped ease his own headaches.

In this building Asa Candler set up the Coca-Cola Company in 1898, at the corner of Edgewood and College Avenues. He believed the structure would be "sufficient for all our needs for all time to come."

It was in Joseph Jacobs' pharmacy (on the old Norcross Corner, site of the present-day First National Bank at Five Points) that Coca-Cola was first sold. The photograph at left dates from 1884; the interior of the pharmacy (below) is shown in 1894. Note the ornate decoration on the support pillar, and the spittoon (at left).

Regenstein's Wholesale & Retail Millinery, which opened in 1872, displayed its finest lady's hatwear out front of the store at its 74-78 Whitehall Street location in the 1880s.

Atlanta's second City seal bears the year of incorporation and the year it began to rebuild from the wartime destruction. The phoenix rises from its own ashes.

Continued from Page 137

enterprises between 1880 and 1900, some of them surviving under their original names.

St. Joseph's Infirmary, Atlanta's oldest existing hospital, was born in 1880 when two Sisters of Mercy arrived from Savannah to establish an institution for the ill, and first began their work at 216 N. Collins (now Courtland). The later hospital was on Ivy Street, but has moved into new northside Atlanta quarters.

Apprentice undertaker Hyatt M. Patterson arrived from Ohio in 1881 to work with George R. Boaz, undertaker and livery stable proprietor. Early in 1882 Patterson was advertising his services as an undertaker in the Markham House block, and a year later separated from Boaz and formed a partnership with Michael Bowden. After Patterson died in 1923, son Frederick opened the Patterson mortuary known as Spring Hill, in 1928.

George E. King was a traveling salesman for a Baltimore metals ware firm before using $9,500 to open a hardware store at Peachtree and Auburn in 1882. He lost $1,839 the first year, but showed a $2,000 profit the second. By 1887 King Hardware was organized, moving to 53 Peachtree, its longtime base, in 1900, and later buying out at least four competitors.

John M. Miller, orphan of a Confederate soldier, was nine when he and his mother arrived en route to Illinois to claim an inheritance. They stayed. Young Miller made pennies selling battlefield shell fragments as junk, then newspapers at the train depot while he worked also in a brickyard and as a cotton factory waterboy. As operator of an exclusive newsstand franchise during the 1881 Exposition, Miller saw financial progress. In 1882 he opened the John M.

Miller stationery store at Marietta and Forsyth, selling newspapers, magazines, cigars and theater tickets. Miller's Book Store was born, and thereafter opened branches still operating.

The Atlanta Journal debuted in February, 1883. The Democratic daily, issued from Alabama Street offices, was launched by attorney and Confederate veteran Edward F. Hoge who promised subscribers a quality paper for 10 cents a week. Shortly before his death in 1885, Hoge sold *The Journal* to John Paul Jones, and in June, 1887, lawyer Hoke Smith became its president/publisher for $10,000. His support of presidential candidate Grover Cleveland won Smith the post of Secretary of the Interior, and in 1900 he sold the paper for $300,000 to laywer James R. Gray and associates. Capping several relocations, *The Journal* was sold for more than $3 million in 1939 to former Ohio Gov. James M. Cox. He also bought the *Atlanta Georgian* that year — and closed it. The *Atlanta Evening Capitol* had already folded.

In 1950 *The Journal* and *The Constitution* were merged; their combined strength overcame the short-lived *Atlanta Times* in the Sixties. It was *The Journal* which brought commercial radio to the South in 1922 by opening WSB, initially a 100-watt facility. That now-powerful station, its sister TV operation and cable TV systems remain, with the two papers, part of the sprawling Cox enterprises. WSB-TV emerged before WAGA-TV or WXIA-TV.

Until 1884 Atlanta was a one-cemetery town, and Oakland was running out of space. That year L. P. Grant, Walker P. Inman, James English, Jacob Elsas, H. I. Kimball, ex-Gov. Bullock, Jacob Haas and

The view is from Peachtree to the south, at Five Points: The tall building is the Fourth National Bank, which faced Marietta. The Jacobs Drug Store was to the right of it. The corner occupied by the Bank is now the site of the First National Bank.

Laurent DeGive secured a charter to open West View Cemetery, purchasing a 577-acre suburban tract—nucleus of its present site—for $25,000. It became the final home of personalities such as Asa G. Candler, Henry Grady, Joel Chandler Harris, Ernest Woodruff, Evan P. Howell, Joseph M. High and some of its originators, including Grant and DeGive.

Another pioneer entrepreneur was pharmacy school graduate Joseph Jacobs. He was an apprentice in the drug business of Dr. Crawford Long (of anesthesia fame) before opening a pharmacy in Athens in 1879. In 1884 Jacobs bought a 30-year-old Atlanta drugstore on the site of the present First National Bank (the Norcross Corner), and before he died in 1929, Jacobs' first pharmacy had become 16 stores. At his popular downtown store, where Coca-Cola was first introduced, Jacobs pioneered the idea of cut-rate merchandising, advertising items for 17¢, 29¢ and 98¢ due to

the shortage of nickels. The idea created a sensation in retail circles, and brought Jacobs threats of lawsuits and violence. The concept remains.

The year after Jacobs arrived in Atlanta, another longtime enterprise emerged. After serving as a clerk in John Ryan's dry goods store and as manager of Rich's carpet department, James J. Haverty (and older brother Michael) opened a Hunter Street furniture store with $600 in borrowed capital, a risky venture since there were already 20 furniture stores. In 1889 James Haverty and Amos G. Rhodes, a pioneer furniture merchant, became partners, and in 1894, after Col. P. H. Snook joined them, Rhodes, Snook & Haverty operated until 1897. The Rhodes-Haverty partnership was dissolved in 1909, whereupon Haverty, oldest son Clarence and other associates formed Haverty Furniture Co. with nine of the 17

Continued on Page 146

Lawyer Woodrow Wilson Had a Brief Stay And Left, Soured

Virginia-born Woodrow Wilson, whose poor health forced him to withdraw from studies at the University of Virginia law school, came to Atlanta in 1882 to open a practice, undaunted by the fact that there were already 143 attorneys in the city.

He chose Atlanta because "it, more than almost every other Southern city, offers all the advantages of business activity and enterprise," he wrote a friend, adding: "I think that to grow up with a new section is no small advantage to one who seeks to gain position and influence."

On his arrival, Wilson joined in a partnership with a former classmate who was already in practice at 48 Marietta Street. Renick & Wilson's office was in Concordia Hall, southeast corner of today's Marietta and Forsyth Streets. Wilson's family sent a desk, book case and elocution chart for the office.

In October, 1882, Wilson took his bar exam, and passed, but Renick & Wilson were hardly besieged with clients. One visitor, New York reporter Walter H. Page, a friend of Renick's, did prove noteworthy much later.

By the middle of 1883, the Renick & Wilson firm ceased to function, and Wilson soon enrolled at John Hopkins University, Baltimore, to pursue his studies. In 1885 he married Ellen Axson, of Rome, Ga.

In Atlanta, Wilson wrote sourly before leaving, "here the chief end of man is certainly to make money, and money cannot be made except by the most vulgar methods. The studious man"—himself, it is presumed—"is pronounced impractical and is suspected as a visionary...."

In 1912, Wilson—having served as president of Princeton University and as governor of New Jersey—was elected to his first term as President. He appointed visiting reporter Hines as ambassador to Great Britain.

143

To Market, to Market...
Where Meats Meet the Streets

Shopping for meat was often a sidewalk excursion in Atlanta nearly a century ago. It might have looked unsanitary (and it was by today's standards), but the meat was usually fresh, not frozen.

On the facing page: The Atlanta Meat Market displayed sides of beef, rabbits, melons and vegetables; ready to serve you were the salesmen of the market on Broad near Marietta. The Marietta Street store with the Pathfinder cigar sign was presumably a neighborhood grocery; the Capital City Meat Market also had a no-nonsense air about it.

On this page: It was shopping day for this trio (above, right). Bananas and whatnot were featured at the J. R. Roseberry grocery (right) at the corner of present-day Marietta and Bankhead. Hanging on the store at left is a mail box. Folsom's Reading-Room Restaurant (below) offered a preview of the menu. It was at 22 Marietta Street in 1892.

The demolition of the City Hall and Court House, which had served Atlanta for 30 years, was completed in November, 1884, and excavation for a building on that site—the state Capitol—was begun. A crowd turned out for the laying of the cornerstone (above) in 1885; four years later the Capitol was completed—costing just under $1 million.

On October 18, 1887, President Grover Cleveland spoke from a platform in front of the Markham House (the hotel is at right, across from Union Station). The view is north on old Loyd (now Central Avenue). The President and his wife of 16 months visited Atlanta briefly.

The railroad passenger cars (foreground) are those of the Richmond and Danville line, which was merged into the Southern Railway System in 1894.

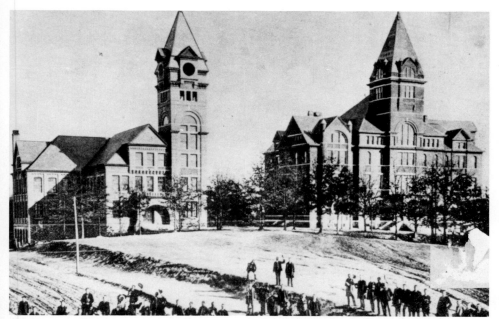

Continued from Page 143

Georgia Tech campus, 1892, four years after it opened: The original Academic building (right) remains. The shop building (left) was destroyed by fire in April, 1892. The street coursing between faculty and students is Cherry.

stores. At first there was only a downtown store; now Haverty's is a corporation with 67 stores in 10 Southern states. Clarence's son Rawson is the president.

Atlanta's most famous business, one whose world-wide product made million-aires, was launched modestly in 1886: Coca-Cola. The originator of it was John S. Pemberton, a Civil War cavalry captain who practiced as a pharmacist (called "doctor") and wholesale druggist in Columbus, Ga., before launching the same business in Atlanta in 1869. Pemberton was known as the developer of formulas and panaceas for various ailments—elixirs such as Globe of Flower Cough Syrup, Triplex Liver Pills, Indian Queen Hair Dye, and French Wine of Coca-Ideal Tonic. With associates including Ed Holland and Frank M. Robinson, the pharmacist organized the Pemberton Chemical Co. to make patent medicines in Holland's two-story brick home at 107 Marietta.

Early in 1886 Pemberton developed a syrup he believed would ease headaches and quench thirst. Expert penman Robinson devised the flowing script to identify the drink by the two names from which the substance was mainly derived: the fluid extract of the coca leaf and kola nut. With a liking for alliteration, the change of one letter and a flourish of the pen, Robinson wrote the world's most famous trademark: Coca-Cola.

Beginning in May, 1886, the syrup was sold in drugstores but not as a carbonated drink. In less than eight months 25 gallons were sold, encouraged by $46 in advertising. Early in 1887 occured one of those incidents which make history: A headache sufferer walked into Jacobs Drugstore, asked soda fountain operator Willis E. Venable for Coca-Cola, and Venable suggested adding soda (rather than tap) water. The customer enthused over the bubbly drink—and word spread.

Soon Pemberton was advertising the soft drink as a "brain tonic and intellectual fountain beverage." But his frail health and meager capital combined to induce him to sell a two-thirds interest in Coca-Cola for $1,200 to George Lowndes and Venable in July, 1887; the material and equipment were moved to Jacobs' store basement. Venable seemed too busy to capitalize on the opportunity. Lowndes, apprehensive about his investment, bought out Venable within weeks. By December, Lowndes sold his two-thirds interest to Woolfolk Walker, one of Pemberton's former employees, and Walker's sister, Mrs. M. C. Dozier. The equipment went back to 107 Marietta.

By mid-April, 1888, Walker had organized Walker, Candler & Co.—having brought Asa G. Candler and Jacobs into it—and bought Pemberton's remaining one-third ownership for $550. (Coca-Cola is a "fine thing," Candler wrote brother Warren; the former, who suffered headaches, had tried it "and was relieved.") Three days after the Company was

The Aragon Hotel, built by George W. Collier in 1892, was at the southeast corner of Peachtree and Ellis Streets. Once a leading hostelry, it was demolished in 1930 to make way for the Collier Building. The fence at left enclosed the yard of Robert F. Maddox, an Atlanta mayor after the turn of the century.

From the 1850s to 1882 Atlanta was protected by volunteer fire departments. They were much admired by residents and often held parades and demonstrations to show off the power of their water hoses and equipment. Photos show them in fine regalia (left) and with their equipment. A trio hold trumpets which were used to shout instructions to firefighters and victims trapped by blazes. The city's first hook-and-ladder unit came into being in 1886. At that time the paid Fire Department had four steamers, four 2-horse reels (one is shown below), 20 horses and 8,500 feet of hose. The fire chief in 1886—W. R. Joyner—received $112.50 per month. He was elected mayor for 1907-1908.

formed, Candler made a major move: He paid $750 for half the two-thirds interest owned by Walker and Ms. Dozier, and thus became majority owner of the firm.

Candler sent his clerk and nephew Samuel C. Dobbs to transfer the equipment to the Candler office and store at 47 Peachtree Street. And four months after disposing of his final part ownership in Coca-Cola, Pemberton died. All Atlanta's drug stores closed, as a mark of respect, during the hour of his funeral. Pemberton had made little from the syrup he introduced two years before.

Soon Candler paid $1,000 for the remaining Walker-Dozier share, and by April, 1891, Candler owned the whole Company for a $2,300 investment. He proved adept at marketing and advertising the drink. As early as 1889 Candler's ads promised a "delicious and refreshing" concoction—two words that still identify it. The rest is amazing entrepreneurial history. The Coca-Cola Company franchised others to bottle the drink—among the first being Joseph Biedenharn of Vicksburg, Miss., in 1894, and Benjamin F. Thomas and Joseph B. Whitehead of Chattanooga in 1899. The fountain drink moved into a new era with bottles.

In 1916 Candler resigned the presidency of the Company to run a successful campaign for mayor. As a mark of Coca-Cola's growth, the 25 gallons sold by Pemberton during 1886 had soared to worldwide sales of 19 million by 1919. That year the Candler family sold the Company to Trust Company of Georgia and others for $25 million. The bank quickly

Continued on Page 154

Horse-drawn vans provided deliveries for the Schlesinger-Meyer Baking Co. (top), Sudan's Butter Milk (center), and Fleischmann & Co., makers of "compressed yeast." Its agent was Robert Dohme.

Atlanta's Remarkable Blacks

Roderick D. Badger is not prominent in Atlanta's history but the ex-slave was the target of an 1859 complaint which signaled a beginning of a long-time dilemma for the town.

On July 15 that year, Atlanta's white dentists complained to City Council that they were "aggrieved...that your honorable body tolerates a negro dentist (Badger) in our midst, and in justice to ourselves and the community, it ought to be abated...".

The young mulatto had been taught dental work by his white master, a dentist, and the few rival dentists were apparently disturbed by the spectre of a black competitor in the struggling town. The Council ignored their complaint; years later Badger became the favorite dentist of many prominent white Atlantans, practicing downtown until his death in 1891.

Badger was but one of Fulton County's estimated 3,000 slaves—25 per cent of the total Atlanta population in 1859—and one of the few who had special visibility. The 1860 County census acknowledged there were "one washerman (negro)," "four washerwomen (negro)" and seven "free negroes" including six barbers and dentist Badger. The menial workers and those few identified as being in "negro trade (nine)" did not trouble the white economic class but, somehow, Badger did.

His brief notoriety is a small anecdote which became a starting signpost in the history of black achievement in one of the nation's most vital black communities.

Pre-Civil War Atlanta was like many young Southern towns. Life was hard for white residents of modest means, but it was often perilous for the town's slaves. Some blacks found rare solace in attending church with their white masters (in segregated galleries, of course), but in 1860 Atlanta there were no formal black schools (indeed, no system of public education for anyone), few organized black churches, little institutional glue to bind a community of the oppressed, no champions of its needs.

In mid-1865 the Federal military ruled Atlanta, but a great problem for blacks, apart from the gaps wrought by lack of education, remained an echo of that which faced dentist Roderick D. Badger: How were they to survive?

The major Atlanta newspaper reported in September, 1865, on the terrible poverty of most residents. Blacks in particular, it said, "are huddled together in most abject wretchedness everywhere, and living in idleness, vice and profligacy." In short, war and freedom had not brought blacks a new day of acceptance—but an era laden with the awesome challenge of mere survival.

The earliest of Atlanta's black institutions of consequence is the Friendship Baptist Church (437 Mitchell), organized in 1862 when blacks withdrew their membership from the white First Baptist Church. Friendship's services were held originally in a freight car purchased by the American Missionary Association—the "car-box" that was also used by the Walton Springs School, an antecedent of Atlanta University. The first pastor of Friendship, "Father" Frank Quarles, and its second, Rev. Edward Carter, encouraged the ties between Friendship and the University. Until 1892 the University's commencement exercises were held at Friendship, whose more recent history was graced by the leadership of civil rights activist Rev. Sam Williams.

While spiritual leadership and some concomitant social activities in the churches were essential, a missing ingredient—one largely suppressed before and during the Civil War—was that which became so prized in the black community: education.

The faintest glimmer of limited hope for blacks came in 1865 when the Freedman's Bureau was given a two-story frame building (onetime Confederate Commisary). It was placed on rollers and moved down Houston Street to the northwest corner of Calhoun (now Piedmont Avenue). It was dedicated in 1866 to the cause of elementary edcucation for black children, named the Storr's School, and served that purpose until it was demolished in 1923.

The freed men of the Bethel Tabernacle (a church organized for slaves by Methodist slaveholders before the Civil War) conducted services and provided social activities. In 1865 the Tabernacle congregation became affiliated with the African Methodist Episcopal Church.

With the support of his congregation, Big Bethel's Rev. Wesley J. Gaines led the drive to establish Morris Brown College in 1881. Until 1885, when a building on Houston Street was acquired, the College (now a part of the Atlanta University Center) held classes in Big Bethel. The Church's present structure (220 Auburn Ave.) was begun in 1891 and completed in 1921, though it was gutted by fire in 1922—the day after its insurance policy expired. Credit is given to Jesse O. Thomas of the Atlanta Urban League for convincing the City Council to donate a substantial sum in the 1920s toward refurbishing the Big Bethel interior after the fire.

In 1867 some blacks petitioned for a

James Weldon Johnson, an Atlanta University alumnus, became executive director of the NAACP.

The Atlanta University campus, 1890

Packard Hall, named for one of the founders of what became Spelman Seminary; the photograph is circa 1893.

Rockefeller Hall, a part of Spelman Seminary, was named for the mother-in-law of one of Spelman's benefactors, John D. Rockefeller Sr. The photograph is from 1885.

church, and initially joined with white members of the First Congregational Church to constitute a Church of Christ. For 17 years the racially-mixed congregation was served by white pastors but in 1894 the congregation, having become nearly all black, called its first black pastor—Dr. Henry Hugh Proctor, who served from 1894 to 1919. First Congregational became the second oldest black Congregational church in the nation (105 Courtland). In that Church in 1894 the National Medical Association was organized, as was the city's first black Boy Scout troop.

The pioneer disciple of black education in Atlanta was Rev. Frederick Ayer who arrived with his wife in November, 1865, and found the first black (private) school had been opened on Jenkins Street by ex-slaves James Tate and Grandison B. Daniels near the present City Auditorium. Not far distant sat a railroad car, purchased in Chattanooga for $310 and brought to Atlanta to serve as a school by partitioning it into two schoolrooms. The "Car-Box" school was opened at Walton Springs, giving Atlanta two black schools.

With the advent of the Storr's School, the Jenkins Street school and the "car-Box" School were soon abandoned, and Edmund Asa Ware (a Yale graduate) became principal of the Storr's School (and later became the first president of Atlanta University).

in 1867 Ayer and Ware were among the petitioners for a successful charter to found a university: Thus was Atlanta University born, with the original 48½-acre tract of its land being purchased in 1869 for $12,500. Its first students, in 1869, were all grammar and high school pupils.

Thus were begun the black educational and religious institutions in Atlanta—but in the late 1860s they could make little dent in the economic, social and political plight of blacks.

Atlanta's black community of the 1870s and 1880s enjoyed greater progress on the educational front. In 1869, when the foundation was being laid for a general public school system in Atlanta, another black college had its inception as a primary school on Fraser Street.

Early that year Rev. and Mrs. James W. Lee opened the school in Clark Chapel and it grew rapidly through the primary impetus of Bishops D. W. Clark and Gilbert Haven. In 1877 it secured a charter as Clark University. The cornerstone of its first brick building on its new campus, Chrisman Hall, came in February, 1880, the building being largely a gift of Mrs. Eliza Chrisman of Topeka, Kansas. In 1941 the University, renamed Clark College, moved to its Chestnut Street site opposite the Atlanta University administration building.

During this period of political turmoil Rev. Andrew Jackson and six parishioners organized the Mt. Pleasant Hill Baptist Church in 1870. The congregation outgrew its old church and built a new one at Fort and Wheat (now Auburn) Streets and renamed it Wheat Street Baptist Church.

In 1883 Gammon Theological Seminary opened near Clark's old site and much residential building for blacks developed along McDonough and Jonesboro Roads.

The progress in black education was so pronounced in postwar Atlanta that an 1870 census showed a total of 6,474 school children of whom 3,129 were black. In December that year an overwhelming majority of Atlanta residents voted in favor of a public school system, and the system finally opened in January, 1872. Black residents helped pave the way for its development.

While there was progress along educational lines, the political growth of black Atlanta was stunted, and economic development remained on the horizon. In December, 1870, two blacks were elected

to the City Council of seven: tailor William Finch and carpenter George Graham. Their terms were brief and almost 100 years would pass before blacks again were elected to City Council.

In 1879 came another advance in black education when the Augusta (Ga.) Institute, founded in 1867, was moved to Atlanta and renamed Atlanta Baptist Seminary, its first local sessions being held in the Friendship Baptist Church. In 1889 it moved to West Fair and Chestnut Streets, was named Atlanta Baptist College in 1897, and renamed Morehouse College in 1913 in honor of Dr. Henry Lyman Morehouse, corresponding secretary of the American Baptist Home Mission Board. From 1906 to his resignation in 1931, Dr. John Hope was Morehouse's president.

Two other present-day units of the Atlanta University Center were born after the end of the Civil War. Morris Brown College came into being in 1881 when a site at Boulevard and Houston Streets was purchased for $3,500; the first building was erected in 1884, and other buildings were added before the College was moved to its Atlanta University Center (A. U. C.) site in 1932. Morris Brown College was named for a bishop of the African Methodist Episcopal Church.

The sixth and final unit of the A. U. C. was originally the Atlanta Baptist Female Seminary, founded by two women from New England. The school opened in the basement of the Friendship Baptist Church in April, 1881. When the founders made an appeal in a Cleveland, Ohio, church for funds in 1882, they were heard by church member John D. Rockefeller Sr.

The latter contributed funds, the school Seminary moved from the basement of Friendship Baptist Church to former U. S. Army Barracks buildings, and as enrollment increased, so did support—from blacks and whites. The Rockefeller family visited the seminary in 1884, were impressed, and gave more funds. The name of the school was changed to Spelman Seminary in honor of Mrs. Rockefeller's mother, Mrs. Lucy Henry Spelman. Rockefeller support continued and the name became Spelman College in 1924.

Initial economic growth of blacks was hardly as impressive as the development of religious and educational institutions. Little businesses—shoe shops, groceries, dining places, beer halls, a billiard room—survived in the jumble of buildings in the Decatur Street area, now the center of downtown Atlanta. Black homes were often tumbling-down shacks in slum areas.

John Wesley Dobbs, a pioneer in the black community's life and grandfather of Maynard Jackson (first black to be Atlanta's mayor), is credited with coining the term "Sweet Auburn." The onetime Wheat Street, renamed Auburn, was for decades the center of black life. The street was energized with activity; it was the avenue where Dobbs, Grand Master of the Masons, had his headquarters in the Prince Hall Masons Building; where the Southern Christian Leadership Conference later established international headquarters, and became the locale of WERD, the first black-owned radio station.

Across from the Masons Building is one of black Atlanta's oldest institutions—the Wheat Street Baptist Church, organized in 1870 as Mt. Pleasant Baptist Church. It moved to its present site (Yonge and Auburn) in 1880, the Gothic structure being begun in 1920 by black contractor Robert E. Pharrow and completed in 1939. Across the street from the Church it opened Wheat Street Towers as a residence for senior citizens. The Church's most prominent minister: Rev. William Holmes Borders.

World famous Ebenezer Baptist

Church (413 Auburn) was under the ministerial leadership of the King and Williams families from inception (1894) until 1975. The pastor in 1894, Rev. A. D. Williams, was succeeded by his son-in-law, Rev. Martin Luther King Sr., who occupied the post for 44 years. "Daddy" King shared the pastorate with his son, the late Dr. Martin Luther King Jr., who used the church as the base of operations for the Southern Christian Leadership Conference. "Daddy" King's wife, a bulwark of the church, was assassinated there. The present structure was completed between 1914 and 1921.

Adjacent to Ebenezer is Dr. King Jr.'s grave, its simple marker etched with a memorable quote: "Free at last, free at last, thank God Almighty, I'm free at last." At 453 Auburn is the Martin Luther King Jr. Center for Social Change, an educational conference and community center which houses Dr. King's papers.

A few feet away (501 Auburn) is Dr. King's birth house, an 1895 Queen Anne style structure owned originally by a fireman. Rev. A. D. Williams bought the house in 1909 and there the late Dr. King was born on January 15, 1929. The home is presently a museum.

The Odd Fellows Building and Auditorium (228-250 Auburn) was inspired and promoted by the editor of *The Atlanta Independent* newspaper, Benjamin J. Davis, designed by white architect W. A. Edwards, and built in 1912-13 by Robert E. Pharrow as headquarters for the Atlanta Chapter of the Grand United Order of Odd Fellows. In its prime the six-story main building included six stores, 42 offices and six lodge rooms, topped by a popular roof garden. A two-story addition contained eight additional stores, 18 offices and a large auditorium. The complex (which included a Yates and Milton Drug Store) was for years the focal point of black economic, political and social activities.

The Herndon Building (239 Auburn)

was built in 1924 and served as locus of black businesses and as headquarters for the Atlanta Urban League until 1964. It also included classroom space for the Atlanta School of Social Work (which later merged with Atlanta University).

The Butler Street YMCA (22 Butler) opened on May 16, 1920, and became of Atlanta's best known meeting places, playing host to local, national and international speakers—black and white—for an exchange of ideas at its "Hungry Club" luncheon forum inaugurated in 1942.

Herman E. Perry, A Texas native who came to Atlanta in 1908 when he was 35, had only a seventh grade education, but in 1911 he organized the Standard Life Insurance Company, and then founded other enterprises: Citizens Trust Company, the National Fuel Corporation, the Service Foundation and firms involved in real estate, engineering, construction, printing, pharmaceuticals and printing. But in 1925 Perry's overextended empire collapsed, reportedly as a result of bad management and high-risk loans. One entity survived: Citizens Trust Bank, whose gleaming building is proud testimony to its major role in black life.

Across from Citizens Trust (75 Piedmont Ave.) was the house of Henry Rucker, one of Atlanta's best-known black citizens. As a reward for his efforts on behalf of the Republican Party, Rucker was named by Pres. William McKinley as Collector of Internal Revenue, a post he held from 1897-1910, the only black ever to hold this position. In 1906 he built the Henry A. Rucker Building (158 Auburn), Atlanta's first black-owned office structure.

The second-largest black insurance company in the nation, Atlanta Life, was founded by Alonzo F. Herndon, an ex-slave born in 1858, who came to Atlanta in 1882 and opened a barber shop which catered to whites and blacks alike, and Herndon ultimately opened three such

The First Congregational Church was built to replace the early Gothic Revival frame structure which had served the black community since 1867.

The 1891 Big Bethel African Methodist Episcopal Church

Alonzo F. Herndon, the barbershop entrepreneur who developed the Atlanta Life Insurance Company

Headquarters of the Atlanta Life Insurance Company

shops employing 75 persons.

In 1905 he amalgamated nine Atlanta insurance firms into the Atlanta Mutual Life Insurance Association, and by 1910 the firm had 43 branches in Georgia and Alabama.

The Walden Building was named for Austin T. Walden, who became Georgia's first black judge, in 1964. As a lawyer, the Georgia native defended black clients in towns small and large, and fought for school integration and voters' rights. As co-chairman of the Atlanta Negro Voters League, he became one of the most powerful men in Atlanta politics. He died in 1965.

Fifteen businessmen in 1925 put up $1500 to establish the Atlanta Mutual Building Savings and Loan Association, which demonstrated its first real growth in the 1930s under president John P. Whitaker, former registrar of Atlanta University. He was succeeded by the nation's first black certified public accountant, Jesse B. Blayton.

Herndon, Perry and Rucker were beacons of achievement in the black community of the early 1900s, as were ministers who served their flocks.

The economic and political struggles upward have been painful for blacks. But the names of achievers make a lengthening list: Dr. Rufus Clement, Lonnie King, Dr. Ralph Abernathy, T. M. Alexander Sr., Fred Shuttlesworth, Don Hollowell, Julian Bond and John Lewis among them.

In the 1970s Atlanta's black community consolidated hard-won gains, and certain individuals gained national prominence as elected officials, appointed leaders and business executives.

Maynard Jackson was elected mayor in 1972 and re-elected, serving two four-year terms (the maximum allowed by law). Dr. Benjamin Mays became the highly-respected president of the Atlanta Board of Education, and Dr. Alonzo Crim arrived to serve as superintendent of the

public schools. Marvin Arrington was chosen head of the City Council. Dr. George Napper was selected as the city's chief of police. Reginald Eaves was chosen a Fulton County commissioner, as was Michael Lomax.

Leroy Johnson's election as the first black chosen for the Georgia legislature since Reconstruction was followed by other blacks selected as state legislators: Alveda King Beal (Rev. King Sr.'s granddaughter), Grace Towns Hamilton, and Billy McKinney among them. Andrew Young, an associate of the late Dr. King, became a U. S. Senator, then U. S. Ambassador to the United Nations, and is now Atlanta's mayor.

Jesse Hill has served for years as president of the Atlanta Life Insurance Company, the second-largest black-owned insurance firm in the world; H. J. Russell Construction Company, founded and led by Herman Russell (named president of the Atlanta Chamber of Commerce in December, 1980, and the second black to hold that post, after Jesse Hill), is ranked as the fifth-largest black-owned firm in the nation. M & M Products Company (Cornell McBride, president) is ranked 13th in the nation, and Gourmet Services, Inc., is ranked 28th. Leading Citizens Trust Bank is I. Owen Funderburg, the institution being ranked as the 7th-largest black-owned bank in the nation. Fletcher Coombs heads the Mutual Federal Savings and Loan Association, ranked as the nation's 11th largest black-owned S. & L. Ms. Freddye Henderson operates a million-dollar travel agency, one of the largest black-owned businesses of its kind; Tom Cordy heads AMC Mechanical Contractors, and Collier St. Clair became the first black in the Southeast to manage an Equitable Life Assurance Society of America agency. The Paschal Brothers restaurant has long been a prominent fixture in Atlanta life.

The role of the Atlanta University

Center in educating, training and inspiring blacks for positions of local, national and international leadership cannot be overestimated. The achievement has been truly remarkable.

A partial list of its distinguished black alumni is a miniature "Who's Who." Among them (with positions they have held) are:

Former Mayor Maynard Jackson; current Mayor Andrew Young; Alice Henderson and Vivian McFadden, first female black chaplains of the U. S. Army and Navy, respectively; James J. Nabrit Jr., president of Howard University; Samuel M. Nabrit, president of Texas Southern University; Albert W. Dent and Samuel DuBois Cook, presidents of Dillard University; Elizabeth D. Koontz, president of the National Education Association, and director of the Women's Bureau of the U. S. Department of Labor; James Weldon Johnson, NAACP executive director; Lerone Bennett Jr., senior editor of *Ebony* magazine and historian; Dr. Louis T. Wright, director of Harlem (N. Y.) Hospital, pioneer in the use of aureomycin; TV star Esther Rolle; Mattiwilda Dobbs, Metropolitan Opera star; Walter White, NAACP executive director; William Bennett, director of the U. S. Information Agency; Atlanta City Council members Marvin Arrington, Ira Jackson and Carl Ware (former president of the City Council); Georgia State Superior Court Judge Horace Ward; Eldridge McMillan, associate director of the Southern Education Foundation; Hugh Smythe, former U. S. Ambassador to Syria and Malta, and Richard Robert White, who formed the nation's first black-owned bank (in Philadelphia).

They and many others represent the remarkable evolution which distinguishes Atlanta, which is light years away from that day in 1859 when black dentist Roderick D. Badger's occupation was regarded with distaste by a handful of whites.

Headquarters of Citizens Trust Bank

153

When people yearn for the "good old days," they imply that groceries cost less, for one thing, as the prices inside this store demonstrate. Rogers' Java and Mocha coffee was 35 cents a pound (three pounds for 95); Fancy Rio coffee was 12½ cents a pound. The well stocked store even boasted a telephone.

Continued from Page 149

announced that a new company would be organized through which "a large amount of stock... will be offered to the public," though members of the Candler family "will also share largely in the new corporation..." It was the largest commercial transaction in Atlanta's history up to that time.

The bank's president, frugal Ernest Woodruff, played the key role in the transaction. His son Robert in 1923 joined The Coca-Cola Company and has been its guiding spirit for almost 60 years.

That in itself is a remarkable story. Robert Woodruff had worked for 60 cents a day in the foundry, as a stockroom clerk for a fire extinguisher company, purchasing agent for an ice and coal firm, and truck salesman for White Motor Company. He served as a major in the motor corps during World War I, and resigned as vice-president of White to join Coca-Cola. His key early aides were lawyer Harrison Jones, who joined the company in 1920 as vice president for sales (and later was chairman of the board), and lawyer Harold Hirsch, general counsel and son of the man who founded Hirsch Brothers clothing firm in 1863.

Woodruff's private philanthropy made him known as Atlanta's greatest "Local Anonymous Donor." His millions aided Emory University, cultural expansion, parks development and numerous other civic, educational and religious endeavors. The Company itself became a huge engine propelling Atlanta's economy, and made rich those farsighted enough to purchase its stock in its early years.

Visionaries realized that an economy based largely on commercial enterprises rooted in cotton, real estate, transportation and distribution required sound financial institutions, and they emerged at a rate more rapid than that of the Seventies, though not all succeeded.

Three which did not survive were launched in 1887: the Capital City Bank (Jacob Elsas, president); Neal Loan and Banking Co. (Thomas B. Neal, president), and the Traders Bank of Atlanta (C. C. McGehee, president).

American Bank & Trust, which began in 1889 with Walker Inman as president, became the Fourth National Bank with ex-Mayor James English as its head. It merged with other banks (including the Lowry Banking Co. and the American National Bank) to form the First National Bank in 1929. The Fourth National is credited with being the first Atlanta institution to employ a woman teller and to establish a savings department.

The Commercial Savings Bank, was chartered in September, 1891 (original incorporators included Joel Hurt, Joseph Hirsch, W. A. Gregg and W. W. Draper), with wholesale grocer Junius G. Oglesby as president and Gregg as vice president. But by December not all the subscribers for stock had remitted payment, and Oglesby, doubtful of prospects and urging return of subscribers' payments, pleaded ill-health and resigned.

Successor president John M. Green was urged by Hurt to turn the Bank into "a large trust company," there being none in the city. Despite the financial panic of 1893, the

The statue dedicated to Sen. Benjamin H. Hill was unveiled in 1886 at the apex of Peachtree (right) and West Peachtree Streets very near today's Peachtree Center. It later was moved to the state Capitol grounds and—in 1912—to Grant Park.

High Victorian Gothic style is evident in St. Philip's Episcopal Church, built in 1881 at the northeast corner of Washington and Hunter (now Martin Luther King Drive). It was demolished in the 1930s.

Bank improved its capital stock. Ernest Woodruff (Hurt's brother-in-law) became a director, the Bank moved into the new Equitable Building and in November, 1893, changed its name to Trust Company of Georgia. Hurt later served as president; so did Ernest Woodruff, for 18 years.

Apart from Woodruff, Trust benefitted from the leadership of Robert Strickland and Thomas K. Glenn; the last two died in 1946 and John A. Sibley became president and chairman until Malcolm Hall was named president in 1948. James D. Robinson, grandson of ex-Mayor English, was then chosen president of Trust Company of Georgia Associates, a subsidiary. Today Strickland's son, Robert, is president of the parent Bank.

In 1893 Gate City National Bank closed, reporting that its assistant cashier Lewis Redwine had "defaulted" to the tune of $66,000. Bank officers kept faith with all its depositors, however, digging into their own pockets to make good the loss. The cashier, a social lion and bachelor who had been living beyond his $1,500 annual salary, was arrested, sentenced, and ultimately died in 1900 in Bowie, La., where he was a bookkeeper.

Atlanta's banks did yeoman service following the panic of '93 when gold was hoarded and left the country, credit was refused in many parts, money became scarce and cotton dropped to five cents a pound. The banks were induced to issue certificates to serve temporarily as money, thus aiding significantly in the movement of cotton. The "splendid financial reputation" of the city was maintained, Mayor Goodwin said, adding that the Forsyth St. bridge was completed, schools kept in operation, the new waterworks almost completed, and the suburb of West End annexed in 1894.

In January, 1896, another bank opened, led by Mississippian Frank Hawkins, who had come to Atlanta only the previous year. The Third National Bank moved into the Empire Building—now the Citizens & Southern National Bank Building—soon after it was erected in 1901. Outgrowing the space, the Third National erected a building across the street and moved into it in 1911. In 1919 the Third National was merged with the 1887-born Citizens & Southern Bank of Savannah, and became the C. & S., with Mills B. Lane Sr. as president. In 1929 the C. & S. bought the Empire Building, remodeled it, and has occupied the structure since 1932. In terms of assets, the multi-branch C. & S. is today the state's largest bank, and is led by

155

The bicycle squad of the Atlanta Police Department posed in 1899 in front of the new police department headquarters on Decatur Street, between Butler and Piedmont.

Bennett Brown, successor to Richard Kattel, who succeeded Lane in the Seventies.

When H. M. Atkinson merged the Georgia Electric Light Co. and the Edison Electric Illuminating Co. in 1891, he strengthened the foundation for the extant firm which emerged after the turn of the century: Georgia Power Co.

There were many other commercial enterprises launched in the 1890s, and which survive. Two insurance men who shared a boarding-house room, John N. McEachern and Isham M. Sheffield, opened an insurance firm in 1891, first renting a $5-a-month office. Their company began as the Industrial Aid Association; today it is known as Life of Georgia.

The High Department Store, founded in 1880 by Joseph M. High, no longer exists but his name survives: Twenty years after his death, his widow gave her home to the Atlanta Art Association as a museum. The High Museum, now part of the Memorial Arts Center, will be housed in a structure now being erected.

Three of High's associates, E. L. Douglas, W. J. Thomas and Beaumont Davison, operated a dry goods store in 1891. After Thomas' death, employee

Thomas L. Stokes became a partner in 1899, and after Douglass retired in 1901, Frederic J. Paxon joined the firm—which became Davison-Paxon-Stokes Co. In 1925 officials of New York's R. H. Macy Co. announced a merger with the firm and built a $6 million store which opened in 1927 on its present downtown site, and is known widely as Davison's, with local area branches and stores in six other communities in Georgia and South Carolina.

Title Guarantee and Trust Co. was opened in 1898 to assure property owners that their deeds had been searched and were secure; in 1943, then known as Atlanta Title & Trust Co., it was purchased by Lawyers Title Insurance Corp. of Richmond, Va. In 1898 former Gov. Colquitt's son Walter T. launched a law firm which today is known as Troutman, Sanders, Lockerman and Ashmore.

The Atlanta Milling Co. opened in 1899, as did the Georgia Savings Bank & Trust Co. In 1920 the Bank purchased the English-American Building (known also as the Flatiron, because of its similar shape, as viewed from above).

The late Henry Grady's advocacy of a municipal hospital for the poor took on

new life in 1890 when councilman Joseph Hirsch urged establishment of such an institution to bear the editor's name. The cornerstone was laid in December, 1890, and the hospital opened in June, 1892, with 15 physicians in charge. The "magnificent hospital," which cost $105,000 for the lot and structure, started with 100 beds, and 10 rooms for paying patients. A children's ward was installed in 1896, a maternity ward in 1903, and other expansion followed.

Cator and T. Guy Woolford in 1899 launched the Retail Credit Co. (now Equifax) to compile credit ratings on those seeking to buy goods; the pair charged 15 cents per report. Business spurted when their reports for life insurance applicants earned $1 each, and with the advent of automobile insurance their income accelerated.

Such enterprises enlarged the need for accommodations for visitors and travelers, and the hotel industry was expanded. A few months after the landmark Kimball House was destroyed by fire in August, 1883, its namesake was launched on the same site, reopening in 1885 and surviving for more than 70 years.

The new Kimball and the Markham faced competition in 1892 when the six-story, 125-room Aragon Hotel opened at the southeast corner of Peachtree and Ellis to the booming of cannon and a banquet

DeGive's first opera House (top left, with balcony) opened in 1870 at the northeast corner of Marietta and Forsyth (site of the present Standard Federal Building). It is shown in 1891. It later became the site of the Bijou Theatre. DeGive's second, *more opulent Opera House (above) opened in 1893; on its site the Loew's Grand succeeded it. The Loew's, where "Gone With the Wind" was premiered in 1939, burned in 1978; the Georgia-Pacific Building occupies the site.*

BILL OF THE PLAY

DeGive's OPERA HOUSE

T. J. COOPER, Chief Usher.   PROF. A. J. WURM. Musical Director.   A. W. SWOPE, Stage Manager.

M. J. DOOLEY. PUBLISHER PROGRAMME. 27½ MARIETTA STREET.

VOL. XII.   ATLANTA, GEORGIA.   No 79

A. M BERGSTROM, PRINTER, 21 EAST HUNTER STREET. ATLANTA, GA.

THE ATLANTA
HOUSE FURNISHING GOODS CO.,

Have just received a beautiful line of 100 white bear skin floor rugs 4x7 feet at $3.55.
100 Grizzly bear skin floor rugs 4x7 feet at $3 90.
50 Black bear skin floor rugs 4x7 feet at $4.99.
50 White wooly sheep rugs 4x8 feet at $6.00.
Wedding Presents a Specialty.
The Atlanta House Furnishing Goods Co.,
41 PEACHTREE STREET.

COMING ATTRACTIONS.

Clemenceau Case......................Nov. 9 and 10
Mr. Wilkinson's Widows..............Nov. 11 and 12
Patti Rosa..........................Nov. 13 and 14

GRAND CYCLORAMA,

OPEN DAY AND NIGHT.

Edgewood Avenue.

1800 STOVES AND RANGES IN STOCK.
Good Stoves with Utensils for $5.00.
Tin Sets, Filters, Coolers, &c.
BABY CARRIAGES!
One Hundred in Stock.
Sole Agents for
Wonderful Gauze Door Range.
Wood & Beaumont Stove and Furniture Co.
85-87 Whitehall, 70-72 Broad.

HAVE YOU SEEN THE

SINGER BUTTONHOLE ATTACHMENT?

It is Not for Sale, but is **GIVEN AWAY** as a Premium
with our **Five Drawer Machines.**

THE SINGER MANUFACTURING CO.,

JOHN Y. DIXON, Manager.

OFFICE, 85 PEACHTREE STREET, OPPOSITE JUNCTION OF BROAD.

The following statement is a correct showing of the sales of Coca-Cola for the year 1890, at the soda fountains in Atlanta:

	Gallons.	No. Glasses 1 oz. 5 cts.	Years Receipts
W. E. Venable........	1,632	132,096	$6,604 80
J. H. Nunnally........	677	86,656	3,332 80
Beermann & Silverman	427	54,656	2,732 80
Elgin, Watson Drug Co.	476	48,128	2,406 40
C. O. Tyner...........	336	43,008	2,150 40
John Venable........	245	31,360	1,568.00
Benjamin & Cronheim	165	21,120	1,0 6 00
S. L. Phillips & Co....	154	19 912	985,60
Other Fountains......	88	11,264	563.20
Total	3,500	418,000	$22,400.00

THE IDEAL BRAIN TONIC.
—DELIGHTFUL—
Summer and Winter Beverage.

Coca-Cola

DELICIOUS.   REFRESHING.
EXHILIRATING.   INVIGORATING.

RELIEVES
MENTAL AND PHYSICAL
EXHAUSTION
CURES
HEADACHE

The Popular Soda Fountain Drink, containing the Tonic Properties of the Wonderful Coca Plant, and the Famous Cola Nut. On draught at all Popular Soda Fountains at 5c. per Glass. Sold at 25c. per Bottle

The front of a DeGive's Opera House playbill in 1891 (above) carried ads for the Cyclorama and (at bottom) for Coca-Cola. In the lower left was The Coca-Cola Company's statement of its sales for 1890: 3,500 gallons of syrup (nearly all of it in Atlanta stores), with that year's receipts of $22,400 from the purchase of 418,000 five-cent glasses of the drink. The drink was then identified as "The Ideal Brain Tonic." On the facing page, an earlier playbill cover from DeGive's includes ads for "Norman's Neutralizing Cordial"—a stomach and bowel remedy—and Bramlett's English Kitchen and Ladies' Cafe, where "those large, fat oysters, quails, rice-birds" were on the menu.

DeGive's OPERA HOUSE PLAY BILL

KRIES & DOOLEY, PROPRIETORS.

A. M. BERGSTROM, THEATRICAL PRINTER, 21 EAST HUNTER STREET.

VOL. V. — ATLANTA, GEORGIA. — NO. 38.

DeGIVE'S OPERA HOUSE.

C. A. HOWARD,	Treasurer.
ARTHUR SWOPE,	Stage Manager.
PROF. A. J. WURM,	Musical Director.
T. J. COOPER,	Chief Usher.

Ushers,

J. B. GLASS, S. W. HOLLAND,
HENRY HETZEL, W. H. DICKINSON.

KRIES & DOOLEY,

CITY BILL POSTERS.

Distributors and Managers of PLAY BILL (the only official Opera House Programme) For rates and space app'y to 18 Loyd Street, Rear of Markham House. Reserved Seat Ticket Office at Phillips & Crew's Book Store, 6, 8 and 10 Marietta Street.

A. J. WURM.

——— Instructor of ———

VIOLIN, CORNET & GUITAR.

Residence, 4 Foster Street.

WE HAVE SAID IT !

WE defy any one to produce a REMEDY that gives better satisfaction than

Norman's Neutralizing Cordial.

It is the only Stomach and Bowel Remedy containing no Opium, Morphine, Laudanum, Paregoric, Sugar of Lead, Chloroform or Ginger. Can be safely given during teething to the frailest infant. It is pleasant to take, and no bad effects follow its use. All we ask is a trial of it. It costs but **25c.** Larger Bottles containing six times as much, **$1.00.** Sold by all Druggists in Atlanta.

THE NORMAN CORDIAL CO.,

ATLANTA, GA.

PITCHFORD'S, ART STORE,
28 Whitehall St.,
STEEL ENGRAVINGS, ANTIQUE, BRONZE AND METAL MOLDINGS.

Wedding Presents and Birthday Gifts.

MAX MARCUS,

16 Peachtree. **THE TAILOR !** 16 Peachtree.

SUITS MADE TO ORDER.

PANTS A SPECIALTY.

Suits Cleaned, Dyed, Repaired at Short Notice

W. R. JESTER,

Carpenter and Builder,

OFFICE & SHOP,

25 EAST HUNTER STREET.

The Ladies' Delight!!!

THOSE LARGE, FAT OYSTERS,

QUAILS, RICE-BIRDS, &C.,

SERVED AT

BRAMLETT'S ENGLISH KITCHEN AND LADIES' CAFE

51 WHITEHALL ST. OPEN DAY AND NIGHT.

J. A. SEATON & CO.,

LEADING

HATTERS

No. 5 PEACHTREE ST.,

ATLANTA, GA.

AGENCY

DUNLAP'S HATS.

Whitehall Street crosses in the center of this 1889 photo of the Union Terminal, the passenger depot. In time, bridges and viaducts were built over the hazardous railroad tracks, thus shadowing the area at right, which lay dormant for decades until revived for a few years recently as a tourist attraction called Underground Atlanta. The second Kimball House is at left, middle of the photo.

for invited dignitaries. The hotel was famed for its sirloin steaks, lobster Newburg, oyster loaves and private dances—one of the first soirees honoring Vice President Adlai Stevenson. The Aragon was equally famed for the entertainers it hosted, including singer Adelina Patti, actor Edwin Booth, Lew Dockstader and actress Anna Held, who reportedly took a milk bath there. As decades passed, the Aragon grew seedy and in 1930 the hotel sold off its silver, furniture and damask. The Collier Building was erected in its place.

Pioneer George Washington Collier, who built the Aragon, had first rejected offers to sell the land until an entrepreneur asked if covering the lot with silver dollars would buy the property. Collier reportedly told him yes—if the silver dollars were stood on edge. The deal collapsed.

Another hotel, in Romanesque style, emerged in 1893 at 97 North Pryor, a development of Marion C. Kiser. The Marion lasted 58 years, then was demolished to make way for a parking garage.

The enterprise which stimulated the biggest—and most lasting—structure before 1900 was politics. Seven years after Atlanta was confirmed by referendum as the state capital, construction began on the Capitol. Kimball's Opera House, at the southwest corner of Marietta and Forsyth,

had served that purpose, but the seat of government demanded a permanent home. In 1883 an Ohio firm won the construction contract and specified Indiana limestone for the exterior rather than "too expensive" Georgia marble, though the latter was used to finish interior walls, floors and steps. To make way for the Capitol, the 30-year-old, $35,000 combination City Hall and Courthouse was demolished. Fulton County officers moved to the newly-erected Courthouse at Pryor and Hunter, and City officials moved to the new Chamber of Commerce Building on Hunter across from the Courthouse.

Thousands viewed the cornerstone laying in September, 1885, and on July 3, 1889, the legislature occupied the new Capitol which Gov. John B. Gordon praised as a "clean, creditable and above suspicion enterprise." There was reason to be proud that there had "been neither jobbery nor thought of corruption," Gordon said: The legislature had allowed $1 million to erect the Capitol, and the cost was $118.43 less. The Capitol gleams, its dome topped with a new, thin sheath of Dahlonega gold. City Hall, which began life on the Capitol site, obtained its present structure in 1930. Five years after the Capitol was opened, Kimball's Opera

Continued on Page 164

The first horse-car barn was on the present site of the Hurt Building. In this photo of the 1880s are (from left) Wade Walker, Robert Dukes, Ed L. Grant, Irby H. Grant and E. C. Peters, general manager of the trolley line.

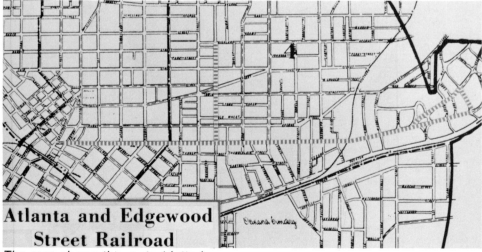

Atlanta and Edgewood Street Railroad

The map shows the route (dotted line) of the Atlanta and Edgewood Street Railroad. Bottom, center, is Oakland Cemetery.

Joel Hurt was a prime mover in the development of intraurban electric trolley systems, and the developer of Atlanta's first suburb, Inman Park. He died in 1926.

The Wren's Nest, the West End home of writer Joel Chandler Harris, remains a tourist attraction.

Poet James Whitcomb Riley (right) visited Joel Chandler Harris in 1898, coming to pay him tribute.

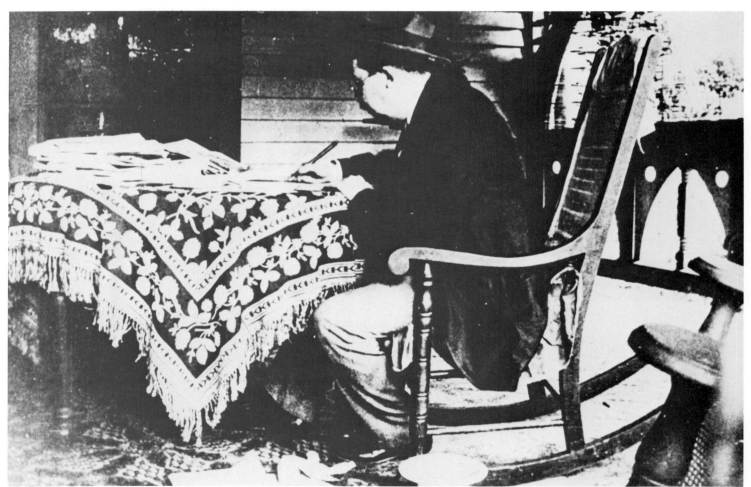

Joel Chandler Harris, who joined The Atlanta Constitution in the mid-1870s at the urging of Henry Grady, was famous for his folklore tales, especially the "Uncle Remus" stories. He is shown working at his porch table at his home, the Wren's Nest, in West End.

Grady Hospital was erected to the memory of the famed editor who, in the last years of his life, had led the campaign to erect such a facility. The original structure was opened in January, 1892, with 100 beds for indigents and 10 private rooms for paying patients. A children's ward was opened four years later.

This unusual photo of the 1880s shows a Jacob Elsas enterprise, the Fulton Bag and Cotton Mill (in the background). The view is from Oakland Cemetery (foreground), and shows the factory houses of Cabbagetown. Some of those modest frame homes still exist.

Three mayors of the period: John B. Goodwin (left), 1883-1884 and 1893-1894; George Hill (above), 1885-1886; and John Thomas Glenn (right), 1889-1890

Beaumont Davison became a key executive in the department store which today bears only his name.

Edwin P. Ansley, entrepreneur for whom the residential development, Ansley Park, was named

Continued from Page 160

House, the temporary Capitol, was so badly damaged by fire it had to be demolished.

To the Capitol temporary and permanent came an unbroken succession of Democratic governors. Colquitt was reelected in 1880 after Sen. John B. Gordon resigned his Federal seat to become counsel of the L. & N. Railroad, and thus repair his financial condition. With that, Colquitt appointed ex-Gov. Brown to complete Gordon's term, and the "Bourbon Triumvirate"—as it was called —was accused of a political deal.

The venerated Alexander H. Stephens, the frail, 70-year-old ex-vice president of the Confederacy, won election as governor in 1882 while he was confined to a wheelchair. He felt, he said at his inaugural, "depression from...the weight of responsibility." Four months later "Little Alec" died.

In April, 1883, a Democratic convention selected editor Henry Grady's choice to succeed Stephens: banker and legislator Henry D. McDaniel, over the most promising opponent, Speaker of the House Augustus O. Bacon. Among those watching McDaniel's inauguration in May was a newcomer to Atlanta, lawyer Woodrow Wilson, who observed in a letter that McDaniel "stutters most painfully." Wilson, who would become president almost 30 years later, had come to Atlanta in 1882 to practice law. "McDaniel is sound enough in other respects, however—not remarkable except for honesty—always remarkable in a latter day politician..." Wilson also quoted one satirical wag who suggested sending someone from Tennessee "for the relief of a state which was about to replace a

governor who could not walk (Stephens) with a governor who could not talk." McDaniel, however, proved to be an able governor, and was reelected in 1884 without opposition.

With Grady's inspired support as campaign manager, Gordon was chosen in 1886, Bacon again losing the nomination, and the Civil War general won re-election in 1888. Gordon left office saying, "Georgia presents a pleasant picture of peace and plenty and prosperity," an alliterative boast that ignored the growing plight of farmers battered by economic failures and the decline in value of the state's chief crop: cotton.

At the close of the Civil War cotton sold for $1 a pound; during the Seventies, 12 cents, and in the Nineties, seven cents. The disaster helped create an "Agrarian Crusade" and a combination of protest groups —Granges, Alliances, Wheels—became in 1889 the National Farmers Alliance and Industrial Union. In Georgia by 1890 its membership exceeded 100,000. By that year the Alliance, with a platform of free and unlimited coinage of silver, government ownership of railroads, tax revision and laws to prevent speculation on the produce exchanges, had become so powerful that *Constitution* owner Evan Howell said, "The Farmers Alliance *is* the Democratic Party." The latter had embraced its principles.

Planter and Alliance leader William J. Northen was elected governor without opposition in 1890. Alliance power brought three-fourths of the senators and four-fifths of the representatives to the General Assembly that year, with Howell's 27-year-old-son Clark named House speaker. Northen was re-elected in 1892 despite the

West View Cemetery, photographed in the 1880s, was the site of the Civil War Battle of Ezra Church on July 28, 1864. The Battle proved a failure for the Union troops of Gen. W. T. Sherman, but five weeks later Atlanta was surrendered.

Atlanta Gas Light Company at 19-21 Whitehall Street in 1885: James Lynch Jr. is at left. Atlanta Gas Light Company is Atlanta's oldest corporate citizen; it began operations in 1856.

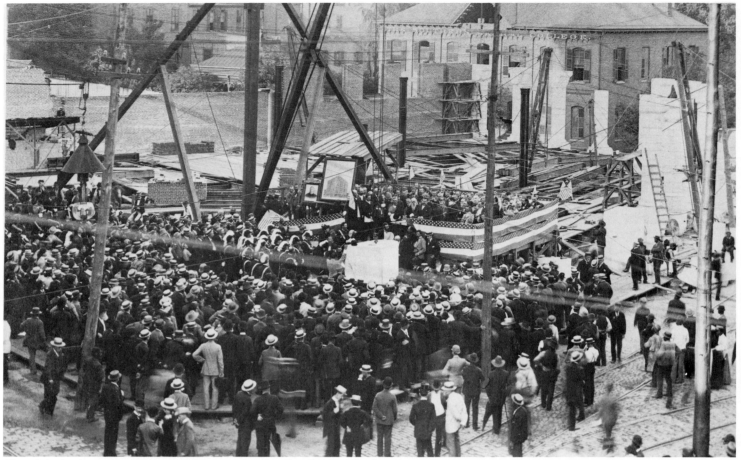

The date is June 25, 1891, and the event is the cornerstone laying of the first Equitable Building, at Pryor and Edgewood Streets. It was built by the East Atlanta Land Company, headed by Joel Hurt, and financed by the Equitable Life Assurance Society. The eight-story structure, completed in 1893, became the Trust Company of Georgia Building in 1913.

The street is Peachtree in the 1890s, and the ornate building housed the Capital City Club.

The Hebrew Orphanage, organized in 1889, was at 478 Washington Street; it was demolished in 1974. Note the Near Eastern themes in architecture: the onion dome atop the clock tower, and the horseshoe arches and flat, lacy ornamentation which reinforced the theme.

emergence of the Populist Party as a significant force. In that same year *Journal* support helped win the Democratic nomination for presidential hopeful Grover Cleveland and running mate Adlai Stevenson. Soon after, *Journal* owner and editor Hoke Smith was named Secretary of the Interior.

Former House speaker and state Democratic chairman William Y. Atkinson succeeded Northen in 1894 in a hot contest wherein the Populist Party, at high tide, backed James K. Hines. Elected with Atkinson as secretary of state was Allen D. Candler, a wounded Confederate veteran who had returned to Jonesboro after the war with "one wife, one baby, one dollar, and one eye." Candler succeeded Atkinson as governor in 1898, and proved an efficient and economical official.

In the same 20-year span Atlanta was served by mayors heavily engaged in civic and mercantile affairs, thus setting a pattern for decades. From the election of 1880 they included banker James English (making his second bid and scarcely nosing out H. I. Kimball); lawyer John Goodwin (two non-successive terms); George Hillyer, John T. Cooper, lawyer John T. Glenn (son of a mayor who served 1859-1860), *Constitution* business manager William Hemphill, and lawyers Porter King and Charles Collier. The man chosen to serve in 1899-1900 was a strong unionist, James G. Woodward, manager of *The Journal's* mailing department. Woodward, a plain-spoken, blunt man who kept the political kettle boiling, served four two-year terms in all, evidence of rising labor strength.

While politics provided much of Atlanta's entertainment, residents also found other growing outlets for their recreational needs. Courtrooms in City Hall were not available for entertainments after 1881. But there were band concerts at the McPherson Barracks, baseball games, the Cyclorama of the Battle of Atlanta (which opened in 1892), Chautauqua events, the zoo (which opened in Grant Park in 1889), football (starting in 1892), events at DeGive's Grand Theatre (opened early 1893) and the Lyceum Theatre (opened 1895).

Twelve German artists arrived from Milwaukee, Wis., in 1885 to survey the battlefield to be replicated in the famed Cyclorama painting. Accompanying them was Theodore Davis, wartime *Harper's Weekly* illustrator who had been with Sherman's troops at the capture of Atlanta. The painting—50 feet high, 400 feet long and weighing 18,000 pounds—was completed in 1887 at a cost of $40,000. It was displayed in cities including Detroit and Minneapolis, then housed in Indianapolis. Financially, it had failed, and Paul Atkinson, of Madison, Ga., paid $2,500 for it in 1890. He brought it to Atlanta, where it was housed in a temporary wooden drum-like structure on Edgewood Street for display in 1892.

But City Council forbade Sunday viewing, and patronage declined. After 12 months Atkinson sold it to H. H. Harrison of Florida, but he failed in his plan to display the "Battle of Atlanta" at the Chicago World's Fair. After a snowstorm caused a roof leak in the wooden building, thus damaging the painting, it was auctioned in mid-1893 to Ernest Woodruff for $1,100. Within days Woodruff had sold it to lumber dealer George Gress and Charles Northern, who moved the work to Grant Park.

In March, 1898, Gress deeded the paint-

Dr. David Marx served as minister of the Hebrew Benevolent Congregation, the first Atlanta synagogue, for more than 35 years, beginning in 1895. It is now known as The Temple and has occupied its present Peachtree Street site (between Spring and Brookwood Station) since 1931. Marx's tenure as a local rabbi has been surpassed by that of Dr. Harry Epstein, who arrived in 1928 to serve the Ahavath Achim Congregation (Peachtree Battle Avenue), where he is still pastor.

The English-American Building, known also as the Flatiron, was constructed in 1897, and remains at the apex of Peachtree (left) and Broad Streets (right) as one looks south. The 11-story downtown building was constructed following the wave of commercial enthusiasm which followed the International Cotton States Exposition of 1895.

The Markham House, which opened in 1876 and became one of Atlanta's finest hotels, was destroyed by fire in 1896. On a preceding page, President Cleveland is shown speaking from the pictured balcony in 1887.

ing to the City, and it remained in its old circular wooden building at the Park until 1921 when a marble building was finished there to house it. The two-dimensional painting went through restoration a dozen years later—under direction of Wilbur G. Kurtz, Victor Llorens and Weiss Snell—who also added a third dimension by inserting plaster figures and artifacts. New restoration of the work, and repair of the Cyclorama building, was completed in the Spring of 1982 at a cost of more than $7 million.

Lumberman Gress had already made a major gift to the City in 1889—the nucleus of a zoo—after he and railroad contractor Thomas J. Jones paid $4,485 at auction for a defunct circus. The purchase included a hyena, two African lionesses, two silver lions, a black bear, two wildcats, a jaguar, gazelle, coon, elk, Mexican hog, two deer, a camel, dromedary, two monkeys and two serpents.

Gress erected housing and cages for the menagerie and contributed other improvements which totaled $6,000 to $7,000 in value. It was the biggest gift "since the donation of 100 acres of valuable land (for the Park) by Col. L. P. Grant, and his subsequent sale of 44 acres at a nominal price," reported Sidney Root, president of the City's park commission.

The "greatest battle known to college athletics in the South" was the local headline heralding Georgia's first intercollegiate football game. It pitted the University of Georgia and Auburn in a Piedmont Park contest on rainy Feb. 20, 1892. The game was under way after festive crowds heard Auburn supporters yelling, "Shoot the billy goat!"—the Georgia mascot—and following a much-applauded clog dance by Dabble, Auburn's black mascot.

The rough game between the unhelmeted gridders ended in an Auburn win, 10-0, and not even a sprained finger resulted. A reporter noted that "The Auburn boys entered an iron-clad pledge before leaving home not to take a drop on the trip" and "the Athens men—football players of a rare order—did the same." The players remained "dry" but many spectators were "wet."

The Georgia Tech-Georgia football rivalry, which began in November, 1893, ended in a 22-6 Tech victory at Athens. There, Lt. Leonard Wood, a parttime student while stationed at Ft. McPherson, paced his teammates; five years later he was commander of Teddy Roosevelt's Spanish-American War "Rough Riders," and later a general for whom an army base was named.

Intercollegiate football nearly collapsed in 1897 when Georgia fullback Richard Von Gammon, 18, suffered a fatal injury during a game against the University of Virginia in Atlanta's Brisbane Park. His death of a brain concussion triggered a regional outcry against football, but his mother wrote University of Georgia trustees an eloquent

Mitchell became aware of Andrew Carnegie's gifts to establish libraries, contingent on support from local tax funds, and enlisted the aid of Walter M. Kelley, southern representative for the Carnegie steel interests. In February, 1899, Carnegie pledged $100,000 to Atlanta to build a library if the City added at least $5,000 annually for maintenance. The gift to Atlanta was his 11th for libraries.

The YMLA, after some debate, agreed to merge its interests with those of the new free library, and by fall a site had been chosen—at Forsyth and Church (the latter being renamed Carnegie Way). Building began in 1900; money ran short (whereupon librarian Anne Wallace secured an added $45,000 from Carnegie), and the structure was opened in 1902. The Atlanta Public Library underwent modernizations through the years until, in the late Seventies, it was demolished for a new building.

Coincidentally, Mitchell's daughter Margaret was born the year the library construction began, and he lived to see her win a Pulitzer Prize for her book, *Gone With the Wind*, 36 years later. Her older brother Stephens became a lawyer and devoted much of his energies to the legal aspects of her book and estate after her death in 1949.

Tremendous strides were also made in Atlanta's educational community with the establishment of Georgia Institute of Technology, Agnes Scott College, Morris Brown College and Spelman College.

With $100 in cash and pledges from the First Baptist Church of Medford, Mass., Misses Sophia Packard and Harriet Giles of New England came to Atlanta to found a school. Legend has it that they knocked on the door of Rev. Frank Quarles, of Friendship Baptist Church, as he prayed for help for black women and children. The result was the establishment of Atlanta Baptist Female Seminary in April, 1881, in the church basement. It opened with 11 pupils.

John D. Rockefeller became aware of its need for funds in 1882, and the following year the school was moved to recently-vacated McPherson Barracks, as enrollment increased along with modest funds and gifts of clothing and supplies. The Rockefeller family visited in 1884, and the family head made a significant contribution, whereupon the Seminary's name was changed to Spelman in honor of Rockefeller's mother. Within 10 years of its founding, the Seminary had 800 students and, as Rockefeller support continued, granted the first college degrees to two students in 1901. It became known as Spelman College in 1924, and is now one of the six units of the Atlanta University Center (A.U.C.).

Morris Brown College, another entity in the A.U.C., was founded in 1880, classes being held early in its building at Boulevard and Houston. In 1932 it moved to its pres-

The Atlanta Mineral Water and Supply Company, at 105 N. Pryor about 1890, delivered the refreshing drink in bottles. Pictured is the staff.

ent site, Tatnall and Hunter. It bears the name of a bishop of the African Methodist Episcopal Church.

Conversation in 1882 between Maj. John F. Hanson, later a railroad president, and Nathanel E. Harris, later a governor, created the idea of a technological school, and later in the year Harris, then a state legislator, introduced a bill proposing one. The postwar financial plight of the State prevented positive action until 1885, when the indefatigable Harris' new bill won legislative appropriation of $65,000. With editor Grady's support, citizens contributed to the project. At one meeting Jacob Elsas observed that "We are selling our old raw materials at $5 a ton to states that have trained engineers who fabricate it and sell it back to us at $75 and $100 a ton." Martin F. Amorous promptly subscribed $1,000, and at least 25 others promptly added $1,000 each. Richard Peters donated four acres of land (and later sold five more to the project), and City Council voted $2,500 annually.

The original $80,000 Academic Building of Georgia Tech was erected in 1888, as was the first shop building. Six professors, including President Isaac S. Hopkins and five foremen of various shops, were the first faculty when Tech opened in 1888 with 130 students. Its 1927 stadium, Grant Field, was named for Hugh Inman Grant,

who died at 11; his father John made possible the purchase of the tract.

The early prime mover in establishing Agnes Scott College was a native Pennsylvanian, ex-Confederate cavalry colonel and an elected governor of Florida who was denied office by Union military authorities. Col. George W. Scott had been a successful Savannah entrepreneur before coming to Decatur to open a commercial fertilizer factory before 1880; later he headed the company which controlled Scottdale Mills. In 1889 his pastor, Rev. F. H. Gaines of Decatur Presbyterian Church, launched the idea of a girls high school, and approached Scott for aid.

In September, 1889, 60 pupils were enrolled for the opening session of the Decatur Female Seminary in a three-story frame residence fronting the Georgia Railroad. (That house was demolished in 1952.) Scott erected a large brick building, Main Hall, and paid $112,500 for it, the grounds and furnishings; he later donated almost $90,000 more. Main Hall was dedicated in 1891, and the Seminary renamed Agnes Scott Institute, honoring the colonel's mother. Rev. Gaines served as president from 1897 to 1923. It became Agnes Scott College in 1906, and later obtained Rockefeller family donations and those of citizens first led by S. M. Inman and J. K. Orr.

The creative power of religious leadership, exemplified in the founding of Agnes Scott, continued to expand with new churches. Grace Methodist, organized primarily to serve the rapid northeast growth of homes along Boulevard and Jackson, opened in 1883 in a small building at Auburn and Jackson. The Unitarian Church, first called The Church of Our Father, was organized the same year, first services being held the previous year in the Senate chamber, Concordia Hall and the U.S. Courthouse. Its first building was at present Forsyth and Carnegie Way.

Mayor Livingston Mims' wife reportedly was healed by a Christian Science practitioner, Julia Bartlett, after she arrived from Boston in 1886 to teach classes. Ms. Mims organized Christian Science work in her home. Growth encouraged moves to other quarters, including the Grand Theatre Building, by 1896, the year a building fund was started. Ground was broken on Baker (between West Peachtree and Spring) in 1898, and the first Christian Science Church in Atlanta, designed as a domed Grecian temple, opened in 1899. It served for a decade, and in 1909 Ernest Woodruff sold land at 15th Street and Peachtree for a new structure. Ms. Mims died before the present First Church of Christ, Scientist, building was completed in 1914.

The same year that East Point was incorporated, 1887, the Second Baptist Church in West End erected a structure on a lot donated by pioneer Jonathan Norcross. A larger building was opened in 1898, and yet

The second naval vessel to be named "Atlanta" was this cruiser, launched in 1884.

another in 1952. Formation of the Sacred Heart Church dates from 1897 when it was established at Peachtree and Ivy, the site being bought by the Marist Fathers for $12,000. It remains Atlanta's only twin-steepled church.

North Avenue Presbyterian Church was organized in 1898, and Rev. Richard Orme Flinn served 40 years until retirement in 1939. The lot at Peachtree and North Avenue, which the Church bought for $18,000, had been the homesite of Edwin R. DuBose; construction began in 1900, dedication was in 1901, and more land was annexed later. St. John's Methodist, at Georgia Avenue and Central, was dedicated in 1898. Inman Park Methodist Church, organized originally in 1868, was re-dedicated in a new building—in 1898—on land donated by Asa G. Candler. Shortly after arrival as pastor of Jones Avenue Baptist Church, Dr. L. G. Broughton launched a project for a larger structure: It became the Baptist Tabernacle, opening in 1899 at Luckie and Harris. The project ultimately grew into today's Georgia Baptist Medical Center.

The moral influence of the churches was felt in the hotly debated question of Prohibition. A Fulton County referendum in 1885 was prefaced by great excitement and mass meetings, and the majority of voters went "dry."

The *Evening Capitol* crowed that "King Alcohol is an exile from Atlanta," but added that "people have pretty well supplied themselves with jugs and barrels and demijohns."

The "deserted saloons," said the paper, "have a ghostly appearance." Bartender Mike Maher hung a sign on his: "Closed in respect to the death of Atlanta." Two years later the Prohibition issue again enlivened the town, and this time Fulton County voted "wet." Atlanta was reborn, as Maher might have rejoiced, and in 1888 the city had 40 saloons.

Despite the progressiveness of a century ago, Atlanta was still troubled by social inequities. There were seamy areas of the city known colorfully and odorously as Pig Alley, Happy Hollow, The Anthole, Beaver Slide, Bone Alley and Hell's Half Acre, where poverty, idleness and vice held many in thrall, the vortex of crime being the area of Five Points.

Pitiful beggars cadged handouts from pedestrians, and the more aggressive appeared at residential front doors to issue scowling demands for food or money. Ninety years ago, Elbow Bend and Hobo Hollow were well known crevices of iniquity, resorts of criminals and prostitutes feeding off the unwary in daily rounds of violence. Policemen had their hands full; the much-praised new patrol wagon bought in 1890 scarcely rested at the new police headquarters erected at 175 Decatur—site of the present modern facility.

The policeman's lot was not a happy one, made even more burdensome when the city's growth led to a successful move in 1895 to extend its corporate limits, the first such expansion in 40 years. It took in areas east of Inman Park to present Little Five Points.

Atlanta's general placidity was shaken early in 1898 with news of the destruction of the battleship U.S.S. Maine in Havana harbor, thus triggering the Spanish-American War. Some residents went to war; a hospital was opened at Ft. McPherson (where Spanish prisoners were also confined), and the Atlanta Relief Association aided the troops. Lt. Thomas M. Brumby, a Mariettan aboard Admiral Dewey's flagship, was credited with suggesting the battle plan which resulted in Dewey's victory at Manila Bay, and Brumby was the first to hoist the American flag over the capital of the Philippines. Brumby was treated as a homecoming hero, and given an elegant sword; he died the following year.

The Atlanta Peace Jubilee of December, 1899, brought President McKinley to the city as a highlight of two festive, socially glittering days of events marking war's end.

Thus did 55-year-old Atlanta close the century—a young city, energetic, reaching for regional prominence, surging to wipe the scars of the past, carried forward by men and women of Civil War memories and 20th Century visions.

The North Avenue Presbyterian Church (607 Peachtree Street) was founded in 1898, and first occupied in 1901.

ATLANTANS AT PLAY

As labor saving devices and new forms of transportation presented Atlantans with leisure opportunities, they responded. On this page: boating on Grant Park's Lake Abana (right) in 1890; picnicking at Vinings (below, left), 1889; the skating rink, merry-go-round, and "Casino" theatre at Ponce de Leon Park (below, right); and bicycling aboard the high two-wheelers (bottom) in the 1880s. On the facing page: a chained elephant was a Grant Park zoo attraction; the Little Tyrol section of Ponce de Leon Park (upper right); swimming at Grant Park; three ladies on an outing at Little Tyrol; and Sunday boating at Grant Park in the 1880s.

176

THE 1895 FAIR

The Cotton States & International Exposition of 1895 in Piedmont Park was the nearest Atlanta has come to staging a "world's fair."

It was a huge commercial success, and drew favorable notice from throughout the world to Atlanta's place in the sun 30 years after its destruction in the Civil War.

On these and the following three pages are scenes from that magnificent burst of showmanship.

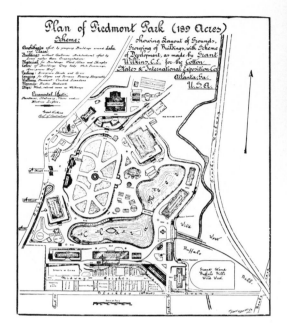

Map (left) shows Exposition's grand design: Piedmont Avenue was at left, with the 14th Street entrance near midpoint; Southern Railway roughly paralleled it (on the right); shoe-shaped Lake Clara Meer separated the Wild West Show (right), the midway (bottom) and the ovoid main exhibition area (upper left). Bleckley Avenue (bottom) is now 10th Street.

"Shooting the chute" was a favorite ride at the Exposition as little cars rode the rails in their plunge into the Lake. Two cars are seen returning to the top for more passengers for the thrill ride.

An artist's skyview rendering of the Exposition showed some of its main features—including the bridged Lake Clara Meer and many of the buildings constructed for exhibitions from throughout the country and foreign nations. The view is from the southeast corner of the Exposition grounds, near present-day 10th Street and Piedmont. Almost one million people visited the fantasy-land during the last three months of 1895.

Placid Lake Clara Meer is in the foreground (note the bridge at right) in this view of the Exposition, taken from the ferris wheel on the midway.

In flesh-colored tights, Nellie White "wowed 'em" as "Trilby Of the Midway."

Stately statues representing the arts topped free-standing columns near a small pavilion. Not one of the large buildings remains.

A mock ship on Lake Clara Meer was one of the numerous attractions. It was anchored near a representational Chinese village (center, left), and could be reached by a tourist boat (foreground).

The Exposition midway was made for strollers, gawkers and curiosity seekers. It included such attractions as the "Mystic Maze" (left of center) and a ferris wheel, (background, left).

The Liberty Bell (right, center) was brought to the Exposition for display, and it drew a crowd to presentation ceremonies in front of the Pennsylvania exhibit building.

Inside the Electricity Building, reflected in Lake Clara Meer, one could view the many usages of the exciting new motive power.

Atlanta children posed primly with the famed Liberty Bell, which had been brought from Philadelphia as an attraction of the Exposition.

Flags of participating nations hung from the high ceilings of the main Exposition building, where those patrons in the balconies could watch the crowds below.

This ramshackle pair of joined huts, seemingly about to collapse, represented "The Old Plantation." The sign at left promised "All Kinds Of Fun" inside.

Alongside an obelisk decorated with hieroglyphics poses a drummer atop a patient camel in the "Streets of Cairo," one of the Exposition's exotic attractions.

The trio in Mideast attire—the one at the left shockingly flaunting a cigarette—were the "Famous Coochee-Coochee" dancers, according to an inscription on the photograph taken at the Exposition. They looked more bored than sexy.

One of the more elegant structures was the columned Art Building, wherein were displayed the latest in paintings. The architect was W. T. Downing, well known Atlantan.

The Chimes Tower (tallest building, foreground) lent an additional lyrical note to the Exposition; the clock was on its four faces. Note the columned statues.

A general view of the expansiveness of the Exposition can be gleaned from this photo of the Grand Plaza, taken from the dome of the U. S. Government Building. The course surrounding the Grand Plaza later became a racetrack.

VICTORIAN ATLANTA

Atlanta's increasing wealth was being demonstrated in its High Victorian homes only 20 years after the Civil War left most of the city destroyed.

By the late Eighties, professional men and captains of industry were turning downtown streets—notably Peachtree—and that first suburb, Inman Park, into showplaces of architecture.

This Revival and Eclectic architecture, named after the reign of England's Queen Victoria (1837-1901), was characterized by fancy woodwork, gingerbread, gables, arches, broad porches, latticework and exterior wall decorations. Multiple angles were much admired and stone was often mingled with wood.

The photos on these and following pages illustrate some of these characteristics, though one—the antebellum Austin Leyden house—dates from 1858 and epitomizes the general view of plantation homes of Greek and Classical derivation.

Perhaps the best collection of the High Victorian homes remains in Inman Park, where residents have lovingly renovated a number of them.

The symmetrically designed residence in the center became the Capital City Club (Ellis Street is to the left). The residence of Mrs. Josephine A. Richards is shown at right.

In 1890 the recently-developed Baltimore Block (right) and the mansion in the background dominated this view of what was Hunnicutt Avenue.

Religious paintings, portraits, glassware, rugs and even a pair of animal tusks (on the floor, center) helped fill this studio of an artist, Mrs. E. J. Bacon, photographed in 1895.

The sketch illustrates the home of Mayor James W. English, at 40 Cone Street. He occupied it for 40 years until his death in 1925.

This was the 1881 West End residence of Evan P. Howell, a major investor in The Atlanta Constitution, with which his family had a long association.

A major locus of Victorian homes was the first Atlanta suburb, Inman Park, developed by Joel Hurt. Some of its residences (shown in the early 1890s) still survive, and recently have been renovated. These splendid homes were along Edgewood Avenue, the thoroughfare on which Hurt operated his electric trolley line in the 1890s.

This view of the northwest side of Peachtree Street (left) is from just north of Ellis Street. Shown are a corner of the Capital City Club (left), the turreted home of Mrs. Josephine Richards (center) and—beyond it— the Austin Leyden house. This area is now occupied primarily by Davison's.

Editor Henry W. Grady's home at 353 Peachtree: It was built in 1891 and demolished in 1921.

Later Grady home was plainer than its predecessor; this was photographed in 1897.

The so-called "house of a thousand candles" (possibly because its numerous angles required them) was built in the 1880s by D. H. Dougherty at the southeast corner of Peachtree and Baker Streets. It served also as the home of the Colonial Club (1900) and the residence of John R. Hopkins, beginning in 1901. It was demolished in 1931. Thus "progress" deprived Atlanta of a fanciful bit of architecture. The photograph is from 1920.

Asa G. Candler obviously did handsomely by his leadership of The Coca-Cola Company. His columned residence was constructed on Ponce de Leon Avenue.

The Austin Leyden house on Peachtree Street (present site of Davison's) was a true Greek-style mansion, erected in 1858, its two-story roof supported on three sides by stately Ionic columns. It served as the headquarters of Union Gen. George H. Thomas in September, 1864. Beyond the home, which was demolished in 1913, stood the John H. James mansion (at the corner of Cain) which became the Governor's Mansion.

Edward C. Peters' residence, built in 1883 at Piedmont and Ponce de Leon Avenue, is Atlanta's finest example of the Queen Anne style residence. Deep porches, half-timbered gables and scalloped wooden shingles marked this hilltop home which still exists, as a restaurant called The Mansion. Tiles in the dining room fireplace were decorated with scenes and symbols from the Peters family's original home city, Philadelphia.

The residence of attorney Jack J. Spalding was called "Deerland," and stood on a Peachtree Road rise which is now the location of Piedmont Hospital.

The "moving" home occupied by W. A. Speer and John Silvey was built in 1885 on Marietta Street. It was moved to 1345 Peachtree Street, and torn down in 1951.

A placid scene at Mrs. Linnie Condon's residence, 388 Spring Street, taken possibly after a satisfying Sunday dinner. There appear to be three generations of two families. Note the bird sitting on the shoulder of the woman by the steps.

When the century dawned, Atlantans could not know that the city's first "Golden Age" was in immediate prospect, that a machine would change it forever, that a riot, lynching, a major fire, a war would scar it for decades. But between 1900 and 1920 the city was also stressed by its expansion as people poured in, commercial activity leaped and many of its present institutions were born to give the place its continuing growth as an educational, commercial and cultural center.

The stubbornness of one man died with him, opening the city to residential growth; the involvement of two merchant-princes in civic affairs saved it from possible ruin; and the vision of yet others propelled its engines of commerce. But it was also a double decade of dislocation, and of racial strife as angry men fanned the embers of economic hardship as rural counties began to empty, and displaced and largely un-skilled Georgians perceived the major city as their opportunity.

There were 90,000 Atlantans in 1900, some 60 per cent of them white. Ten years later the population was 154,000 and, by 1920, almost 200,000. The population shift became more marked as farms dried up and agriculture was forced to share the spotlight with manufacturing. In 1900 Fulton County's population represented five per cent of the state; 70 years later the metropolitan Atlanta area was home to half of all Georgians, a stunning change in the 130 years since Marthasville held a handful of pioneers.

One of them, George Washington Collier, lived in Atlanta for 60 years prior to his death in 1903. In his early 30s he had acquired some 600 acres north of the hamlet, all the while playing active roles in its development, ranging from postmaster to builder of the Aragon Hotel. Those 600 acres were largely intact when he died, the city growing to the edge of his forested acreage known as "Atlanta's Chinese Wall" and the "North Side Dam," because it had not been breached. The land now includes prime residential and commercial acreage including Ansley Park, Sherwood Forest and land between the Peachtrees north of 15th, including the Memorial Arts Center.

On Collier's death in 1903, his acreage was broken up for development, and the emergence of the auto after 1900 acceler-ated the movement of homes to such an extent that about 1915, homes had gener-ally vanished from downtown Atlanta, replaced by office buildings and hotels. The suburbs began their explosion.

They owed their growth mainly to the advent of the auto.

Bicycle dealer William D. Alexander brought the first cars to Atlanta: three, 650-pound, steam-driven Locomobiles which arrived in crates, ready for assembly, in February, 1901. They had no lamp, no top, no horn: Each had only a buggy with a boiler under the seat and an engine on the

A Tarnished Age of Gold

1900-1920

Banker John W. Alexander, an early motorist, was photographed taking a spin in his 1901 Locomobile. For a brief time, Alexander had no other motorized traffic to contend with. And now look at the expressways!

189

Carnegie Library, circa 1910

Groundbreaking for the Carnegie Library, on May 15, 1900: $100,000 gift from Andrew Carnegie stimulated the project. It was replaced recently with a larger structure on the same site, Carnegie Way.

axle. Alexander's first test run was a two hour, nine-mile ride from Pryor to Ft. McPherson and return. Soon thereafter banker John W. Alexander bought one car for $925 and on the maiden run it was forced into a ditch when a startled mule backed into it.

Nonetheless, Dr. John Earnest bought Alexander's third Locomobile, and in 1902 the latter formed a company with C. L. Elyea and became the first Oldsmobile agency. The first inevitable accident came soon thereafter, one of the bruised victims arguing that, "I am in favor of a law against this automobile business."

The mishap led to City ordinances in 1904 limiting speed to 15 m.p.h., auto registration and requirements that drivers prove competence before they were licensed. A few weeks later there occurred the first auto fatality when chemist Frank Reynolds lost control of his White Steamer.

Despite mixed reviews on the safety and desirability of autos, there was no stopping them: Eight years after Alexander brought in the Locomobile, there were 35 dealers offering such makes as the Premier, Pierce-Arrow, Cartercar, Maxwell, Hupmobile, Silent Selden, Hudson, Stearns, Pullman, Lambert and Ford. That year, 1909, the Atlanta Taxicab Co. began with eight "neat and clean" vehicles.

In a few years horse-drawn cabs had disappeared, and the State passed laws penalizing anyone who "shall throw glass, nails, tacks or other obstruction upon the public highwasy..." By 1915 Model T's were being assembled at the Ford Motor Co. plant on Ponce de Leon; the facility moved to Hapeville in 1947.

Veteran carriage-maker John M. Smith, in business since 1869, had seen the handwriting on the wall. In 1913, reported *The Journal,* he burned 25 "phaetons, victorias and sulkies" valued at $30,000, signaling the close of an era. Ironically, he died later that year. His only son and successor, John E., reported in 1916 that Atlanta then had 6,000 cars at an average cost of $700, one-fourth the approximate tab for a fine rig and pair of horses. By 1917 Atlantans could choose from 34 makes of cars, including the Hanson Six, an Atlanta-produced vehicle of a firm headed by a onetime wholesale grocer, George W. Hanson. He promised to deliver 2,000 cars the first year for residents of "a section that is destined to be the garden spot of the United States in the next 10 years...the logical automobile center of the great southeast." The $1,000 Hanson Six sold respectably but competition was too fierce and in 1925 production ceased.

Studebaker salesman L. L. Boyes glowed about the auto's prospects in 1917, especially its appeal to the fair sex: "I have yet to see any woman who has not been materially benefitted by driving. The fresh air, the coordination of eye, mind and muscle, the exhilaration of feeling that you are master of the powerful and yet tractable motor, and that it will answer your every whim, cannot help but have a beneficial effect on the nerves..." That was years

The view is south from the juncture of Pryor (left) and Peachtree Streets. At left was DeGive's Grand Opera House, later the Loew's Grand, where the premiere of "Gone With the Wind" was shown in December, 1939. The Grand was destroyed by fire in 1978; the Georgia-Pacific Building is now on the site. The steeple rises from the First Methodist Church, which has moved elsewhere.

President Theodore Roosevelt tipped his hat from the carriage he rode while on an Atlanta visit in 1905.

The first Confederate Soldiers' Home, on Confederate Avenue, in 1901: The building burned shortly after this photo was taken.

before "women drivers" became a pejorative phrase among impatient males. Boyes' claims helped sell cars.

The advent of cars was not lost on the Fire Department, which began to replace its horse-drawn vehicles with motorized trucks in 1916. The popularity of cars also led the Asa Candlers, Senior and Junior, to organize the Atlanta Automobile Association in 1909, and build the Atlanta Speedway racetrack on a site which later was occupied by the old Atlanta Airport. One of its more unusual races pitted a new device, the airplane (sponsored by Lindsey Hopkins) against an auto and a motorcycle. The car won.

Hopkins, a car dealer, bought a Curtiss biplane in 1911, and he and a Navy pilot made history delivering the first American air mail between two New York cities. The 1911 air meet at the Atlanta raceway featured aviators Lincoln Beachey, C. C. Witmer and Thornwell Andrews. Their aerial acrobatics thrilled the crowd.

The emergence of the auto accelerated movements to bridge the downtown railroad tracks, and change Atlanta. The span linking Peachtree and Whitehall, scene of some pedestrian deaths, led one dedication speaker to express the hope that the "jealousy...between the two sections"—north and south Atlanta—"will soon be obliterated."

The auto also led the impetus to construct more downtown buildings prior to World War I. Asa G. Candler, with loans from his Coca-Cola Company to the Candler Investment Co., erected the 17-story Candler Building in 1906, and school children loved riding the elevators to the top of Atlanta's tallest structure, built on the site of the First Methodist Church.

The likenesses of Candler's parents, as well as those of such historic personages as Alexander H. Stephens, Gen. John B. Gordon, Sidney Lanier, Eli Whitney and Joel Chandler Harris, were sculpted in marble and still adorn the lobby frieze. Carved exterior panels represent aspects of the arts. On the ground floor of the building, first deemed remote from the business section, Candler installed his own Central Bank and Trust Corp. It survived 16 years before merging with Citizens and Southern in 1922.

Chamber of Commerce president Robert F. Maddox began pressing in 1904 for a city auditorium. A Courtland and Gilmer Street site was purchased for $59,000, and the building completed in 1909 at a total cost of $190,000. The "old" post office and Federal Courthouse on Forsyth at Walton was completed in 1911, and two years later work began on its neighbor across the street, William T. Healey's office building.

The appealing Peachtree Arcade was erected in 1917, fronting Peachtree and running west to Broad, at a cost $500,000; and the Transportation Building (later Western Union Building, at Forsyth and

The Spanish-themed Terminal
Station on Spring Street was
completed in 1905, but no longer
exists.

The ornate entrance of Terminal
Station

Marietta), was erected in 1918 on the site of the temporary State Capitol, which had been an opera house. The extant YMCA Building on Luckie opened in 1914.

The thrusting city demanded more hotels, and between 1900 and 1920 several famed ones came onstream. The Piedmont, dubbed for its elegance as "our New York hotel," opened in 1903 to great festivities, its first guests being owners Hoke Smith and George W. and S. F. Parrott. The site, Peachtree and Luckie, had served the homes of pioneers William Ezzard and Dr. James F. Alexander; later, the Piedmont was razed to accommodate the present Equitable Building.

Joseph Gatin's 10-story Georgian Terrace Hotel opened at Ponce de Leon and Peachtree in 1911, billing itself as "a Parisian hotel...in a metropolitan city." It survives, having played host to opera stars who appeared in the Fox Theatre across the street.

The million-dollar Ansley Hotel, named for builder Edwin P. Ansley, opened in 1913 and was renamed the Dinkler-Plaza after enlargement and modernization in 1953. All that remains presently is a hole-in-the-ground parking lot.

Another hotel opening in 1913, the Winecoff, named for builder William Winecoff, drew the usual lavish praise from the press. But 33 years later Atlanta's worst fire tragedy almost destroyed the Peachtree structure and took 119 lives, including those of builder Winecoff, his wife and many young people attending a YMCA meeting. In 1951 it was completely renovated and reopened as the Peachtree on Peachtree Hotel. Prior to World War I the Ponce de Leon Apartments, across from the Georgian Terrace, were opened, and recently have undergone renovation.

Other pre-1920 buildings also survive downtown. The 16-story Fourth National Bank Building, built on the site of pioneer Jonathan Norcross' frame store at Peachtree and Marietta, later became the renovated nucleus of First National Bank's present facility. It was there that Coca-Cola was first served as a fountain drink in Jacobs' Drug Store. The old Fulton County Courthouse survived from 1881 to 1911, when it was razed for the structure which has remained since 1914—"the handsomest courthouse in the South," claimed *The Journal* then, "and one of the largest and costliest in the nation."

Perhaps it was his 1880s residency in Atlanta which influenced President Woodrow Wilson to favor a Federal Reserve Bank branch in the city. It opened in 1914, after heavy lobbying by the financial and political community, and its first building opened on its present downtown site in 1918. There had stood the First Presbyterian Church.

The blooming of commercial structures

The heart of downtown in 1905: The skyline view (looking north) was made from the top of the Piedmont Hotel (where the Equitable Building now stands). The steeple tops the First Methodist Church.

Mrs. William Lawson Peel was photographed in the music room of her Peachtree Street home circa 1905.

Just Where the Ex-Competition Candidates Stand and Just What They Are After.

This cartoon was distributed during the street railway consolidation disputes about 1900. The figure on top the trolley is a caricature of railway magnate Joel Hurt; the balloon reads, "Joel is on top as usual." Initials on the conductor's cap are "H. M. A."—for Henry M. Atkinson, hard-driving electric power executive.

Alonzo F. Herndon's Tonsorial Palace, at 66 Peachtree Street; he was the barber who ultimately formed the Atlanta Life Insurance Company.

The A. G. Rhodes home, completed in 1904, stands on Peachtree Street, opposite Rhodes Center. The mansion sat originally amid 100 acres of land owned by the furniture executive, and was modeled after several Rhineland castles.

and displacement of downtown residences led to northward development, a process which coincided with the emergence of the auto. *The Journal* in 1909 lamented the disappearance of fine downtown homes: "All is going...every last shred of brick, every last crumb of old mortar, every last vestige of the days gone by. For the city has outgrown them. They are downtown, where they don't belong..."

The first residential development after the breakup of Collier's princely 600-acre domain was Ansley Park (first called Peachtree Garden). After E. P. Ansley launched it in 1903, he even staged a street-naming contest which led to the designations of La Fayette Drive, Westminster Drive and The Prater (after the Vienna location), now called The Prado. Peachtree Heights Park was the original name of a

kindred development beginning in 1910 in the present Paces Ferry-Peachtree Battle-Habersham Road-Andrews Drive area. Rivers Road and Andrews Drive are named for two of the key developers, Eretus Rivers and Walter P. Andrews. Both had been Collier's executors; they sold the land for $375,000, and *The Journal* prophesied accurately that "Atlanta will boast a residence section excelled nowhere in beauty and desirability..." Today there is no prettier section when the dogwood dances.

One of the first residents of elite West Paces Ferry Road in early 1900 was an extraordinary civic leader, banker Robert P. Maddox, whose home gave way in the Sixties for the Governor's Mansion. Maddox was one of two prime businessmen (Asa Candler being the other) drafted to serve as mayor between 1907 and 1916. Maddox had not sought office, but shortly after two-time Mayor James G. Woodward, a pleasure-loving printer, won the Democratic primary (tantamount to election), he was arrested for being drunk and rowdy on a downtown street.

Hundreds of indignant citizens met and nominated Maddox, an independent, to oppose Woodward, and Maddox won. (Woodward later served two more terms.) Maddox's election was a fortunate matching of a man to meet the City's needs; its rapid expansion greatly strained the treasury, and citizens had been reluctant to vote a bond issue.

In 1910 more than 80 miles of streets lacked water mains or sewers; sewage disposal was inadequate; water pressure was insufficient for adequate fire protection; Grady Hospital could accommodate only a fraction of the public need, and half the schools were firetraps. Thus, the Chamber in 1909 urged a $3 million bond issue, and

Livingston Mims, mayor, 1901-1902

Thomas Egleston: His will provided funds for a hospital

John Temple Graves: first editor of The Atlanta Georgian newspaper; he said editor Grady died "literally loving a nation into peace."

Eugene M. Mitchell: father of novelist Margaret Mitchell

Mrs. Eugene Mitchell: mother of Margaret and Stephens

W. R. "Cap" Joyner: onetime fire chief, and mayor in 1907

Joseph M. Brown: Georgia governor (1910-11 and 1912-13) and son of Georgia's Civil War governor

Courtland S. Winn, mayor, 1911-1912

James R. Gray: In 1900 he and associates bought the 17-year-old Atlanta Journal from Hoke Smith for $300,000.

The fashionable Piedmont Hotel (right) opened in 1903 at the site now occupied by the Equitable Life Building. Because it was sophisticated in appearance, it was referred to by Atlantans as "our New York hotel." Prior to the Piedmont, the corner site had held the homes of pioneers William Ezzard (a mayor) and Dr. James F. Alexander, successively. The photo, taken in 1908, includes a residence (left) at the corner of Broad and Luckie Streets. Below, the rich interior of the Piedmont lobby.

Atlantans Go Clubby

The growing elite, suburban shift and advent of the auto led to the growth of private country clubs after the turn of the century.

In the summer of 1904 *The Atlanta Journal* reported the formation of what became the East Lake Country Club, with a golf course, tennis courts and promises "a complete chain of all sports known to modern civilization..."

Members of the Jewish community inaugurated the private Standard Club in January, 1905, its first site being a Washington Street home; the second was a new facility at 400 Ponce de Leon. After two decades, it moved to its present site in Brookhaven.

The Piedmont Driving Club had closed for almost two years following destruction by fire in 1906, but staged its reopening in November, 1907.

In 1910 members of the Mechanical and Manufacturers' Club announced they had purchased 150 acres, on north Peachtree Road, to establish the Brookhaven Country Club. It opened in December, 1911, and in 1913 became a part of the Capital City Club, so the latter had both intown and suburban facilities. In 1911 the Capital City Club opened its new downtown building at Peachtree and Harris.

In that same year the first Debutante Club was organized, holding its first major dance at the Piedmont Driving Club. The debutante organization was more than merely social: The objective of the group was charity, initially the furnishing and maintenance of a ward at the Home for Incurables, in the A. G. Rhodes mansion.

The Ansley Park Club dates from 1912, beginning as a semi-public golf course; the Druid Hills Golf Club emerged the same year, beginning with plans for an 18-hole golf course on its 1,650 acre site.

Other social and civic organizations emerged in the double decade following 1900: the Progressive Club (now off Moore's Mill Road); the Atlanta Art Association (chartered in 1905), to which Mrs. Joseph High gave her home, at 15th and Peachtree, as an art museum in 1926; the Atlanta Writers Club, organized in 1914; and the Atlanta Junior League in 1916, formed by members of the Debutante Clubs. The Atlanta Historical Society was founded in 1926 under the leadership of Walter McElreath, Eugene M. Mitchell and others.

The Piedmont Driving Club closed for almost two years following destruction by fire, but reopened in November, 1907. It is on its original site in Piedmont Park.

The Junior League's focus was charity: It managed a school of Household Arts, raised funds for the Buford Memorial Home for Girls, furnished free school books and lunches to underprivileged children, worked with hospitals, and sponsored the *Gone With the Wind* ball the night before the movie's premiere in 1939. The League remains service-oriented, and one of its recent beneficiaries is the Atlanta Preservation Center.

Citizen aid to sufferers of the February, 1905, snow and ice storm was spearheaded by lawyers Joseph C. Logan and Robert Zahner. That led to the formation of Associated Charities, an antecedent of today's United Way.

Atlanta's first Rotary Club dates from 1913 (with the late Ivan Allen Sr. as prime organizer); the Kiwanis entered the Atlanta scene in 1917, the Civitans in 1920, and the Atlanta Exchange Club in 1922.

Tenor Enrico Caruso (far left) was pictured during the 1913 visit of the Metropolitan Opera (above) and was photographed in a dramatic scene from St. Saens' "Samson and Delilah" (below).

Continued from Page 200
college that seeks to maintain, in Weltner's charge, "a superlative academic program." Manning M. Pattillo now heads the institution.

As Atlanta's educational community enlarged, so did its medical facilities. The elegantly-dressed bachelor Thomas Egleston, a widely known insurance executive who served as director of key companies, left a remarkable will at his death in 1916: It had bequests for children of old friends, relatives, friends and servants, as well as money to buy land and equip a 50-bed hospital for children. The hospital finally opened in 1928, and was named for Egleston's mother, Henrietta.

The work of the Atlanta Circle of King's Daughters and Sons led in 1912 to founding the Home for Incurables, on Carnegie Way. On land donated by furniture magnate A. G. Rhodes, a new home was built later for the institution at South Boulevard and Woodward.

Wesley Memorial Hospital got under way in 1904 when Asa Candler paid $17,500 for a downtown home, and promised $12,500 more if Methodists would match the latter gift. They did, and 50-bed Wesley Memorial opened in 1905. By the time its new structure had opened on the Emory campus in 1922, Candler had donated about $1,250,000. Other Candler family members made donations to expand it, and in 1925 title to the medical facility was turned over to the school and renamed Emory Unversity Hospital.

Amster's Private Sanitorium, founded in 1905, was reorganized in 1908 as Piedmont Hospital, and later moved to its present Peachtree Road location, occupying the site of "Deerland," home of lawyer Jack J. Spalding.

Drs. E. C. Davis and Luther C. Fisher took over the building of small Atlanta Hospital when it closed, and launched the Davis-Fisher Private Sanitorium. It soon became inadequate, and a larger facility was built on Linden Street, opening in 1911. (In the first operation there, a patient's gall bladder was relieved of 167 stones.) An adjacent building opened in 1922, and in 1931 the facility was renamed Crawford W. Long Hospital; in 1938 the Hospital was given to Emory. The medical complex remains on the site of the onetime Alexander Luckie family cemetery.

Commercial enterprises kept pace with educational and medical expansions.

George W. Connors perceived a need, and in 1901 launched the Atlanta Steel Hoop Company, and soon expanded. In 1907 it became known as the Atlanta Steel Company (Connors resigning and moving to Birmingham). The firm weathered hectic years and financial reorganizations, and in 1913 became a Delaware corporation known as Atlantic Steel.

The Atlanta Freight Bureau was launched in 1902 to seek more equitable alignment of rates from the South whose firms argued the discriminatory charges hurt commerce. The Seaboard Air-Line completed its rail link between Atlanta and Birmingham in 1904 as Terminal Station was being built on Spring Street. The new Station, an improvement over the long-outmoded facility at Wall Street, opened in

Decades ago, as now, it was quite the thing to be photographed with stars of the Metropolitan Opera. The picture (circa 1910) captures a genial moment between strawhatted tenor Enrico Caruso (left) and H. M. Atkinson, the prime mover of the company which became Georgia Power.

Movie House Opens In 1904; Patrons Supply The Peanuts

A few years after the first local showing of rudimentary movies flopped at the Exposition of 1895, journalist Smith Clayton screened *The Black Diamond Express* at the Grand Opera House, and a bullfight film was shown at the Lyceum before it burned in 1901.

Only in 1904 did the first regular movie house open—John B. Thompson's The Star, at 36 Decatur; he opened a second, The Eldorado, at 146 Marietta, in 1906. A new industry was born: By 1907 there were 14 movie houses, all except the Piedmont Park being in the downtown area; one, the Gayoso, was for "colored," noted the city directory of 1908.

As a rule the early films ran about 15 minutes, and admissions were 5 cents. Patrons brought their own peanuts and candy as they often sat through several showings. City Council feared the darkened halls were dangerous to young ladies, and other patrons held on to their wallets for fear of pickpockets.

The Montgomery Theatre, 87 Peachtree, was the most elaborate of the period when it opened in 1911, featuring a four-piece orchestra in tuxedos. *The Birth of the Nation* created a sensation when the movie played here in 1915.

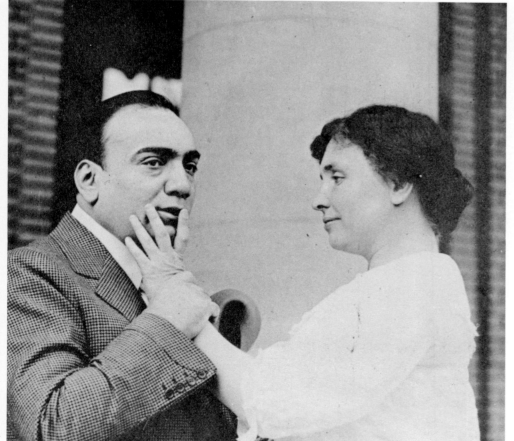

During one of his Atlanta visits with the Metropolitan Opera, tenor Enrico Caruso "spoke" with the famed Helen Keller, her fingers "reading" his lips.

Atlantans have always been visionaries, and this is an artist's 1910 conception of how Peachtree Street would appear a century later—less than 30 years from now. The artist correctly anticipated skyscrapers and buses, but the lagoon (at bottom) seems unlikely, and the air age brought jets instead of dirigibles.

1905, the year the Louisville and Nashville Railroad began serving Atlanta. Brookwood Station opened in 1918, and now is an Amtrak facility. Atlanta thus continued to confirm its rail prominence.

The Atlanta Coca-Cola Bottling Co., licensed in the spring of 1900 with J. B. Whitehead as manager, became the second Coca-Cola bottling plant in the U. S. Mississippi native Arthur Montgomery left his nine-year job as Atlanta agent for the Southern Express Co. to buy an interest in the bottling firm, and assumed active management from 1903 until his death in 1940. Montgomery, who spearheaded establishment of other Coca-Cola bottling plants in Georgia, brought nephew LaFayette F. Montgomery into the firm in 1908, and the latter succeeded to the presidency on his uncle's death.

John Temple Graves, well known journalist, became editor of a colorful paper, the *Atlanta Georgian,* on its founding by Fred L. Seely in 1907. In 1912, however, Seely sold it to William R. Hearst, but the sprightly, sensationalist journal never provided the profits Hearst sought, and it was sold and ceased publication late in 1939. That left Atlanta with two hardy survivors: *The Constitution,* launched in 1868, and *The Journal,* which debuted in 1883. By 1950 they, too, had merged into one company with separate staffs. Now the two papers have one reporting staff. (*The Atlanta Times* emerged in 1964 but survived only 15 months.)

The black press got firmly underway in 1903 when Benjamin J. Davis established the weekly *Atlanta Independent,* but that Republican organ died in 1932. Four years earlier the W. A. Scott family launched a more enduring paper, *The Atlanta Daily World,* which survives as one of the nation's major black dailies.

Dr. William J. Blalock, a physician, was the primary force behind establishment in 1909 of Fulton National Bank (unrelated to the Bank of Fulton which died in 1864), and its first president. Its first offices were in the English-American (Flatiron) Building, but in 1913 it occupied part of the Empire Building (now site of the C & S National Bank), and in 1921 moved to 18-20 Marietta. After years of expansion, Fulton — recently renamed Bank of the South —paid $275,000 for the old Federal Customshouse and post office site which had served as City Hall, at Marietta and Forsyth. The Bank erected a 25-story building in 1955. Fulton had launched a "first" in 1921: the initial southeastern bank to inaugurate a school savings plan for children.

Atlanta further signaled its business importance in 1911 by hosting a three-day Southern Commercial Congress, which drew former President Theodore Roosevelt, then-President William H. Taft, and a future one, Woodrow Wilson. (*The Journal* thinly disguised a joking allusion to Taft's startling heft by

noting that "his descent from his private [rail] car was thoroughly impressive.") Booming cannon, cheering crowds and festive decorations greeted Taft, and City Auditorium was alive with applauded speeches designed to awaken the "South (to) reach speedily her destined place of national leadership."

In that same year Northwestern Mutual Life Insurance Co.'s general agent W. Woods White founded the Atlanta Savings & Loan Co. in the Candler Building. It was renamed the Morris Plan Co. of Atlanta in 1921. In 1946, having moved 10 years before to 36 Peachtree (site of Alamo No. 1, a movie theater), it was renamed Bank of Georgia. Today, the National Bank of Georgia's majority owner is an Arabian construction magnate.

Close by, on Marietta Street, was ample evidence that one of the most aggressive and industrious black citizens was creating a major enterprise. Soon after 24-year-old ex-slave Alonzo F. Herndon arrived from Jonesboro in 1882, he became partner in Dougherty Hutchins' barbershop. Herndon later operated his own 12-chair parlor in the Markham House (the hotel burned in 1896), and a successor parlor at 66 Peachtree. So successful was Herndon with his elite white trade that he bought real estate in Atlanta and Florida. His largest Peachtree shop, with 25 chairs and 18 basement baths, was an elegant enterprise, its fixtures copied from those Herndon admired in Europe.

In 1905 Herndon acceded to black citizen requests that he buy the 35-year-old, financially troubled Atlanta Benevolent and Protective Association, which offered burial insurance. The price was only $140, but Herndon and associates were also

obliged to pay the State $5,000 to meet new insurance company regulations. The institution became Atlanta Mutual, fed by additional Herndon funds, and the Auburn Avenue firm aggressively sold insurance, surviving problems with untrained salesmen.

In 1922 it was renamed Atlanta Life Insurance Co., and five years later Herndon died, leaving a sterling record of entrepreneurship and philanthropy. His son Norris succeeded; the current chief executive is Jesse Hill, former Chamber of Commerce president. The columned Herndon mansion, near Atlanta University, is being converted into a museum and research center.

Another visionary was Isadore M. Weinstein who, during hospitalization for wounds received in France in World War I, conceived the idea of a linen service. The Atlanta Linen Supply Co. was launched in April, 1919, by Weinstein, who contributed $1,500, and associate Herman Gross, who invested $200. Now known as National Service Industries, the company—which opened in a 10 x 12-foot room of an old Walker Street home—has grown to be a conglomerate of firms, a hugely successful enterprise (now led by Erwin Zaban) which expects to be a billion dollar company within a few years, according to its own projections of sustained growth.

Other enterprises of current prominence were spawned shortly after 1900. In 1905 B. M. Grant founded a real estate firm, and soon took in A. S. Adams as partner. When Grant retired, Adams and Alvin B. Cates Sr. formed a new partnership as A. S. Adams-Cates Co., and on Adams' death in 1926, the firm was incor-

Atlanta, 1906: The view is south—with the English-American Building (the Flatiron) in the center foreground, Broad Street at right, and Peachtree at left, leading to Five Points. The photo was made from the 17th floor of the Candler Building. Central City Park is now in the upper left of the picture.

Banker Robert F. Maddox, mayor in 1909-1910, and one of Atlanta's most progressive chief executives

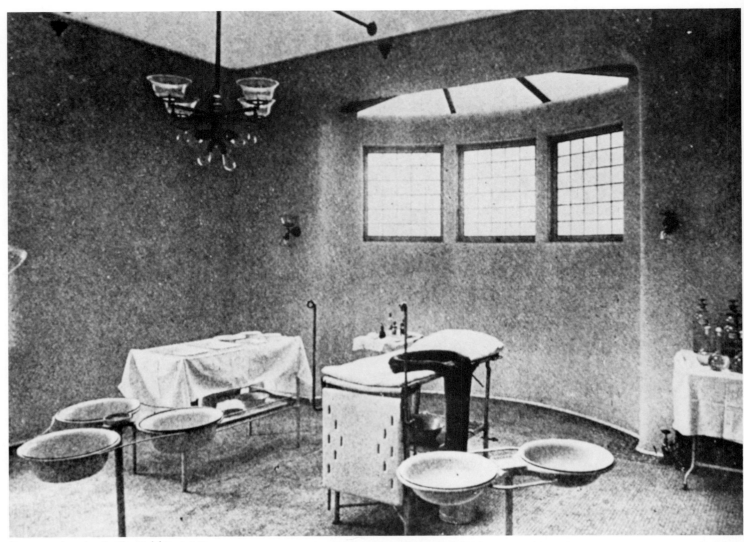

By our standards the tables were
rudimentary, as was the rest of the
operating room equipment. This was
Grady Hospital in 1912.

Medical students, faculty and an
attendant posed seriously with a
classroom corpse in 1911—but some
wag inked in the line, "He lived for
others, he died for us."

porated under its present name, Adams/Cates Co.

Other enterprises date from this period: William H. Brown and James L. Mayson, with $100,000 cash, obtained the charter for Greenwood Cemetery in 1904; its first direct interment was in 1907. Greenwood is known for its special Greek, Jewish and Chinese sections.

The Chamber of Commerce took a far-reaching step in 1912 when it organized the Atlanta Convention Bureau; its present-day successor is a prime player in what has become one of Atlanta's key industries. Another is real estate, and the Atlanta Real Estate Board began with informal luncheon meetings in 1908. The Central Atlanta Improvement Association (antecedent of today's Central Atlanta Progress) was launched in 1909.

The newspapers took note of such new enterprises, but the commercial issue which captured headlines was the continuation of a war which had erupted in the last decade of the old century. The chief contenders were Joel Hurt's Atlanta Consolidated Street Railway Co. (renamed Atlanta Rapid Transit Co. in 1902) and H. M. Atkinson's Georgia Electric Light Co.

The competitors continually filed rival streetcar franchise applications with City Council; in the seven-year period from 1895 they filed 17 injunction suits against each other, and even backed rivals in the mayor's race of 1900.

Their war ended at the conference table in 1902: Georgia Electric bought the Hurt interests, and later became Georgia Power Co. Its transit interests were sold in 1950 to the Atlanta Transit Co. Before then, the system had added gas buses and converted from fixed-rail to trackless electric trolleys. The last streetcar ran in 1949, and the last electric-powered vehicle in 1963. The Atlanta Transit Company was the predecessor of today's Metropolitan Atlanta Rapid Transit Authority.

The first of four tragic events to scar Atlanta between 1902 and 1918 was the "Pittsburg Riot." It was triggered on the evening of May 16, 1902, when former policeman Samuel A. Kerlin was attacked by blacks led by Will Richardson, who threatened to kill Kerlin for putting him in the chain gang. The unarmed Kerlin retreated under a barrage of knife thrusts and stones, and his cries brought help from two soldiers and two policemen. Richardson locked himself in a store, and fired his gun. A policeman was killed.

A crowd gathered, police were called, a gun battle ensued and the store was set ablaze. At the end of the fray, Richardson was dead, as were three officers and two other citizens. Five other men were wounded, and a city block was in ashes.

A violent race riot occurred in 1906. Some of its seeds were sown that year in the heated gubernatorial contest between Hoke Smith, *The Journal's* candidate and its onetime president/publisher, and *The*

The Georgia Tech Evening School was at 223 Walton Street when this sketch was made. In 1931 it became part of the school that has emerged as Georgia State University—no longer on Walton, of course.

Shortly after the turn of the century, fashionable hotels emerged, such as this one, the Majestic.

Sculptor Gutzon Borglum's model of the first concept for Stone Mountain memorial; the figures were reduced to three.

Sculptor Augustus Lukeman and workmen on June 7, 1928: The figure of Robert E. Lee astride Traveler is clearly defined.

Gutzon Borglum's (bald man, left) and guests shared a 1924 meal on the granite ledge which became Lee's shoulder.

Borglum with model for T. J. "Stonewall" Jackson's head in 1925; on the carving Jackson emerges hatless.

55 Years from Idea To Its Completion

From conception to completion, the 80-foot-tall carving on the side of Stone Mountain required 55 years.

Mrs. Helen Plane, of the United Daughters of the Confederacy, was quoted in 1909 as proposing the Mountain for a memorial.

Sculptor Gutzon Borglum, then being acclaimed for his statue of Abraham Lincoln, was consulted, and he said the project would require 10 years and cost $3 million. In 1915 he envisioned Confederate leaders riding around the Mountain.

After being deeded the face of the Mountain and 10 adjoining acres in 1916, the UDC started to act. But World War I halted real work, and only in 1923 did Borglum report his designs were finished and he was ready to carve. Soon after he began, personality rifts between the UDC and Borglum increased and in 1928 he destroyed his models and left Georgia.

Augustus Lukeman was chosen to succeed Borglum. But before major work was finished, donors of the Mountain face and acreage reclaimed their property, in accordance with the terms of the original deed. Thirty years later the State purchased the Mountain and 3,800 surrounding acres for a park, and Walter K. Hancock was chosen in 1963 to finish Lukeman's plan. Completion of the three figures in the carving came in 1970.

Interior of the main office of Atlanta Gas Light Company, at the corner of Alabama and Broad Streets at the turn of the century

Constitution's favorite, Clark Howell, its former editor.

Part of Smith's platform was advocacy of a constitutional amendment to disfranchise blacks, and the vitriolic Populist Tom Watson was an outspoken supporter. Smith won; *The Constitution* called the lopsided balloting of August, 1906, a "Smith Deluge."

While historians agree that Watson's inflammatory anti-black statements contributed to the onset of the riot which erupted a month later, the immediate trigger was a series of assaults upon white women by blacks over several months. Inflamed reportage by the papers and contagious rumors added to the rising anger. "It is time," editorialized *The Journal* in August, 1906, "for those who know the perils of the Negro problems to stand together with deep resolve that political power shall never give the Negro encouragement in his foul dreams of a mixture of the races."

The explosive situation erupted the evening of Sept. 22: Four attempted assaults on white women by blacks that day were reported in sensationalized news stories. That night a crowd gathered at Pryor and Decatur, and some white boys —with too much to drink—attacked a black bicycle messenger, ultimately rescued by police. The mob enlarged to about 2,000, and blacks were chased in the downtown area until fire department hoses cooled the hotheads. Attacks were made on blacks riding the trolleys, the police

were called, and the chief himself engaged in a hand-to-hand fight on one car. Soon whites were rushing hardware stores for guns and ammunition. The worst battle of the night ensued at Marietta and Forsyth, where the mob dragged two black barbers from their shop and killed them, along with another black on the Forsyth Street bridge.

Other segments of the mob descended on blacks working near the Union depot, killing a porter. At this stage Mayor Woodward pleaded with the crowd to "go to your homes quietly...I beseech you not to cause this blot on the fair name of our most beautiful city..." His remarks were in vain, and he called on the fire department which swept Decatur Street from Peachtree to Ivy with heavy jets of water. But when a streetcar stopped at Marietta and Peachtree, mobs assaulted its blacks, leaving seven on the floor—three of them beaten to death.

By early Sunday morning, Sept. 23, 600 soldiers commanded the city's center, and the town was quiet. The following night, blacks held mass meetings; the largest—at Brownsville—was broken up by police, who arrested some of them. But the force was ambushed as it returned to town, and one officer was killed; others were wounded.

On Tuesday afternoon leading citizens met and called for calm, denounced the mob, and named a committee, headed by clothing merchant George Muse, to raise a relief fund for families of victims.

Ponce de Leon Park, across from the Sears, Roebuck Company store, included a baseball diamond and covered stands.

George Muse Clothing Company headquarters at 1-3-5 Whitehall Street was erected in 1902; the 1917 photograph includes its motorized delivery van. Muse's moved to its present Peachtree and Walton location in 1921.

By Wednesday, the riots had ended and Atlanta had a large black eye. The toll, apart from property damage: 12 dead (10 blacks, two whites), and 70 wounded (60 blacks and 10 whites).

The commercial expansiveness of the double decade after 1900 was matched by the development of numerous special-interest clubs and organizations designed to enhance the city's social, cultural, recreational, business and sports life. Increasingly, famed personalities—especially in the music world—found Atlanta more cosmopolitan, and the "New York of the South," as some began to call it, played joyous host to their performances.

Polish pianist-composer Ignace Jan Paderewski's recital in 1900 drew wild applause. In the same year William Jennings Bryan lectured on trusts and the gold standard, months later being defeated again in his presidential bid, against William McKinley. (The following year, McKinley, who had been a Union officer with Sherman's troops in the Battle of Peachtree Creek, was assassinated.)

Ex-Confederate Gen. Joseph Wheeler attended a Veterans Reunion—accompanied by his daughter, an Agnes Scott student—in Piedmont Park, where later that year was held the "first great fashionable horse show" in the South. Other distinguished visitors during a few years after 1900 were the inquisitive Chinese Ambassador Wu; President and Mrs. Theodore Roosevelt (who visited his mother's home, Bulloch Hall, in Roswell); President-elect William H. Taft; novelist Mary Roberts Rinehart, evangelist William Ashley "Billy" Sunday, and Irish tenor John McCormack in a recital that brought tears to many of the 5,000 who heard him.

(One of the unwilling visitors was writer Julian Hawthorne, son of the late author of *The House of Seven Gables*. The younger Hawthorne arrived in 1913, and became convict No. 4435 when he was clapped into Atlanta's 10-year-old Federal penitentiary. Hawthorne, sentenced for a year for using the mails to defraud, was released after seven months.)

But the crime that rocked Atlanta in 1913—and left shock waves for decades— was the murder of Mary Phagan, not yet 14, and the trial of her accused employer, Leo Frank. In a highly-charged trial, heated by anti-Semitic and racial overtones that steamy summer, Frank was convicted on testimony of another employee, James Conley, despite the latter's private confessions he himself had murdered the child.

Following a vain series of appeals and a gubernatorial commutation of sentence, Frank was snatched from his prison cell by a lynch mob more than two years after his conviction, and hanged from a tree near Marietta, where Phagan was born.

Sixty-nine years after the murder, the *Nashville* (Tenn.) *Tennessean* published a copyrighted section featuring the sworn statement of another former Frank

Flag-raising day in 1917 included a Peachtree Street parade (the view is south through Five Points) that demonstrated citizen support for the war effort.

employee, Alonzo Mann, that, "Leo Frank did not kill Mary Phagan. She was murdered instead by Jim Conley."

Mann, now in his eighties, reported seeing Conley carrying Phagan's limp body that Saturday in 1913, but had been warned by his own mother to remain silent. Mann testified at the trial almost 70 years ago, but said nothing then of seeing Conley. The Nashville newspaper subjected Mann to lie detector tests to weigh the truth of his revelations; he passed them all.

About noon on Saturday, April 26, 1913, Phagan appeared in Frank's second-floor office of the National Pencil Factory, 39 S. Forsyth St., between Alabama and Hunter, there to collect the $1.20 due her for the previous Monday's work. Frank testified that he gave her the money, and she left; that he never saw her again.

About 14 hours later her lifeless body was found by Newt Lee, the black night watchman for the factory, in the building basement. He promptly phoned police. Examining physicians reported that Phagan had not been molested, and that she had died—probably of strangulation—between noon and 3 p.m. that fateful Saturday.

Lee and Frank, who was Jewish, were both questioned. Both denied knowledge of the crime, and Frank even employed detectives to find the murderer. Lee said he saw Frank at the factory about 4 p.m. that Saturday, and was told to leave the premises, have a good time, and return about 6 p.m. When he did, Frank was there, but left for home, and phoned about 7 p.m. to ask if everything was all right. That sort of phone call was unusual for Frank, and it damaged his protests of innocence.

Early in May, police arrested Conley,

the black sweeper of the factory, when he was observed washing a shirt thought to be flecked with the victim's blood. Conley had been in and out of the chain gang, and was known to be a dissolute and shiftless character who often cadged coins from fellow employees for alcohol, as Mann recalled.

Conley swore that Frank had murdered the child, then asked him to burn her body in the basement after forcing him to pencil two notes—left by her body—that tended to implicate Lee as the murderer.

Four weeks after the murder, Frank was indicted. He pleaded not guilty. Lawyers Luther Z. Rosser, Reuben Arnold and Henry A. Alexander defended him. The chief prosecutor was Solicitor General Hugh M. Dorsey, assisted by lawyer Frank A. Hooper Sr. The judge at the trial, which began July 28, was Leonard S. Roan. The jury consisted of 12 men, 11 of them married.

The prosecution charged that Frank hurt Phagan accidentally or otherwise, then strangled her. Conley's testimony, said Frank, was "the vilest and most amazing pack of lies ever conceived in the perverted brain of a wicked human being." But the defense failed to break Conley's testimony which included charges that Frank had intrigued with female employees. Character witnesses, including employees, defended both Conley and Frank.

On August 18, Frank made a four-hour statement. His wife and mother wept. The jurors sat entranced, one of them saying later, "Frank acquitted himself. No man could talk like he did, and lie."

Public feeling ran high; the courtroom was packed; some spectators ate lunch at their seats rather than leave during recess; throngs shouted outside the courtroom.

Admiring smiles greeted Gen. John J. Pershing in 1919 as he left the Georgian Terrace Hotel to inspect army camps. Pershing commanded the American Expeditionary Force during World War I.

Among the Atlantans in the army during World War I was 2nd Lt. Stephens Mitchell, photographed in 1918. Mitchell, older brother of novelist Margaret Mitchell, became a well known lawyer.

Captured German officers and crew members from a submarine were interned at Ft. McPherson in 1917.

On August 26, after the jury had sat for 29 days and deliberated for four hours, the verdict was "guilty," and Frank was sentenced to be hanged on Oct. 10. An appeal was filed but on Oct. 31 Judge Roan denied a motion for a new trial. On appeal to the State Supreme Court, it affirmed Roan's ruling (4 to 2) on Feb. 17, 1914. On March 7, Frank was again sentenced to die, on April 17.

The Journal editorialized that, "Leo Frank has not had a fair trial," and added: "The very atmosphere of the courtroom was charged with an electric current of indignation... The courtroom and streets were filled with an angry, determined crowd, ready to seize the defendant if the jury had found him not guilty..."

The newspaper's appeal did not earn a new trial for Frank, but brought it the vitriolic condemnation of Tom Watson in his own publication, *The Jeffersonian.*

Frank obtained a new stay of execution on April 16, 1914, on an extraordinary motion for a new trial; it was denied, and the case went to the U.S. Supreme Court on a writ of error. On December 7, the high court decided against Frank, and on Dec. 9, he was sentenced for the third time, to be hanged on Jan. 22, 1915. But the case came before the high court again on application for a certificate of reasonable doubt. It was dismissed April 19, 1915. The courts offered no further relief.

Frank's attorneys appealed to Gov. John M. Slaton for commutation of sentence to life imprisonment. Despite the hundreds of letters the governor received, threatening him with death if the sentence were commuted, the governor told his wife his decision early in the morning of June 21: "It may mean my death or worse, but I have ordered the sentence commuted."

It is reported that Mrs. Slaton kissed him and said, "I would rather be the widow of a brave and honorable man than the wife of a coward."

Slaton, whose term was to end the next day, noted that the case had been marred by doubt on the part of the trial judge (Roan), two judges of the state Supreme Court, two on the high court, and one of the three prison commissioners. The night Slaton wrestled with his decision, Frank was sent to the prison at Milledgeville.

Watson's columns in *The Jeffersonian* had assaulted the Governor, declaring that he had sold out to the Jews, and urged the mobs to lynch Frank and "get the governor."

Two companies of the National Guard and county police protected Slaton's Buckhead residence the day he announced the commutation of sentence, and drove off riffraff who attacked that day and again that evening, capturing 26 men along with some dynamite and pistols. Most of those arrested were indicted, tried and punished.

On July 17, as Frank slept on his prison cot, fellow prisoner William Creen slashed his throat. A month later, before he was fully recovered, Frank would die.

On the night of August 16, 25 armed men, some masked, arrived in Milledgeville in eight autos. Calling themselves the Knights of Mary Phagan, they cut prison wires to the world outside, detained the superintendent and warden in their homes, overpowered prison guards, and in 10 minutes had seized Frank and disappeared toward Atlanta.

Early in the morning of Aug. 17, Frank was hanged from a tree on land of former Cobb county sheriff W. J. Frey. Frank was cut down, and his body hurried off to the Greenberg & Bond mortuary at Houston and Ivy Streets, where thousands filed by to view the body. By midnight Frank's body was on a train taking him to burial in Brooklyn, N.Y.

The identities of the 25 men who kidnaped Frank were never discovered, despite an investigation by Slaton's successor, Gov. N. E. Harris. Atlanta Mayor Woodward, addressing a meeting in California the day after the lynching, said that Frank had suffered the "just penalty for an unspeakable crime."

According to Allen L. Henson, an assistant State's attorney in 1913, Conley admitted to his own attorney, William Smith, that he had killed the girl. Conley made the same confession to Annie Maud Carter, she swore in an affidavit supporting one of Frank's appeals. And an insurance agent said, in a sworn affidavit, that Conley had also confessed the killing to him.

Judge Roan, according to the autobiography of associate Arthur G. Powell, told Powell he believed Frank was innocent. Indeed, in *The Atlanta Constitution* of July 14, 1914, Conley's attorney, Smith, said he was convinced that Conley had lied, that Frank was innocent, and promised to work for Frank's exoneration.

Nothing came of it all, and justice apparently was murdered along with Frank. The obvious anti-Semitism surrounding the Frank trial led to the formation of the B'nai B'rith Anti-Defamation League, organized to fight prejudice and discrimination in any form, whoever its intended victims might be. All the principal members of the terrible drama are now dead—save Alonzo Mann, and in 1982 his conscience spoke to clear Frank's name—69 years after angry passions fouled it and took his life.

Perhaps emboldened by the lynching of Frank in August, 1915, the Ku Klux Klan was revived fewer than four months later. On the night of Thanksgiving, preacher and traveling salesman William J. Simmons and 33 friends—two of them members of the Reconstruction-era Klan which had been quiescent since the early 1870s—held a ceremony atop Stone Mountain.

The Klan's new charter was issued by the State, and the movement spread nationwide, though slowly. In 1921, when the Klan had branches (or "klaverns") in virtually every Northern state, the organi-
Continued on Page 218

Advocating women's right to vote, three ladies—Ms. Mary L. McLendon, Mrs. Hardin and Mrs. Leonard Grossman— were in a 1913 parade.

Long Road to Woman's Suffrage

In March, 1894, a women's suffrage league was organized in Atlanta, and was affiliated with the statewide movement which began in Columbus, Ga., four years before.

The first Atlanta members were Mrs. Mary L. McLendon and Mrs. Kate M. Hardwick, and their efforts led to the annual meeting in Atlanta of the National American Women Suffrage Association in 1895. Ninety-three delegates from 28 states attended, and heard an address by 75-year-old Susan B. Anthony, the Association's president.

Ms. Anthony noted that one of the nation's two equal suffrage states then had three women in its legislature. "I know that there are men who will say it is a shame," she said, but in the minds of such men "it is no disgrace for women to keep the legislative hall in order, to clean the spittoons and to keep the dust from settling on the floor..." It is only when they sit in the legislature and vote is an objection made, she added.

In 1902 Atlanta women asked City Council for the right to vote, but were denied on that occasion and later. In 1913 the Georgia Equal Suffrage League was formed in Atlanta with Mrs. Frances Whiteside, principal of the Ivy Street School, as president; that year a Georgia Men's League for Woman Suffrage was also formed, led by attorney Leonard J. Grossman.

Finally, in May, 1919, the Democratic Executive Committee of Atlanta voted 24-1 to permit women to vote in city primary elections, and in June, 1919, the Federal woman suffrage amendment was submitted to states for ratification. The 19th Amendment went into force on August 26, 1920, and in 1921 the Georgia legislature passed an act enabling women to vote and hold office. Only in 1970 did the legislature ratify the 19th Amendment.

Tom Watson stirred racial passions during the Leo Frank trial; he later became a U. S. senator.

Gov. John M. Slaton commuted the sentence of Leo Frank—but the latter was kidnapped and hanged.

215

Almost 2,000 structures were destroyed in the 1917 fire, which began at the corner of Decatur and Fort Streets (above). Despite brave efforts of the firemen, commercial buildings (upper right), shanties (below, left and right) and homes were swallowed up in the inferno which cast a pall over much of the city. Ten thousand persons were made homeless.

View of the destroyed area from Angier Avenue to Houston Street, along Forrest Avenue (now Ralph McGill Boulevard), Boulevard and Jackson Street: Ruins include those of the Jackson Hill Baptist Church, Westminster Presbyterian Church, Grace Methodist Church and many apartments.

This view of the destruction was taken from Jackson Street, showing Ponce de Leon Avenue (indicated by the line of trees), where the fire was finally arrested. The May fire laid waste some 300 acres; property loss was set at $5.5 million.

1917 Fire Wastes 300 Acres, 1938 Buildings

Atlanta's second of two great fires came almost 53 years after Gen. Sherman set the first. Late in the morning of Monday, May 21, 1917, three isolated blazes broke out on Murphy Avenue, York and Gordon Streets, and at Woodward and King. A total of 15 houses were destroyed. An hour after the first alarm, however, came the report of the fourth blaze that day—Atlanta's "big fire."

It erupted on the roof of the so-called "old Negro pest house," then used by Grady Hospital as a storage depot. It stood north of Decatur Street between Fort and Hilliard. Brisk winds caught sparks from burning mattresses and flung them north. Said *The Journal* the next day: "The north side, along Boulevard and Jackson Street (now Parkway Drive), from Decatur Street almost to Piedmont Park, has been swept as bare as a billiard table... Scarcely a stick is left standing... It is one long field of cinders stretching for nearly two miles straight..."

Dynamite was used to halt the path of destruction. Firemen from other cities were called, as were local soldiers and Boy Scouts. By 10 p.m. "the great red wall was finally stopped, halfway between Ponce de Leon Avenue and Piedmont Park," reported *The Journal*. Attractive homes and business places were consumed, as were many shacks owned by blacks.

After 10 hours the fire was under control. The following morning some 200 to 300 people awoke from makeshift beds in Piedmont Park; many blacks occupied a vacant lot on Edgewood.

Relief work began immediately; funds were raised for the destitute, the Red Cross established a clearing house for refugees, and trucks hauled stacked household effects to Municipal Auditorium for safekeeping.

A survey showed that despite the usage of 22 million gallons of water, 300 acres were laid waste, 1,938 buildings were destroyed, and 10,000 people—most of them black—were made homeless. Property loss soared to $5.5 million. Only one person died: Mrs. Bessie Hodges, of a heart attack triggered by shock following the burning of her Boulevard home.

Marietta Street, looking northwest from Peachtree, in 1917: Horse-driven vans, mule-pulled carts, electrified trolleys and gasoline autos didn't stop pedestrians from crossing where they wished.

The Empire Building (erected 1901) became, after remodeling, the Citizens & Southern National Bank building in 1929, still at Broad and Marietta Streets.

Continued from Page 215

zation bought the former Edward Durant Home (corner Peachtree Road and East Wesley Road) for its "Imperial Palace." (It is now owned by the Roman Catholic Church.)

By 1924, it has been said, Klan membership was at 6 million, its peak as it turned out, and it influenced national elections and local politics. Though its power waned by 1928, it grew strong again during the Depression, but curtailed its activities during World War II. In 1947 Georgia revoked the Klan's charter; the most powerful replacement for it was the Association of Georgia Klans, which was placed on the list of subversive organizations by the U.S. attorney-general in 1949.

More than three months before President Wilson formally asked Congress to declare war on Germany in April, 1917, Gen. Leonard Wood, former Georgia Tech student and then Chief of Staff of the U.S. Army, wired Ivan Allen Sr., president of the Chamber of Commerce. Wood wanted to inspect sites for a cantonment, and the next day he and civic leaders toured a two-county area.

On June 1 Atlanta was notified it had been chosen as one of the sites to train soldiers; in June a 2,000-acre tract in the Cross Keys district of DeKalb County was chosen, and on July 16 it was named Camp John B. Gordon. Two days after the declaration of war was signed (April 6), recruiting offices were jammed with volunteers. Ft. McPherson took on new life as one of 14 sites to train applicants for commissions.

Citizens soon seeded vegetable gardens for the war effort (some at Maddox, Mozley and Piedmont Parks); parades heightened the civic zeal, residents subscribed to Liberty Bonds, and more than 21,000 Fulton Countians signed up for the draft. On June 5 seven Atlantans—including two blacks—held the first number drawn: 258.

By Sept. 5 Camp Gordon was receiving the first contingent of soldiers-to-be, three months before the Camp—with 1,400 buildings—was completed at a cost of $6 million. Between September, 1917, and November, 1918, more than 233,000 men had passed through it, including those of the famed 82nd (Rainbow) Division and five Engineer Service Battalions composed of black soldiers.

By war's end, Atlantans were telling tales of manpower shortages (women drove elevators, for example); of Camp Jesup (near McPherson), where army vehicles came for repair; of meatless days and wheatless days, of joy-riderless Sundays due to gas rationing, and "lightless nights" due to cutbacks in electrical service. Young women knit socks, staged dances to boost soldier morale and performed other kindred chores. "Four-Minute Men" clubs offered civilian speech-makers to disseminate data about war work and civilian

"Atlanta's Great Two-Mile Speedway," where first auto races were held Nov. 9-13, 1909. This area, Candler Field, was the site of the first Atlanta Airport.

defense measures. The War Camp Community Service organized entertainments through various civic clubs to amuse area soldiers.

The day after the Armistice was signed, Atlanta residents spent themselves on a grand downtown parade which included 10,000 troops, swooping airplane displays, joyous flag-waving and ear-splitting pandemonium. Five weeks later the 1,400 German prisoners confined at Ft. McPherson were allowed to observe Christmas according to the customs of their homeland.

Fulton County sent 8,733 men to war (7,890 of them being from Atlanta); DeKalb County, 765. Of the almost 9,500 servicemen, 124 died from service-connected disabilities not later than 1920.

Except for the Atlanta homes made sorrowful by the deaths of loved ones, the city closed the first 20 years of the new century on a hopeful note. In 1919 the Chamber of Commerce successfully foiled an attempt to move the capital to Macon. In the same year Atlanta women obtained the right to vote in local elections; the 19th Amendment was approved the following year.

It augured well. The Twenties could bring only normalcy and prosperity, and it did—for a time.

Candler Field racetrack featured grandstands for viewers.

Atlanta Finds New Business

1920-1929

Atlantans who served in Europe during the Great War saw first-hand that two modern inventions had passed beyond mere hobby status: airplanes and wireless voice transmission. Both were to become familiar parts of life in Atlanta by the end of the Twenties. The aviation role Atlanta carved out for itself in the Twenties, in fact, was to prove a dominant fact of economic life for the region thereafter.

If those same servicemen had acquired a taste for European wines and brandies, however, there was little opportunity to pursue that interest. Atlanta had been more or less dry under state law since 1908. In 1920, when the city's population had just passed 200,000, the 18th Amendment extended Prohibition to the entire nation.

As Americans were losing the right to drink, women were gaining the right to vote by virtue of the 19th Amendment. And soon they were serving in public office in Georgia. Miss Bessie Kempton, a *Constitution* reporter, was elected to the Georgia House from Fulton County in 1922. In that same year, Mrs. Rebecca Latimer Felton became America's first female senator when Georgia Gov. Thomas W. Hardwick appointed her to the vacancy caused by the death of Sen. Tom

There was no passenger service in 1927, when the City of Atlanta still was leasing land at the old Candler racetrack for this airport facility.

Downtown Peachtree Street was Atlanta's "theater district" when this was shot in 1921. Visible are the Lyric at junction with Forsyth, and the Howard, later known as the Paramount before it was razed.

The scissors and the date—October, 1928—suggest these Spring Street school children may have been at work on some Halloween decorations.

When it opened in 1920 on Peachtree Street near the junction with Forsyth, the Howard Theatre was the most opulent in Atlanta. In later years it was known as the Paramount. It has long since yielded to office construction.

Watson. (She did not seek election to the remainder of the term, and the seat was won by a former Georgia Supreme Court justice named Walter F. George. He held it till 1957.)

Hardwick's gesture to the new female vote did him little good when he stood for re-election in 1922. In 1920, before women were enfranchised, Hardwick had defeated Clifford Walker. In 1922, with women on voters' roles, the results were reversed. Since "exit polls" were unheard of in those days, there's no record of how the vote went along sex lines.

Along racial lines, it can be stated categorically that the vote for both Walker and Hardwick was 100 per cent white. Blacks were to remain barred from the crucial Democratic primary until the late Forties. The civil rights movement was even further away.

Black progress in the Twenties consisted primarily of improved municipal services and establishment of some durable institutions. The first branch library for black Atlantans was authorized in 1920, and the first municipal swimming pool in 1922 (in Washington Park on the West Side, which already was becoming a more prestigious residential neighborhood than the Decatur Steet-Auburn Avenue area east of Five Points).

Of great long-range import, the compact which has developed into the six-member Atlanta University Center was inaugurated in 1929. It provided that Morehouse College would offer undergraduate education for men and Spelman College for women, and that Atlanta University would serve exclusively as a graduate school. Morris Brown and Clark Colleges and Gammon (now Interdenominational) Theological Seminary joined the group later.

Atlanta's first black-controlled bank,

Atlanta State Savings Bank, had been organized in 1909. It failed in 1922. But in 1921 Herman E. Perry, then president of Standard Life Insurance Co., organized Citizens Trust Bank. Over the years, it has been an important influence in Atlanta's black community. Its handsome modern headquarters on Houston Street led the way for redevelopment of that downtown area.

In 1928 William Alexander Scott founded a weekly that later developed into the *Atlanta Daily World,* one of the oldest black-owned newspapers in America.

Every era adds its own veneer to the accumulation of events we call history. Sometimes change in a given era is multi-faceted, sometimes concentrated in one field. The Twenties in Atlanta exemplify the latter. The decade's most profound contributions were in business development, above all in commercial aviation.

Aviation's importance is widely recognized and customarily observed in any economic analysis of Atlanta. It deserves the emphasis it receives, because Atlanta's bold seizure of a central role in air routing has produced one of its greatest economic assets: an extraordinary network of direct passenger and freight air connections with the rest of the United States and an increasing number of foreign cities.

But another economic accomplishment of the Twenties also has had profound though subtler impact on the city's character. For in the Twenties, Atlanta emerged as a branch office city. It became somewhat less blue collar and somewhat more white collar.

The trend naturally affected Atlanta's politics. The labor vote became less potent than in the days when union leader James G. Woodward repeatedly was elected mayor. And Atlanta's economic underpinnings became better balanced, so that in future hard times, Atlanta was not hit so severely as some industrial cities.

Much of Atlanta's Twenties boom can be credited to the Forward Atlanta campaign of the Atlanta Chamber of Commerce. It was a three-year, $825,000 advertising program to tout nationally Atlanta's favorable climate, work force, natural resources and location.

The campaign was the brain child of W. R. C. Smith, publishing executive and Chamber president. When he proposed it in October, 1925, Atlanta was in the economic doldrums. Business and construction has been brisk in the early postwar years. By 1925, the pace had slowed, in part because of the attention and investment being attracted by the soon-to-collapse Florida land speculation bubble.

A social event of 1922 was the marriage of Margaret Mitchell to Berrien K. Upshaw, against her family's wishes. Before the end of that year, Upshaw had left her, and she won an uncontested divorce by the end of 1924. In mid-1925 she married the best man at her wedding, John Marsh. The Mitchell-Upshaw wedding picture shows (from left) Dorothy Bates, Marsh, Augusta Dearborn, Aline Mitchell Timmons, Upshaw, Margaret Mitchell, Winston Withers, flower girl Clara M. McConnell, Martha Bratton, and Margaret Mitchell's brother Stephens.

The bunting-draped main hall of Atlanta's Municipal Auditorium in 1925 could seat 6,000. Here it looked ready to host a political convention.

Wrong-Way Run Gilds Tech's Golden Year

One of the greatest football teams in Georgia Tech's history was the "Golden Tornado" assembled by head coach Bill Alexander in 1928.

It rolled over all its regular season opponents, including such heavyweights as Notre Dame and arch-rival Georgia, and earned an invitation to the Rose Bowl.

Tech won the bowl game, too—with a little help from the captain of its opponent, the University of California Golden Bears. Captain Roy Riegels recovered a fumble on the Tech 30, became confused and raced 69 yards to his own one-yard line before a teammate tackled him. The Bears' kickoff was blocked and Tech scored a safety—the two points Tech needed for its 8-7 victory.

With office supply executive Ivan Allen Sr. as chairman and a board that read like Who's Who of Atlanta business, the 1926-29 campaign was notably successful. It is credited with attracting 762 new enterprises that created 20,000 new jobs with payrolls totaling $34.5 million a year. The jobs were especially welcome because of the heavy Twenties influx of rural people driven off their farms by boll weevil infestation and general depression in agriculture.

The Forward Atlanta experience had impact far beyond those impressive numbers. It reinforced Atlantans' belief that they could achieve ambitious goals through aggressive and intelligent promotion—that the boast could become reality. The concept was not new. It underlay the three expositions of the 1880s and 1890s. And it was to be reiterated in the second Forward Atlanta campaign of the 1960s (proposed by Allen's son, Ivan Jr.).

Much of the development Forward Atlanta generated came from national corporations that established regional management, sales, assembly and distribution operations.

Major businesses attracted to Atlanta in the Twenties include Sears, Roebuck & Co., which completed its enormous Ponce de Leon facility in 1926, and General Motors, which opened a Chevrolet and Fisher Body assembly plant in 1928.

Atlanta businessman Carlyle Fraser established an auto parts company at Baker and Ivy Streets in 1928 with a $25,000 inventory. It has grown into a successful nationwide company, Genuine Parts.

The investment firm of Courts & Co. was started on a small scale in 1925 by Richard W. Courts Jr. and Sr. to specialize in bank and local stocks.

A local department store founded in 1891 and known under various names was acquired by New York's R. H. Macy & Co. in 1925. Construction of its new headquarters was launched that same year and today remains the core of Davison's downtown store.

J. P. Allen & Co. opened a new downtown headquarters at Peachtree and Cain (International Blvd.) in 1928.

A long-developing series of bank mergers culminated in 1929 with the creation of the First National Bank. Because of the charter of its earliest antecedent, Atlanta National, it is able to date its birth to 1865.

Georgia's first commercial radio station, WSB, went on the air March 16, 1922, in an unpartitioned section of *The Atlanta Journal's* fifth floor. Radio was a pet interest of *Journal* president and editor John S. Cohen. He hired an electrical engineer from the Georgia Railway &

Electric Co. to design and build the facility. Its antenna was on the building's roof.

The Journal promised not only local programming, but retransmission of distant broadcasts: "Weather, News, Crop Reports, Musical Concerts and Other Matters of Public Interest."

The competitive *Constitution* tried to beat the Journal to the airwaves by utilizing equipment of the Georgia Railway & Power Co. to broadcast news. *The Journal* won the race by one day.

The entire Twenties decade was a boom time for construction, both commercial and residential. One measure of real estate values was the 1927 sale of property at Peachtree Street and Edgewood Avenue downtown for $13,000 per front foot.

It is a commentary on Atlanta development patterns that many of the Twenties' fine buildings have yielded to wreckers' balls and dynamite to provide room for higher-density construction. The Twenties landmarks included:

• The Palmer Building at Forsyth and Marietta, built on the site of the original DeGive Opera House, later known as the Columbia Theatre and then the Bijou. The Palmer's clean lines qualify it as an early example of architecture now called "Deco." It in turn was wrecked for today's Standard Federal Savings & Loan.

• The Glenn Building at Marietta and Spring, and Rich's main downtown store, both survivors, and the 101 Marietta Building, now replaced by a structure with the same name.

• The elegant $6 million Biltmore Hotel,

The legendary matinee idol Rudolph Valentino was among the visitors at radio station WSB in 1922, the year it was launched by The Atlanta Journal.

Henry Ford (seated, wearing earphones) was one of the early visitors at the WSB "studios," which started in a section of The Atlanta Journal building's fifth floor in 1922. WSB was the state's first radio station.

Opening of the Spring Street viaduct in 1921 gave Atlantans an important new route from Brookwood to the industrial area south of Five Points. Here is part of the parade that followed the ribbon-cutting.

site of many top Atlanta social events, closed but standing at this writing. The Robert Fulton Hotel, later Georgian, now the planned site of a new downtown YMCA. The Cox-Carlton bachelor's residence, now operating as the York Hotel.

• **The Henry Grady** Hotel, built on the site of the old Governor's Mansion and itself long since dynamited to make way for the 70-story Peachtree Plaza. After lodging governors for a time in private residences, the State leased and later purchased the Edwin P. Ansley home on The Prado in Ansley Park. It served as the Governor's Mansion until the late Sixties.

• Several mid-rise apartment buildings on Peachtree and West Peachtree south of Pershing Point. Some survive; the Bell System Long Lines Building occupies the site of one.

• Southern Bell's Ivy Street building, started in 1929.

• The Rhodes-Haverty Building, at 21 stories, Atlanta's tallest when it opened in 1929.

• **The opulent Fox** Theatre, which opened shortly after the stock market crash and nearly was razed in the Seventies until saved by a public subscription campaign.

Viaduct construction in the late

Twenties removed some serious bottle-necks and raised street levels and "ground floor" throughout the railroad gulch area. Ever since Atlanta was born around the rail lines, train traffic had been a menace to man and beast. Gradually, streets were elevated to bridge the tracks. (The first, today's Broad Street, earlier was called Bridge Street.)

The Spring Street viaduct was completed in 1923, and dedicated amidst speeches, band music and parades. The total project transformed rambling up-and-down Spring Street and another minor road into a major traffic artery from Brookwood to the industrial area south of Five Points.

An even more ambitious project was completed in 1929: viaducts for Pryor Street and Central Avenue, with laterals connecting Hunter (M. L. King Dr.), Alabama and Wall Streets. The work was done with $1 million in municipal bond money and $1.25 million more supplied by Georgia Power Co. and the railroads. Although the job included some lowering of tracks, owners of property along the raised streets had to elevate their entrances or tear the buildings down. In the late Sixties, the old area hidden by the viaducts became the now defunct Underground Atlanta entertainment and boutique development.

Residential neighborhoods launched in the Twenties included Brookwood Hills, Ansley Park Annex and Cascade Heights. In 1924 George Francis Willis, who had made a fortune in proprietary medicines, acquired the little DeKalb County town of Ingleside and an adjoining 950 acres, and developed the heart of today's Avondale Estates.

Throughout the Twenties, Atlanta was annexing areas all around its periphery, including the town of Kirkwood (incorporated in 1899), Virginia-Highlands, Ormewood Park, a section of Cascade, Morningside Park, the town of East Lake (incorporated in 1910), a sizable nearby section of unincorporated DeKalb County and an undeveloped section now known as Johnson Estates.

Atlanta had three mayors during the decade. Lawyer James L. Key, the incumbent, was re-elected in 1920. He did not seek another term in 1922, and was succeeded by Walter Sims, another lawyer, who ran on a police-reform platform. In 1924 Sims won a second term against Key's challenge.

Isaac N. Ragsdale, who had prospered in the grocery and livestock businesses, was elected in 1926. In an unusual tribute to his popularity, he had no opposition in 1928.

In retrospect, however, the most sig-nificant election of the period may well have been that of a young lawyer who won the Third Ward alderman's post in 1922: William B. Hartsfield.

Later, he was to serve longer than any other person—nearly 24 years—as Atlanta's mayor. As soon as he was seated in 1923, however, he was named chairman of the new Council Aviation Committee. It was no happenstance. Hartsfield had fallen in love with airplanes when he saw his first at the old Candler racetrack in 1909.

By 1923 the auto racetrack had become an informal aviation center. During World War I, aviators had appeared there to promote war bond sales. An aviator taking off from Candler scattered political leaflets east of the city in 1920. He crashed when he ran out of gas, and so did the campaigns of the three candidates he was promoting. Barnstormers and wing-walkers performed at Candler in the early Twenties. Atlanta air pioneers Doug Davis and Beeler Blevins used the field as their base to take daring Atlantans for flights over the city on Saturdays at $5 per passenger.

In 1925 Asa Candler offered the City a five-year lease on the 297-acre property, with an implied purchase option, provided he was excused from any taxes on it while it was under City control. Mayor Sims asked Hartsfileld to evaluate the site, as

The old railroad gulch area rose from the ground in 1928-29 with construction of a network of new viaducts. Buildings had to construct new entrances for the new "street" level. Here is Alabama Street, looking east.

Doug Davis was an Atlanta aviation pioneer. He operated his own flying service in the Twenties. In 1930 he piloted one of the inaugural passenger flights out of Atlanta for Eastern Air Transport, later Eastern Airlines.

Fulton's Last Hanging Executed in Style

Georgia executions used to be carried out in the county where a felon was convicted, rather than at the State Penitentiary in Reidsville.

The last hanging in Atlanta was performed Sept. 1, 1922, at the Fulton County jail. The convict was Frank DuPre, a 19-year-old who had killed a detective during a jewelry store robbery.

With some 5,000 spectators in the streets below, DuPre put on a show of bravado to the end, demanding that his hair be brushed back before the deputy sheriff slipped the death cap over his head.

The Name Is Columbia; The Site Is Decatur

Columbia Theological Seminary was nearing the century mark when it moved to its present campus in Decatur in 1927. It had begun in Lexington, Ga., as the Theological Seminary of the (Presbyterian) Synod of South Carolina and Georgia, but moved to Columbia, S. C., two years later. Young Woodrow Wilson first professed his faith in a service there.

In time the synods of Florida, Alabama, and Mississippi joined in its support, and a campaign was begun to move it to a more central location. A $500,000 endowment and equipment fund raised in the Atlanta area helped make the move possible.

well as others proposed for a municipal airfield.

In the ensuing weeks, with Blevins or Davis or pilot George Shealy at the controls, Hartsfield surveyed sites all over the Atlanta area from the air. He drove to them by auto, too. He concluded that Candler was best—close to the city, fairly flat, and free of swampy areas. Fulton County agreed to forego tax collection, and the deal was on.

Many Atlantans were dubious about spending tax money on something they considered a dangerous sport. Charles Lindbergh helped change a lot of minds when he visited in 1927 not long after his historic nonstop solo flight across the Atlantic. "Lindbergh Day" was marked with a motorcade, VIP visits, a banquet and a speech by "Lucky Lindy" to 20,000 at Grant Field. Soon afterward, Mayson Avenue, running from Peachtree to Piedmont, was renamed Lindberg Drive.

The Air Commerce Act of 1926 provided for establishing air mail routes from New York to Miami and New York to San Francisco. Since air navigation instruments in those days were unsophisticated and unreliable, the routes were to include beacon lights every 10 miles to guide night flights.

Hartsfield and other Atlantans recognized the importance of this first official routing web, and were alarmed at reports that Birmingham rather than Atlanta might be on the north-south line. Hartsfield arranged for an invitation to the U.S. Assistant Secretary of Commerce for Aeronautics from the governor, mayor and leading Atlanta businessmen. That Federal official received the full VIP treatment, including a motorcycle escort, banquet and top-level meetings. A week later Atlanta was designated for the route.

In 1929, Atlanta purchased Candler Field for $94,500. Pitcairn Aviation (predecessor of Eastern Airlines) announced that it would build a new hangar and shops there, and the City began improving the runways. Within a year, Atlanta Municipal Airport was handling 16 passenger and air mail flights a day.

Today the original 297 acres are part of the vast air complex named for Atlanta's most enthusiastic supporter of aviation: Hartsfield International Airport.

Charles Lindbergh gave aviation a big boost in 1927 when he visited Atlanta not long after his solo trans-Atlantic flight. In this 1934 shot, he is with Constitution Publisher Clark Howell Sr.

Hundreds of Atlantans came to Candler Field on May 1, 1928, for ceremonies inaugurating the first airmail service to New York. The hero of the day was pilot Gene Brown, an Atlanta native who made

the daring flight. Pictured are (from left) postmaster E. K. Large, Brown, Harold Pitcairn (owner of Pitcairn Aviation, later named Eastern Airlines), and Mayor I. N. Ragsdale (standing, right).

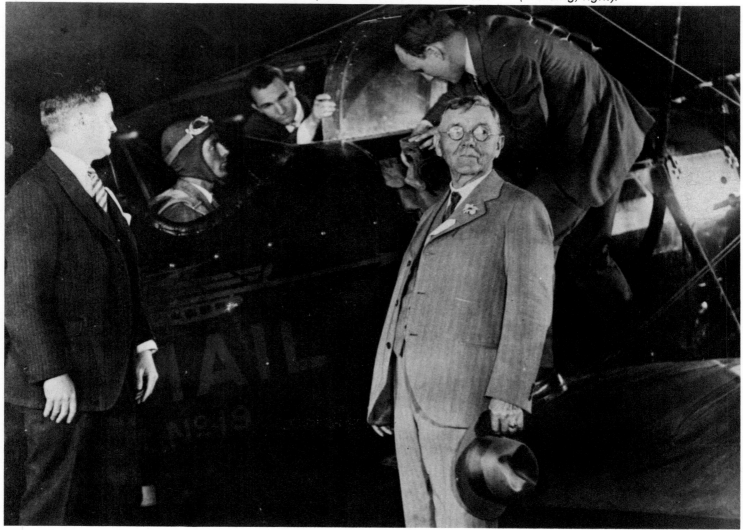

When the Fox Theatre opened, the stock market had just crashed, talking movies were the rage, and the neighborhood still was residential.

Fabulous Fox Has Survived Depression, Wrecker's Ball

The Moorish courtyard feeling of the Fox's main auditorium is repeated in the mezzanine lobby (upper photo). Many details or original decor, such as "F" design with stars in crescent in stairwell carpeting, are being restored.

When it was completed in 1929, the Fox Theatre was the ultimate expression of Silver Screen fantasy, with its Moorish lines, set director's amalgam of Egyptian and Middle Eastern decorative motifs, "tented" balconies and a ceiling that twinkled with simulated stars. However, the Fox's biography reads less like *The Sheik* than *The Perils of Pauline*.

The Theatre was an afterthought—or rather a last-minute economic necessity —in ambitious plans Yaarab Temple Shriners had been laying since 1915.

As their dreams grew more elaborate and expensive, they struck an income-generating deal with movie magnate William Fox to incorporate retail space and a 5,000-seat theatre. (They already were planning a huge auditorium.)

Records have been lost, but the Fox cost about $3 million, or three times its contemporary, Atlanta City Hall. Today's replacement cost would be at least 10 times that figure.

The Fox opened Christmas Day, 1929, less than two months after the stock market crash, with a program including dancing girls, a community sing, music on the 3,610-pipe Moller organ, an orchestral interlude conducted by Enrico Leide, the first Mickey Mouse cartoon and a forgettable feature film entitled *Salute*. Ticket prices ranged from 15 to 75 cents.

Neither Fox nor the Shriners could survive the Depression economics. Both declared bankruptcy in 1932, and the Theatre was closed for two years. The City of Atlanta took possession for nonpayment of taxes. The Theatre reopened with movies and occasional orchestral and Atlanta Music Club concerts.

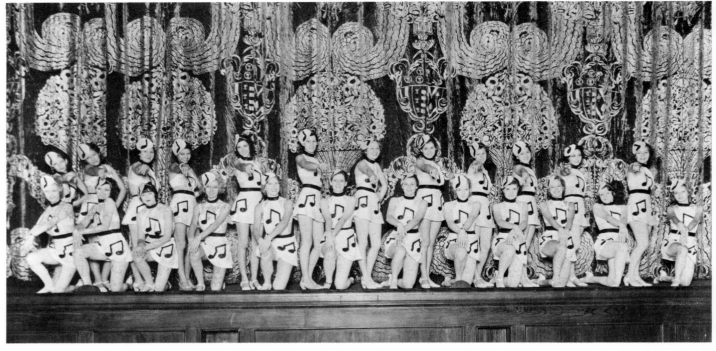

The ladies in noted costumes were the Fanchon & Marco troupe, who were regulars in the early days of the Fox.

Management was assumed in 1935 by Mosque Inc. (Paramount Pictures and Atlantans Arthur Lucas and William Jenkins). The Fox became profitable with movies, concerts by notables and dancing in the Egyptian Ballroom. The Metropolitan Opera appeared annually from 1947 to 1966.

Wilby-Kincey (Robert B. Wilby and Herbert F. Kincey) took over the Fox in 1951 and hired Noble K. Arnold, a spit-and-polish manger who restored much of the Theater's original reputation. The Fox was unsurpassed as a place to see wide-screen, stereophonic-sound films.

But shifting residential patterns and changing film distribution contracts that required long-run guarantees spelled doom for the Fox as a movie house. It almost was sold and wrecked to make may for Southern Bell's new headquarters.

Fox-lovers banded together as Landmarks, Inc., to save the structure. Southern Bell cooperated fully in their efforts. At first Landmarks consisted almost solely of grass-roots volunteers like Joe Patten, who spent 10 full months restoring the Moller organ. Later an expanded board of directors was able to attract large-scale donations.

A combination of big and small contributions saved Pauline from the tracks. The Fox today is making its way as a concert hall. Occasionally it offers Atlantans a reminder of what movies were like before screens were reduced to postcard dimensions.

The lounge in the upper photo was for the Shriners, who built the Fox but lost it in the Depression. Main men's lounge (lower photo) has strong Egyptian accents.

The horizontal bands of cream and buff brick, the arches and the onion dome of the Fox have become Atlanta landmarks.

The Fox's orchestra pit rises and lowers on elevators. It can accommodate a small symphony orchestra. Famous Moller organ is at left.

Hard Times And World War

1930-1945

America's economy crashed along with the stock market in October, 1929, but the impact of such a fall is not felt overnight. In the new year 1930, many Atlantans remained skeptical about talk of a depression. Signs of the Twenties' boom remained vigorously visible.

The opulent new Fox Theatre was drawing big crowds. The William-Oliver skyscraper and the million-dollar neo-Gothic City Hall were under construction. A new central Post Office had been authorized. Natural gas lines reached Atlanta in 1930, and dial telephones were due the next year. Union (railway) Station was about to open on Forsyth Street.

Out at recently purchased Candler Field, plans were underway for the nation's first air passenger terminal. Financiers may have been alarmed, but nobody was leaping from high-rise windows into Peachtree Street.

Like an unwound clock, though, Atlanta's pace slowed and for a while seemed to grind to a standstill. By the time Franklin Roosevelt was inaugurated in March, 1933, there had been a hunger march on the Fulton Courthouse; salaries of City and County employees had been slashed; and local officials were improvising relief programs with almost no funds.

Until Roosevelt's New Deal pumped millions into public works programs, municipal and county governments

Continued on Page 237

Franklin Delano Roosevelt, who had recuperated from polio at Warm Springs, Ga., was a great favorite of Georgia voters. Here he campaigns in Atlanta in 1932, with daughter and wife Eleanor (right). Driver is Atlantan A. L. Belle Isle. Note lack of security.

234

When Prohibition finally was repealed in Georgia in 1938, state law required customers to sign a register when making purchases. The most frequently used names were those of the governor and the revenue commissioner.

'Tobacco Road' Shows, Booze Sells in Thirties

Bible Belt mores won some and lost some battles during the Thirties and Forties, but they were a force to be reckoned with in any confrontation.

Official censors previewed and sometimes banned movies and plays. It was 1933 before Atlanta voters approved commercial amusements on Sunday; at first, movie houses cautiously donated Sunday receipts to charity and Depression relief.

After Mayor James L. Key publicly advocated repeal of Prohibition, he was ousted as teacher of a Sunday school class at Grace Methodist Church. (The next month, Key started his own nondenominational Sunday school class in the Capitol Theatre; he drew some 1,000 to his first session.)

In May, 1933, after adoption of the national Repeal amendment, Atlanta authorized sale of 3.2 beer (for the first time since 1916). Forty-nine establishments wre licensed on the first day, and some had 3.2 signs in their windows while City Council was still debating. Beer sold so fast that one bartender complained: "We can't even get it cold."

Sale of anything stronger was forbidden by state law for several more years. Georgia voters in 1935 approved beer and wine sales, but narrowly defeated liquor. In 1938 the Georgia General Assembly passed a local option liquor law. Fulton County wasted no time in holding a referendum, and liquor sales were okayed by a lopsided 11,884-3,658 vote.

The most enduring anecdote of Atlanta's censorship era was censor Christine Smith's agonizing over Rhett Butler's climactic line in the movie version of *Gone With the Wind:* "Frankly, my dear Scarlett, I don't give a damn." Art triumphed, and she decided to let Clark Gable utter "damn" from the screen in Atlanta.

In its own day, however, the *Tobacco Road* issue received far more notoriety. A traveling stage production of Erskine Caldwell's classic was scheduled to open at the Erlanger Theatre on the night of Nov. 21, 1938. At their insistence, members of the library board's censors committee attended a private performance that afternoon.

They were so offended by the play's earthy escapades and language that they banned the whole play. ("I don't see how these people who don't have to are sitting through the performance," said one woman who turned out not to be an official board member.)

Attorneys for the show promptly obtained an injunction, though Judge E. D. Thomas did order a sign barring persons under 16. The curtain went up that night —and for another week—before capacity audiences.

Atlanta continued to have an official censor (Mrs. Christine Gilliam, *nee* Smith) until the mid-Fifties, when her authority was effectively removed in litigation over the movie *The Blackboard Jungle.*

'Margaret Puzzles Me'

Soon after *Gone With the Wind* was published, Margaret Mitchell had a letter from Mrs. Eva W. Paisley, one of her teachers at Washington Seminary in Atlanta.

Mrs. Paisley recalled a conversation she had with Margaret's mother: "Margaret puzzles me," the teacher quoted the mother. "I don't know whether she is headed for success or failure, but in any event she will be her own honest self."

EASTERN AIR TRANSPORT
ATLANTA-NEW YORK PASSENGER SERVICE
DECEMBER 10, 1930

NEW YORK
NEWARK
PHILADELPHIA
BALTIMORE
WASHINGTON

RICHMOND
GREENSBORO
CHARLOTTE
SPARTANBURG
GREENVILLE
ATLANTA

Atlanta's first air service to New York via Eastern Air Transport (now Eastern Airlines) in 1930 took eight and one half hours with nine intermediate touch-downs, including a lunch stop in Greensboro.

Atlanta Airport's first passenger terminal was opened by Eastern in 1930. The second floor was added in 1931.

The City of Atlanta built its first air terminal in 1932. The tower in this shot was added in 1938.

Continued from Page 234

patched together programs of light street work for heads of family, farming of government-owned land and very limited direct relief payments to families with no able head of household. The Chamber of Commerce sponsored a "back to the farm" movement for unemployed Atlantans.

It was the end of the decade before city and county tax digests returned to pre-Crash levels, and the early Forties before a war-stimulated economy absorbed the remaining job-seekers.

Yet if Atlanta was ailing in the Thirties, it did not suffer so much as some parts of the country—certainly not so much as rural Georgia, nor so much as cities of the East and Midwest whose economies depended more heavily on manufacturing.

Alone among America's larger cities, Atlanta suffered no Depression bank failures. Aviation continued to be a growth industry, and the Depression itself brought a new role for the city: Atlanta became a Federal subcapital.

Perhaps in part because FDR's home-away-from-home was nearby in Warm Springs, Ga., and in part because of close political ties with Atlantans like Treasury Undersecretary L. W. "Chip" Robert, Atlanta fared well in distribution of Federal work-relief funds. Techwood Homes became the pilot for Federally assisted public housing. Administration of these and other New Deal programs created even more jobs.

The Depression was no joke for those who lost homes, savings, businesses and health, but there's a kernel of truth in one wealthy Atlantan's jesting recollection: "We all suffered during the Depression. The maid suffered. The gardener suffered. The chauffeur suffered." Though things were scaled down, in short, life did go on.

In government and politics, the Thirties began with scandal in City Hall: graft involving municipal purchasing practices. *The Atlanta Constitution* won the 1931 Pulitzer Prize for its coverage. As the Associated Press recapitulated the story, "...not one pint of disinfectant, not one pound of lavatory supplies could be sold or bought by the City without the payment of graft." One grand jury estimated taxpayers were being bilked in excess of $1 million a year.

More than 50 City officials and businessmen were indicted, and a substantial number went to prison.

Lawyer James L. Key, a former City Councilman, won the mayor's race in 1930 on a clean-up platform. Key was reelected in 1934 but lost in 1936 to another lawyer, William Berry Hartsfield, who was to become Atlanta's most enduring mayor.

One of Hartsfield's earliest accomplishments was one of his most important: He secured the Legislature's adoption of a model budget law that forbids the City from appropriating more than 99 per cent of the previous year's receipts. The law ended the City's chronic deficits and earned it excellent bond ratings.

When Eastern inaugurated Atlanta passenger service, stewardesses were wearing these official uniforms.

237

The Terminal Hotel fire was Atlanta's worst up to that time (1938). Two minutes after the first alarm was turned in, most of the five-story structure was ablaze. Thirty-four died. Origins are believed accidental.

Hartsfield lost his first reelection bid in 1940 by 83 votes to insurance executive Roy LeCraw, but when a special election was called in May, 1942, after LeCraw answered a call to military service, Hartsfield won that and every subsequent contest until he retired in 1961.

In 1932 economic reality prevailed over political ambition when two bankrupt counties—Milton to the north and Campbell to the south—merged into Fulton County. It was the first and only reversal of Georgia's 19th- and early 20th-Century balkanization. To give Fulton better access to Campbell, a Cobb County grand jury transferred the largely rural Roswell district to Fulton as well.

In 1937 Fulton, Atlanta and the Chamber of Commerce hired Dr. Thomas Harrison Reed, a nationally recognized authority on government organization, to study relationships between the County and City. His wide-ranging report in 1938 recommended, among other things, consolidation of various City and County services.

Hartsfield already had begun proposing annexation of suburbs north of Peachtree (Brookwood) Station. It was more than a decade before either man's suggestions were adopted.

Depression or no, Atlanta continued to enhance its status as a transportation center—by air, rail and highway.

In 1935 a motorcade celebrated paving of the last link between Atlanta and Savannah. And in 1938, Georgia's first four-lane "superhighway" (U.S. 41) was opened between Atlanta and Marietta.

Atlanta's aviation growth was even more

impressive. In 1930 the city won a spot on the new east-west air mail route. The next year, it opened America's first air passenger terminal—after the fact of passenger service, for in December, 1930, Eastern Air Transport (later Eastern Airlines) had inaugurated Atlanta-New York service.

The trip in a twin-engine Curtiss Condor, with a crew of three and 18 VIP passengers, required eight touchdowns and eight hours' flying time. The next month service was extended to Miami, with stops in Macon, Jacksonville, Daytona Beach and Palm Beach.

Passenger service continued to expand throughout the Thirties. In 1938 Atlanta Municipal Airport inaugurated the nation's first air traffic control tower, and in 1942 the first instrument approach system.

After Southerners had complained, officially and otherwise, since Reconstruction days that rail freight rates were higher in the South than in the North, Georgia Gov. Ellis Arnall decided to take the matter directly to the U.S. Supreme Court. His victory there also was a victory for economic development throughout the South—notably in Atlanta, the rail hub.

Many trends were converging in the Thirties to rid Atlanta of its insularity: air and highway ties to the rest of the America, network radio, the proliferation of New Deal programs with their national standards and perspectives. But it was still very much a Southern city with strong if not dominant Bible Belt mores.

The races remained totally segregated by law. Relatively few blacks voted since they were barred from Democratic pri-

Continued on Page 246

Bobby Jones displays the swing that would make him famous; photographed in 1916.

Bobby Jones, Other Sports Idols Lifted Spirits in Depression-Plagued America

Atlantans seemed to appreciate—even savor—their celebrities all the more during the lean times of Depression. These notables' achievements in sports, literature, politics and other fields became vicariously shared triumphs over challenge and adversity.

Bobby Jones gave Atlanta plenty to cheer about in 1930. Robert Tyre Jones had won Atlanta's Junior Championship golf cup in 1911 at age nine, the U.S. Amateur in 1916 and 1919, and two or more major tournaments every year afterward. But in 1930 he scored an unprecedented "grand slam": victories in golfdom's four most prestigious competitions—the British Amateur, U.S. Open, British Open and U.S. Amateur.

Atlanta had to share Jones that year with New York, which gave him a ticker-tape parade and testimonial dinner after he had won the first three. Atlanta outdid that after the grand slam with an exultant Bobby Jones Day parade down Peachtree.

Jones was honored so many times that year that Will Rogers wrote in *The Journal* that, "Atlanta no more than gets cleaned up from one Bobby Jones celebration till another comes along. You can easily exist in Atlanta by eating only at Jones testimonial dinners."

Jones retired from tournament golf that year, but remained an influential figure in the sport. He was president of the Peachtree Golf Club and helped organize and design the Augusta National Golf Club, site of the annual Masters Tournament. A lawyer by profession, he later became an executive in various ventures including Scripto, Inc.

Another Atlantan, Charles R. Yates, won the British Amateur eight years later. His tournament career extended into the Fifties, and included honors in the National Intercollegiate, Western Amateur and Masters Tournaments, and as both playing member and captain of the U.S. Walker Cup Team.

After business careers in banking, textiles and railroads, he was chosen as president of the Atlanta Arts Alliance.

Yet another native son kept Atlanta in the minds of sports fans during the Thirties —and beyond. Bryan M. "Bitsy" Grant won the U.S. Clay Court tennis championship in 1930 and again in 1934 and 1935. He was a member of the 1937 Davis Cup Team.

Two sports stars who brought glory to Atlanta: golfer Bobby Jones (left), and baseball great Ty Cobb, photographed in 1925.

Margaret Mitchell's GWTW, Written As a Diversion, Won Pulitzer, Movie Honors, Lasting Place in Local Lore

The manuscript of the massive novel Gone With the Wind was typed by diminutive author Margaret Mitchell Marsh on the comparably small portable pictured here.

Margaret Munnerlyn Mitchell was born in 1900 to Eugene Mitchell, lawyer and amateur historian, and Maybelle Stephens Mitchell, who so loved literature that she paid her children to read books. "Peggy" Mitchell was enrolled at Smith College in a pre-med program when her mother died of influenza during the post-World War I epidemic. Peggy, whose soldier-fiance died during the war, returned to Atlanta to run the house and serve as hostess for her father.

She was married briefly and unhappily during a few months of 1922. Her husband vanished from Atlanta before year's end, and she won an uncontested divorce in 1924. In December, 1922, she joined the staff of *The Atlanta Journal Sunday Magazine,* forerunner of today's *Atlanta Weekly.* In the next four years she established herself as a witty and disciplined reporter, though she showed no ambition to try novels.

Her social life centered in a group of writers and artists whose views then would have been considered *avant-garde:* opposed to Prohibition, the Klan and Puritanism. In 1925 she married John Marsh—best man at her first wedding, former English teacher and newspaper-

Cat-lover Peggy in pensive pose at age 20

As Journal Magazine reporter, she often posed on assignment: here on cowcatcher...

Here with matinee idol Rudolph Valentino...

And here with elephant and trainer.

Seated in the Loew's Grand audience for the premiere of Gone With the Wind are (front, left to right) Herbert Bayard Swope, Claudette Colbert, Mrs. David Selznick, Georgia Gov. E. D. Rivers; (next row) John Hay Whitney, Margaret Mitchell, John Marsh, Clark Gable, Carole Lombard (Mrs. Gable) and Atlanta Mayor William B. Hartsfield.

man who by then was on the advertising and publicity staff of the Georgia Power Company.

She left the *Magazine* staff in 1926 but continued free-lance contributions. Later that year she sprained an ankle that had been injured twice before. Her recovery involved many weeks in a cast, in traction and on crutches.

Marsh encouraged her to relieve her heavy schedule of reading by trying to write a novel. Thus *Gone With the Wind* was launched.

Later, she insisted that none of the characters was biographical, but she obviously drew on lore of family, friends and people she had interviewed, as well as her reading. She stopped work on the manuscript in 1929. It was untitled but lacked only an opening chapter and some transitions.

Peggy stored it in a closet. There it remained until Macmillan editor Harold Latham took a manuscript-searching tour of the United States in 1935. A mutual friend urged him to look up Peggy Mitchell. He asked her about her novel, and she said it wasn't finished. Latham persisted.

She delivered her bulky manuscript, and he took the train for his next stop, New Orleans. She wired his hotel there: "Send the manuscript back. I've changed my mind." Latham ignored her request.

Among the changes between manuscript and publication: "Pansy" became "Scarlett" O'Hara; "Fontenoy Hall" became "Tara"; *Tomorrow Is Another Day* became *Gone With the Wind* (taken from a phrase in the 19th Century poet Ernest Dowson's *Cynara*).

The novel's success is one of the

legends of modern publishing. More than a million copies were printed in the first six months alone. The figure now is well beyond 20 million, including dozens of translations. David O. Selznick paid $50,000—then a record—for movie rights. In 1937 the book won a Pulitzer Prize.

Margaret Mitchell Marsh was ill-prepared for fame: for the phone calls, letters, speaking and social invitations, legal actions. She resented the intrusions into her privacy as much as she was pleased by the novel's success. The problem only grew worse amidst the hoopla over casting, filming and premiering the movie.

But for other Atlantans, every scrap of information about the impending movie was savored and shared with friends. Atlantans felt a proprietary interest in the film, and naturally assumed the premiere would be in Atlanta. Rumors that it might be New York instead could give cold chills and hot flashes to everyone from Mayor Hartsfield to the citizen on the street.

Atlanta *did* get the premiere: on Dec. 15, 1939, at Loew's Grand Theatre, the erstwhile deGive Opera House and now part of the Georgia-Pacific headquarters site. (The Theatre burned in 1978.)

Notables began arriving on the 13th. The next day there was a Peachtree Street parade in the late afternoon and a *GWTW* ball at Municipal Auditorium in the evening, part of which was broadcast on the NBC network.

The orchestras of Kay Kyser and of Enrico Leide played. The choir of Ebene-zer Baptist Church (later famous as the pulpit of Dr. Martin Luther King Jr.) sang spirituals. Sponsor of the ball was the Junior League, which had snubbed teen-aged Margaret Mitchell. For that or other reasons, she did not attend the ball.

The Loew's Grand facade was redecorated to suggest a Greek Revival plantation house, with a medallion of Rhett (Clark Gable) and Scarlett (Vivien Leigh) above the pediment. The 2,031 seats were filled with notables from Hollywood and Atlanta (as well as governors of five Southern states). The author did attend, and afterward praised the "absolutely perfect cast."

The triangle across from the premiere site today is known as Margaret Mitchell Square.

GWTW was as much a phenomenon in film history as it was in publishing. It won 10 Academy Awards, including best picture and acting Oscars for Leigh and for Hattie McDaniel, the first black so honored. It has been revived several times, and has shown on TV. It has grossed far in excess of $100 million.

Margaret Mitchell never wrote another novel. During World War II she did Red Cross and war bond work and christened the cruiser *Atlanta*. She took part in 1948 ceremonies marking Atlanta's centennial. But she stayed as much as possible out of the public eye.

On Aug. 11, 1949, while crossing Peachtree Street at 13th Street en route to a movie, she was struck and severely injured by a taxi. She died five days later and was buried in Oakland Cemetery. John Marsh died three years later.

"Rhett" and "Scarlett" with their creator: This photo of Clark Gable, Vivien Leigh and an orchid-bedecked Margaret Mitchell Marsh was taken during 1939 ceremonies attending the premiere of the movie Gone With the Wind.

In scene from movie, bored widow Scarlett
scandalizes Atlanta by dancing.

Leslie Howard played Ashley and Alicia Rhett his
sister India.

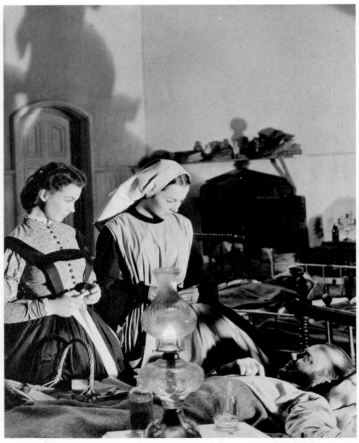

The realities of war come home as Scarlett, Melanie
tend wounded.

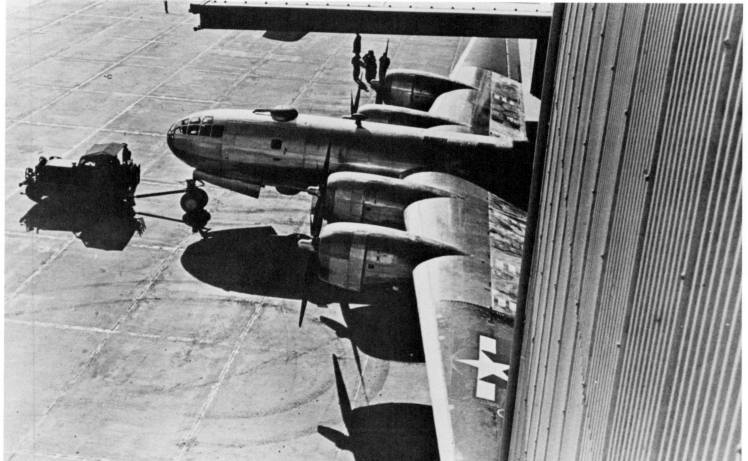

Bell Aircraft in Marietta not only provided jobs, but inspired postwar Atlanta to seek other sophisticated industry. Scenes show assembly line and roll-out of B-29. Facility now is operated by Lockheed-Georgia.

Atlanta Journal Editor Wright Bryan's coverage of the European Theater of Operations during World War II won him the Medal of Freedom, here being presented by General of the Army Dwight D. Eisenhower, in 1947.

Patriotic sentiment is reflected in this World War II scene in the entrance promenade of the Fox Theatre.

The City sponsored a "Buy Now" campaign, and streetcars ran free one day to encourage participation in downtown bargain sales.

Public housing became a dramatic and highly visible symbol of the New Deal. Like other Atlantans to follow, developer Charles F. Palmer was quick to take advantage of new Federal programs that could benefit the city. He put together plans that resulted in the nation's first public housing projects: Techwood Homes, which replaced white slums near Georgia Tech, and University Homes, which cleared slums in a black area near the Atlanta University complex.

The President came to dedicate Techwood in 1935 in nationally broadcast ceremonies. By 1941 Atlanta had eight Federally funded housing developments. They were all managed by the Atlanta Housing Authority, created in 1938 with Palmer as its first chairman.

Public housing was not universally admired in Atlanta. Rumors abounded about the projects. Herbert Porter, publisher of the *Georgian,* reported that a female phone caller insisted machine guns were being installed on the roofs of Techwood "to put down the impending revolution."

Despite the hard times, or perhaps because of them, organized labor in some industries grew more aggressive. In September, 1934, strikes closed all but one Atlanta textile mill. Martial law was declared to restore peace after some two weeks of sporadic violence connected with the strike. In 1936 there was a three-month strike at the McDonough Boulevard plant of Fisher Body.

Population growth had slowed in the Thirties, but the 1940 census showed an increase of nearly 12 per cent in the decade, to 302,288 in the city (about one third black). If Atlantans needed a symbol for improving times, it came in May with the return of the Metropolitan Opera's annual tour.

The guns of war were rumbling in Europe. Most Americans still expected the United States to stay out of this one, but the nation was taking some preparedness steps. Work began in October, 1940, on a Naval Air Station (today's DeKalb-Peachtree Airport) at the old Camp Gordon site.

Other military installations in Metro Atlanta during World War II included Fort McPherson, which became a major induction center; Atlanta General Depot at Conley and Lawson General Hospital in Chamblee.

The Bell Aircraft plant in Marietta served the war effort, too. It also had far-reaching impact on the future of Metro Atlanta and Georgia.

The plant was announced less than three months after Pearl Harbor, and began producing B-29s in September, 1943. At its peak, it employed 30,000— many of them women handling industrial

jobs for the first time. Some experts considered it a gamble to operate a high-skill industry in the South, which suffered a reputation of poor training and worker inefficiency. The Georgians proved to be quick learners and willing workers.

The bomber plant experience not only impressed investors in other parts of the country, but also inspired local economic development promoters to tackle more ambitious prospects.

Bell closed the plant at the end of the war, but it was reopened in 1951 during the Korean War as Lockheed-Georgia. It manufactures a variety of craft, primarily heavy-payload freight haulers.

The Chevrolet Lakewood plant was converted during the war to produce munitions.

Margaret Mitchell had christened the cruiser *Atlanta* in September, 1941. When it was sunk off Guadalcanal in 1942, Hartsfield led a war bond drive to raise $35 million for a new one. The campaign surprised everyone by raising $165 million. The new cruiser *Atlanta* was commissioned in December, 1944; Margaret Mitchell again swung the Champagne.

Many Atlantans had had to do without in the Thirties because of hard times. Most Atlantans had to do without a lot of things in 1942-45 because of wartime shortages. Gasoline was among the first rationed items, and a tire shortage led the City to cease collection of leaves, limbs and cuttings. Mayor LeCraw and Gov. Talmadge led a bike parade in Piedmont Park to promote independence from automobiles.

Georgia Power brought some old-style trolleys out of retirement, and it eliminated 560 bus and streetcar stops to improve efficiency (if not convenience).

Housing already was in short supply because of relatively little Depression-era construction. With a war-swollen population, the shortage grew worse. Many families took in boarders for the first time. Quarters near streetcar and bus lines were particularly in demand.

Scrap drives, rubber drives and blackout drills brought the war a little closer to home.

The Office of Price Administration froze rents and then many other prices, beginning in 1942.

Hartsfield instructed the police force to crack down on honky-tonks and individuals who might try to take advantage of servicemen. City Council adopted a midnight curfew for all houses of entertainment.

Traveler's Aid desks in rail, bus and air terminals listed Atlanta families who offered servicemen dinner and weekend accommodations invitations. Many who were so hosted moved to Atlanta after the war.

The scenario for Atlanta's impromptu celebration of Japan's surrender in 1945 was played out in cities across America that day: Joyous, raucous, unabashedly drunk servicemen and civilians flooded the streets and cheered far into the August night. But the setting was uniquely Atlanta's: Focus of the celebration was Peachtree Street, under the big red Coca-Cola sign and adjacent to the movie house where *Gone With the Wind* had premiered.

Over, over there—part II: Servicemen and civilians flooded Peachtree Street on Aug. 14, 1945, to celebrate Japan's surrender to the Allies. The setting is today's Margaret Mitchell Square.

Youth Orchestra Became An Adult Symphony

Although the name "Atlanta Symphony Orchestra" had been used before, today's ASO was seeded in a 1944 Atlanta public school program. Students enrolled in a new instrumental music program organized what was called the "In and About Atlanta High School Orchestra."

The next year, with a commission from the Atlanta Music Club, Henry Sopkin came from Chicago to found an Atlanta Youth Symphony Orchestra. In 1948 it was renamed Atlanta Symphony Orchestra, and two years later it was classified by the American Symphony Orchestra League as one of the major orchestras of the United States and Canada.

ASO has had only two full-time music directors/conductors: Sopkin and, since 1967, Robert Shaw, who gained fame earlier as a choral conductor. ASO's home is Symphony Hall in the Atlanta Memorial Arts Center. It tours both regionally and nationally, and has made a number of critically acclaimed recordings.

Concentrating On the Basics

1946-1959

Atlanta's streetcars were gradually replaced by trackless trolleys, which drew electricity from overhead but ran on tires. The last streetcar made its Chattahoochee River run in 1949.

World War II had brought the grief of death notices to Atlanta's service families. It had meant shortages, crowded housing and other inconveniences. But it also had been a boom time after the lean years of Depression.

In the national psyche, the humbling experience of Depression was recent enough to cloud the euphoria of military victory. Atlantans wondered whether business activity would falter with conversion to a peacetime economy.

Instead, Atlanta hummed with hundreds of new businesses and expansions in the late Forties. Among the encouraging economic signs were a new Ford assembly plant in Hapeville (1947) and General Motors in Doraville (1948). Rich's department store opened a $7 million store-for-homes addition in 1948. The Bell bomber plant in Marietta shut down in 1946 but reopened as Lockheed-Georgia in 1951 during the Korean conflict.

By 1954, 800 new industries and 1,200 offices of national corporations had been established in Metro Atlanta. The following year, annual retail sales hit $1 billion for the first time, and the first skyscraper started since the Depression was dedicated—the 22-story headquarters of the Fulton National Bank (now Bank of the South).

A housing shortage developed in the immediate postwar years after 15 years of Depression and wartime housing inactivity. Atlanta's population was growing, and with the return of prosperity more families could afford their own homes. In 1948 Hartsfield turned his attention to another neglected aspect of housing: The City hired 10 new inspectors to supervise upgrading or destruction of 34,000 units of substanddard housing.

Atlanta's leaders recognized that sustaining growth involved more than luck. From the time Atlanta was incorporated and city fathers petitioned for it to be Georgia's capital, Atlantans have been ambitious (or "pushy," in words from *Gone With the Wind*). But they also have had the sense to develop the resources to accomplish their goals: rail network, air service, highways, water, higher education, work force, cooperative governments.

So postwar Atlanta began building the infrastructure to transform a regional center—many lovingly referred to it as an "overgrown country town"—into a national city. Few in 1945 would have dreamed or divined how altered Atlanta would be a mere 15 years later, much less a quarter century. But they were determined Atlanta would keep ahead of its competitors.

They concentrated on basics: expressways, a bigger if unglamorous air terminal, a water supply adequate for the 21st Century, a great regional public hospital, and government reorganization to provide more efficient services.

At the same time Atlanta's black leadership, which heretofore had exerted itself

With Death Toll of 118, Winecoff fire in 1946 Was America's Worst

It was an ominous date: Dec. 7. But the year was 1946, and World War II had been over more than a year. The Christmas seasons was at hand. Atlantans were feeling good about the strength of the postwar economy. There was no way to anticipate the horrors to come that day.

In the early hours of the morning, fire broke out in the supposedly fireproof Winecoff Hotel at Peachtree and Ellis Streets. The cause never was officially fixed, and it is only an educated guess that it started on the third floor.

Despite its masonry construction, the Hotel had enough woodwork and furnishings to fuel the flames. Stairwells and elevator shafts became chimneys, creating powerful drafts. Near this tower of flame, enamel bathroom fixtures cracked and wood was reduced to charcoal.

Most of the 119 victims died of suffocation, however. The fire department had no ladders to reach the upper floors, and some leaped to their deaths.

When firemen finally were able to survey the building, they found tableaux ranging from the pitiful to the grotesque: a fully dressed, headless woman; a man seemingly in prayer by a window; a family of four clustered together in a bathroom with wet towels wedged futiley under the door. Ropes of blankets and sheets swung mournfully from several windows.

Among the victims were 32 high school children attending a conference.

The tragedy at the time was the nation's worst hotel fire disaster. It inspired stricter safety codes not only in Atlanta but throughout America. After refurbishing, the building operated for several years as the Peachtree on Peachtree Hotel, later as a retirees' home and then as an office building.

With the windows of neighboring Davison's department store decorated for Christmas, the Winecoff Hotel is seen ablaze on Dec. 7, 1946. One hundred nineteen died in the tragedy, at the time the nation's most devastating hotel fire. In lower photo, firemen aid one of the fortunate survivors.

Adding Buckhead and the Northside to Atlanta was voted down several times before it finally succeeded. Here, in a 1947 scene, Buckhead annexation opponents celebrate one defeat with a mock funeral for Atlanta Mayor William B. Hartsfield, The Atlanta Journal, The Atlanta Constitution (both annexation supporters) and "one government."

mainly within its strictly segregated milieu, began working on its own basic priorities: voting rights, access to public facilities, elective office. Though white Atlanta frequently regarded their efforts as rocking the boat, these goals also were vital to the national and international status Atlanta would achieve.

The era 1946-59 could well be called "the Hartsfield years." Bill Hartsfield's tenure as mayor began almost a decade earlier, and extended a year beyond. But during these 14 years in particular, Hartsfield's amalgam of civic goals, boosterism and flexibility on the race issue epitomized the evolution of Atlanta itself.

In 1944, when manpower shortages made their proposal no more than a wishbook, Atlanta and Fulton planners offered a scheme to handle anticipated postwar traffic: Build a parking plaza over the downtown railroad tracks and four-lane highways above the radiating rail lines. The next year national traffic consultant H. W. Lochner prepared a multifaceted traffic improvement plan for the region.

Its total price tag was beyond the City's means, but officials decided to concentrate on its major feature: a north-south limited access freeway.

In 1946, 10 years before the Federal interstate highway program was born, Atlanta voters approved $16 million in bonds to begin acquiring right-of-way. It was a piddling sum, measured by today's investment in a vastly expanded expressway system, but then it was a bold act of self-reliance.

With State and Federal funding assistance, construction began in 1949. By 1956, the year Congress approved 90 per cent Federal funding for an interstate highway system, Atlanta's freeway already was

handling levels of traffic that had been projected for 1970.

Atlanta began facing up to its surface street traffic as well. Since the early days of automobiles, Atlantans had been accustomed to parking on main downtown streets. They knew the auto population was increasing when they had to circle blocks to find a spot convenient for shopping or other business.

Parking bans were politically so unpopular that City Council had postponed or vetoed them for years. Finally, in 1948 Council administered the first big dose of needed medicine with a ban affecting 11 major thoroughfares.

Since horse-powered cars began operating on the West End Line in 1871, streetcars had been a familiar part of the Atlanta scene. But they passed into history on April 9, 1949, when the last one clattered down the River line. Streetcars gradually had been supplanted by gas buses and, since 1937, by trackless trolleys. The latter ran on balloon tires and were much quieter than their predecessors, but their power poles frequently jumped off the overhead electric lines.

Until they were phased out by the end of 1963, it was a familiar sight to see a harried driver leap out of his trolley and yank on cables at the rear to guide the two power poles back into place.

Georgia Power Co. and its predecessor had operated the transit system since 1902, but after divestiture was ordered by the Securities and Exchange Commission, a group of local businessmen headed by attorney Granger Hansell and bankers James D. Robinson Jr. and James M. Shepherd purchased the operation in 1950 and incorporated it as Atlanta Transit Co.

Its chief operating official for many years

was a jovial and popular native Scotsman, Robert Sommerville. Atlanta Transit in turn was purchased in 1972 by the Metropolitan Atlanta Rapid Transit Authority (MARTA).

To accommodate real and anticipated air passenger traffic, the City erected a new terminal in 1948. "Now Atlanta can treat a passenger like a king on the ground," Mayor Hartsfield boasted. In truth, even a deposed king might have complained: The building was an ugly corrugated metal Quonset-style structure.

Its beauty lay in its price: an incredibly cheap $180,000. Since his days of promoting old Candler Field, Hartsfield always had placed his priorities on land, runways, lights and controls rather than buildings. The low-budget terminal served Atlanta for a dozen years.

No area can grow without a reliable water supply, so the Corps of Engineers' completion of Buford Dam in 1956 is an especially important milestone. Besides impounding enough Chattahoochee River water to supply 2 million residents, the dam also created a lake with 540 miles of shoreline. Lake Lanier has become a favorite of Atlantans for water recreation and second homes. It is the most-used Corps of Engineers lake in America.

Hartsfield lobbied untiringly for Buford Dam, but much credit also belongs to Georgia Sens. Walter George and Richard Russell, as well as area congressmen, who guided the necessary legislation through Congress.

On a far smaller scale, Hartsfield achieved another long-held dream when Plaza Park was dedicated in 1949. The pocket-sized park was built above the railroad tracks between Peachtree Street and Central Avenue just south of Five Points. Detractors predicted it would become a haven for derelicts; unfortunately, they were right.

The "Plan of Improvement" was an unequivocal victory, however, and Hartsfield unquestionably was its father. Almost as soon as he was elected in 1936, he proposed annexing of the Northside. City boundaries then ended on the north a couple of blocks beyond Peachtree (Brookwood) Station. In 1947 he campaigned to add Buckhead on the north and Cascade Heights on the south, but voters rejected the referendum.

The Plan of Improvement was proposed by a citizens' study commission and closely tracked recommendations made in a professional study (the Reed Report) completed in 1938. Backers of the plan assiduously avoided the buzz-word "annexation," though it did propose annexing densely populated areas north and south of the city.

Cake, Re-enactment Mark Atlanta's Centennial

As a chartered municipality, Atlanta was 100 years old in 1948. It was an opportunity not to be overlooked by that consummate showman, Mayor William B. Hartsfield. His principal consultant on history matters at the time was no less than Margaret Mitchell Marsh, author of *Gone With the Wind.*

Several historians used minutes of the first Atlanta Council meeting (Feb. 2, 1848) to write the script for a public re-enactment. When possible, descendants of the first councilmen took the parts of their ancestors.

John Ashley Jones summarized the 11 years of Terminus/Marthasville/Atlanta before incorporation. Franklin Garrett traced the family trees of the first municipal officials. And Hartsfield waxed eloquently on Atlanta's future.

Another day, Margaret Mitchell cut the city's birthday cake at City Hall for the mayor, councilmen and aldermen.

In 1948, Atlanta conducted various celebrations of its 100th birthday as a chartered city. Here, Gone With the Wind author Margaret Mitchell Marsh hands the first slice of birthday cake to Mayor Hartsfield in City Hall's Council chamber.

Mayor William B. Hartsfield, Atlanta's most notable aviation supporter, was more interested in runways and control equipment than fancy terminals. This one, erected in 1948 for a mere $180,000, served until 1961.

The program also proposed realignment of government duties between Atlanta and Fulton County, and eliminating duplicated services. The City was to take over parks and police and fire protection; the County would assume health, welfare and tax collections.

This time, voters approved, and the Legislature passed some 40 pieces of implementing legislation. On Jan. 1, 1952, Atlanta's land area trebled (from 37 to 118 square miles) and its population jumped about 100,000.

No attempt was made in discussions of the Plan of Improvement to annex densely populated contiguous areas of DeKalb County. Adding that controversy seemed to risk approval of the basic plan. Yet much of DeKalb even then was stitched to the city with an invisible seam. Actions in each jurisdiction affected the other intimately.

Therefore in 1947 the General Assembly approved a two-county Metropolitan Planning Commission with authority to recommend plans for orderly growth and development. MPC has evolved into today's Atlanta Regional Commission, with a much expanded planning role for seven counties: Fulton, DeKalb, Cobb, Clayton, Gwinnett, Rockdale and Douglas.

Another example of two-county cooperation during the period was construction of the present Grady Memorial Hospital under the aegis of the Fulton-DeKalb Hospital Authority. The gigantic facility was dedicated in 1958, and is operated by the Emory University Medical School. Primarily, it serves emergency and charity patients. In the segregated era, the associated Hughes Spalding Pavilion was the only adequate hospital in the area for black paying patients.

Anticipating Atlanta's expansion as well as reflecting changing mores, the School Board in 1947 ended the old system of sexually segregated white high schools. Gone were Boys High, Girls High and Tech High; in their place were coeducational neighborhood high schools.

Atlanta Journal-owned WSB had been the first of the city's commercial radio stations. In 1948, WSB went on the air with Atlanta's first TV channel. It was a novelty then; few Atlantans owned receivers. Few could anticipate the impact TV would have in the coming years—including an evening news audience that would chew into the circulation of the parent *Journal*.

The Journal made news again in 1950 when owner James M. Cox acquired the rival *Atlanta Constitution* in a stock trade. The papers' production, ad sales and Sunday editions were merged. At the time, *The Journal* was the larger paper. But a national trend to get evening news from TV ultimately weakened the *Journal;* newsgathering staffs were merged in 1982, though the newspapers retained their separate identities.

Improvement of services, facilities and legal rights for black citizens in the Forties and Fifties closely paralleled growth of black voting polls. Before 1946 blacks could and did vote in general elections, special elections and bond elections, but they were barred from the Democratic primary at a time when Georgia was a one-party state. Such limited franchise, compounded with long waiting periods, poll taxes and the weight of custom, severely

discouraged black registration.

In 1944, however, the U.S. Supreme Court outlawed Texas' white primary. Before that precedent could be applied to Georgia, Atlanta's black citizens had an unusual opportunity to make their influence felt: Fifth District Congressman Robert Ramspeck resigned to accept a Federal appointment, and a special nonpartisan election was held in early 1946 to fill the vacancy. Nineteen candidates filed for the post.

Because it was a special election and involved no party primary, it was conducted under unrestricted popular vote. Blacks were eligible. The County Unit System did not apply, so there was no threat that DeKalb and Rockdale Counties, with far less popular vote than Fulton, could reverse the total popular mandate for the three counties.

Black leaders invited all 19 candidates to meet with them and answer questions. Among the few who accepted was Mrs. Helen Douglas Mankin, a member of the Georgia House of Representatives. Other major contenders looked upon any contact with black voters as a political kiss of death.

At the time only about 7,000 black voters were registered. *The Atlanta Daily World* and black community leaders like attorney A. T. Walden and Atlanta University history profesor Clarence Bacote mounted an intensive and highly successful get-out-the-vote drive.

Turnout was so large at bellwether precinct 3-B (E. R. Carter School) that it was an hour after poll-closing time before the final ballot was cast. It was the last precinct to report. Mrs. Mankin was trailing in the count until she logged 963 of 3-B's 1,040 votes. She went to Congress.

It was 1962 before the County Unit System was ruled unconstitutional, but Georgia's white primary was invalidated shortly after that special 1946 election. In a remarkable 51-day campaign sponsored by the Atlanta NAACP, 18,000 new black voters were registered.

Leaders included Bacote, Walden, Mrs. Grace Hamilton (then head of the local Urban League and later member of the state House of Representatives), union leader John Wesley Dobbs, C. L. Harper (head of hte local NAACP and principal of Washington High), businessman John Calhoun, Urban League executive Robert Thompson, Butler Street YMCA executive Warren Cochrane, the Rev. Martin Luther King Sr., the Rev. William Holmes Borders and *Atlanta World* publisher C. A. Scott.

Thereafter, black voters were an increasingly significant factor in all local elections. Few serious candidates ever again ignored invitations to their rallies.

Black citizens' treatment by Atlanta's all-white police force was a particularly raw grievance in the black community. As early as the Thirties, Walden and Cochrane had asked Mayor James Key to hire black policemen. Key was sympathetic, but told them political realities made that impossible. Later, he discussed the matter with his policeman/driver Herbert Jenkins—Atlanta's future, much respected police chief. I'm old enough that it won't happen in my lifetime, Key told Jenkins, but you will live to see the hiring of black policemen.

The growth of American aviation can be measured by this view of the main waiting room of Atlanta Municipal Airport's 1948-61 terminal. Even then, Atlanta was one of the busier airports in the country.

Small in-city parks were a pet project of Mayor William B. Hartsfield. He was especially fond of this one, Plaza Park, spanning the railroad gulch. It was dedicated in 1949. Critics predicted it would attract derelicts. They were right.

Key and Jenkins both lived to see it. The first eight were appointed in 1948.

In 1977 Bacote told *Atlanta Journal* interviewer Raleigh Bryans that in his early days as mayor, Hartsfield "was not what you call a racist, but he didn't pay any attention to blacks...there weren't enough of them voting." When black leaders made requests such as appointing black policemen, Hartsfield told them in effect: If you had 10,000 votes, we might be able to talk.

By 1948 they had more than 25,000 votes, and Hartsfield *did* talk. His private "kitchen cabinet" of black advisers included Walden, Cochrane, Mrs. Hamilton, Bacote and Dobbs.

At first, black policemen were assigned solely to black areas of the city, and were not authorized to arrest whites. In fact, they dressed and showered at the Butler Street Y rather than at police headquarters.

If there had to be a segregated "black precinct," the Y was its perfect headquarters. For one thing, seven of those first eight black officers had been recommended by the Y. More to the point, in addition to its traditional role of recreation and training for boys, the Butler Street YMCA had become the single most important "clubhouse" of the adult black community.

Since 1945 it has hosted the weekly luncheon meetings of the Hungry Club, whose motto is "food for taste and food for thought for those who hunger for knowledge and information." Each week, the speaker is some newsmaker in politics, government, business, education or some other field. In the Club's early days, white guests were rare; later, politicians of all hues eagerly sought invitations.

The Y also was headquarters of the Atlanta Negro Voters League, which was established after black Democrats and black Republicans supported different candidates in the 1948 race for solicitor general (district attorney). With Democratic (Walden) and Republican (Dobbs) cochairmen, the League for many years screened candidates for local office and published a "ticket" that generally won more than 90 per cent of the black vote. The League no longer exists.

Despite its bipartisan origins, the League was most influential in Democratic primaries, since the Republican party was too small to conduct primaries and only rarely fielded candidates in general elections.

The 1953 municipal election was the last conducted along party lines. Hartsfield foresaw growing Republican strength, especially in the newly annexed Northside. He had many friends among these Republicans and reasoned that he was more likely to win their votes in a nonpartisan election. The local delegation in the General Assembly approved his idea.

That 1953 election included a milestone in Atlanta race relations. Dr. Rufus Clement, black president of Atlanta University, was elected to the Atlanta Board of Education in a citywide vote. At the time, whites held a substantial majority in voter registration. Clement carried many predominantly white precincts as well as all the majority-black boxes.

If such gains in black rights seem modest today, they were viewed with alarm and no little demagoguery by some white state politicians. After Hartsfield addressed the national convention of the NAACP in Atlanta in 1951, for instance, a photograph of the mayor and a biracial group of NAACP leaders was widely distributed by segregationists around Georgia.

The County Unit System gave thinly populated counties as much as 99 times the voting power of the most populous, Fulton. But it applied only to primary elections. Mrs. Mankin's election and subsequent black voter-registration drive raised fears that black voters would influence future general elections, so Gov. Herman Talmadge urged that the Unit System rules be extended to general elections.

His proposal, in the form of a constitutional amendment, was soundly defeated in a statewide vote (conducted without Unit System weighting).

The U.S. Supreme Court's 1954 school desegregation decision stirred political rhetoric and racial tensions throughout the South. The Georgia Legislature enacted a set of "massive resistance" laws, and Georgia voters in 1954 narrowly approved a constitutional amendment that would allow the State to give a school child tuition grants in lieu of providing a public education.

But the first scene of court-ordered desegregation in Georgia was a golf course rather than a schoolhouse. A group of black citizens led by Dr. H. M. Holmes had filed suit two and one half years before against segregation of park facilities. At the time, "separate but equal" was the prevailing doctrine, and plaintiffs could argue correctly that there was no public golf course for blacks.

After the Supreme Court ruled in favor of Holmes' group, some Atlanta citizens heatedly urged closing the golf courses. Hartsfield, however, declared that the parks were for all Atlanta's citizens. He was worried, though, and quietly negotiated with black leaders to keep publicity about their first use of the golf courses at a minimum.

On Christmas Eve, 1955, a special force guarded the North Fulton course, and reinforcements trained for riot duty were on call. By prearrangement, a quintet of black players led by Holmes arrived two hours later than they had announced, after TV cameras and reporters had left. They played the course in two groups—without incident.

Desegregation of public transit four years later had far more impact on the daily lives of Atlantans. In the segregation era, transit passengers had to play a cumbersome game of musical seats. Blacks sat or stood in the back, whites in front. If a seat

emptied behind a black passenger while any white was standing, the black had to move back.

A few days after Dr. Martin Luther King Jr. and his nonviolent movement won their challenge of such rules in Montgomery, Ala., a group of ministers decided to force desegregation in Atlanta.

On Jan. 9, 1957, more than 30 black adults including the Revs. William Holmes Borders, M. L. King Sr., R. H. Williams and B. Joseph Johnson boarded a trolley at Peachtree and Mitchell, and took seats in the front. The driver pulled down the trolley wires and busied himself with the vehicle's machinery. A second trolley picked up most white passengers, and the first was relabeled "Special." When it ran again, the only whites aboard were the driver, some reporters and one elderly man who got off a few blocks away.

So the ministers had no arrest to appeal. They vowed to try again the next day on a larger scale. At Wheat Street Baptist Church that night, Borders vowed: "We're going to ride these buses desegregated in Atlanta, Georgia, or we're going to ride a chariot in heaven or push a wheelbarrow in hell."

At first Hartsfield was furious because he had not been forewarned. But he and Chief Jenkins negotiated with the protesters to make an appealable arrest the following day. It was two more years before the final appeal was decided and the transit system actually desegregated.

Horace Ward, a black Atlanta college graduate, sought to break the color barrier

Kimball House, seen from Plaza Park, was on its last footings in the this Fifities shot. The once elegant hotel yielded to wreckers' balls soon afterward.

Enrico Leide, shown with his cello in this 1955 portrait, conducted his own orchestra, which for decades entertained Atlantans at public concerts as well as private parties.

While many state politicians were proposing to close public schools rather than integrate them under court orders, HOPE (Help Our Public Education) was gathering 10,000 signatures on an open-school petition. In this January, 1960, photo, Mrs. Beverly Downing exhibits the petition at the State Capitol.

Martian Visitors Proved To Be Monkey Business

In July, 1953, at the height of American interest in unidentified flying objects, three Atlantans were driving home to their apartment after a night of "honky-tonking."

According to their account, their truck headlights suddenly revealed three small creatures and a saucer-shaped red vehicle in the middle of U.S. Hwy. 78 near Austell.

The driver braked too late to avoid striking and killing one of the creatures. The other two returned to the saucer, which turned blue and soared away.

Two Cobb County policemen drove by, heard the story and saw the creature, but took no action. The men took the 21-inch, four-pound creature home, stored it in their refrigerator and contacted news media.

The story went out on national news wires. Some 25 newsmen and photographers beseiged the trio's apartment. Two Air Force representatives interviewed them about the UFO, and one of the three sketched for them. Newspapers were flooded with calls about the incident.

An Emory University associate professor of anatomy, however, commented that, "If it's a creature from outer space, they haven't invented anything new." Except for its hairless condition and lack of tail, he opined, it resembled a rhesus monkey.

Later, experts detected traces of a dipilatory and signs the creature had been shaved. An injury on the lower spine suggested removal of a tail. Two of the tale-bearers were barbers and the third a butcher. Dr. Herman Jones of the State Crime Laboratory confiscated the beast.

After Cobb authorities charged the trio with cruelty to a domesticated animal, they confessed they had bought a monkey, killed it while it was under ether, and then shaved it. The ringleader was forced to pay a $40 fine for obstructing a highway. Other charges were dropped.

at the University of Georgia Law School, but after University officials swore they had no policy of segregation (despite an all-white student body), a U.S. District Court in 1957 ruled against Ward. Georgia's moment of truth on the school issue was nearly four years away. Ward subsequently became a Fulton County Superior Court judge.

Atlantans meanwhile kept a watchful eye on other Southern cities where "massive resistance" was challenged and desegregation sometimes erupted into violence. The 1957 Little Rock confrontation with its protracted damage to economic development was especially sobering.

With state government continuing to take a defiant stance, a growing number of Atlantans took the initiative to assure peaceful compliance when desegregation inevitably was ordered. In November, 1957, ministers representing 80 major Protestant churches signed a manifesto supporting obedience to law and preservation of public schools. It was widely circulated by the United Churchwomen of Georgia. (A far larger group of ministers signed a subsequent manifesto.)

Others reacted to the inexorable course of desegregation with frustrated violence. During the dark of night in October, 1958, The Temple of the Hebrew Benevolent Congregation on Peachtree Road was dynamited. No one was in the sanctuary, but part of it was severely damaged.

Arrests were made, but no one was convicted of the deed. Motives were understood, though. Rabbi Jacob Rothschild had been outspoken in his support of preserving public schools in the face of desegregation.

Leading Atlantans rallied to aid the congregation in word and contribution. *Constitution* editor Ralph McGill's eloquent column titled "A Church, A School" later was cited when he was awarded a Pulitzer Prize. "It is the harvest," McGill wrote, "of defiance of courts and the encouragement of citizens to defy law on the part of many Southern politicians...It is not possible to preach lawlessness and restrict it."

McGill, Hartsfield and other Atlantans were helping earn the city a national reputation as an island of moderation. The Mayor's famous remark that "Atlanta is a city too busy to hate" apparently was printed for the first time in a 1959 *Newsweek* article.

But the uncertainty surrounding school desegregation and possibility of violence were having their impact. In 1959, just as Metro Atlanta's population unofficially reached 1 million (a figure confirmed in the 1960 census), the number of jobs declined for the first time since the Depression.

Atlanta Constitution Publisher Ralph McGill ignites fuse of the "Henry Grady cannon" to celebrate John F. Kennedy's election as President in 1960. The cannon had not been fired since Grady saluted election of the first Democratic President after the Civil War (Grover Cleveland). Raising his fist is Constitution Editor Eugene Patterson. Both he and McGill won Pulitzer Prizes for their editorials.

Pulitzer-Winning Editor Ralph McGill Known as 'Conscience of the South'

In his later years, Ralph Emerson McGill was an Atlanta institution as well as editor of *The Constitution*.

An interview with McGill was *de rigeur* for fellow journalists from other parts of America and the world who were writing on the South. Diplomats and exchange students regularly sought his insights. Universities bestowed the laurels of honorary doctorates.

He came to be known as "the conscience of the South" largely because of his unending battle against bigotry. In awarding him a Pulitzer Prize in 1959, Columbia University trustees specifically cited his column blaming Southern officials' defiance of desegregation orders for a climate of violence that had inspired church and school bombings.

Yet the race issue was not McGill's one-note theme. His strength sprang from his love of what was good about the South as well as his fight against its wrongs. He traveled widely and read broadly. He knew the mighty and the humble, presidents and tenant farmers, and wrote with equal compassion about them all.

McGill was born in 1898 in a farming community north of Chattanooga. His family moved to that city when he was six. He graduated from the McCallie School there and enrolled at Vanderbilt Univer-sity. During World War I he interrupted his studies to join the Marines, but never was in combat.

Back at Vanderbilt and not far from graduation, he was dismissed for a pair of transgressions: In the student newspaper, he asked why University officials never had built the student center specified in a donor's will. Then he and a friend distributed bogus invitations to a rival fraternity's dinner dance to the campus at large, as well as to bootleggers and bawdy houses.

From 1922 to 1929, he wrote for the *Nashville Banner*. Though he was sports editor during his last five years there, he wrote on a broad variety of subjects throughout his stay. He moved to Atlanta in 1929 as assistant to *Constitution* sports editor Ed Danforth.

Again, McGill ventured beyond his sports assignment. Publisher Clark "Papa" Howell Sr. assigned him to some political coverage in 1936, and later he traveled throughout Georgia, studying and writing about its economy, agriculture, politics and people.

On the basis of this latter work he was awarded a Rosenwald Fellowship which allowed him to spend six months in Britain and on the continent as Hitler was moving toward war. Later, McGill counted this travel one of the most broadening experiences in his life. He was always a prodigious writer who could produce under pressure. During his six months abroad, he wrote more than 200 columns and articles for *The Constitution*.

After his return to Atlanta in 1938, publisher Clark "Major" Howell Jr. appointed him executive editor and editorial columnist. He became editor, with full-time editorial duties, in 1942.

McGill had married Mary Elizabeth Leonard in 1929. Death in infancy of their first two children brought lasting grief to both parents. Their third child, Ralph Jr., was born as McGill was rushing home from one of his several overseas tours as a war correspondent.

McGill continued his globe-trotting throughout the rest of his life. He covered political conventions and outfiled reporters half his age. His contacts in government, politics, academia and business gave him extraordinary access to ideas and information.

He was a man whose curiosity led him to study and write in many fields, but he is best known for his support of racial justice.

His ideas evolved gradually. At one time, for example, he could defend segregated education. But he always sought fairness and even-handed justice. He condemned lynching and race-baiting politics with the thunder of an Old Testament prophet.

He stood, in short, as far ahead of the times as a Southern editor could; ultimately, that meant total break with all forms of segregation. He was the devil incarnate to segregationists, but only death stilled his voice.

In 1960 his close friend Eugene Patterson became editor and McGill was given the title of publisher. It was largely honorary, but he continued his daily page-one column.

Mary Elizabeth died in 1962 after an extended illness, and McGill's loneliness showed in his face. His marriage to Dr. Mary Lynn Morgan in 1967 restored a springtime cheer.

McGill died of a heart attack early in 1969. He was at his typewriter until his last few hours. His enthusiasm for life lasted till the end.

The annual performance of the Metropolitan Opera of New York has been a major social event in Atlanta since 1911. Here, in 1960, Met diva Zinka Milanov is escorted by Mayor William B. Hartsfield and Alderman/businessman Jesse Draper.

King's treatment was far more sensational. A few months before in DeKalb County, he had received a probated sentence for driving without a valid Georgia driver's license. (He had an Alabama license.) Following King's sit-in arrest, the DeKalb judge revoked probation on the license conviction and ordered King to serve six months at the State Penitentiary in Reidsville.

King went to prison in the final days of the 1960 presidential campaign. He was released after nationally published news that candidate John F. Kennedy had telephoned on his behalf.

That concern is credited with winning enough black votes in critical states to cinch the closely contested election. Later, various persons claimed credit for masterminding the telephone idea. Atlanta's Mayor Hartsfield said he released word of Kennedy's concern on his own initiative, after failing to reach the campaigning candidate; Kennedy, he said, approved after the fact.

The student issue was settled in a manner typical of Atlanta in those days—in private negotiations among adults. Rich's executives were as stubborn as the students, and refused to deal directly with them. The settlement began with two venerable lawyers, one black and one white. A.T. Walden, son of slaves and one of the first black lawyers in Georgia, called on Robert B. Troutman, Rich's attorney and partner in an "established" law firm.

Their discussion led to a meeting of 25 leading store executives, who authorized negotiation of a settlement. The students

came out on bail, and there followed five weeks of secret sessions at the Commerce Club (theoretically segregated at the time). A key negotiator was Ivan Allen Jr., President of the Atlanta Chamber of Commerce and soon to be elected Mayor. This was their agreement:

The stores would desegregate all their facilities as the students requested. To lessen tensions surrounding the planned Aug. 30, 1961, desegregation of Atlanta schools, the agreement would not go into effect until the end of September.

The delay did not sit well with some students, especially since lunch counters in Savannah and several other cities already had been desegregated. At a mass meeting in Wheat Street Baptist Church, some threatened to take to the streets again. The group fell silent when King entered, however. This is how Allen recalls his words:

"I'm surprised at you. The most able leadership you could have to represent you has made a contract with the white man, the first written contract we've ever had with him. And now I find people here who are not willing to wait another four or five months, after waiting 100 years and having nothing to show until now..."

King saved the day, but it was the last time young militants deferred so unequivocally to the white and black "power structure." Two years later sit-ins were renewed with broader targets—restaurants, hotels, theaters.

Though many businessmen followed the lead of peers like Herren's restaurateur Ed Negri in voluntarily desegregating their

Continued on Page 270

Arts Center Honors 106 Crash Victims

The 106 Atlantans who boarded a charter flight at Paris' Orly airport on June 3, 1962, greeted one another like members of a big family. All were members of the Atlanta Art Association, or relatives. They had been touring Europe, concentrating on its art treasures. Most had known each other for years.

Their Air France 707 jet roared down the runway but could not reach takeoff power. The pilot tried to abort. With locked wheels and disintegrating tires, the jet skidded off the end of the runway across 1,200 feet of field, crashed into a small stone cottage an burst into flames. The only survivors were three stewardesses who were in the tail section when it broke off. The field was strewn with sorrowful souvenirs: small art works, bottles of Champagne, a roll of film, books, purses, clothing.

Mayor Ivan Allen later summarized the city's grief and shock: "These were my lifelong friends. This was my generation. This was also the backbone of Atlanta's cultural society, the city's leading patrons of the arts."

Allen took the first available flight to Paris to coordinate the necessary grim arrangements. The American embassy and the French government provided unstinting assistance.

Out of the tragedy came the triumph of a Memorial Arts Center. Atlanta voters earlier in 1962 had defeated a bond issue that included an arts center for Piedmont Park. Now through private donation, Atlantans raised $13 million for a center built around the High Museum. It became the home not only of the High, but also the Atlanta Symphony Orchestra, The Atlanta College of Art, Alliance Theatre and Atlanta Children's Theatre.

When the Center was dedicated in 1968, the French government donated a casting of Rodin's *"L'Ombre."* He stands on the north staircase, his head dipped in perpetual mourning.

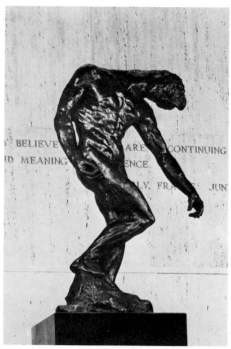

The French government donated this casting of Rodin's "L'Ombre" to the Memorial Arts Center in honor of the 106 Atlantans who died in a Paris air disaster in 1962.

The Atlanta Memorial Arts Center is home of the Atlanta Symphony Orchestra, High Museum, Atlanta College of Art and Alliance Theatre.

Wealth Robert W. Woodruff Earned As Head Of The Coca-Cola Company Has Enriched City's Medical, Cultural, Civic Facilities

Atlanta's most influential citizen for more than half a century has been one of its least public figures. His position, wealth and generosity could have earned him the celebrity of his company's leading product, Coca-Cola.

Robert Winship Woodruff instead has chosen to cloak his philanthropy in anonymity, to eschew most press interviews, and to exercise his influence through opinions quietly stated to the right leaders.

Woodruff's business acumen is well known, though his *modus operandi* is not.

When he became president of The Coca-Cola Company in 1923, the soft drink firm was deeply in debt and narrow in its marketing approach. Within four years it had paid off its notes, split its stock two-for-one, and established its national reputation.

In the ensuing years, the Company has become international and multifaceted. Whether president or "semi-retired" as the board's Finance Committee chairman, Robert Woodruff remained the dominant force in The Coca-Cola Company.

This business success alone has meant much to Atlanta. It has provided employment. It has made many of the Company's executives and investors rich, and that wealth has flowed back into the community.

But this success also provided Woodruff leverage to exercise profound and positive influence at two other levels, philanthropic and governmental—the latter even less publicized than the former.

Five foundations or funds controlled by Woodruff have given more than $400 million to educational, artistic, civic, medical and other projects—mostly in Metro Atlanta.

Woodruff's anonymity vanished in 1979 when he turned over all assets of the largest fund to Emory University's endowment program. They were worth about $100 million. But he already had given more than $110 million to Emory to develop one of the nation's finest medical centers.

Other Atlanta-area philanthropies include: $8 million for Atlanta Memorial Arts Center, a $10 million operating endowment for the Arts Alliance, $7.5 million for the High Museum, $9 million for Central City Park, $8 million for the Atlanta University Center's main library, $1 million for the Martin Luther King Jr. Center, $1 million for a park in Buckhead, and $2 million for a park between the Peachtrees downtown.

In the Depression year 1934, The Coca-Cola Company advanced the City of Atlanta $800,000 for its operating budget, but Woodruff became even more involved in city affairs after his boyhood friend William B. Hartsfield was elected mayor in 1936.

Just before Hartsfield was inaugurated, municipal employees were being paid in scrip. Woodruff announced that The Coca-Cola Company would stand behind the December payroll, so banks honored scrip at face value.

Woodruff strengthened Hartsfield's hand by passing the word to executives of financial institutions that he had confidence in the new mayor. With a new model budget law and improving times, Hartsfield had Atlanta out of debt by the end of 1939. Hartsfield drew on Woodruff's advice throughout his 23½ years in office.

So did Ivan Allen Jr. during his two terms. "During Hartsfield's and my terms ...we had three mayors—Hartsfield, Allen and Woodruff," Allen remarked later.

Woodruff was especially useful in providing entree to national business leaders when Allen and the Forward Atlanta campaign began a concerted effort to draw new and expanded corporate operations to the Metro area.

Woodruff also offered a steadying hand when the civil rights movement was shaking the South.

Allen recalled that when he proposed to 19 Commerce Club officials that the Club drop its racial barriers, he couldn't get a second for his motion until Woodruff approved. Then the vote was unanimous.

Later, many leading Atlanta businessmen balked at honoring Martin Luther King publicly for his Nobel Peace prize. Woodruff let it be known that he would support a testimonial dinner; Atlanta's business luminaries were well represented in the sold-out banquet hall.

Allen later wrote of the call he received from Woodruff the night King was assassinated in Memphis: "Ivan, the minute they bring King's body back

tomorrow—between then and the time of the funeral, Atlanta, Georgia is going to be the center of the universe. I want you to do whatever is right and necessary, and whatever the City can't pay for will be taken care of. Just do it right."

The man who wielded such quiet and powerful influence in Atlanta is no ideologue, no academic intellectual. He dropped out of Boys High School and earned his diploma at Georgia Military Academy. He went to college—Emory at Oxford—for only one year, then went to work as a 60-cent-a-day apprentice at General Pipe and Foundry.

Not that he had to: His father was president of the Trust Company of Georgia and later was head of the syndicate that bought The Coca-Cola Company from the Candler family.

Robert Woodruff was born in Columbus, Ga., in 1889 and has lived in Atlanta most of the years since 1893.

After various blue collar, clerical and sales jobs, he proved such a good salesman for White Motor Co. that he became Atlanta branch manager within one year. After motor corps service in World War I —he was a major at discharge—he

became White Motor's vice president for sales, with offices in Cleveland and New York.

He left that $85,000-a-year job to become The Coca-Cola Company's $35,000-a-year president. He loved Atlanta, but he has explained that he also was protecting his substantial investment in Coca-Cola stock.

In 1912 Woodruff married Nell Hodgson of Athens. They maintained homes in New York, Wyoming and in South Georgia (Woodruff's beloved Ichauway Plantation) as well as Atlanta. She was a trained nurse, and the nursing school at Emory is named in her honor. She died in 1968.

In business as well as behind the scenes in government, Woodruff deals with the big picture rather than detail. "He listens to people," observed his longtime friend, banker/lawyer John A. Sibley. He delegates corporate administration to executives he trusts.

In his office at The Coca-Cola Company is an engraved motto: "There is no limit to what a man can do or where he can go if he doesn't mind who gets the credit."

Despite their close association, these three men who profoundly influenced Atlanta rarely were photographed together. Left to right: Robert W. Woodruff, philanthropist and Coca-Cola Company executive; and former Mayors William B. Hartsfield and Ivan Allen Jr.

After years of Ugly Duckling status, Atlanta Municipal Airport got a modern terminal in 1961. It was almost immediately too small and was replaced 18 years later.

Continued from Page 266
facilities, others refused.

The agitation ended only after enactment of the 1964 public accommodations law.

In resolving the sit-ins, Atlanta had to overcome the internal restraints of tradition and public sensibilities. Public school desegregation presented formidable external restraints of state law.

Following the U.S. Supreme Court's *Brown* decision in 1954, Georgia's Gov. Herman Talmadge secured legislative and narrow voter approval of the so-called "private school amendment." It modified Georgia's Constitution to allow the State to provide students tuition for private schools.

It fell to Talmadge's successor, the late Marvin Griffin, to propose the legal framework for implementing the amendment. Griffin, a fire-breathing segregationist, won easy General Assembly approval of his "massive resistance" package.

Such laws were typical in Deep South states during the first years after the *Brown* decision. Among other things, Georgia's laws required closing all public schools in an integrated district and withdrawing all State funds from the district. Teaching an integrated class was made a felony.

To this day it is not clear whether Griffin believed massive resistance would survive court challenge or he merely was carrying out the extremist pledges he had made on the stump in his 1954 campaign. Low-profile moderates in his administration and the Georgia Attorney General's office defended the laws later as buying time for Georgians to observe the course of massive resistance in other states.

That course was inexorable. In Norfolk, Little Rock, New Orleans and elsewhere, Federal courts found such laws in conflict with the Constitution, and struck them down. Desegregation proceeded despite challenge, but state defiance frequently led to rioting which disrupted the education of children and severely damaged economic development.

The first organized opposition to Georgia's official position came from ministers and the grass roots. In the late Fifties more than 100 local clergymen signed two "ministers' manifestos" supporting preservation of public schools. An organization called HOPE (Help Our Public Education) waged a campaign of information and persuasion. Editor Ralph McGill and the editorial pages of *The Atlanta Constitution* and *The Journal* grew increasingly outspoken about the futility of massive resistance.

Ernest Vandiver was elected governor in 1958 on a platform of preserving segregated education. But before he took office the U.S. Supreme Court in the Little Rock case held that not even public disorder could excuse delaying desegregation orders. Thus was decommissioned the last remaining weapon in the arsenal of massive resistance.

Vandiver asked a panel of lawyers to study his legal dilemma. Its chairman was Griffin Bell, an Atlanta attorney who later

270

The last of Atlanta's unsightly overhead wires for trackless trolleys were removed in 1963. The Atlanta Transit System completed its conversion to diesel buses that year.

served as Judge on the U.S. Court of Appeals and Attorney General of the United States.

After consulting with governors and legal authorities throughout the South, Bell concluded Georgia's laws would be invalidated as soon as tested, and that the State would be in a more flexible position if it had no mandatory segregation statutes.

As a lawyer, Vandiver concurred. But he had campaigned on a promise that "no, not one" instance of integration would occur in his term. Furthermore, his inner circle of advisors was sharply divided on the question.

Bell suggested a commission to hold hearings throughout Georgia, inform Georgians of their choices in light of recent court decisions, and let them have their say. Vandiver liked the idea but warned it could get out of hand without a strong chairman.

He and Bell discussed a few names and concluded the ideal choice was Bell's senior partner, James Sibley. A bill to create the commission was approved, but not identified as an administration proposal.

The Sibley Commission, as it came to be known, held hearings in each of Georgia's 10 Congressional districts. It heard from hundreds of witnesses, ranging from individuals who merely identified themselves and said "I'm for segregation" or "I'm for open schools" to representatives reading carefully written statements on behalf of thousands.

As Bell observed many years later, letting people speak publicly relieved some emotional tensions in the situation. But more important than anything any witness said was the statement Sibley read at the start of each hearing. He outlined existing Georgia law and court rulings on similar laws in other states. The only alternatives before Georgians, he concluded, were accepting some degree of desegregation or abolishing public education outright.

Atlanta's newspapers and HOPE statements, among others, had been saying the same thing, but Sibley was more credible in Georgia's rural areas. Though he was a big-city lawyer (with King & Spalding) and banker (with Trust Company of Georgia), he came across as a cheerful country squire who could discuss crops with

Victim of progress: The glass-roofed Peachtree Arcade, which provided a covered passageway from Broad to Whitehall (now Peachtree) Street, was razed to make way for the First National Bank Tower, completed in 1966. This fish-eye lens view shows its three levels of shops—and dwindling patronage.

farmers, and grandchildren with housewives. He made it clear he was unhappy with the courts himself.

Besides Sibley's unambiguous statement of the alternatives, the hearings also surprised much of Georgia by the widespread open-school sentiment they uncovered. "It was a time when you could hear minds clicking all over Georgia," remarked *Gainesville Daily Times* editor Sylvan Meyer.

Most of the Sibley Commission proposed repeal of the school-closing laws, but neither the governor nor the legislature acted until faced with crisis in January, 1961, when U.S. District Court Judge W.A. Bootle ordered two black Atlantans, Charlayne Hunter and Hamilton Holmes, admitted to the University of Georgia.

Citing existing law, Vandiver ordered the University shut for a week to allow the General Assembly to consider new legislation. Even this degree of control was denied the State. While University officials stalled implementation of the closing, plaintiffs obtained an injunction and were promptly enrolled.

During Miss Hunter's first night on campus, some 2,000 students and outsiders rioted in front of her dorm, and Vandiver ordered the two blacks removed "for their own safety." The Federal court overruled this action, too, and massive resistance in Georgia was over.

The Atlanta school board thus was legally free to implement its ultra-cautious plan to desegregate one grade per year, starting with the senior class. More than 200 black juniors applied for transfer. Ten were chosen, and one of these accepted a college scholarship instead. So on Aug. 30, 1961, nine black children made history by enrolling in four formerly all-white high schools.

The event attracted some 300 reporters and cameramen from around the world. They found none of the yelling mobs nor armed resistance they had observed in other Southern cities.

Police efficiently but quietly barred outsiders from school campuses. Mayor Hartsfield established a huge, well equipped press room at City Hall. Desegregation went so smoothly that Hartsfield offered the visiting press bus tours of the city that afternoon and a cocktail party—integrated —at the Biltmore Hotel that evening.

At his afternoon news conference that day, President Kennedy congratulated Atlanta's officials and citizens, and urged other communities "to look closely at what Atlanta has done and to meet their responsibility, as the officials of Atlanta and Georgia have done, with courage, tolerance and, above all, respect for the law."

As the President observed, Atlanta's achievement resulted from months of

Pickrick restaurant owner Lester Maddox became a symbol of protest against racial change in the Sixties. He closed the Pickrick rather than comply with the 1964 Public Accommodations law and later won the Georgia governorship despite running second in popular vote. In this photo he leads a boycott group outside Journal-Constitution offices.

community preparation. HOPE expanded to become OASIS—Organizations Assisting Schools In September—and continued its public information campaign. Local newspapers reported unfolding preparations in great detail.

Elected officials, leading businessmen, Police Chief Herbert Jenkins and others recorded radio spot announcements promising that public order would be maintained. Press representatives who wanted to be present outside the integrated schools were issued special credentials, but they and all others with no school connections were barred from the grounds.

As school desegregation approached, Atlanta was in the midst of a heated campaign to succeed retiring Mayor Hartsfield. All the candidates—even outspoken segregationist restaurant owner Lester Maddox—urged citizens to be law-abiding.

Atlanta's self-control in facing that emotion-laden break with tradition was a vital part of the positive national reputation the city earned in the Sixties. In a subtler way, the mayor it elected in the momen-

tous year 1961 had equally long-ranging impact.

Ivan Allen Jr. was in one sense the last hurrah of the old political coalition of blacks and white-collar whites. He was the quintessential power structure insider who could settle major policy matters over lunch or over the telephone. At the same time, he was a harbinger of the future. Faced with the tough realities of changing times, this silver-haired patrician reexamined his own assumptions and became the advocate of the poor and the poorly represented.

Allen's father was drawn to Atlanta from Dalton, Georgia, by the glamor of the 1895 Cotton States Exposition. Starting as a typewriter salesman, he later built his own prospering office supply business. His public service included a term as state Senator and numerous civic and advisory positions. He promoted the Atlanta Chamber of Commerce's first highly successful "Forward Atlanta" industry-seeking campaign in the 1920s.

Young Ivan grew up in the comfort and

Continued on Page 278

Atlanta Stadium, built in less than
one year, is home of the Atlanta
Braves and the Atlanta Falcons.

Another achievement of the Allen
mayoral years was a new Civic
Center, with auditorium and
exhibition space on same grounds.

M. L. King Jr., America's Apostle Of Nonviolence, Was Native Son

The Rev. Dr. Martin Luther King Jr. returned to his native Atlanta in 1960, and eight years later returned permanently to its soil.

King was born on Auburn Avenue in 1928, and followed in his father's footsteps by studying for the ministry. He came to the world's attention as a leader of the successful boycott protesting segregation of buses in Montgomery, Alabama.

He moved to Atlanta in 1960 for several reasons. The bombing of his home underscored the danger not only to himself but to his family in Montgomery. Atlanta was a safer and more central headquarters for the Southern Christian Leadership Conference, through which he aided nonviolent protest movements throughout the region. And he had an invitation to share the pulpit of Ebenezer Baptist Church with his father.

King's brief jailing in the state penitentiary at Reidsville, Ga., on a driver's license charge led to an expression of concern by presidential candidate John F. Kennedy, and may have tipped the close election to Kennedy. Most of King's public activities were outside Atlanta, however, though the Rev. M.L. "Daddy" King Sr. was long active on the local scene.

In 1964 the powerful impact of King's philosophy of nonviolence won him the Nobel Peace Prize. That presented many of Atlanta's leading white citizens with a dilemma. Some resented his role in the sit-ins and other direct action campaigns. Yet to ignore the Nobel award would sully Atlanta's national image. In the end, some 1,500 blacks and whites—including most of Atlanta's business leadership—gathered for a dinner in King's honor.

When King was assassinated in Memphis in 1968, many of the nation's black ghettoes exploded in flaming riots.

When this residence at 501 Auburn Avenue was built in the 1890s, the neighborhood was not racially distinct. Later it became a black neighborhood, and the house the birthplace of civil rights leader Martin Luther King Jr.

The medal representing the award of the Nobel Peace Prize was shown proudly in a photograph by recipient Dr. Martin Luther King Jr. (seated, left), with his wife Coretta. Standing (from left) are his mother, father (Rev. Martin Luther King Sr.), sister Christine King Farris and brother Rev. A. D. King.

During the "long hot summers" of the mid-Sixties, Atlanta had suffered no serious or sustained disturbances, but now the city held its breath as preparations were made for his funeral.

Mayor Ivan Allen got a phone call from The Coca-Cola Company's Robert Woodruff, who counseled: "...the minute they bring King's body back tomorrow—between then and the time of the funeral—Atlanta, Georgia, is going to be the center of the universe. I want you to do whatever is right and necessary, and whatever the city can't pay for will be taken care of. Just do it right."

Some 200,000 persons marched in King's funeral procession—the poor and unheralded along with all major presidential candidates and a galaxy of other celebrities. The peacefulness of the day was a fitting tribute to the apostle of nonviolence.

King's simple marble tomb is a focal point of today's King Center, an institution of education and research headed by his widow, Coretta Scott King.

Beautiful Swan House, a private residence when completed in 1928, now is showpiece of the Atlanta Historical Society.

Tullie Smith House, in the 1840s "plantation plain" style, originally was in DeKalb County but was moved to the Historical Society grounds.

Architect Philip Shutze's loving attention to detail is apparent in this stairway at Swan House.

Though Atlanta had been capital of Georgia since 1868, it was a century before the State built a mansion specifically for its governors. This Greek Revival-style mansion on West Paces Ferry Road was dedicated in 1968.

The simple tomb of Dr. Martin Luther King Jr. is inscribed with a phrase he quoted just before his assassination: "Free at last. Free at last. Thank God Almighty I'm free at last."

Atlanta has been the site of the Sixth District bank headquarters ever since creation of the Federal Reserve system. The present Marietta Street building has preserved columns from an earlier Federal Reserve Bank at the same address. The bronze eagle is by Elbert Weinberg.

Continued from Page 273
comfortable assumptions of Atlanta's Northside. This is how he summarized it in *Mayor: Notes on the Sixties* (written with Paul Hemphill; Simon & Shuster, 1971):

"When I looked around (in the late Fifties) to see who was with me in this new group of leaders, I found my lifelong friends. Almost all of us had been born and raised within a mile or two of each other in Atlanta. We had gone to the same schools, to the same churches, to the same golf courses, to the same summer camps. We had dated the same girls...We were white, Anglo-Saxon, Protestant, Atlantan, business-oriented, nonpolitical, moderate, well-bred, well-educated, pragmatic, and dedicated to the betterment of Atlanta."

Ivan Jr. not only entered the family business but also accepted his father's *noblesse oblige* attitude toward civic service. A brief term as excutive secretary to Georgia Gov. Ellis Arnall just after World War II whetted the younger Allen's political appetite.

As head of the Community Chest drive in 1947, Allen for the first time seriously confronted the problem of racial segregation. Black banker L.D. Milton invited him to attend a dinner launching the black community's fund drive. Such an unprecedented invitation created a crisis for the 36-year-old civic leader. He consulted various friends but received no satisfactory advice.

Finally he went to his father. The elder Allen replied: "My generation has com-pletely failed in every way to enlighten or solve the major issue which our section of the country has: the racial issue...the Southeast will never amount to anything until it brings its level of citizenship up...It's time for some major changes. Your genera-tion is going to be confronted with it, and it will be the greatest agony that any generation ever went through."

Ivan Allen Jr. attended the dinner.

In the late Fifties he made speeches around Georgia to test the waters for a gubernatorial campaign. He withdrew before he formally entered, candidly asses-sing himself as unmarketable in Georgia's political climate at that time.

He focused his extra-business energies instead on Atlanta civic endeavor. After serving in lesser positions, in 1960 he was about to succeed to the presidency of the Chamber of Commerce. He did not accept the role routinely; he drafted a white paper addressing the serious problems Atlanta was facing: school desegregation, a net loss of jobs as the postwar boom sputtered, traffic congestion, slum housing, and a negative national image of Atlanta as revealed in private poll data.

Allen's position paper became the basis not only for the Chamber's enor-mously successful "Forward Atlanta" in-dustrial development campaign of the Sixties, but Allen's winning 1961 campaign for mayor.

It included keeping public schools open; speeding construction of freeways; press-ing for a large-scale rapid transit system;

expanding and accelerating urban renewal and construction of low-income housing; building an auditorium/coliseum and a stadium; and mounting a well-financed advertising, educational and research program to promote Atlanta nationally.

The coliseum and financing of rapid transit had to wait till the term of his successor, Sam Massell, but all the other goals were achieved before Allen retired after two four-year terms as mayor.

Old warrior Hartsfield had a hard time retiring from battle. He was 72 and slowing down, though he had a vigorous decade to live. He wanted to marry Tollie Tolan, a widow 34 years his junior, and he was convinced voters would not forgive the divorce he sought. Still he hesitated to make the gate-locking retirement announcement.

Finally Allen visited Hartsfield's office and offered $10,000 as well as his personal support if the Mayor were planning to run again. But Allen asked Hartsfield to make it official if he weren't, so other candidates could make their plans. Hartsfield wandered to a window and reminisced aloud, almost to himself. Then he agreed to make a statement the next day.

Allen had planned a noncontroversial campaign stressing the goals he had set the year before. But before the first joint appearance with his four rivals, intuition told him to go for the jugular of one opponent, Lester Maddox.

Personal contrasts between Allen and Maddox could hardly have been more pronounced. Maddox grew up in a poor Atlanta family and dropped out of high school. After a variety of blue-collar jobs and entrepreneurial efforts, in 1947 he established the Pickrick, a restaurant popular with working-class residents of the neighborhood northwest of Georgia Tech.

In the Fifties, Maddox began peppering his weekly advertisement in *The Constitution* with political comment. It grew increasingly strident and segregation-oriented, and Maddox became a symbol of resistance to racial change. In 1957, after Hartsfield had won the mayoral primary, Maddox entered the general election and was trounced.

At that first 1961 mayoral campaign rally, speaking without notes, Allen laid into Maddox: "You represent a group which would bring another Little Rock to Atlanta...You spread hatred and lawlessness, but we will settle it this summer, with God's help."

Maddox was caught by surprise but not without his litany of "Communists...freedom...racial pride." The five-man race in effect shrank to two that night. In the run-off, Allen overwhelmed Maddox 64,313-36,091.

(Maddox lost a third race—for lieutenant governor of Georgia—in 1962, but became governor in 1967 after the write-in candidacy of former Gov. Ellis Arnall made the three-way 1966 election so close that the choice was thrown to the General Assembly. Constitutionally barred from succeeding himself, Maddox successfully ran for lieutenant governor in 1970. He

Colony Square (upper photo) is a "micropolis" in Midtown. The connected buildings include offices, a hotel, retail stores, restaurants and condominia. Sculpture (below) in front of original building is made of weathering steel which has developed a dark patina.

John Portman's Regency Hotel created a revolution in hotel design. Portman himself has repeated the dramatic atrium lobby in other cities, and the idea has been widely copied.

lost to George Busbee when he sought to return to the Governor's Mansion in 1974.)

The rapid collapse of legally mandated segregation was the most profound social change in Georgia in nearly a century, but the U.S. Supreme Court's "one-man, one-vote" decision in 1962 initiated a political revolution almost as far-reaching.

Georgia had no copyright on legislative and Congressional malapportionment. The ailment afflicted most states in the union, in all regions. But in Georgia, it had an unique twist. The County Unit System could dilute urban votes in statewide races by as much as 99-1.

Unit System arithmetic was based on seating in Georgia's House of Representatives. All of Georgia's 159 counties had at least one House seat; 30 larger counties had two; the eight largest had three. A county had twice as many Unit Votes as House seats. Statewide and multi-county primaries were determined by Unit Votes rather than popular vote totals. The plurality winner in a county took all of its Units Votes. (In those days the Republican party was so small that races were settled in Democratic primaries.)

Thus it sometimes happened that governorships and seats in Congress were won by candidates who had lost in popular vote. Mere existence of the Unit System tended to discourage urban and politically moderate candidacies.

The Unit System had survived earlier court attacks, but when the Supreme Court decided *Baker vs. Carr* to "enter the political thicket," its days were numbered. Atlanta attorney Morris Abram, later president of Brandeis University, had anticipated the *Baker decision.*

Within minutes of its announcement, he filed suit against the Unit System on behalf of businessman James O'Hear Sanders. Nine days later attorney Francis Shackelford filed suit against legislative malapportionment on behalf of Atlanta architect Henry Toombs and other plaintiffs.

The General Assembly made a half-hearted effort to make the Unit System fairer, but the new law was invalidated, and the 1962 primaries were decided by popular vote. In the belief that *Baker* applied to only one house of a bicameral legislature, Georgia's Assembly reapportioned the Senate. In 1965 it was required to redraw House lines as well.

"One-man, one-vote" meant far more than a mere trading of seats. It meant far more than election of black senators and representatives for the first time since early in the century. It altered the rhetoric and the focus of state politics. Former Gov. Eugene Talmadge had bragged he never campaigned in counties where streetcars ran. But in the Sixties, statewide candidates not only had to start campaigning in urban counties; they had to speak to urban issues, and deliver when elected.

Symbolizing Atlanta's business boom of the Sixties and Seventies is this reflection of the Hyatt Regency, with its rotating dome, in the facade of the Coastal States Building.

281

The old Equitable Building, eight stories high, was Atlanta's first "skyscraper." It was designed by Burnham and Root of Chicago and developed by Joel Hurt. Later it was headquarters of the Trust Company of Georgia.

benevolent oligarchs of the business leadership without broader community input.

Bringing Big League sports to Atlanta was important to Allen not only because it would symbolize the city's growing national status, but also because news coverage of games would repeat the name "Atlanta" thousands of times a year throughout the country.

In private discussions, owner Charles O. Finley promised to move his American League Kansas City Athletics to Atlanta if the city would build a stadium. Allen drove him around to three sites under consideration; Finley didn't like any of them. Allen suddenly thought of an urban renewal tract near downtown and near the interchange of three interstate highways. Finley approved.

Allen showed the site to his friend Mills B. Lane, head of the C&S Bank. Lane was enthusiastic.

"How bad do you want this stadium, Ivan?" he asked.

"Bad," replied the mayor.

Lane suggested reconstituting an old Stadium Authority with himself as treasurer and Atlanta Coca-Cola Bottling Company's executive Arthur Montgomery as chairman; Lane pledged the full credit of the bank to the project.

American League officials then informed Atlanta Finley didn't have enough League votes to move the franchise. Montgomery heard stockholders of the National League Milwaukee Braves were interested, however, and arranged a lunch meeting of Braves stockholders and Atlanta executives.

With no formal Braves agreement, and with no approval yet from the City or County, Lane supplied the money for the architect/engineers (Finch/Heery) to get started. As Allen observed later, they were planning a stadium on "land we didn't own, with money we didn't have, for teams that didn't exist." Only after a handshake agreement that the Braves would move in 1965 was the project publicly announced.

Atlanta's Board of Alderman and the Fulton County Commission approved the plan, and the local legislative delegation rushed through authorization for revenue anticipation certificate funding.

To accommodate the Braves' 1965 deadline, the Stadium Authority paid a $600,000 premium to assure construction within one year. The handsome circular arena was completed in 51 weeks. Then, ironically, the Braves became ensnarled in litigation with Milwaukee, and could not move until 1966. The Atlanta Crackers played their last season in a new stadium.

To secure a professional football team, Allen called on Cox Broadcasting executive Leonard Reinsch. Atlanta would have preferred to be in the stronger National Football League, but after talks with both leagues' executives and attempts to buy two existing teams, Reinsch concluded

The changes had dramatic results immediately. In 1962 moderate State Sen. Carl Sanders defeated segregationist former Gov. Marvin Griffin in the governor's race, young attorney Charles Weltner ousted ultraconservative U.S. Rep. James C. Davis, and black Atlanta attorney Leroy Johnson was elected to the State Senate. Beyond such highly visible examples, though, the new system wrought slower but comparably profound changes in the priorities of the State's bureaucracy.

When he took office in 1962, Ivan Allen realized that his ambitious development program would be expensive, and that he would have to seek funding from many sources.

Unlike some cities, Atlanta never had been bashful about seeking Federal money. When Lyndon Johnson's "Great Society" legislation greatly expanded the Federal largesse for urban renewal, low-cost housing, "Model Cities" and various other antipoverty programs, Atlanta generally was near the head of the application line. Wooing and prodding accelerated Federal funding for interstate freeways. Voter-approved bonds built the auditorium/trade show Civic Center complex.

The story of how Atlanta got a stadium and Big League sports is especially fascinating because it was the last time such a major civic decision could be made by the

After its old headquarters was demolished, Trust Company saved three of the ornate columns seen here and placed them free-standing in front of its new building (background).

that Atlanta's best shot was to establish an American Football League expansion team. With his own negotiating skills and a good word from Robert Woodruff of The Coca-Cola Company, Reinsch won an AFL franchise contract.

Before Reinsch could present it to the Stadium Authority, Commissioner Pete Rozelle decided the NFL should be represented in Atlanta. Although he had discouraged Atlanta representatives earlier, now he was offering an expansion franchise. Reinsch had made it possible, but the new team was organized by insurance executive Rankin Smith, who had been recommended to Rozelle by Gov. Carl Sanders.

Thus in 1966 Atlanta became the first city ever to obtain major-league baseball and football in a single year.

Meanwhile, the Atlanta Chamber of Commerce was vigorously implementing another of Allen's 1960 proposals. With $1.5 million raised from local businesses, in 1961 it launched a three-year "Forward Atlanta" campaign. It proved so successful that it was renewed three years later, and ultimately incorporated on a permanent basis into the Chamber's budget.

Forward Atlanta allowed the formerly low-profile Chamber to build a professional staff, publish economic research data, actively seek new business and advertise Atlanta's virtues in national publications. It also underwrote a slick city magazine, *ATLANTA*, which was written for Atlantans but also widely distributed to industrial prospects all over the country. (*ATLANTA* remained a Chamber publication until late 1977, when it was sold to private interests.)

"Forward Atlanta's" aggressive activity capitalized on the good name Atlanta had won for peaceful handling of desegregation. Favorable articles about Atlanta began appearing in numerous national publications.

Large corporations established or expanded operations in Metro Atlanta; some made it national headquarters. Job rolls expanded by tens of thousands a year. The 1960 census showed Atlanta had risen from 25th to 21st in national population rank, and throughout the Sixties it was among the top 10 in such indicators as downtown construction, bank clearings, air traffic and employment. Unemployment fell as low as 1.9 per cent during the Sixties.

Peaceful desegregation and "Forward Atlanta" promotion aside, Atlanta's prime economic development assets continued to be central location in the booming Southeastern region, outstanding transportation and distribution facilities, moderate climate, a good labor pool and relatively low cost of doing business.

During 1960-73 Metro Atlanta further secured its transportation leadership in the air and on the ground.

From the time he was an aviation-minded alderman, Bill Hartsfield had placed his airport priorities on routes, lights, runways, control towers and modern guidance equipment rather than elaborate terminal buildings. The homely corrugated metal terminal he built in 1948 for $180,000 was a case in point.

In Hartsfield's final year in office, however, Atlanta dedicated a modern $20 million terminal. As chairman of the American Municipal Association's Aviation Committee, Hartsfield had lobbied succesfully for expanded Federal aid to airport construction. Atlanta's share, augmented with municipal bond money, funded the handsome building.

Though it looked better than the old Quonset-style terminal, the new one never could keep up with the explosion of air traffic, despite millions of dollars spent for additional concourses, runways and parking. Only 19 years after it was opened,

The under-the-viaducts railroad gulch area blossomed into an entertainment and boutique development called Underground Atlanta in the Sixties and Seventies. At this writing it is inoperative, but hope remains it can be revived.

the "new" terminal yielded in 1980 to a gargantuan complex—the world's largest terminal—immediately to its west.

Some six months after Bill Hartsfield's death in 1971, Mayor Sam Massell proclaimed a new name for the municipal airport: William Berry Hartsfield International Airport—an appropriate tribute to the man who more than any other individual deserved to be called the father of commercial aviation in Atlanta.

The "International" was mostly boast at the time, though Eastern Airlines already had begun nonstop flights to Mexico. Atlanta's international thrust lay ahead.

On the ground, Atlanta finally completed the basic gridwork for a freeway system by the late Sixties. Like the air terminal, though, the freeways are continually being expanded after use far outruns projections.

Through its history, Atlanta's residential areas have expanded as its means of transportation became available. West End developed as a suburb because of the rails. Joel Hurt built his Inman Park residential suburb simultaneously with an electric streetcar line tying it to downtown. The automobile made Druid Hills and the Northside possible in the Teens and Twenties.

In the Sixties, Metro Atlanta began moving out its freeway arteries into rural parts of surrounding counties. This time there was significant difference: Industry and retail trade moved out as well as homes.

Atlanta was perhaps the last major American holdout against suburban shopping centers. One man was primarily

responsible for the delay: Richard Rich, chief executive of Rich's department store. He believed Metro Atlanta's population should reach 1 million before any major suburban center was launched, and that Rich's should have a comprehensive downtown store with a large parking facility. So critical was Rich's to any shopping center financing that he had his way.

Lenox Square in the heart of Buckhead was Metro Atlanta's first regional shopping center when it opened in 1959. It has been expanded frequently, and become the magnet for an "Uptown" complex of office, hotel and high-rise apartment developments. Most subsequent regional shopping malls have been built adjacent to the freeway system.

Though Atlanta was late to embrace suburban shopping centers, it was a pioneer in office parks. The idea was so novel when developer Mike Gearon began promoting it in the early Sixties that he had trouble finding financing.

Some lenders feared it would hurt the downtown boom that was just taking off. Others feared the site—a former dairy farm at North Druid Hills and I-85—simply was too far out. Gearon's Executive Park was such a success that he sold it at a handsome profit three years after it opened. By then, imitators were dotting the suburban landscape with office parks.

Despite occasional periods of overbuilding, office park development continues to be an important element of Metro Atlanta's growth. By far the greatest number are in a crescent northeast to northwest of the city. Industrial parks and trucking facilities have tended to cluster to the west and south.

The most dramatic evidence of Atlanta's economic boom in the Sixties, however, was the downtown skyline's transformation. Except for construction begun before The Crash, the only high-rise building completed between 1930 and 1960 was the brick Bank of the South (then Fulton National Bank) tower, opened in 1955.

The skyline began sprouting in 1960. One of the first new buildings was a million-square-foot Merchandise Mart developed by a young Atlanta architect, John Portman. It became the nucleus of a complex of office towers, hotels, retail shops and mart space called Peachtree Center.

Portman's design for a Hyatt Hotel, with its floor-to-roof atrium, revolutionized hotel architecture and won him international recognition and business.

From 1960 forward, several downtown buildings a year usually have been under construction. Downtown space became so valuable that a Fifties motel and a Sixties office tower have been razed for larger projects.

As Atlanta development spilled into the suburbs, the demography and politics of the central city were shifting. The black vote had become increasingly important since the late Forties; usually it one-sidedly supported candidates chosen by the white business leadership. By the time of the 1969 mayoral election, blacks were nearing a majority of registration, and they wanted a far bigger voice in calling the shots on candidates.

Retiring Mayor Allen had great respect in the black community. He had negotiated a compromise in the 1960-61 sit-ins. He personally had integrated City Hall's cafeteria and hired the first blacks for prominent municipal jobs.

He had testified before Congress in favor of the 1964 Civil Rights Act despite opposition from his business peers and even liberal *Constitution* editor Eugene Patterson, who had argued for voluntary desegregation of public accommodations.

When other cities were burning during the "long hot summer" of 1966, Allen walked into the middle of a relatively minor but potentially dangerous riot in the black Summerhill community.

But black voters rejected Allen's favorite for a successor, insurance executive Rodney Cook. With overwhelming black support and only a small white vote, the winner was Vice Mayor Sam Massell.

The winning coalition of more than 20 years' standing was shattered.

Massell had been vice mayor during the eight years of Allen's tenure, but they had not campaigned or operated as a ticket. Though Massell was a fairly affluent real estate executive who lived on the Northside, he was not in the "power structure" inner circle.

Massell, 42 when elected, was Atlanta's first Jewish mayor, but his political base was not the small Jewish community. Ever since his graduation from Georgia State University and Atlanta Law School, he had been a joiner and a server: civic clubs, fund drives, political committees. He had been an officer or board member of at least 45 organizations. He had forged solid political contacts though eight years' service on the City Executive Committee, which used to supervise municipal elections.

Massell's four years were dogged by controversy, much of it involving the police department. Even before he was elected, newspaper articles alleged his brother Howard and a vice squad officer were pressuring nightclub operators for contributions. Rumors of Howard's influence within the police department plagued much of Massell's term. His choice for police chief frequently was criticized from within the department and without.

Nonetheless, Massell could boast of solid accomplishments both in continuing Atlanta's economic development and in furthering the aspirations of the city's emerging black majority.

His most lasting achievement was the birth of Atlanta's rapid transit system. By constitutional amendment, voters had

In 1970 marchers along Auburn Avenue protested the Vietnam War and deaths of anti-war protesters in the United States. Front-line protesters included civil rights leaders, labor leaders, presidential aspirant George McGovern and Atlanta Mayor Sam Massell.

Mayor Sam Massell (right) dedicated a commemorative gas lamp and plaque in 1972 on the occasion of Atlanta's 125th anniversary. Others in the photo are W. L. Lee (left), then president of Atlanta Gas Light Company, and Norman Shavin, who conceived and promoted the celebration.

authorized planning of a regional unified transit system in 1964. But until 1971, MARTA (Metropolitan Atlanta Rapid Transit Authority) had only limited planning funds and none to build or operate a system.

In 1968, Fulton and DeKalb voters rejected a proposal to underwrite MARTA bonds with property taxes. MARTA officials and staff returned to the drawing boards and substantially altered route and funding proposals. In 1971, voters were asked to approve a 1 per cent sales tax for MARTA.

Informal polls indicated the new initiative was doomed. Many voters simply opposed any new taxes or the basic rapid transit idea. Black voters in particular complained that sales taxes are regressive—hit poor people the hardest.

To make the proposition more attractive to low-income voters, Massell hit on the idea of a no-fare system. His close advisors warned him the MARTA Board would never agree to that, and urged him to have a compromise alternative: a low, single-price fare. Thus was born the MARTA Board's pledge to reduce fares to 15 cents and hold them there for seven years.

Massell campaigned all-out for the referendum. He flew in a helicopter over stalled freeway traffic and with a bullhorn called out: "If you want to get out of this

mess, vote 'yes.'" He boarded buses to distribute pro-MARTA brochures. On blackboards at community meetings, he showed how the 15-cent fare meant poorer citizens would get their one-cent sales tax back or even more.

The sales tax referendum was held in all five counties involved in MARTA planning: Fulton, DeKalb, Cobb, Gwinnett and Clayton. It was agreed that at minimum Fulton, DeKalb and Atlanta voters must approve the funding. All three jursidictions did so by slim margins; the 15-cent deal converted enough black votes to save the day. Voters in the other counties rejected the tax.

A few weeks after the referendum, MARTA purchased the old Atlanta Transit System and began extending its routes, replacing its old buses, and engineering a rapid rail system. Despite subsequent financial squeezes and proposals to raise fares, MARTA stuck by the 15-cent fare for the full seven years.

Inaugurating rapid transit had been one of Ivan Allen's two unfinished goals. Massell also was able to achieve the other: a coliseum.

Allen had been lucky in starting a stadium on "land we didn't own, with money we didn't have, for teams that didn't exist." In the Seventies, it was generally agreed the taxpayers would not sit still for such a tightrope act again. The teams would have to come first, and then the building.

Investors headed by Tom Cousins, a successful young developer, supplied the first requirement by buying an existing National Basketball Association team, the St. Louis Hawks. They played at first in Georgia Tech's Alexander Memorial Coliseum, but the NBA insisted on a larger permanent home.

Various sites were proposed for a coliseum. Cousins lobbied for the area near Atlanta's birthplace—the sprawling rail yards north of the Spring Street viaduct. A sports arena was key to Cousins' plans for large-scale development of the area. A few years before, from another private investor, he had acquired an option to develop the State-owned air rights. To meet a deadline for starting investment, he first built parking decks.

An economist's study of the railroad gulch envisioned multipurpose usage: office buildings, hotels, etc. But it advised that a strong amusements element was needed to generate sufficient patronage in an area that was then off the beaten commercial path. A coliseum used for sports and large-audience entertainment events fit the bill perfectly.

Because building a tax-supported coliseum in the air-rights area obviously would benefit a private developer (Cousins), many taxpayers, politicians and spokesmen for various interest groups opposed using tax funds there. Yet a private developer would have had difficulty obtaining financing for such a venture, and

Tens of thousands filled the
downtown streets of Atlanta in April,
1968, for the funeral march honoring
the late Dr. Martin Luther King Jr.
The route of the march took
participants past the State Capitol
and City Hall, King's body being
carried on an old wagon pulled by
mules.

Among those in the King funeral
march were Ethel Kennedy (above,
left), and entertainers Sidney Poitier
and Sammy Davis Jr. (above, right).

Two months later, Mrs. Kennedy's
husband Robert was assassinated in
California.

First Seventies building in the railroad gulch area northwest of the Spring Street viaduct was the Omni Coliseum, home of the Atlanta Hawks. Its developer, Tom Cousins, then built the Omni International megastructure next door, and the State developed the World Congress Center just beyond.

Atlanta's leadership strongly approved of building a coliseum somewhere.

Massell put his 20 years' real estate experience to work to package a plan for building an air-rights coliseum without tax funds: Use bonding power of the Recreation Authority that operated the stadium; pledge net revenues from coliseum events to pay bond principal and interest; further pledge net revenues from Cousins' parking decks, if needed. "It was a terrific deal for Atlanta and the envy of other cities," Massell said later.

Atlanta's Board of Alderman and the Fulton County Commission approved, and so the 16,000 seat Omni coliseum with its unusual "waffle iron" roof and weathering steel facade was built for $17 million. It was inaugurated in the fall of 1972 with an ice hockey game featuring Cousins' new Flames team (who subsequently moved to Calgary). The project was not entirely tax-free, since the City paid some $3 million for improvements to adjacent Magnolia Street, but Massell observed that Atlanta frequently encouraged major developments by paying for traffic improvements.

At one stage of Omni negotiations, five black aldermen held up the deal until they had guarantees of black employment by the coliseum's contractors. Their action

symbolized an evolving focus of black political interests. In the Fifties and early Sixties, the goal had been eliminating segregation enforced by law and custom. With the battle won, the focus by the early Seventies had turned to "affirmative action"—a required share of the pie, rather than mere removal of barriers to the pie.

The emerging attitude applied also to political office. As a substantial minority of the electorate in the previous three decades, blacks often provided margins of victory for sympathetic white candidates. With a voting majority within the city, they turned increasingly to black candidates.

In his 1973 bid for re-election, Massell could report that municipal jobs for blacks had risen to 42 per cent during his four years, but even if his administration had been free of controversy, he probably could not have survived black voters' overwhelming urge to elect a black mayor.

Massell barely made the runoff, and then lost decisively to Maynard Jackson, the articulate lawyer who had served the prior four years as vice mayor. Black voters did not vote a straight racial line in 1973, however: In the same election a white candidate, Wyche Fowler, defeated a controversial black, Hosea Williams, for the number-two post (renamed "president of City Council" that year).

The Nature
Of Atlanta

This 16-page unit of color photographs captures Atlanta in some of her finery—ranging from the general benevolence of nature to the charms of recreation and the spiritual warmth of some of her churches.

The "Dogwood City's" favorite trees provide an April dance unrivaled anywhere else.

Azaleas in white, pink and red rise amid the city's protective trees in Spring, and the forested green ferns and trees of Summer offer cooling vistas.

Autumn brings Joseph's coat of vari-colored maples, and rare Winter ice creates intricate patterns.

*Atlantans live a variety of lifestyles—
in the Villa Apartments, echoing
Italy, and (below) in the rich
elegance of a Northside home.*

Inman Park, Atlanta's first suburb, is the site of Victorian restoration.

The lobby that revolutionized hotel design is that of the Hyatt Regency, a gawker's paradise.

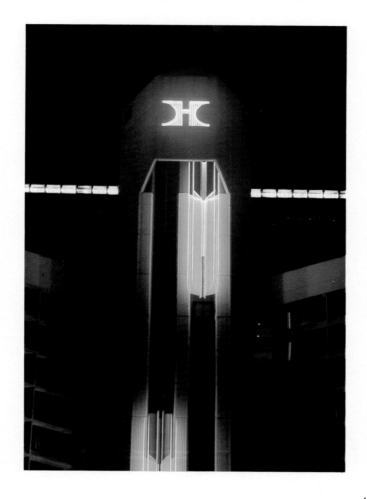

Hotel attractions: the Hilton's
exterior elevators (above) and the
Peachtree Plaza's massive columns
and interior lake

Overleaf: the breathtaking roller
coaster ride at Six Flags Over
Georgia, the giant amusement park

295

The Stadium is the home of baseball's Braves and football's Falcons

Byzantine-style mosaic icons are a stunning feature of the Greek Orthodox Cathedral of the Aunnication.

At left, a processional in the Episcopal Cathedral of St. Philip

*The Second Ponce de Leon Church,
in Buckhead*

The classical interior of The Temple,
the reform Jewish house of worship
on Peachtree Street

*Ebenezer Baptist Church, where the
late Dr. Martin Luther King Jr. was
co-pastor*

In today's Atlanta, Forrest Avenue, commemorating a father of the Ku Klux Klan, has been renamed Ralph McGill Boulevard, after the *Atlanta Constitution* editor who championed racial justice. A street whose eastern end passes the State Capitol is known now as Martin Luther King Jr. Drive. Cain Street, named for a son-in-law of Atlanta pioneer Hardy Ivy, has been extended to the Georgia World Congress Center and renamed International Boulevard.

DeKalb, the quiet farming county from which Atlanta and Fulton County were carved in 1853, rivals the City of Atlanta in population. After aggressively courting economic development in the post-World War II years, DeKalb officials have begun looking askance at proposals to create commercial centers matching downtown Atlanta in density.

In Cobb, there is growing a *de facto* new city of prestigious office centers, shopping facilities and affluent residential neighborhoods.

In the current era, most of what is said about Atlanta refers to Metropolitan Atlanta. The U.S. Bureau of Census identifies it as 15 interrelated counties. Statewide political candidates recognize its five inner counties—Fulton, DeKalb, Cobb, Gwinnett and Clayton—as the dominant though diverse area where they must concentrate their campaigns.

These are a few highlights from a complex portrait of today's Atlanta, a

New Patterns For Tomorrow

Post 1974

Maynard Jackson enthusiastically slices huge cake with a sword during a street celebration. This photo was shot while he was vice mayor, not long before his election as Atlanta's first black mayor.

The gargantuan C-5 transport plane, its nose open to accommodate heavy payload, dwarfs executive jet at Dobbins Air Force Base. Both planes are manufactured by Lockheed-Georgia.

national and international metropolitan area. Like any city, it has evolved from its past. It also reflects the contemporary American mobility that tends to attract citizens from many areas and homogenize regional differences. Yet it remains distinctive, a place unlike any other, imbued with a belief that it can be whatever it wills itself to be.

As there are many visions, so there are many Atlantas. The region is diverse enough to elect an Atlanta mayor who was a U.N. ambassador and lieutenant of Martin Luther King Jr., and a suburban congressman who is a Birch Society member. It encompasses "urban pioneers" who enthusiastically revive in-town neighborhoods as well as families who rarely come inside the Perimeter Highway for business, shopping, schools or entertainment.

Within the municipal boundaries of Atlanta, the 1980 census showed population declining. It was no surprise that black citizens accounted for 66.6 per cent of the 425,022 citizens.

It was perhaps startling to learn that only one in six families within the city comprised the traditional mother, father and children. Barely more than two in five children were growing up in two-parent homes, and an almost equal number with only one parent. Atlanta exaggerated a national trend toward unmarried households: singles, divorced persons, widows, widowers, apartment-sharers, gays, couples living together.

Just as these figures show the core city was attracting a segmented rather than

cross-sectional population, so was its business becoming more specialized.

Downtown increasingly has become a government center, concentrated in a strip stretching from the gold-domed State Capitol, past City Hall and the Fulton Courthouse complex, to the Richard Russell Federal Building.

It remains headquarters for major banks, savings institutions, accounting firms and law firms, together with various support services. Computer technology and modern telecommunications have loosened downtown's ties on stock brokerage/investment counseling firms, and many have moved to Buckhead. Some large law firms have supplemented downtown offices with suburban branches.

Several of Atlanta's most important corporations easily could have moved out, but chose to keep their headquarters in downtown or midtown: Georgia Power, The Coca-Cola Company, Georgia-Pacific, Atlanta Gas Light Company and Coastal States Life among others.

Beginning in the late Sixties, Georgia State University and Georgia Tech began central-city campus expansions that are ongoing: GSU on platforms over city streets and railroad tracks, Tech in acreage to its north and west.

Beginning in the Seventies, convention activity mushroomed so dramatically that conventions and trade shows almost can be counted a new industry—one that contributes significantly to the character and vitality of downtown. From a mediocre rank in convention activity, Atlanta soared to third in the nation.

Fernbank Science Center, operated
by the DeKalb Board of Education,
includes telescope, planetarium,
library, museum, nature preserve.

Scene at Six Flags Over Georgia, a
top tourist attraction, showing
Crystal Pistol and tram

Shopping malls have become
community centers in modern
Atlanta. Attractive fountain graces this
one at Perimeter Mall.

Modern Georgia Archive building
near Capitol houses books,
photographs, maps and other
historic documents.

Part of this increase can be attributed to a vigorous Convention & Visitors Bureau, but it would not have been possible without the necessary infrastructure: outstanding air service, six interstate highway legs, a rail network, a continual blossoming of spectacular downtown hotels, a doubling of the original Merchandise Mart and addition of a separate Apparel Mart.

The State-built World Congress Center near the Omni coliseum put Atlanta's convention/trade show in even bigger leagues. Dedicated in 1976, it offered the nation's largest single-floor exhibition space and a commodious auditorium with built-in simultaneous interpretation facilities. The Center became so heavily booked that the Georgia General Assembly authorized doubling it, thus allowing Atlanta to bid for the nation's biggest conventions.

International activity began expanding so extensively in the Seventies that it, too, could be considered a new industry. International growth is another example of Atlanta's bragging itself into a goal. When the Atlanta Chamber of Commerce began advertising its early-Seventies slogan, "Atlanta: The World's Next Great City," there was far less to support the claim than today.

Most of the Atlanta-posted career consulates, some honorary consulates,

international trade offices and international tourism bureaus are in downtown, and an internationally affiliated World Trade Club was established downtown in 1982.

Atlanta's major banks have developed active international departments, and more than a dozen foreign banks do business in downtown Atlanta offices.

This ongoing growth of international offices reflects the vast expansion of international trade and foreign investment in America's Sunbelt, and Atlanta's central role in the Southeast.

Though downtown remains economically vigorous, it no longer is the dominant multipurpose shopping center of the region. Its Rich's and Davison's headquarters department stores, for instance, increasingly are rivaled by the same chains' outlets at Lenox Square in uptown, Cobb County's Cumberland Mall and DeKalb County's Perimeter Mall.

It is difficult to find a wide selection of hardware or groceries in downtown. Several traditional names in downtown retailing are found today only in the suburbs. Trucking firms, the old southern downtown garment district and warehousing generally have moved out.

Permanent residences are notably few. In 1980, there were only two downtown

The Georgia World Congress Center, a massive facility for conventions and trade shows—but flexible enough to handle small seminars—is already being expanded.

Several thousand fairly recent Oriental arrivals have stimulated more Oriental restaurants, market items.

Ethnic Newcomers Tend To Spread Through City Rather Than Clustering In Neighborhoods

Since Atlanta's earliest days, when many of the railroad-builders were Irish and German, the population has included some immigrants. But unlike cities in the Northeast and Midwest, Atlanta never has experienced significant waves of immigration, nor developed lasting ethnic neighborhoods.

Instead, ethnic interests have been preserved primarily through cultural and religious societies, and through personal networks. By the 1980s there were several dozen such organizations—some with large memberships, many with only a handful, and a few dating from the 19th Century.

Their purposes are varied: Some concentrate on the literature and arts of their native countries; others offer help to newer arrivals; some are primarily religious in orientation. Their public activities range from Scottish games to annual festivals of the Greek community.

Georgia State University's Anthropological Department has traced this pattern in Atlanta's history of immigration:

In 1850 most of the 130 first-generation immigrants were Irish and German. A decade later, immigrants also included quite a few English and some Italians. In 1880 Germans and Irish comprised about one third each of Atlanta's immigrant population (which was only 3.7 per cent of the total).

From 1890 to 1920, there were significant numbers of Russians, Poles, Germans, Greeks, Syrians, Lebanese, Hungarians and Jews from various countries. During the rise of Nazism, immigration of German and Austrian Jews rose considerably.

In the 1950s, the major new groups were Cubans, Koreans, Japanese and Chinese. In the 1970s new Atlantans included Latin Americans, Vietnamese, Indochinese and Russians.

Immigrants still comprise only a small part of Metropolitan Atlanta's population. It is estimated there are about 50,000 first-

generation Latin Americans—mostly Cubans—in the area; 5,000 Koreans; 2,500 Japanese; 3,000 Chinese and 1,000 Vietnamese.

The greatest number of immigrants tend to cluster in the northeast quadrant of the city, but they do not form distinct ethnic neighborhoods. Stores and restaurants in Broadview Plaza, for example, indicate that the shopping center services a concentration of Oriental and Latin American clients, but the surrounding neighborhood is not divided along ethnic lines.

At one time, Atlanta did have identifiable Greek and Jewish neighborhoods. These groups still tend to cluster in certain areas of the city, but not to the extent of forming distinct ethnic neighborhoods. Even among the more recent arrivals, the pattern is more typically to disperse to other parts of the Metro area after a few years in immigrant-cluster areas.

The Jewish Community Center, nine synagogues and other voluntary organizations have helped retain Jewish identity. Similarly, Greek identity and voting power are held together through the Orthodox Cathedral of the Annunciation, the Hellenic Center and various voluntary groups. The Greek community members about 3,500.

One of the oldest ethnic organizations in the area is the Burns Club of Atlanta, founded in 1896 as a Scottish literary and cultural society.

Atlanta's ethnic diversity is reflected not only in societies and religious institutions, but in restaurants, retail stores, annual festivals and cultural entities such as Germany's Goethe Institute.

A multicultural directory of Metro Atlanta's ethnic societies and other international activities is available through Georgia State University.

addresses: high-rise apartments (now condominia) on West Peachtree Street and Piedmont Avenue. Some planners believe the more recent Renaissance Park condominia and apartments in the Bedford-Pine urban renewal district are harbingers of future downtown living.

On the fringes of downtown, however, are several vigorous residential neighborhoods. Ansley Park, between Peachtree and Piedmont north of 14th Street, led the way. Though never seriously deteriorated, it began attracting young renovators in the mid-Sixties. As values in Ansley Park began soaring, others attracted to in-town living staked out other neighborhoods: Midtown (even closer to downtown), Morningside, Virginia-Highlands, Candler Park, Little Five Points, West End.

The biggest gamblers were the early renovators in Inman Park, the erstwhile prestige address for Atlanta's elite, built by Joel Hurt in the late 19th Century at the end of his electric streetcar line.

Its Victorian mansions were deteriorated and subdivided into rooming houses. The area was laced with dilapidated former homes of factory workers. Initially, financial institutions considered the area too risky for loans. Only the personal labors and investments of several "pioneers" turned the situation around, and Inman Park is once more a desirable address.

The in-town renovators tend to be young and politically active. Their neighborhood organizations, loosely tied together in a Citywide League of Neighborhoods, have become a new and effective political force, not only in supporting or opposing candidates, but also in fighting unwanted commercial rezoning and helping kill two Seventies freeway projects.

This new-found political strength has been recognized by the City's established Neighborhood Planning Units (NPUs), through which planning and zoning matters are submitted to advisory votes in public hearings.

Whereas the central city has had to adjust to neighborhood activism, specialization of its downtown business activities, and a shift from white to black majority, the suburban counties above all have had to grapple with sheer growth.

It has been the stuff chambers of commerce's dreams are made of, and county commissioners' sleepless nights. The freeway system opened the gates for a torrent of subdivisions, apartment complexes, office and industrial parks, regional shopping centers and commercial strip developments.

These in turn created extraordinary demands for water, sewers, traffic improvements, schools, law enforcement and administrative officials. Revenue needs

The Musical Museum was one of the attractions in the heyday of Underground Atlanta.

Crazy and chaotic annual Chattahoochee Raft Race finally was banned because of litter, safety hazards.

Arts Festival of Atlanta was born in a Buckhead back yard in 1954, but has been held in Piedmont Park ever since.

Atlanta's suburbs are dotted with spacious homes.

generally grew faster than tax bases, and infrastructure rarely kept up with growth. (One notable exception was DeKalb County's post-World War II extension of water service into areas that still were rural then.)

Rocky politics was the inevitable symptom of growing pains—of rising taxes, traffic bottlenecks, homeowners' resistance to apartments and commercial incursions, etc. DeKalb was the first to feel the suburban spillover, and first to reflect it politically. Scott Candler was DeKalb's sole county commissioner from the Thirties to the Fifties. Since then, no commission chairman has ever won a second term.

By the mid-Seventies, it had become good politics in DeKalb to put brakes on growth. The issue was epitomized in 1982 when the county rejected two simultaneous proposals that would have created office and commercial development along the Perimeter Highway rivaling the density of downtown Atlanta.

Suburban growth has been fed both by in-migration and exodus from Atlanta. Schools in particular have been a factor. As Atlanta's school population has risen to more than 90 per cent black, the average school child is from a poorer family than he or she was two decades ago. School priorities necessarily have been more job- than college-oriented than before, despite special curricula like the remarkable performing arts program at Northside High.

White (and some middle- and upper-income black) families with school-age children therefore have tended to settle in the suburbs. The trend partly explains Atlanta's skewed population figures, with relatively fewer children and more childless adults than in the suburbs.

When Maynard Holbrook Jackson Jr. was inaugurated as mayor of Atlanta in 1974, he sailed into uncharted governmental seas. Under recently enacted legislation, he had to implement a government reorganization that gave the mayor administrative powers formerly shared with the Board of Aldermen. (The same law renamed aldermen "councilmen" and the vice mayor "president of council.") Far more difficult, he had to balance the expectations of his black constituency against the wishes of the white business leaders who still oiled and operated the engines of Atlanta commerce.

Jackson was a unique man for a unique set of challenges. He was 35 when elected. Though born in Dallas, Tx., he grew up in Atlanta, and had deep Atlanta roots. His maternal grandfather, John Wesley Dobbs, had been a community and labor leader who had championed black voter registration. His aunt, Mattiwilda Dobbs, was a distinguished operatic soprano. His father

313

The Alonzo F. Herndon home, near
the Atlanta University Center
campus, is being turned into a
museum and study center.

Many of Atlanta's well-to-do black
families occupy spacious homes on
the city's South side. Among the
residences are the one above, at top
and bottom (left) of the facing page.

was pastor of Atlanta's historic Friendship
Baptist Church from 1945 until his death in
1953.

Jackson, a lawyer with mellifluous ora-
torical abilities, came to political attention
in 1968 when he challenged Sen. Herman
Talmadge in the Democratic primary. He
had no chance, but the effort was not
purely quixotic. He garnered a quarter of
the statewide vote—no bad show for a
black newcomer—but more to the point,
ran up a 6,000-vote majority within the city
of Atlanta.

The next year he parlayed his political
recognition into a successful bid for vice
mayor. Four years later he decisively
unseated incumbent Mayor Sam Massell.

Tensions between the black mayor and
the white business leadership mounted
during his first three years in office. Their
differences were rooted part in perception,
part in reality.

First, government reorganization itself
and second, the appointment of Jackson's
team to high posts meant that the business
leadership had to deal with a new cast of
characters in matters ranging from zoning
to building permits, traffic improvements,
sales contracts and major policy decisions.
Jackson became notorious for inaccessi-
bility because of a sheath of protective
assistants.

Jackson's priorities were far greater
irritants. "I come to the job as an advocate," he said. "I believe in actually changing how the system operates. We're going

to build a human system, regardless of sex, race, religion..." Jackson implemented a sweeping program to guarantee the black community a substantial share of city business.

It included affirmative-action hiring requirements for city suppliers and joint-venture arrangements to involve black contractors. Beyond its substance, however, the program was condemned for the snail's pace of its operation and the contentiousness of its administrator, Emma Darnell. Even so vital a project as a new airport terminal was delayed at least a year because of compliance controversy.

The business community's grievances surfaced publicly in the so-called "Brockey letter." Harold Brockey at the time was Board chairman of Rich's and of Central Atlanta Progress (CAP).

CAP for years has been a catalyst for implementing projects considered important by Atlanta's downtown business interests. In this instance it prepared a draft paper cataloguing Atlanta's pressing problems and invited some 50 black and white leaders to the Commerce Club to discuss them. It was a tough and specific document.

Among the problems it listed, the one that received the most publicity was the perception of some white businessmen that the Jackson administration was anti-white. Consensus of the meeting was to submit a list of problems to the mayor in written form.

Among the fine residences occupied by some of Atlanta's black families are these—above and below.

Henry Aaron made sports history with the Atlanta Braves as he knocked out his 715th homer, thus beating Babe Ruth's record.

315

The onetime Nunnally mansion on Blackland Road was one of the sites for filming a recent Tim Conway movie, "They Went That-a-Way and That-a-Way." That's Conway, in formal attire, posing as a Japanese; in geisha clothes is Chuck McCann. The mansion is now owned by a Saudi Arabian prince.

Atlanta's newest skyscraper, Georgia-Pacific's headquarters building, towers in the background.

In the foreground, the venerable English-American (Flatiron) Building, dating from 1897.

Gigantic Hartsfield International Airport, largest in the world.

The State Capitol, its dome of gold sheath, and (below) the Hall of Flags, inside.

Sailing on nearby Lake Lanier, and the
showing of discipline at the Hunter-Jumper
classic

The Midnight Sun restaurant overlooks a
fountain, and the Memorial Arts Alliance
Galleria provides a warm meeting place for
patrons of the arts.

Maestro Robert Shaw has served as musical director of the Atlanta Symphony Orchestra since 1967.

Rich wood and appointments set a graceful atmosphere in the Atlanta Historical Society.

Restoration in West End homes

Through a curve of a sculpture at Peachtree Center, a city within a city, one views the world's tallest hotel, the cylindrical, 73-story Peachtree Plaza.

A North Avenue vista, near midtown, provides views of Georgia Tech's tower, the cylindrical C&S Building, and the Life of Georgia skyscraper.

Shopping malls are always thronged: At left, a circular sculpture in Lenox Square; at right, festive mobiles in Perimeter Mall.

The sculpture-rich
staircase in the opulent
Candler Building, with its
ornate facade (below)

At left, the striking office facility,
Tower Place

For participants and spectators—the Peachtree Road
Race (above) and daredevil auto racing

Citizens & Southern's National Bank's main lobby reflects a classic age, and the Hyatt Regency Hotel's flag-draped entrance welcomes the city's arrival as an international center.

At Emory University, the Woodruff Medical Center (above) and a modern chemistry building

Part of Georgia State University's campus downtown (above), and festivities at Georgia Tech (below), where the "Ramblin' Wreck" is a tradition

Harkness Hall, on the Atlanta
University campus

Oakland
Cemetery

Since Oakland Cemetery opened in 1850, more than 100,000 persons have been buried there.

They include Confederate generals and unknown soldiers, slaves and wealthy pioneers, children whose lives were cut short in infancy, eccentrics and citizens average and famous.

There, among others, sleep Margaret Mitchell, author of *Gone With the Wind*, and Martha Lumpkin Compton, for whom Atlanta was first officially named.

The funerary architecture varies from the plain to the ornate, from simple markers to tombs with stained glass. It is a marvel to visit.

Shown on this and two following pages is a representative sampling of Oakland's treasures.

The marker of Martha Lumpkin Compton: For her Atlanta was first given the name Marthasville. Her father was a major proponent of a railroad system, and a Georgia governor.

The tomb of Dr. Nedom L. Angier: He is credited with suggesting the name Fulton for the county which Atlanta dominates. He served also as mayor.

Anton Kontz was buried under this Egyptian structure in the midst of his family's plot.

Jasper Smith sits in stone serenity above the door of his tomb. On Jasper's head, a bird has found a momentary resting place.

Gen. Alfred Austell's substantial tomb reflects the strength of that early-day Atlantan who is credited with founding the Atlanta National Bank in 1865.

The tomb of George Washington Collier, whose grocery was at Five Points in the 1840s; Collier became a major landowner and developer.

The final resting place of Samuel M. Inman, entrepreneur regarded by many as "Atlanta's First Citizen" between 1870 and the time of his death, 1915. The first suburb is named for him.

Co-Sponsors Of the History

Two prime Atlanta civic organizations agreed, at the conception of *ATLANTA: Triumph Of a People,* to serve as co-sponsors of this book.

They are the Atlanta Preservation Center and Central Atlanta Progress. They are dedicated to the maintenance of historic structures of value, and to the quality growth and viability of Atlanta.

Their early support and continuing aid on behalf of this project have been of inestimable value. Their key executives have consistently responded creatively to the requests for guidance and assistance. For their help, the authors are deeply grateful. Special appreciation is paid to Dan Sweat of Central Atlanta Progress and Jim Cumming of the Atlanta Preservation Center.

The profiles of their agencies are on the next two pages.

The need for an organization like the Atlanta Preservation Center, dedicated to promoting the preservation of the city's architecturally, historically and culturally significant buildings and neighborhoods, was not recognized until recently.

Busy with rebuilding itself after Gen. William T. Sherman's incendiary March to the Sea, Atlanta was more interested in the future than in the past.

The lure of progress, the relative newness of its structures and the availability of land prevented conflict between history and the wrecking ball until the late 1960s and early 1970s.

The early skirmishes over architectural preservation occurred in Atlanta's intown neighborhoods, which had suffered from the exodus to the suburbs and which were threatened by plans for highway construction.

The Seventies saw a revival of interest in such close-in neighborhoods as Ansley Park, Candler Park, East Lake, Grant Park, Inman Park, Midtown, Virginia-Highlands and West End, which have undergone remarkable renovation.

The successful campaign in 1974 to rescue the "Fabulous Fox" Theatre from demolition applied the same sentiments to an architecturally significant public building.

Historians, architects, city planners, neighborhood activists and business leaders became convinced that Atlanta needed an organization to educate Atlantans and visitors about the cultural heritage embodied in the city's buildings and neighborhoods, and to propose economically realistic methods for their preservation.

A task force of the Junior League of Atlanta studied the idea for a year and a half and recommended that the Atlanta Preservation Center be created to work on already identified preservation needs.

The Junior League provided substantial funding for three years. The first year's funding was matched by a grant from the Heritage Conservation and Recreation Service of the U.S. Department of the Interior, and was administered by the Historic Preservation Section of the Georgia Department of Natural Resources.

The Atlanta Preservation Center developed several programs to increase awareness of Atlanta's heritage. Its volunteers staff a speakers' bureau, conduct walking tours of historic areas and publish a quarterly newsletter.

Other activities include seminars and workshops on preservation issues, and an annual fall course on Atlanta history and preservation. The Center cosponsors Archifest, including coordination of downtown walking tours, in conjunction with the annual event of the Georgia Chapter of the American Institute of Architects.

Supporters of the Atlanta Preservation Center believe progress is compatible with preserving those parts of the past that testify to the visions of successive generations of Atlanta's leadership.

Atlanta Preservation Center

Three of the four houses along Edgewood Avenue shown in this 1895 photograph still stand. These houses in Inman Park exemplify the architectural heritage of Atlanta's first suburb.

Walking tours are one way the Atlanta Preservation Center makes Atlantans aware of their architectural heritage. Participants in a tour of the Fairlie-Poplar district are shown near Central City Park. In the background at left is the Flatiron Building (1897), Atlanta's oldest standing skyscraper.

341

Central Atlanta Progress

Central Atlanta Progress represents the commitment of 175 businesses, organizations and institutions to maintain, through cooperation between the public and private sectors, an economically vibrant central business district.

CAP traces its lineage to 1941, when commercial interests in the Five Points area organized the Central Atlanta Improvement Association. It and the Uptown Association, formed in the 1960s to seek improvements in the Ponce de Leon/North Avenue corridor, merged in 1967 to become Central Atlanta Progress.

Their merger recognized that Atlanta's central business district over the years had grown beyond Five Points. Along the corridor formed by Peachtree, West Peachtree and Spring Streets, there was an identifiable business district of similar interests bounded on the north by Brookwood Station, by The Coca-Cola Company on the west, and the Sears Roebuck building on the east.

While membership in private, nonprofit CAP is by invitation, in reality it is open to all businesses whose leaders are willing to work for the collective interests of the downtown community.

Annual membership dues are assessed on the basis of a business' size and property holdings. Governance is through a 35-member board of directors drawn from the membership; the board meets quarterly, and a 20-member executive committee meets monthly. CAP has a seven-person, full time staff and an annual operating budget of about $300,000.

CAP's influence stems from the nature of its members, the way they organize themselves to tackle perceived problems and the resources they are able to draw upon.

With few exceptions, members are the chief executives of their organizations. In addition to their personal commitments, they have authority to commit their firms. Each issue is dealt with by development of a task force. Finally, the organization is able to marshal outside financing for public improvements.

Task force members often contribute financially or donate materials or services.

In addition to these reasons for its effectiveness, CAP counts City government as a partner, an alliance that dates from the joint planning process begun in 1969 on the "Central Area Study." Most studies by CAP since then have involved public sector participation, with public and private oversight.

This cooperation and coordination was present in the "Back-to-the-City Housing Strategy Study" completed in 1974. It encouraged 15 Atlanta banks and savings and loan associations to pledge $63 million for intown mortgages over a five year period.

The Fairlie/Poplar Project, the rejuvenation of a 21-block area downtown, was organized and executed in a similar way, with the City contracting with CAP to produce the master plan.

In other instances, Central Atlanta Progress has adopted different organizational structures. In the redevelopment of the 78-acre Bedford-Pine area with intown housing, CAP formed a private development company, Park Central Communities.

This organization is made up of six banks, six private developers, Rich's, Inc., The Coca-Cola Company, and a nonprofit CAP subsidiary, Central Atlanta Civic Development, Inc.

Many CAP projects take the view that the health of downtown is inextricably related to the entire city. This was illustrated in development of the intown mortgage pool, and in the rapid formation of a fund drive to rebuild the Bowen Homes Day Care Center after a disastrous explosion in 1980.

During the summer of 1981, 160 representatives of CAP's member firms participated in a series of task forces to forge an agenda for the 1980s. From that effort emerged a series of objectives and recommendations for activities in human services, economic development, housing, public safety, urban design, transportation and marketing.

The agenda represents a work program for CAP's continued role as a catalyst for cooperative action between Atlanta's public and private sectors.

Robert Maddox (left), who was first president of Central Atlanta Progress, greets Jack J. McDonough, then president of the Atlanta Chamber of Commerce, at Maddox's 88th birthday celebration in the mid-Fifties. Maddox, formerly mayor of Atlanta, was president of the First National Bank at the time of CAP's founding.

Partners In Prosperity

Since Atlanta's inception as a railroad terminus, its most powerful engine has been commerce, and the opportunities which the city developed attracted entrepreneurs and visionaries who shaped its character, lifestyles and culture.

The leaders of commerce have been involved in Atlanta's political destinies, and in rebuilding the city from the destruction of the Civil War. They have played key roles in the city's emergence as a prime transportation, education, medical, communications and government center.

Their contributions and dedication are manifest in the city's shape, its skyline, its parks, its entertainments, its suburban development, and its growing posture as an international marketplace.

They helped create the Atlanta spirit, and exemplify its motto, *Resurgens*.

As Atlanta has grown and benefitted from their leadership, so have they become partners in its prosperity.

ATLANTA: Triumph Of a People identifies the origins of some in the main history portion. But this section, Partners In Prosperity, is devoted to detailed profiles of 89 select, top Atlanta firms which are among the elite of its enterprises. The origins of some date from Atlanta's infancy and early youth; others are younger; all are vigorous, and justifiably proud of their roles in Atlanta's forward thrust.

Their stories are positioned alphabetically on pages 344 through 447, except for a few intervening leaves titled "Some Faces In Our Past," devised so companies whose profiles occupy more than one page could display them on facing pages.

The assistance of these Partners In Prosperity was essential to the successful development of *ATLANTA: Triumph Of a People*, and to them the authors express deep thanks in this enterprise which offers their stories as well as that of Atlanta, a time and place to which we and the Partners are dedicated.

Contents

Aaron Rents, Inc.

R. Charles Loudermilk, president and founder, Aaron Rents, Inc.

Aaron Rents, Inc., corporate headquarters in Buckhead, the heart of uptown Atlanta

One of Aaron Rents' earliest stores, at 14th and West Peachtree Streets

R. Charles Loudermilk, a native Atlantan, is founder and chief executive officer of Aaron Rents, Inc. In 1955, at age 28, Loudermilk began the business with $500 borrowed from a local bank. He chose the name of his company simply to ensure that it always would be the first of its kind listed in the Yellow Pages of the telephone book.

Aaron Rents is now a $50 million corporation, headquartered in its own impressive office building in Atlanta's uptown, Buckhead.

The progress of Aaron Rents closely tracks the evolution of Atlanta as the commercial capital of the Southeast. In 1955, when Loudermilk seized on the idea of providing rental furnishings for large parties and banquets, he was working with his mother in her Pershing Point restaurant, the Rose Bowl.

At first, his rental business was strictly a sideline for the young entrepreneur, but within a couple of years the business had grown enough to need a store of its own. In 1957 he opened the original Aaron Rents party equipment rental store on Peachtree Road at Peachtree Battle, today the site of the Peachtree Battle Shopping Center.

In the moderately expanding economy of the late Fifites, Loudermilk needed a means to enlarge his market base; he chose patient care equipment rental as the logical companion to his thriving party rental business. Late in 1957 he opened the second Aaron Rents store on Peachtree, this one near downtown, across from the Doctors Building.

But it was in the mid-1960s that the excitement began. At this point, Atlanta was attracting corporate newcomers and their employees in greater numbers than most had foreseen. As a consequence, there was an acceleration of apartment building that was to continue unabated for a decade or more.

In the years since 1955, Loudermilk had become a seasoned veteran of the business community, closely attuned to the city and its changing fortunes. So, in 1964 he opened his third store, on Buford Highway, and began renting furniture.

From that point, Aaron Rents' operations expanded at a dizzying rate. Young families poured into the city throughout the Sixties and Seventies, and most needed furniture. They found they could get what they needed within hours from Aaron Rents, and tens of thousands did just that.

In 1967 Loudermilk took the first major step toward making Aaron Rents an integrated furniture company. He opened his first retail sales store on the Northeast Expressway, the main corridor to the city's most concentrated area of residential growth. This move gave his company a profitable sales outlet for its large quantity of previously rented furniture.

In 1972 Loudermilk took another step toward vertical integration by establishing the company's own furniture manufacturing facility in Duluth, on the far northeast side of metropolitan Atlanta. This 60,000 square foot plant supplies Aaron Rents with all its living room furniture and bedding.

It was also in 1972 that Loudermilk expanded his business to include the rental and sale of office furniture. Again, it was a case of capitalizing on an opportunity presented by the city and the nation.

During the Seventies, Aaron Rents expanded not only in Atlanta but also into other growing markets in the Southeast, Southwest and Midwest. And in 1981 Aaron Rents opened its first store in Denver, the doorway to its expansion to the West.

It was also during this decade that Atlanta's reputation as a convention city rose almost meteorically. So it was all but a predictable certainty that Aaron Rents would initiate a convention furniture division, which it did in 1980.

Today, Aaron Rents fairly boasts that it is "the second-largest and one of the fastest-growing furniture rental companies in the industry." In fact, it is the largest privately held furniture rental company in the nation.

Aaron Rents now employs more than 700 people and operates 31 rental showrooms in 14 major cities throughout the Southeast and Southwest, along with 16 retail furniture stores, 18 office furniture showrooms, two manufacturing plants and the original party and patient-care division.

AFCO Realty Associates

AFCO Realty Associates began with an idea: professional on-site management for investor owners. From a single account and a 10-by-15-foot office in 1971, AFCO has grown to a full-service real estate company handling lease and sales transactions in excess of $70 million a year throughout the Southeast.

That beginning was a result of an idea conceived by Samuel G. Friedman Jr., president and chairman of the board of AFCO.

"My idea was to start a full-service property company to offer specialized real estate services to users and owners of real estate property," says Friedman.

In negotiating the sale of the nine-story 148 International Boulevard building, Friedman saw firsthand the need for a quality management program. He then convinced the new owners of that building that he could handle the management of their business.

So, with an account already in hand, AFCO Properties, Inc., was formed in October, 1971.

It was a start based on applying sound business principles to a real estate company and utilizing innovative selling techniques, thorough market knowledge and personal service.

In 1982 AFCO employs 24 associate brokers and salesmen.

Within six months of the start in 1971 Friedman had acquired his second account, the Cities Services Building, and added his first full-time leasing agent, Thomas J. Wesley III, now a vice president and partner of the company.

The combination of professional management and aggressive marketing techniques in leasing enabled AFCO to lease fully the Cities Services Building in 18 months during a soft market, land the Corporate Square office park exclusive leasing account, and start construction of the National Data Building in Corporate Square by negotiating the 82,000-square-foot lease with National Data Corporation.

Those deals coupled with creative selling helped AFCO build a reputation for reliable and consistent results, a reputation put to the test during the 1973-74 real estate depression.

"You couldn't give real estate away," recalls Friedman. "It was an incredibly overbuilt market."

Yet the company prospered with a combination of hard work, conservative business practices and consistent results.

"We learned that there are many opportunities in bad times," says Friedman. "After only two years in the business we were facing a time when some of the biggest names in the industry were in financial trouble. We were able to grow by learning the importance of sound management and filling a niche in the marketplace."

After negotiating several brokerage deals considered noteworthy in a depressed marketplace, AFCO's reputation as a brokerage company was firmly established.

"Everybody wanted to hire us. We weren't tarnished by the recession," says Friedman.

During that period the management business provided a steady ongoing base while the company developed other facets of its real estate business: office leasing and consulting.

In 1976 J. William Butler joined AFCO to head the commercial investments division. Butler, now a vice president and partner, also heads the counseling program.

With a continuing expansion of the company's services, a need arose for a new name that encompassed all of AFCO's activities. In 1977 the name AFCO Realty Associates was adopted.

That same year the company reorganized, adding a fourth division: industrial leasing and sales.

Deals such as Allstate's 84,000-square-foot office in 1980, Ernst & Whinney's 53,000-square-foot lease in Peachtree Center in 1981, and a 100,000-square-foot Institute of Nuclear Power Operations lease in 1982 have highlighted AFCO's leasing successes.

In management, AFCO has achieved status as an AMO—Accredited Management Organization—the industry standard for excellence in management, awarded by the Institute of Real Estate Management.

Continuing professional education by individuals of AFCO has resulted in achievement of such professional designations as the CCIM, CRE, CPA and RPA. That same involvement extends to such major civic and professional organizations as the Atlanta Chamber of Commerce, Central Atlanta Progress, The World Trade Club and the Atlanta Board of Realtors.

AFCO Realty Associates

Sam Friedman (center), chairman and president of AFCO, participated in ground-breaking festivities for the National Data Building, along with George Thorpe (left), then chairman of National Data, and Dick Sorenson.

T. M. Alexander Sr. and Company, Inc.

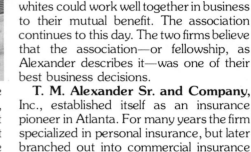

T. M. Alexander Sr. (right) in front of his Auburn Avenue office, with his longtime friend and business associate W. L. Calloway

T. M. Alexander Sr. with executive vice president Horace A. Tory

With $100 in cash in 1931, during the desolate days of the great Depression, Theodore Martin Alexander created what is now one of the oldest and most successful minority-owned insurance agency companies in the United States.

From that lean beginning more than 50 years ago, T. M. Alexander Sr. and Company, Inc., in 1981-82 recorded several million dollars in business and listed many well-known local and national organizations among its clients.

In the early years in his career, Alexander formed an affiliation with John Charles Whitner, a white businessman who owned an Atlanta insurance firm. Insurance specialist Donald Oberdorfer bought out Whitner and thus became associated with Alexander.

The association was a loose one, and allowed the two men to combine their technical expertise and expand the scope of their economic opportunities. Alexander maintained his separate office on Auburn Avenue, the center of the black community, from which he and his staff developed a substantial book of clients.

At a time of segregation in Atlanta and throughout the South, the integrated business enterprise was a testimonial to the belief of both firms that blacks and whites could work well together in business to their mutual benefit. The association continues to this day. The two firms believe that the association—or fellowship, as Alexander describes it—was one of their best business decisions.

T. M. Alexander Sr. and Company, Inc., established itself as an insurance pioneer in Atlanta. For many years the firm specialized in personal insurance, but later branched out into commercial insurance and employee benefits.

Alexander took a great risk in first setting up his insurance business in what was a white-dominated field, but risk-taking seems to come naturally to him. In 1971 he and Oberdorfer formed a joint venture to serve as insurance brokers and consultants to MARTA. Two other companies joined the firms in taking an initial eight-year contract with the transit authority.

The Oberdorfer and Alexander firms together have formed a special risk commercial lines department, with consulting and advisory services available to the insured. Alexander's latest venture is the formation of a multi-line insurance company in Atlanta.

Personal risks have been no less a part of Alexander's life than business risks. He was the first black in 90 years to try for an alderman's seat in Atlanta. He lost, but tried again for public office when he ran for a seat in the Georgia Senate in 1961. Although he lost, he is credited with having opened the political arena to black candidates, and in doing so earned recognition in *Who's Who in America*.

As a result of his friendship with Dr. Martin Luther King Jr., T. M. Alexander Sr. became active in the civil rights movement, from its first confrontations in the Montgomery, Ala., bus boycotts in 1955. Alexander remains a staunch civil rights supporter and an advocate of black business opportunities.

The present operations of Alexander and Company are carried on by executive vice president Horace A. Tory, who, like Alexander, is a Morehouse College graduate. Tory joined the Company in 1975 and has directed the firm's growth in areas previously unexplored by a minority firm.

Alexander spends much of his time in Washington, D.C., where he is an adjunct professor of insurance at Howard University.

AMC Mechanical Contractors

"Daylight never catches me at home," says Thomas O. Cordy, president and owner of AMC Mechanical Contractors. "I'm in the office before dawn, and I leave after dark."

According to Cordy, hard work is the reason his company, founded in 1972 with five employees, is now the largest minority-owned mechanical contractor in the nation.

With 110 employees, the privately held company is usually working on at least 15 projects at a time. AMC's projects have included the Schlitz Brewery in New York, the Georgia Power Company's Plant Vogtle in Waynesboro, and Hartsfield Atlanta International Airport's new terminal.

Cordy began modestly as a residential heating and air conditioning contractor in partnership with Edward Alston, a mechanical engineer. For the first two years the going was tough. "About the time we got started, the bottom fell out of the economy," says Cordy. "We were in serious trouble."

Alston Mechanical Contractors, as the company was then known, was the first minority-owned mechanical contractor in Atlanta. As residential business continued to drop off in 1974, Cordy and Alston began to look for commecial work. Expanding the company's services to include plumbing and commercial boiler work, they were awarded their first commercial contract in 1974.

That first project, the Bolton West Ltd. Office Building, was followed by projects at the Hemphill Pumping Station and the Georgia-Hill Street Neighborhood Center the same year.

While business had begun to pick up, the company was still in debt. It was a $2 million contract with Schlitz Brewing Co. in August, 1976, that got the company back on its feet and allowed it to expand, dropping out of the residential market.

In November, 1976, Cordy bought out Alston and changed the company's name to AMC.

AMC specializes in commercial and industrial plumbing, heating, ventilating, air conditioning and process piping. It also provides design engineering assistance.

The company and its owner have what some might consider a handicap. Being black, they must overcome racial bias and skepticism "from those who are not used to dealing with blacks," Cordy says.

"We do not market this company as a minority-owned firm. If you compare us with any other mechanical contractor in Atlanta, we are in the top five in size, depth and management quality."

The articulate, self-confident Cordy personifies his company's motto, "We dare to excel." In addition to his responsibilities at AMC, he serves as chairman or as chief executive officer of Urban Communications, Inc., Urban Trans Media, Inc., Urban Cable Training Center, and Atlanta Airport Shuttle. He employs more than 400 persons in the various ventures.

Cordy is involved in nearly every aspect of AMC's day-to-day operation. For example, when the company began the Schlitz project, he moved to New York to serve personally as project manager. He says he is constantly working to ensure that AMC produces "high quality work."

"We deliver a quality product. We deliver what we promise at a fair profit with honesty and integrity."

AMC's growth in 10 years has made relocation necessary three times. Founded in 1972 at 255 Spring St., the company moved in 1973 to 242 Walker St. It occupied its present building at 463 Plum St. in 1977, and expanded the facility in 1981.

Headquarters of AMC Mechanical Contractors, 463 Plum Street

Arthur Andersen & Co.

From eight people in 1940 to more than 500 in 1982, the Atlanta office of the public accounting firm of Arthur Andersen & Co. has grown to become the largest professional practice in the Southeastern United States.

Today clients include approximately 40 per cent of Atlanta's 50 largest public companies and nearly half of all Georgia-based companies listed on the New York Stock Exchange. At the same time, service to small- and medium-size companies constitutes a major share of the office's practice.

This full-service approach is further emphasized by the fact that the office's audit practice is augmented by dominant tax and management information consulting divisions, each with more than 100 specialists.

When Arthur Andersen & Co. made the decision to open here 42 years ago, it was with the knowledge that Atlanta was destined to lead the Southeast into a new era. From the outset, the Atlanta office of Arthur Andersen & Co. made a point of participating in civic and educational matters while structuring its own growth so it could develop along with the emerging industries of the city and region.

That commitment to industry specialization is evident in a quick look at the office makeup today. Industry teams, each consisting of professionals in accounting, auditing, consulting and tax matters, are active in such areas as banking, the carpet industry, construction, education, electric and gas, health care, high technology, hospitality, international business, insurance, manufacturing and service, real estate, small business, retail/distribution, state and local government, telephone and transportation.

Arthur Andersen & Co. is proud of its Atlanta heritage and considers its commitment to the city a major reason for its success. This commitment is underscored by the continuity and leadership of the managing partner group.

From William J. Nettles, who opened the firm's first Atlanta office in the William-Oliver Building, to Albert J. Bows Jr., to Samuel E. Hudgins, to James D. Edwards, who will lead the office into new headquarters in the Georgia-Pacific Building in 1983, the office has had only four managing partners in 42 years.

Arthur Andersen's Atlanta strategy—commitment to the city and to the industries which would lead the region—has resulted not only in an outstanding growth record, but has enabled the firm to parallel the city's own growth as a regional leader.

From its Atlanta base, Arthur Andersen & Co. has opened offices in Charlotte, Birmingham, Chattanooga and Tampa. Today these offices, combined with Atlanta personnel, total more than 1,000 people throughout the Southeast.

The future looks better than ever. Atlanta has clearly established itself as the heart of the Southeastern portion of the Sunbelt and is well positioned to share in our country's turn towards the sun.

Just as it has for 42 years, Arthur Andersen & Co. will support Atlanta's government, civic and business leadership as it continues to make the future happen, and make Atlanta what it will be tomorrow.

William J. Nettles, managing partner (1941-1959)

James D. Edwards, managing partner (1979-present)

Arnall, Golden & Gregory

Former Governor Ellis Arnall (left), Sol Golden (center), and the late Cleburne Gregory Jr.

When former Georgia Governor Ellis Arnall, Sol Golden and the late Cleburne Gregory Jr. organized their law practice in 1949, they were relatively young, but each had already achieved remarkable records in public service and in the law.

Arnall was only 40 but had already been speaker pro-tem of the Georgia House of Representatives, attorney-general and Governor (1943-47).

Gregory had been assistant attorney-general. And Golden had developed a national reputation as a skilled corporate attorney; indeed, it was a prominent New York corporation president who introduced Golden to his future partners.

Arnall's skills as a litigator were nationally known. While he accomplished numerous reforms during his years in public life—including abolishing the voting poll tax, revoking the state charter of the Ku Klux Klan and introducing the planned teacher retirement system—his political career will likely best be remembered for his successful legal battle to bring economic equality to the South.

Up through World War II the South had remained primarily agricultural, and poor. Manufacturers in the region couldn't operate plants economically because of unequal railroad freight rates favoring Northern industrial states. The railroads charged 39 per cent more to ship finished goods from the South to the North than from the North southward.

Arnall, working closely with Gregory when they were both in the attorney-general's office, brought suit on behalf of the people of Georgia against the then-powerful Pennsylvania Railroad. In 1945, when Arnall was Governor, the case was heard by the U.S. Supreme Court, and he personally argued it before the high court, which sided with the state.

The decision opened the way for the postwar economic boom not only in Georgia but throughout the South and West, which also had been discriminated against.

In the same spirit, the firm of Arnall, Golden & Gregory has represented corporations and industries wrestling against unfair trade practices.

In the 1950s, for example, the firm received national attention when it successfully represented Hollywood's independent movie producers, including Walt Disney and David Selznick, who complained the large studios, through ownership of the major theater chains, had an unfair advantage in getting theater bookings. The suit forced the major studios to divest their theater chains.

Through its work the firm has attracted a wide range of clients. They include such major Atlanta organizations as Rollins, Inc., National Distributing Co. and Ackerman & Co.; such national firms as Eastman Kodak, Rich Products Corp., General Foods and Burlington Northern, Inc.; and such international firms as Hexalon Real Estate, Inc., Wilma, Inc., and the Canadian Pacific Railroad.

To handle its ever-increasing workload, the firm has enlarged its professional staff, particularly since 1975. It has 30 partners and some 40 associates. Its Washington office is headed by Charles White, former chief trial attorney for the Interstate Commerce Commission.

Among Atlanta law firms, according to the *American Lawyer Guide,* Arnall Golden & Gregory has in recent years the lowest associate turnover, the highest growth in the number of professional personnel, and provides the greatest opportunity for professional advancement.

Periodically, attorneys of the firm leave to pursue careers in public service: U.S. Rep. Elliot Levitas and Fulton County Superior Court Judge Joel Fryer are former partners; State Supreme Court Justice Charles Weltner and former U.S. Rep. Ben Blackburn were associates.

The Atlanta Coca-Cola Bottling Company

Arthur Montgomery, working in 1900 as a shipping agent for Southern Express Company, watched with interest as increasing numbers of crates of bottled Coca-Cola were sent from Atlanta to outlying towns.

Knowing a good thing when he saw it, Montgomery sought out J. B. Whitehead and J. T. Lupton, owners of The Chattanooga Coca-Cola Bottling Company, and secured a job in 1902 as manager of their Atlanta bottling plant. Later that year, the Company was reorganized, and Montgomery bought a one-third interest for $6,000.

The Atlanta Coca-Cola Bottling Company was born on January 30, 1903, when Whitehead, Lupton and Montgomery were granted a charter by Fulton Superior Court.

L. F. Montgomery

Arthur Montgomery

Arthur L. Montgomery

The first Atlanta bottling plant was largely a one-man operation, with most of the work done on a foot-powered bottle washer and filler. From its facility at 78 Auburn Ave., the Company served 35 counties stretching from Atlanta to the Tennessee line.

The Company grew rapidly the first few years as the popularity of Coca-Cola increased throughout the South. The Atlanta plant bottled 10,391 gallons of syrup in 1903, and by 1912 its volume had increased to 53,429 gallons.

Joining the Company in 1908 was L. F. Montgomery, Arthur's nephew, who eventually learned every aspect of the Company's operation by assuming a wide range of responsibilities.

Arthur Montgomery died on September 5, 1940, but the tradition of steady growth was carried on by L. F. Montgomery who led the Company until shortly before his death in 1965.

Always an innovator, The Atlanta Coca-Cola Bottling Company's introduction of new products and packages has made it an industry leader over the years. It was among the first to introduce soft drinks for home consumption in the 1940s, and it pioneered the production of metric containers in the 1970s.

Other innovations have included the first returnable quart bottles, the first plastic-coated, non-returnable bottles, and the first liter returnable bottles. These industry firsts have helped make the Company one of the top three bottling companies in the United States.

In 1979 the Company was bought by The Coca-Cola Company for $65 million. Until that time, third-generation bottler and part-owner Arthur L. Montgomery, son of L. F. Montgomery, had served as board chairman.

Today, The Atlanta Coca-Cola Bottling Company has increased its territory to 40 counties and serves about one-third of the state's population. Its three plants in Atlanta, College Park and Marietta produce and sell the equivalent of more than 45 million cases of 6½-ounce bottles each year.

The Atlanta Coca-Cola Bottling Company has always been an involved good citizen in the community in which it operates, a commitment which undoubtedly has contributed to its success as a local enterprise. That practice continues today.

According to Richard H. Horsey, current president and chief operating executive since 1965, "In spite of our notable growth, we've not forgotten the importance of the small things, the human things, that give a 'soul,' if you will, to a business in its relations with its customers, its employees, and the community from which it draws its livelihood. And may we never forget them in the long and successful future we see ahead."

Some Faces In Our Past

The Boys High School football team of 1914, led by Coach Wood, ended the season with five wins and two losses.

The Atlanta Crackers looked cheerful enough as they sat for this 1909 photograph. That year they won the pennant. They have been identified as (from left, front row) Lattimer, Winters, Leidy, Bush, Krug and Frank; back row (from left), Creighton, Storch, Ely, Baker, Pabst (with mustache), Henley, Wilson and Hoffmeister. Ah, where are they when we need a pennant winner!

In the 1920s this member of the Atlanta Cracker team showed real promise, and fulfilled it: That's Leo Durocher, later a major league coach.

The Atlanta Falcons

Leeman Bennett

Running back William Andrews (#31)

When ground was broken April 15, 1964, for Atlanta-Fulton County Stadium, the American and National Football Leagues began to seriously consider this city as the home for a new professional football team.

On June 20, 1965, the National Football League owners voted to expand to Atlanta. Ten days later the new franchise was awarded to Rankin M. Smith, 41-year-old executive vice president of the Life Insurance Company of Georgia, for approximately $8.5 million.

After several months of organizing the new club, a radio contest was held to select a nickname for the team. The name "Falcons" was suggested by Julia Elliott, a Griffin school teacher.

The first players joined the Falcons Sept. 9 when Bob Paremore of Florida A&M and Gary Barnes of Clemson were signed. In November the team's first-round draft choices were Tommy Nobis, All-American linebacker from the University of Texas, and quarterback Randy Johnson of Texas A&I.

Atlanta was soon caught up in the excitement of its newest professional sport. By Dec. 24 season ticket sales had to be stopped at 45,000.

The Falcon's first head coach was named in January, 1966. Formerly a member of Vince Lombardi's staff at Green Bay, Norb Hecker immediately went to work selecting the 42 players to be signed in the February expansion draft. Three players were chosen from each of the 14 established teams.

In July, a month after the AFL and NFL merged to form today's National Football League, the Atlanta Falcons opened their first training camp at a YMCA facility near Asheville, N.C.

The team played its first regular season game Sept. 11, 1966, losing to Los Angeles,

19-15. A 53-yard pass from Randy Johnson to wide receiver Gary Barnes netted Atlanta its first touchdown.

The Falcons' first win came Nov. 20 against the New York Giants at Yankee Stadium. The score was 27-16.

Although the first season ended with a 3-11 record, the Falcons had established themselves as a young, aggressive team not to be taken lightly.

In 1967, Frank Wall was appointed general manager, and the training camp was moved to the campus of East Tennessee State University. Although the team's record that year was a disappointing 1-12-1, linebacker Tommy Nobis provided excitement throughout the season, becoming the first Falcon to be named All-Pro.

The following year, Hecker was replaced as head coach by Norm Van Brocklin. The change in leadership came midway through a season in which the Falcons won only two games.

As Van Brocklin began his first full year as head coach, the Falcons won their first season opener, beating San Francisco, 21-7. In October, 1969, Junior Coffey, last of the original team members, was traded to the Giants.

The highlight of the 1969 season was a 10-7 win over Minnesota, stopping the Vikings' 12-game winning streak and giving the Falcons a 6-8-1 record, best in the club's history up to that time.

In January, 1970, Frank Wall was named team president, and Rankin Smith became chairman of the board. Van Brocklin was given the additional title of general manager.

Though the 1970 season began on an optimistic note (the best pre-season in the team's history, 4-1), the Falcons' overall record slipped to 4-8-2.

The following year, the club moved to

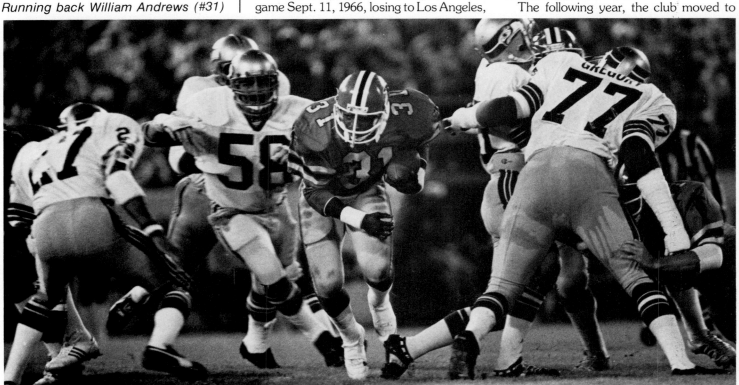

Mick Luckhurst

Mike Kenn

Steve Bartkowski

another training camp, Furman University, in Greenville, S.C. With a 24-20 victory over New Orleans in the final game of 1971, the Falcons completed their first winning season (7-6-1).

In the 1972 home opener, the Falcons crushed Los Angeles, the first time they had beaten the Rams. The highlight of the game was the performance of running back Dave Hampton, who scored two touchdowns and rushed for a team record of 161 yards. Unfortunately, the team managed only a 4-8-2 record for the season.

When the 1973 season opened with a 62-7 rout of New Orleans, 35 team records were smashed during the game. Another team record was set that year as the Falcons won seven games straight on their way to a 9-5 season.

Van Brocklin was fired in 1974 after the season began with three straight losses. Defensive coordinator Marion Campbell replaced him as head coach, but the Falcons managed only a 3-11 record.

In 1975 Pat Peppler was named general manager, quarterback Steve Bartkowski was drafted, and Hampton rushed for more than 1,000 yards. The team's record, however, showed little improvement: The Falcons won four and lost 10.

When the 1976 season got off to a 1-4 start, Campbell was fired and Peppler stepped in as interim coach for the remainder of the season.

After 11 years and only two winning seasons, changes made in 1977 turned the Falcons around. Eddie LeBaron joined the club as general manager, Rankin Smith Jr. was named president, and Los Angeles defensive coordinator Leeman Bennett was hired as head coach.

"Somehow, some way, we'll find a way to win," Bennett said. His attitude was reflected in the team's performance his first year; the Falcons went 7-7 and established a new 14-game NFL record for fewest points allowed, 129.

As Bennett prepared for his second season, the Falcons moved their offices from the Stadium to a year-round training

facility at Suwanee, Ga., described by many as the finest in the NFL.

The 1978 season brought a record of 9-7, and the first playoff appearance in the club's history. Atlanta got national attention as the "Miracle Falcons" won game after game with dramatic plays in the closing minutes of the fourth quarter. A high point of the season came on "Monday Night Football" when Tim Mazzetti kicked five field goals to give the Falcons a 15-7 victory over Los Angeles.

In their first playoff game, the NFC Wild-card contest, the Falcons beat Philadelphia, 14-13, with two Bartkowski touchdown passes in the final eight minutes. The next week the Falcons lost a closely contested playoff game, 27-20, to Dallas after leading 20-13 at the half.

The 1979 season was not so kind to Bennett and the Falcons; they slid to a 6-10 mark. But Bennett remained confident in his long-range strategy for building the team. A bright spot in the season was rookie William Andrews, a running back who set team records for most yards in a game, 167, and most in a season, 1,023.

Bennett's non-wavering philosophy paid off in 1980 as the Falcons won their first Western Division title, made their second appearance in the playoffs and went 12-4 for the best record in pro football.

Many predicted the Falcons would reach the Super Bowl in 1981, but they finished way short with a record of seven wins and nine losses. Though disappointed, Bennett did not lose his confidence or enthusiasm for the next season.

According to Bennett, "A lot of things went wrong last year, but we still have a solid young nucleus that is capable of winning a lot of football games."

The Atlanta Falcons entered the 1982 season with an improved defense and the same offense that was second in the NFL last year in points scored.

With his characteristic optimism, Bennett predicts that the 1982 team will "find a way to bounce back into the winning ways."

Buddy Curry

Atlanta Gas Light Company

The most important single event in the history of the Company occurred in 1929-30 when it began serving natural gas rather than manufactured gas. Soon the cleaner, cheaper fuel replaced coal as the dominant heating fuel in Atlanta homes. This preference for natural gas as a home heating fuel continues today.

Although founded originally to provide street lighting for the City of Atlanta, the Company began selling gas for cooking in the early 1880s. This "new" use began to catch on with the public, due partly to such sophisticated advertising as shown in this early 1900s photo.

On Christmas Day, 1855, the first gas lamp was lighted on Atlanta's streets, bringing gas service to the young city. Hundreds of the town's more than 6,000 residents attended the festivities.

The gas street lamps were instituted partly as a deterrent to nighttime crime, a problem faced by the growing community, but they were also symbolic of the progress of the town once known as "Terminus"—the southern end of the Western and Atlantic Railroad.

Atlanta's oldest business, Atlanta Gas Light Company has evolved from serving one customer—the City of Atlanta—into the largest on-site energy supplier in the state and the largest natural gas distribution company in the Southeast. The Company was incorporated on February 16, 1856, by an act of the Georgia legislature. Today, it operates under the same charter, one of the few such charters still existing.

During Sherman's Atlanta campaign in the spring and summer of 1864, the city's gas supply survived three battles and a 40-day siege. The gas plant buildings suffered only minor damage in the relentless bombardment.

In mid-November Sherman ordered the destruction of the city as his troops prepared for the infamous "March to the Sea." On November 13, 1864, the gas works were demolished, leaving the city without service.

After service was restored on September 15, 1866, the Company's growth paralleled the city's—rising from the ashes of war stronger than ever.

A new use for gas was introduced in 1881 when the Company began selling ranges to Atlanta homemakers. Later, gas-fired water heaters came into use, prompting a change in the utility's charter to allow it to sell gas "for any and all purposes."

Soon the Company's major stockholder, City of Atlanta, sold its original Atlanta Gas Light stock to finance various activities: $50,000 for land for the founding of Georgia Tech; $15,000 for the Cotton States Exposition Building at Piedmont Park; $25,000 for Boys' High School, and $5,635 for a school building in the Fourth Ward.

By 1903, Atlanta Gas Light had 122 miles of gas main, 11,000 meters and an average daily distribution of 1,629,500 cubic feet of gas.

The most important event in the Company's history was the change—on April 4, 1930—from manufactured to natural gas. The new gas, piped in from wells in Louisiana by Southern Natural Gas Co., was cleaner, safer and more economical. Soon it began to replace coal in home and industry, creating a far cleaner Atlanta.

In its more than 125-year history, Atlanta Gas Light has undergone a number of ownership changes. In 1884, United Gas Improvement Company (UGI), of Philadelphia, began distributing gas in Atlanta, and two years later the two companies merged, with UGI gaining financial control. Local control returned in 1903 when Georgia Railway and Electric Company acquired UGI's gas properties. Although additional changes occurred, the Company continued under its 1856 charter. In 1935 it began a series of purchases and mergers that eventually made it the region's largest gas distribution company.

On November 1, 1947—after 61 years as part of a holding company—Atlanta Gas Light became an independent company serving 138,000 customers.

The Company's greatest period of expansion occurred in the 1960s during which it added 35 new communities between Brunswick and Macon to the pipeline system, purchased the distribution systems of Mid-Georgia Natural Gas and Mid-Georgia Gas companies, and extended service into northeast and northwest Georgia. By October, 1970, the Company was serving more than 600,000 customers. A merger in 1966 with Savannah Gas Company had added over 34,000 customers.

In 1972 construction was finished on the Company's first complete liquefied natural gas plant in Riverdale. The $15 million project has a storage capacity of 2,538 million cubic feet of natural gas and a daily send-out capacity of 200 million feet.

A second plant, with storage and regasification facilities only, was completed in 1977. Located in Middle Georgia, the facility has a 19-million gallon storage tank for liquefied natural gas. These LNG plants, along with eight propane plants throughout the state, and underground storage of natural gas, provide supplemental gas supplies on the days of maximum use when delivery contracts with the pipeline companies do not provide enough gas for customers' needs.

In 1981 the Company was serving more than 850,000 customers in more than 200 Georgia cities and towns, and reported operating revenues of nearly $830 million with a net income of $14 million.

Some Faces
In Our Past

This proper little girl became well known as the wife of one of Atlanta's major mercantile entrepreneurs, the founder of Rich's department store. She is Mrs. Morris Rich.

This handsome couple, who are unidentified, sat in photographer Julius Kuhns' studio for this portrait in the 1880s.

Photographer C. W. Motes, seen earlier in this book (dressed in his Confederate uniform), took this photograph of proud Mrs. Annah Gibson on June 23, 1886.

Louise Kuhns was sure her picture would turn out well: It was taken by her husband, photographer Julius Kuhns.

Mrs. John Thomas Glenn was the wife of a noted lawyer who died in 1899.

Atlanta Life Insurance Company

The Atlanta Life Insurance Company is the legacy of a child born a slave on a plantation near Social Circle, Ga., in 1858.

This child, Alonzo Franklin Herndon, mastered the art of barbering in his early years and moved to Atlanta to open what was reputedly the grandest barber shop in the world.

There, in the shop on Peachtree Street, Herndon earned a living with razors and clippers. But his life was devoted to a larger quest: to encourage economic independence and growth among black Americans.

Seventy-seven years later—just blocks from the site of that first barber pole—stands the symbol of what Herndon achieved: Atlanta Life Insurance Company, the largest proprietary insurance company owned and operated by blacks nationwide, and the largest black-owned business in the United States based on net worth.

The sleek headquarters at 100 Auburn Avenue is the home office to more than 60 offices in 12 states, with assets totaling $112 million, insurance in force amounting to $1 billion, and more than one million policyholders.

Thousands have obtained employment; homes, businesses and churches have been financed, and the burdens of illness and death have been lessened by the millions of dollars paid to policyholders.

This mission began humbly, however, as Herndon and several other prominent black entrepreneurs purchased the Atlanta Benevolent and Protective Association in 1905.

The Association had been founded by the Wheat Street Baptist Church to help members through financial crises and provide funds for burial. Herndon renamed it the Atlanta Mutual Association and set up a one-room office in the Rucker Building.

A few weeks after registering with the State and paying a $5,000 deposit to insure policyholders' contributions, the Company moved to a Herndon-owned structure at 202 Auburn Avenue, and dedicated itself to giving every policyholder financial relief and a "square deal."

Herndon and his management team hired black men and women throughout the state as Atlanta Mutual agents—employment opportunities not available in the few white-owned companies that insured black risks.

The early years were hard, but Atlanta Mutual's appeal to the black community to support a company that offered both employment and insurance against illness and death was answered in force.

In September, 1916, 11 years after its founding, Atlanta Mutual was reorganized as a stock company with capital stock of $25,000. Six years later it became a legal reserve institution with authority to write all classes of insurance—and was renamed Atlanta Life.

Herndon died in 1927, leaving his son Norris Bumstead Herndon to fulfill his mission as president in 1928. The 45 years that Herndon headed Atlanta Life brought many Company milestones.

Herndon led the business through the great Depression, paying every justified claim, and through the personnel shortages brought by World War II. Under his

Atlanta Life Insurance Company grew out of a barber's vision.

Alonzo Franklin Herndon

Norris Bumstead Herndon

A. F. Herndon's 25-chair barbershop:
"The Finest In the World"

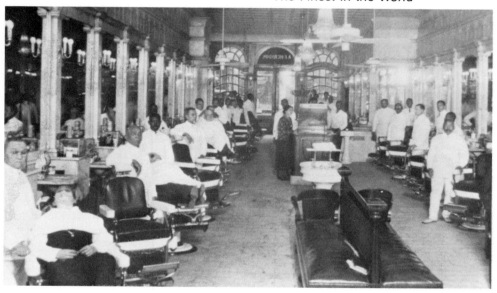

guidance, the firm moved to the top of the insurance industry as the largest stock company organized and operated by blacks.

In 1950 Norris Herndon established the Alonzo F. and Norris B. Herndon Foundation, Inc., as a memorial to his father and a means of ensuring that Atlanta Life would remain a major black-owned enterprise. This also meant that his philanthropy and the legacy of the Herndons would continue.

In 1973 Norris Herndon retired, passing the mantle to Jesse Hill Jr. Hill's election as the Company's third president and the rise of a new management team constituted the first major reorganization of Atlanta Life since the 1920s.

Throughout this period Atlanta Life continued to be a strong source of mortgage loans for the black populace while maintaining a record of community service in the areas of housing, jobs and black business gains. The Company charted a future course: to increase service to the growing black middle class.

The 104,000-square-foot Atlanta Life Insurance headquarters building at 100 Auburn Avenue testifies to the growth and maturity of the major corporation that grew out of a barber's vision.

Completed in 1980, the striking marble edifice houses hundreds of employees serving policyholders nationwide.

The atrium and halls of the home office provide a fitting backdrop for the work of black artists recognized by the Company through its national annual art competition.

This commitment is one more reminder of the quest for economic dignity that Atlanta Life's founder undertook, and the importance that insurance has played in enabling black wage earners to obtain employment and build a strong economic foundation.

Former home office: 148 Auburn Avenue

Atlanta Market Center

For more than 20 years the Atlanta Market Center (AMC) has played a significant role in the efficient wholesaling of consumer products in this country.

Since its inception as a 1 million square foot mart in July, 1961, this giant marketing facility has grown to encompass three trade buildings—the Atlanta Merchandise Mart, the Atlanta Apparel Mart and the Atlanta Decorative Arts Center.

Today, AMC provides more than 3.5 million square feet, or 81 acres, of display space for wholesale goods.

The Atlanta Market Center is a marketplace for manufactureres and wholesalers to sell to retailers and designers who, in turn, market these products to the consumer.

Approximately $10 billion in orders for domestic and foreign merchandise are placed in the Market Center each year by buyers representing retail stores across the U.S. and the world. Designers and architects from throughout the East Coast purchase and specify design-oriented items from the Decorative Arts Center for resale to clients for homes and offices. These sales support manufacturing and retail employment throughout the Southeast.

The three facilities annually attract 300,000 buyers and visitors to Atlanta, generating one-fourth of the city's convention business.

The Atlanta Market Center was the brainchild of architect/developer John C. Portman Jr., principal owner of the complex. A successful trial market in 1957 convinced Portman of the viability of an Atlanta wholesale market facility.

Construction of the first mart began in 1959. In July, 1961, the 22-story Merchandise Mart opened its doors at the corner of Peachtree and Harris Streets as a showcase for home furnishings, floor coverings, gifts, decorative accessories and apparel.

In 1968 the building was doubled in size to accommodate the sustained growth of buyer activity and showroom demand. AMC annually hosts more than 40 "markets," or week-long buying periods when various industries invite specialty retailers to place orders.

The Atlanta Decorative Arts Center (ADAC) also came to life in 1961. To complement the Merchandise Mart's service to retail buyers, ADAC serves interior designers and architects with high quality furnishings, drapery and upholstery fabrics, wall and floor coverings and decorative accessories in a facility on Peachtree Hills Avenue in Buckhead. Expanded twice, ADAC is the largest single display facility for design furnishings east of the Mississippi River. It is owned by Mrs. Jan Portman.

Plans for major expansions, starting in 1982, of the Merchandise Mart and the Decorative Arts Center will add 1 million square feet to the market center complex.

Signaling Atlanta's heightened stature in world trade, a third AMC facility—the Apparel Mart—opened adjacent to the Merchandise Mart in November, 1979. The apparel industry's move into its impressive new home, four times larger than its previous space in the Merchandise Mart, established Atlanta as the fashion capital of the Southeast. The Apparel Mart is a major sales outlet for Southeastern manufacturers, generating jobs in Georgia's second largest industry.

Reflecting its growing involvement in international trade, the Atlanta Market Center worked with other Atlanta companies such as Coca-Cola, C&S Bank and the international business community to launch the World Trade Club of Atlanta.

The Club opened atop the Merchandise Mart in 1982. Sam A. Williams, general manager of the Atlanta Market Center and chairman of the World Trade Club of Atlanta, said, "The Club provides an important base for international business dealings that encourage greater foreign investment in, and exports from, the Southeast."

Rooted in the Southeast's stable economy, the Atlanta Market Center in just two decades has become an anchor for international marketing activity. "Given the opportunities for trade and investment in the Southeast and the Market Center's record of development, the Atlanta Market Center will continue to provide important leadership in consumer products marketing for many years to come," Williams predicts.

A fashion show in the Atrium Theatre of the Atlanta Apparel Mart

The Atlanta Apparel Mart (foreground) and the Atlanta Merchandise Mart (right rear of the Apparel Mart)

Bank Of The South

Erected in 1955, the Bank of the South Building at the corner of Marietta and Forsyth was Atlanta's first major "skyscraper." The Bank was known as Fulton National from its inception in 1909 until the name was changed in 1980.

Bank of the South began in 1909 at a time when many Atlanta banks were being merged on the theory that the bigger the institution, the better the ability to compete for large corporate accounts.

A physician, Dr. William J. Blalock, is credited with recognizing the need for a bank serving individuals and smaller businesses. In December that year, the Fulton National Bank, as it was known until 1980, opened at Peachtree and Forsyth Streets, with Dr. Blalock as president.

Early in the Bank's history, three individuals became major investors, and their descendants have remained actively involved, both as officers and directors.

The first was Bolling Jones, at the time postmaster of Atlanta, who served as Bank president in 1928 and was chairman from 1929 to 1933. His great-nephew, Gordon Jones, was president from 1958-81 and chairman of the executive committee after that, leading the Bank through its period of greatest growth.

The second was Clarence Haverty, president of Haverty Furniture Cos., who became a director in 1910 and was chairman of the board from 1939 to 1958; his son Rawson, became the Bank's chairman in 1977, a position he still holds, and he also became head of the retail furniture chain.

The third was Marion Smith, partner in the prominent law firm of Kilpatrick & Cody. Various partners in the law firm have continued as directors following Smith.

A major event occurred in 1955 when the bank's 25-story headquarters tower opened. The 527,000 square-foot building at the corner of Marietta and Forsyth Streets was the city's first major skyscraper.

The brainchild of Dallas developer Leo Corrigan, it was erected on the site of the old Federal Building, used also as City Hall. The Bank occupied the plaza level plus five stories, and Corrigan set out to lease the rest. Some thought he wouldn't succeed. With offices leasing for $2 a square foot, they said no one would pay the building's price of $4.

But soon after it opened, the new building was occupied by major corporations seeking a prestigious downtown location. In 1980 the building underwent extensive renovations, and a handsome limestone exterior was overlayed on the original brick exterior.

Over the years the institution became an important source of financing for major corporations as well as for individuals and smaller firms. A trust department was established, and the Bank became a major depository for City, County and State funds. To prepare for the future, in 1968 a parent holding company was established; within a decade, banks in DeKalb, Clayton, Gwinnett, Cobb and Fulton Counties were acquired.

The 1980s began with the Bank changing its name to Bank of the South, and the holding company to Bank South Corporation. In 1981 Gordon Jones, who has served the bank for 41 years, was succeeded by Robert P. Guyton, a nationally known executive who had been chief executive officer of three other banks before joining Bank South.

The institution now competes for business nationally and has established broad experience in international trade, particularly to South America. With resources of $1.4 billion, Bank South has grown to become the fourth largest bank in Georgia and one of the 200 largest in the nation.

Beers Construction Company

Clayton General Hospital

The Coca-Cola Company headquarters

Southern Bell Telephone Company headquarters complex

Harold W. Beers entered the concrete construction business in 1907 as chief engineer of the Southern Ferro Concrete Company.

At that time, the Company, founded two years earlier by Charles Loridans, was helping pioneer in the use of reinforced concrete in construction. Reinforced concrete, as an alternative to structural steel, was a new concept that was quickly gaining acceptance.

Southern Ferro assisted in the construction of the Atlanta Terminal Station, the Bibb County Courthouse, the Andrew Jackson Hotel in Nashville, Tenn., and several railroad terminals in the Southeast.

When the U.S. entered World War I, the entire Company was taken over by the Federal government and employed in the construction of Camp Gordon, the Dublin Army Hospital and several other military facilities.

The Company resumed normal operations after the war, but its activity ground to a halt with the onset of the great Depression.

To continue and complete the work that had been initiated prior to that time, Beers Construction Company was formed in 1935.

In the ensuing years, the Southeast experienced unparalleled growth. The population upsurge resulting from economic expansion created a tremendous demand for building construction.

Just 20 years after its formation, Beers Construction Company's sales totaled nearly $100 million. H. W. Beers served as president until 1950, when his son H. W. Beers Jr. assumed control of the business.

Today, the Company's growth continues under the leadership of Larry Gellerstedt Jr., president and majority owner. Hired by Beers in 1946, Gellerstedt says that while the Company's gross work volume has increased each year, growth has been permitted to proceed only at a rate that allows the Company to maintain its traditional high-quality work.

"We do all our work in Georgia," he says. "We have no desire to go national."

Because of the confidence the Company has earned over the years, all of its contracts in the past decade have been negotiated—not secured in competitive bidding. The fact that Beers is capable of negotiating its contracts is a tribute to its reputation for good work and low costs.

According to Gellerstedt, obtaining a contract through negotiation allows his Company to work closely with the architects and engineers each step of the way.

"With a team approach, you can test the market, analyzing every piece of the job, and save a great deal of money for the customer," he says.

A contractor that began as a concrete company, Beers has not forgotten its roots: Today, most of its work still is done with reinforced concrete.

Most recently, Beers constructed the two million square foot Southern Bell headquarters complex using reinforced concrete. Other Beers projects have included The Coca-Cola Company headquarters and AT&T Southern Region Headquarters.

Since 1975 Beers has completed work on 15 hospital projects at a total cost of more than $100 million. The hospitals include Piedmont, Egleston, Northside, Emory, Cobb General, Clayton General, and Crawford W. Long.

Century 21 Of the Southeast, Inc.

For several years prior to 1971 California real estate brokers Art Bartlett and Marsh Fisher shared a growing concern that the real estate brokerage business in many quarters suffered from an "unprofessional" image.

From early discussions of the problem grew the concept of a nationwide network of independent brokers bound by a common dedication to professionalism and improved marketing.

That concept came to fruition as Century 21, a national organization headquartered in Irvine, Calif. More than 7,000 locally owned, independent real estate firms are franchised affiliates of Century 21. Brokers and sales associates now number more than 80,000.

Training programs by Century 21 are designed to help brokers and associates list and sell property more effectively, serve their clients and customers better and generally raise their level of professionalism.

In addition, Century 21 brokers participate in a national referral system which is made more effective by Century 21's aggressive national advertising program.

In 1979 Century 21 was acquired by Transworld Corporation, which brought new strength and scope to the organization with no lessening of Century 21 commitment to professionalism. Affiliation with Transworld enabled the company to provide benefits to the full-service broker, not only for residential sales but also in sales of commercial and investment property and property management.

In 1976 Century 21 established its Southeastern office in Atlanta in recognition of the city's growth as a regional business center. Today there are more than 100 Century 21 real estate firms in metropolitan Atlanta, with over 1,300 brokers and sales associates.

Each firm retains its separate name and identity but uses the familiar Century 21 logo, which is known from coast to coast. Century 21 agents are trained to *look* professional as well as act professional. Many wear the traditional Century 21 gold blazer or other standard items of clothing when showing property.

Fred K. Rhoden, an experienced real estate professional, is president and regional director of Century 21 in the Southeast. Mr. Rhoden, before joining Century 21 of the Southeast, Inc. as its president, served as vice president/regional marketing director.

The familiar Century 21 logo is known to buyers and sellers of homes from coast to coast. In Metro Atlanta there are more than 1,300 Century 21 brokers and sales associates.

Fred K. Rhoden, president, Century 21 Of the Southeast, Inc.

Training to help brokers and sales associates list and sell property is an integral part of the Century 21 program.

361

The Citizens and Southern National Bank

The headlines of the Sunday morning *Atlanta Constitution* and *Journal* announced the opening with great anticipation. Full-page ads confirmed the announcement with the declaration, "No account too large, none too small."

Such was the manner in which The Citizens and Southern Bank first opened its doors in Atlanta at the corner of Broad and Marietta Streets on September 29, 1919. Coming to Atlanta with over $50 million in assets, C&S was already the largest bank in Georgia.

Today, it is still the largest, with assets exceeding $5 billion and more than 150 banking locations throughout Georgia.

The history of C&S dates from a time when Atlanta was just beginning to recover from the burdens of Reconstruction, and Savannah was the economic center of the state.

The Citizens Bank of Savannah was chartered in September, 1887. In 1888 the board of directors invited Mills B. Lane to buy into the institution and serve as vice president.

Lane had worked with his father's bank, the R. Y. Lane Banking Company in Valdosta, and had introduced several new, efficient techniques into the banking system. Among these procedures were to-the-penny balancing and checks drawn against a customer's personal account.

Until that time, all balancing had been rounded to the nearest nickel, and checks had been drawn against the bank itself.

Lane brought his banking expertise to Savannah, becoming president of The Citizens Bank of Savannah in 1901 and leading the institution to become what was then the second largest bank in Georgia. The largest bank in the state at that time was the Southern Bank of The State of Georgia, also in Savannah.

In February, 1906, these banks merged, creating the forerunner of the C&S system today—The Citizens and Southern Bank.

From that point on C&S grew as Georgia grew, branching throughout the state. The first move was made in 1912, just six years after the merger, when C&S opened an office in Augusta. C&S later expanded to Macon, Athens and Valdosta. In 1919, C&S made the move that proved to be the pivotal point in the Bank's history.

Mills Lane realized that Atlanta was destined to become the economic hub not only of the state, but of the entire Southeast.

When it became known that the Third National Bank of Atlanta was for sale, C&S bought this Bank and, on September 29, 1919, opened its doors in a building directly across the street from where it is headquartered today.

It was from this historic moment that C&S began to take an active part in Atlanta's development and to share in the young city's vibrant, healthy growth.

In May, 1927, C&S received its national charter. In 1929 C&S moved to its present location in Atlanta at 35 Broad Street, then the second largest office building in the city. The Bank retained the services of award-winning architect Phillip Trammel Shutze to renovate the building in a style that would represent the financial solidarity of the Bank.

Shutze did just that, designing the lobby to be a replica of the Pantheon in Rome. Today, The Citizens and Southern National Bank corporate headquarters building is listed on the National Register of Historic Places.

The Citizens and Southern Banks in Georgia continued to grow even though the great Depression, and by the mid-1940s had become a system of 22 banking locations managing assets of more than $300 million.

In the summer of 1945, Mills B. Lane Sr. died, ending an era of banking in Georgia. His legacy was to live through his son, Mills B. Lane Jr., who became president of C&S in 1946.

Mills Lane Jr. inherited from his father the ability to direct banking operations in an innovative manner. During his 25-year tenure as president of C&S, the Bank experienced rapid growth, seeing its $300 million in assets multiply almost 10 times to nearly $3 billion. His flamboyant, creative style was well known in banking circles and around the state.

Mills Lane Jr. also believed in the sound fundamentals of banking. Two innovative programs that had a significant impact on the banking industry and the public came about in the late 1950s.

The first was the C&S Charge Card. When introduced in 1958, it was the first independent credit card to be issued by a bank in the nation. The second innovation came a year later as an extension of the C&S Charge Card service. It was called Instant Money.

Instant Money enabled a C&S customer to make a loan without taking the time to complete additional paperwork or to await further approval. Using a C&S Charge Card, a loan could be made from a teller, either in the Bank or at a drive-in window location.

C&S has always taken pride in making banking more convenient for its customers. Mills Lane Jr. also led C&S to become a working citizen in towns and cities all over Georgia.

His father had said that, "What's good for the community is good for the Bank," and Lane believed wholeheartedly in this philosophy. As a result, in the late 1960s C&S responded with a very tangible ex-

The laying of the foundation of the first C&S main office in 1907: the Savannah building was constructed on the site where stood the first business establishment in Georgia.

A familiar and well known sight to Atlantans is The C&S Round Building. Erected in the late Sixties as the country's first landscaped office building, it is as much a symbol of C&S' progressive ideas as 35 Broad Street is of the Bank's strong traditions.

pression of corporate responsibility, an event called "Spring Cleaning"—a Bank-sponsored program in which C&S worked with community leaders to organize residents to clean their neighborhoods.

The idea caught on, spread rapidly and evolved into what was known as The Georgia Plan. The success of this program reinforced what Mills Lane Jr. believed: Any community could, on a do-it-yourself basis, revitalize its living and business environment; and a clean, stable neighborhood tends to encourage responsible banking customers. The idea was that simple.

The work involved, however, was a little more difficult. Banking regulations at the time prohibited commercial banks from direct involvement in all the activities that Lane felt necessary to accomplish sound economic redevelopment. Therefore, the Community Development Corporation (CDC) was formed as a subsidiary of C&S Holding Company.

The CDC, capitalized with $1 million taken directly from Bank profits, was intended to encourage the development and improvement of both residential and business communities in the inner-city Atlanta area.

When banking regulations were eventually modified, eliminating the need for the CDC to operate as a separate entity, the Bank assumed these responsibilities. The CDC was merged into the Bank, and later the Enterprise Banking Department was created.

During this period a change occurred in the leadership of the Bank. Mills Lane Jr. retired in 1973 and was followed by Richard L. Kattel, who was succeeded by Bennett A. Brown.

Brown became the chief executive officer in 1979. Brown's beliefs were closely aligned with those of Lane; he believed that he had a personal responsibility to Atlanta, and he stressed that all officers of the Bank should take an active role in their communities.

Brown himself became chairman of Central Atlanta Progress, a nonprofit organization dedicated to the enhancement and economic health of the downtown business district.

Brown's beliefs, along with C&S' philosophy of corporate responsibility, resulted in the Bank's becoming involved in the City of Atlanta Business Improvement Loan Program.

This program was to be a joint venture between the City and C&S Bank, wherein C&S would act as an agent for the City in a direct loan program.

The purpose of this effort was to enable the City to lend funds directly to qualified borrowers at below-market rates to encourage the revitalization of intown Atlanta.

Initially there were two targeted neighborhoods: Little Five Points and Lakewood Heights. As the program grew in popular-

ity, the number of communities expanded to include the Peachtree Walk, Sweet Auburn, Kirkwood, Fairlie-Poplar, University West, Heart of Atlanta (central business district), West End, Bankhead Highway, Home Park and Cascade neighborhoods.

Both the city and C&S benefitted, and the inner core of Atlanta was once again becoming a healthier, more economically stable area.

Cooperation between the City and the Bank continues today. The Enterprise Banking Department is maintaining its course of expanding opportunities for businesses throughout Atlanta.

Through this department, C&S participates in the Renaissance Park Project, an effort to revitalize the old 87-acre Bedford Pine neighborhood, vacant since urban renewal efforts in the mid-1960s.

These current projects are a continuation of C&S activities over the years. C&S was an integral part of the building of Atlanta-Fulton County Stadium, a prime factor in bringing professional sports to the city. Additionally, the Bank has long had a full time economic development department which has been important in bringing new industry to Atlanta and Georgia.

Citizens and Southern Georgia Corporation, parent company of The Citizens and Southern National Bank, is the largest bank holding company in Georgia, and C&S is well aware of the responsibility that comes with such a franchise. Not only has it grown in size, but also in terms of social commitment.

The directors of the Company voluntarily contribute a portion of their annual compensation to a special fund to support institutions of higher education in Georgia. The Bank is also recognized as an industry leader in providing special services to those whose hearing, speech or vision are impaired, offering the first Braille checking account in the Southeast and providing a telecommunications device for the hearing and speech impaired.

The Bank has come a long way from 22 Bull Street in Savannah. Today, C&S and its subsidiaries have offices throughout Georgia, in nine other states and six foreign countries, and employ more than 5,000 persons.

At December 31, 1981, it was the 53rd largest bank holding company in the nation in terms of assets. However, C&S remains committed to its origins and dedicated to continue its leadership as a responsible corporate citizen in Atlanta and other cities that it serves.

The Citizens and Southern National Bank's corporate headquarters is at 35 Broad Street, in downtown Atlanta. The building is listed on the National Register of Historic Places.

Former Atlanta Mayor Ivan Allen visited with Atlantans involved in the Bank's "Spring Cleaning" program. The program began in Savannah in 1968 and became known as The Georgia Plan as it was implemented throughout the State.

Citizens Trust Bank

L. D. Milton

The creation of Citizens Trust Bank was the realization of a dream and a lot of effort by five prominent Atlantans. In 1919 Herman E. Perry headed a committee, including J. A. Robinson, T. J. Ferguson, W. H. King and H. C. Dugas, to establish a bank to serve the urban black community of Atlanta.

Two years later, on August 16, 1921, Citizens Trust Bank opened at 212 Auburn Avenue.

The Bank's founders saw the country on the verge of tremendous growth; they also saw the South moving from an economy dominated by agriculture to one based on industrialization. The change would bring large numbers of people from the rural areas to the city.

The goal of Citizens Trust was service to the community—offering its customers better financial security, promoting better living conditions and better business methods, stressing the principles of thrift and, not least, making home ownership possible for a larger portion of Atlanta's black population.

Those basic goals have not changed, though the Bank has grown to reflect the improved economic status of many of its clients. Citizens Trust, with assets of $60 million, is a full-service bank serving individuals, corporations, small businesses and non-profit organizations.

One of the Bank's early employees was L. D. Milton, a young Morehouse College teacher with an M.A. in economics from Brown University. Milton had saved enough money to buy three shares in Citizens Trust when he asked the Bank officers for a job. Milton started out in the general accounting department but left the Bank two years later to go into business with a partner, C. B. Yates. The two men bought a failing drugstore, turned it into a profitable property and eventually bought four others.

In the meantime, Citizens Trust had suffered from poor management and was floundering. There was even talk of liquidating the Bank.

The National Benefit Life Insurance Company, of Washington, D.C., purchased the Bank and, knowing of Milton's experience and qualifications, asked him to return and rehabilitate Citizens Trust.

Milton, who then owned 56 shares of the Bank's stock, took up the challenge in August, 1927. He managed to place the Bank on such a sound footing that it weathered the stock market crash of 1929 and the succeeding Depression years.

Citizens Trust was among the first banks in the country to reopen their doors after the "bank holiday" in the early 1930s.

Milton became president of Citizens Trust in 1937 and served in that capacity for 34 years. He continued to teach at Morehouse and was later named dean of Atlanta University's Graduate School of Business Administration. The banker served on a number of corporate and institutional boards and was active in community, civic and international affairs.

During his presidency, Citizens Trust opened its 12-story building at 175 Houston St., in downtown Atlanta. The Bank has two other branch offices.

In 1975 I. Owen Funderburg became president. Funderburg, a native Georgian and a graduate of Morehouse College and the University of Michigan School of Finance, was the first black to finish the Stonier School of Banking at Rutgers University.

Funderburg notes the changing philosophical role of Citizens Trust Bank. The Bank's goals have not changed, but its role in the community has.

When society clearly discriminates, as it did at the time the Bank opened and for a number of years thereafter, the role of the black institution is to bring together the resources of the community and hold those resources for their use.

As discrimination lessens, the institution's role is to go beyond the community to create a pool of resources sufficient for the community's needs and to provide access to those resources.

Though Citizens Trust Bank will always identify with the black community, the Bank is not exclusively for that group, and it has expanded its role to provide services to the general Atlanta population. It is a bank that truly reflects the growth and the changes in the city and its people.

The first home of Citizen's Trust, 212 Auburn Avenue

Coach & Six Restaurant

In every great city there is one restaurant where business people, politicians, sports figures and local celebrities gather, the place to go to make a deal over lunch, dinner or for a not-so-casual run-in with an important client.

In Atlanta's history there have been several such places—like the Markham Hotel's dining room in the 1880s and the Kimball House at the turn of the century. Since the 1960s that place has been Beverlee Soloff Shere's Coach & Six Restaurant.

What makes a restaurant the city's informal meeting place? First, it must serve consistently superior food. But there is more. The owner personally must be on hand, building a rapport with patrons, letting them know they are truly welcome and appreciated.

Mrs. Shere's late husband Hank Soloff opened the Coach & Six at 1776 Peachtree Rd. in 1961. While competitors predicted its quick demise because the restaurant was far from downtown, Soloff, once a partner in New York's Coach House restaurant, quickly built a reputation with a gourmet American menu and attentive service.

Soloff, a gregarious man, was always on hand to greet customers and soon became as much a local personality as the people who frequented his restaurant and lounge. As an added touch, he erected a 25-foot long mural behind the bar where artist Peter Jacobsen oil-painted the portraits of regular patrons.

When Soloff had a heart attack in 1968, his wife Beverlee, a former nightclub singer-comedienne, learned the business while he recovered. Then, in 1975, when another heart attack took his life, she took over at the Coach & Six.

Like her husband, Mrs. Shere, who married attorney Ralph Shere in 1977, is on hand each day talking with regular customers. She gives credit to her staff of 105, especially manager Heinz Mielert. Mielert has been with the Coach & Six since it opened, as have the pastry chef, sous chef and broil chef.

Under Mrs. Shere's control the restaurant has maintained its reputation for fine food. The Coach & Six was one of only 50 restaurants presented "A Taste of America" award, which came with an invitation to serve its famed black bean soup during Inaugural Week in Washington. In addition, the restaurant has received awards which it has won annually, like the Business Executives' Dining and the Holiday Magazine Awards.

And the Coach & Six remains the city's premier meeting place. Mrs. Shere likes to recall how in 1976 Jimmy Carter's presidential campaign headquarters was next door. There were numerous nights when campaign workers and party leaders would virtually move into the restaurant and lounge for their meetings.

After 20 years since its founding, the Coach & Six retains its personality. While more casual, trendier dining places have sprung up, the Coach & Six remains a bastion of traditional dining and the unofficial gathering place for Atlanta's elite.

Owner Beverlee Soloff Shere, with the mural of 450 portraits of leading Atlantans behind her.

A landmark for outstanding dining since 1961: the Coach & Six at 1776 Peachtree Road.

The Coca-Cola Company

Created in Atlanta on May 8, 1886, in a druggist's backyard, refreshing Coca-Cola has achieved extraordinary success as the world's favorite soft drink. It is asked for more than 250 million times a day in 80 languages around the globe.

As the world's leading producer and distributor of syrups and concentrates for soft drinks, The Coca-Cola Company today provides more than 35 per cent of all soft drinks enjoyed worldwide, sold through about 4,000 fountain wholesalers and distributors and about 1,500 bottlers in more than 145 countries.

But that success was not overnight in coming. It took the perseverance and dedication of leaders who believed in the product and its potential for greatness—men like Atlantans Asa Candler and Robert Woodruff—to create a legacy for today's management.

According to legend, pharmacist Dr. John Styth Pemberton produced the first batch of syrup for Coca-Cola on a spring day nearly a century ago by mixing the ingredients in a three-legged brass pot in his backyard on Marietta Street.

As the story goes, Dr. Pemberton carried a gallon jug of the syrup down the street to Jacobs' Pharmacy, and whether by design or accident, carbonated water was added to the new syrup to produce a drink that was at once delicious and refreshing.

Frank M. Robinson, one of Pemberton's partners, named the beverage after two of its ingredients, the coca leaf and the kola nut. Thinking that "the two C's would look well in advertising," Robinson calligraphed "Coca-Cola" in the Spencerian script of the day.

Hand-painted oilcloth signs on store awnings soon read "Drink Coca-Cola," and on May 29, 1886, the first print ad for the product appeared in *The Atlanta Journal.*

During the first year, sales averaged 13 drinks per day. Only $50 was realized from the sale of syrup for Coca-Cola—while $73.96 was spent on advertising. This emphasis on advertising has continued for nearly a century, mirroring the changing lifestyles of America and capturing the public's imagination through famous slogans and colorful memorabilia.

In ailing health, Dr. Pemberton soon sold a two-thirds interest to several Atlanta businessmen. In 1888 all of his remaining rights to the product were purchased by Asa Candler, owner of a pharmaceutical company, who proceeded to buy additional rights and acquire complete control. Candler became sole proprietor of Coca-Cola on April 22, 1891, at a cost of $2,300.

Candler had a flair for merchandising, and by 1892 the sales of syrup for Coca-Cola had increased nearly tenfold. With his brother, attorney John S. Candler, Frank Robinson and two other friends he formed a Georgia corporation that year named The Coca-Cola Company, with capital stock of $100,000.

Under Candler, the Company began its vigorous program of trademark protection, which continues today. The trademark "Coca-Cola" was registered in the U.S. Patent Office in 1893. "Coke," first used on labels in 1941, was officially registered in 1945, and the famous 6½-ounce contour bottle, created in 1916, was registered in 1960. Few other packages have been accorded this honor.

Also in 1893 the first dividend was paid to stockholders at $20 per share. Every year since then, dividends have been paid on the Company's common stock.

Joseph A. Biedenharn, a candy merchant, became the first to put Coca-Cola in bottles in 1894 in Vicksburg, Miss., to sell at a picnic. Using syrup shipped from Atlanta, Biedenharn's innovation created a new marketing concept that opened the way to wider distribution of Coca-Cola.

By 1895 branch syrup manufacturing plants had been established in several cities, and Candler stood before the stockholders at the annual meeting in 1895 and announced, "Coca-Cola is now drunk in every state and territory in the United States."

In the first year of the new century,

Atlantan John S. Pemberton (left) first created the syrup for Coca-Cola in a three-legged brass pot in his backyard on Marietta Street. The refreshing beverage became a household word thanks to the powerful leadership of Asa Candler (center), founder of The Coca-Cola Company, and Robert Woodruff, former president and chairman and currently chairman emeritus of the finance committee of the board of directors.

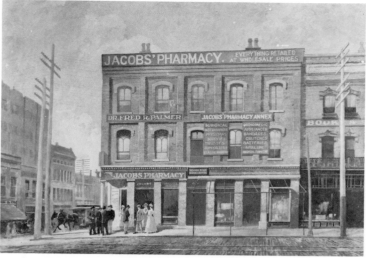

in Victoria and Vancouver, British Columbia. Later that year the beverage was served at a fountain in London where Charles Howard Candler, eldest son of the Company's founder, took a jug of syrup along on a vacation trip.

Others were added to the growing list of countries where Coca-Cola could be purchased in 1900, and from such small beginnings the overseas distribution of syrup began.

Large-scale bottling of Coca-Cola was made possible when Benjamin Franklin Thomas and Joseph Brown Whitehead of Chattanooga, Tenn., secured from Candler in 1899 the exclusive rights to bottle and sell Coca-Cola in practically the entire United States.

Realizing the tremendous task of covering the nation with bottling plants, a search was begun for competent individuals with sufficient capital to run community bottling operations. This marked the beginning of the unique franchise system of bottling plants owned and operated by independent businessmen in specific territories. Today, the Company's commitment to its bottlers remains strong.

To meet the needs of the expanding business, the first headquarters building of The Coca-Cola Company was erected in 1898 on the corner of Atlanta's Edgewood and College Avenues (now Coca-Cola Place).

Candler hailed the new three-story structure as "sufficient for all our needs for all time to come." With the fantastic growth in demand for Coca-Cola, however, the building was inadequate in 10 years.

(Earlier "homes" had included 42½ Decatur Street, on the site of the original Trout House, a leading antebellum hotel that was burned by General Sherman during the Civil War; and 77 Ivy Street, previously the site of Wesley Memorial Methodist Church.)

After outgrowing the Edgewood Avenue location, the Company moved to 1909 Magnolia Street, only a half block west of Dr. Pemberton's home on Marietta Street, where it all began.

By 1919 the Magnolia Street location was overcrowded, and the Company moved its executive offices to the 17th floor of the Candler Building at the corner of Peachtree and Houston Streets. A year later the Company moved to the present location on North Avenue.

In 1919 The Coca-Cola Company was sold to Atlanta banker Ernest Woodruff and an investor group he had organized, for $25 million. The business was reincorporated as a Delaware corporation and its common stock put on public sale for $40 per share.

An investor holding one share since the original offering would have collected more than $5,000 in dividends and, after adjust-

Expansion of the business has taken Coca-Cola to nine "homes" throughout the city. Coca-Cola was originated in 1886 at the Pemberton residence at 107 Marietta Street and first sold at Jacobs' Pharmacy at 2 Marietta Street. In 1898 The Coca-Cola Company built its first headquarters building at 179 Edgewood Avenue (now known as Coca-Cola Place). In 1920 the Company moved to 310 North Avenue where the red brick headquarters, familiar to many Atlantans, remains part of today's modern office complex.

Early advertising depicting the trademark design included popular "calendar girl" promotional giveaways.

The Company never faltered in its effort to maintain the morale of American GI's during World War II.

ing for stock splits, would now have 192 shares worth about $6,600.

A victory in the Company's never-ending battle against imitators came with a landmark decision rendered in 1920 against the Koke Company of America. Justice Oliver Wendell Holmes of the United States Supreme Court ruled not only that the name "Coke" could mean only Coca-Cola, but that the trademark Coca-Cola "means a single thing coming from a single source, and well known to the community."

Robert Winship Woodruff was elected president of The Coca-Cola Company in 1923, four years after his father had purchased the Company. Under Woodruff's half century of imaginative leadership, Coca-Cola was destined to become a world-famous drink that would reach unrivaled heights in commercial history.

At 33 Woodruff had risen from truck salesman to vice president and sales manager of White Motor Company before accepting the presidency from The Coca-Cola Company's board of directors. He succeeded Charles Howard Candler, Asa's son, who remained on the board.

Technological innovations developed under Woodruff—including the six-bottle carton, the metal-top cooler and the automatic fountain dispenser—revolutionized the soft drink industry.

The declaration of war in 1941 brought an order from Woodruff "to see that every man in uniform gets a bottle of Coca-Cola for five cents wherever he is and whatever it costs the Company."

This effort was underway when an urgent cablegram from General Dwight Eisenhower's Allied Headquarters in North Africa in 1943 requested shipment of machinery for operating 10 bottling plants. Equipment for a total of 64 bottling plants to provide Coca-Cola was shipped abroad during World War II and set up as close as possible to combat areas to help maintain morale among American GI's.

Although originally a firm advocate of the one-product, one-package policy, Woodruff, with his executive management team, wrote new chapters of Company tradition in the 1950s and 1960s by making the changeover to a multi-product, multi-package corporation.

In addition to leading The Coca-Cola Company to unparalleled success, Woodruff has earned the nickname "Citizen Woodruff" for his generous contributions to Georgia, and especially to Atlanta.

His philanthropies over the years have aided, among many others, the Robert Winship Memorial Clinic at Emory University, which evolved into the Emory University Clinic; land purchases for four Atlanta parks; Fernbank Science Center; funding for the Atlanta Historical Society's new archives building, and the greater part of funds for the Atlanta Memorial Arts Center. The nationally known Centers for Disease Control are located in Atlanta due essentially to Woodruff's influence.

In 1955 Woodruff retired at the age of 65. He continued to serve on the board of directors and as chairman of the finance committee; in 1981 he was named chairman emeritus of that committee.

Through the 1960s and 1970s, under the leadership of J. Paul Austin, the Company continued to prosper. Austin spearheaded a highly successful effort to expand the markets for Coke and other Company products around the world.

Two major achievements were attained in 1979 with the re-entry of Coca-Cola into China, and the introduction of Fanta Orange in the Soviet Union.

Following 90 years of dramatic growth, the business that Candler purchased in 1891 for $2,300 now achieves annual net sales of almost $6 billion.

The 1980s brought a dynamic new management team to the Company: Roberto C. Goizueta, chairman of the board and chief executive officer; and Donald R. Keough, president and chief operating officer. Their implementation of a well-defined corporate strategy for the decade of the 1980s has become the driving force behind the Company.

Central to that strategy is continued dedication to the Company's leadership position in the soft drink industry. In

Introduced in 1982, the new advertising theme, "Coke is it!", reflects the direct, assertive nature of America and The Coca-Cola Company in the 1980s.

addition to Coca-Cola, soft drinks of the Company include the Fanta line of flavors, Sprite, Sugar-free Sprite, TAB, diet Coke, Fresca, Mr. PiBB, Sugar-free Mr. PiBB, Hi-C soft drinks, Mello Yello, and Ramblin' Root Beer. Other brands are available overseas.

Complementing the success of the world's number one soft drink, Coca-Cola, it is notable that another Company brand, Fanta Orange, is the world's third most popular soft drink. In fact, if Fanta Orange were produced by a separate company, that company would be the third largest soft drink firm in the world.

The Coca-Cola Company Foods Division, based in Houston, is among the largest citrus processors in the United States, producing and marketing the well-known Minute Maid brand of chilled and frozen citrus juices, ades and lemonade crystals; Snow Crop Five Alive frozen concentrates and juice drinks; Bright & Early frozen concentrate; Hi-C fruit drinks, and Maryland Club and Butter-Nut coffees. Other Company subsidiaries produce disposable plastic wrap, bags, cutlery and straws, and bottled water.

Wine is the fastest-growing segment of the Company's domestic beverage business. The Wine Spectrum division of the Company is the fourth largest wine producer and marketer in the United States, and encompasses Taylor and Great Western New York State wines as well as Sterling Vineyards, The Monterey Vineyard, and Taylor California Cellars wines.

Consistent with its strategy for profitable growth in a compatible consumer market, the Company diversified into the entertainment industry with the acquisition of Columbia Pictures Industries, Inc., in 1982.

While maintaining its status as the premier producer and marketer of the highest quality beverage products in the world, through Columbia the Company will also have an entry in the film and leisure-time entertainment business, including the rapidly growing cable television industry and the expanding home video entertainment market.

Beyond its dedication to producing quality products, The Coca-Cola Company is committed to good corporate citizenship in every community in which it conducts business.

The Company takes an active interest in the growth and betterment of Atlanta through support of many organizations, including the United Way of Metropolitan Atlanta and the Atlanta Arts Alliance. In addition, management has played a major part in the development of the nationally known Atlanta University Center, Inc.

The phenomenal growth of Coca-Cola from a bubbly brew in an Atlanta backyard to its worldwide fame today is a proud legacy for both the Company and its home city. Nearly a century old, the beverage continues to bring a moment of pleasure into the lives of millions of consumers every day.

In the 1980s The Coca-Cola Company is committed to continued growth based on the fundamentals of quality products, expanding availability, innovation, and creative advertising.

The challenges of future markets lie ahead. Continuing consumer confidence that, as asserted in the Company's new advertising theme, "Coke is it!," perhaps is best demonstrated by the many applications received over the years by the Company for bottling franchises...on the moon.

Adding to Atlanta's modern skyline, the 26-story North Avenue Tower, international headquarters of The Coca-Cola Company, opened in 1979.

Roberto C. Goizueta (right), chairman of the board and chief executive officer, and Donald R. Keough, president and chief operating officer, have brought dynamic new leadership to the Company in the 1980s.

Cousins Properties Incorporated

Omni International Atlanta, an example of downtown, mixed-use development by Cousins Properties, Inc.

One Live Oak Center, the newest addition to the Live Oak office complex at 3475 Lenox Road, Atlanta

Cousins Properties Incorporated is a publicly owned, diversified real estate development and investment company headquartered in Atlanta—a company dedicated to creating outstanding values in real estate.

CPI was founded in 1959 by I. W. Cousins and his son Thomas G. Cousins, who is now chairman of the board and chief executive officer.

Cousins saw the potential for housing in Atlanta and started a residential construction company. The company soon diversified into purchasing large land tracts, installing roads and utilities and then subdividing the property into lots for sale to other builders.

Through the years the company has built and maintained a solid and enviable reputation for creative development and leadership within the real estate industry. Evidence of CPI's contributions can be found throughout Atlanta: in office complexes which include Corporate Square, Piedmont-Cain Building, Live Oak Center, Wildwood and Interstate North; and in residential developments including Hidden Hills, Huntcliff, Woodfield, Indian Hills, Martin's Landing and Lee's Crossing.

CPI is known not only in Atlanta but throughout the Southeast for downtown mixed-use developments like Omni International Atlanta and Omni International Miami, and regional shopping centers like Hickory Hollow Mall, Rivergate Mall and The Mall at Green Hills in Nashville, Tenn.; Haywood Mall in Greenville, S.C.; Orange Park Mall in Jacksonville, Fla.; University Mall in Pensacola, Fla.; Greenbrier Mall in Chesapeake, Va., as well as 60 strip centers throughout the Southeast.

The success of Cousins Properties can be attributed largely to the corporate philosophy upon which the company was founded: that there is absolutely no substitute for integrity and quality; that land must be held in highest respect so that it continues to have meaning when fitted to the needs of the people who occupy it; that attention to detail is mandatory; and that every aspect of a project must be undertaken with an ultimate goal — that of pride.

With this philosophy as a base, Cousins Properties Incorporated continues to grow and distinguish itself as a dynamic development leader within Atlanta and the numerous communities it serves.

Residential development representative of Cousin's contribution to Atlanta's housing opportunities

Davison's

In 1890, when Atlantans still watered their horses at an artesian well at Five Points, Douglas-Thomas & Company opened a dry goods store in modest quarters on Whitehall Street. The enterprise prospered and a year later the firm became Douglas-Thomas and Davison with the addition of British-born Beaumont Davison as a partner. By 1894 they were able to relocate to larger quarters one block north.

Thomas L. Stokes, an employee, became a partner in 1899 and Frederick J. Paxon joined the partnership in 1901. With the death of Thomas and the retirement of Douglas, the firm became Davison-Paxon-Stokes Co.

The Company grew with Atlanta and even as early as 1911 was progressive enough to install the first escalators in the South. Strangely, Atlantans refused to ride these newfangled contraptions, so they were quietly sold to a firm in Texas where, presumably, the residents were more daring.

In 1925, the Company was acquired by R. H. Macy & Co. of New York. This was a homecoming for Jessie, Percy and Herbert Straus, then the executive heads of Macy's, since their grandfather, Lazarus Straus, had settled in Talbotton, Ga., in 1848.

The day after the purchase, Davison's announced plans for a six-story department store to be built at 180 Peachtree Street, then owned by Asa G. Candler, Inc. The property was eventually donated to Emory University which later sold it to R. H. Macy Co., Inc.

The site where the store operates today is one of great historical interest. It was the location of the Leyden residence, known before the Civil War for its lavish entertaining and used during the war as headquarters for Confederate Gen. John B. Hood. After the War, the Governor's Mansion was next door.

Prior to the 1920s all of Atlanta's department stores were south of the railroad tracks. Davison's was the first major retailer to locate on the north side, creating what many consider Atlanta's choicest downtown shopping area.

Completed in 1927, the new Davison's boasted the largest store window expanse in the country as well as the most modern and luxurious facilities to be found in any department store. In fact, it incorporated a small vaudeville theater which operated on the site for 20 years. In 1949 an additional 180,000 square feet were added to the facility, bringing the store's total size to almost 600,000 square feet.

The name of the store was changed in 1963 one last time: It was shortened to Davison's.

In keeping with the desires of today's shoppers, new stores have opened in major regional shopping malls.

Davison's launched an extensive expansion program beginning in 1944 and established branch stores in Macon, Augusta, Athens, Columbus and Sea Island, Ga., and Columbia, S.C. In 1959 its first suburban Atlanta store opened in the Lenox Square regional shopping mall. This was followed by stores at Columbia, Northlake, Cumberland, Southlake, Shannon and Perimeter Malls.

Davison's has changed greatly over the years from the small store on Whitehall Street run by 30 emloyees. Today more than 3,500 employees, led by chairman and chief executive officer Herbert Friedman and president Harold Kahn, have made this department store chain a vigorous and vital part of Atlanta and the South.

Davison's Peachtree Store opened in 1925 and had the largest expanse of window front of any department store in the country.

Days Inns
Of America,
Inc.

Days Inn motel

Cecil B. Day Sr. was founder of Days Inns of America, Inc., currently the sixth largest lodging chain in the United States.

Established by Day in March, 1970, the Atlanta-based company now operates and franchises more than 300 Days Inns and Days Lodges.

Day, a native of the Savannah area and a Georgia Tech graduate, was a successful Atlanta realtor who specialized in building and operating apartments in the area.

The budget-luxury concept of Days Inns began with an idea Day had while traveling with his wife and five children. He realized the void in the lodging industry for meeting the needs of middle Americans and families traveling on a limited budget.

As a result, Day designed a motel which combined budget luxury features and construction techniques in offering the unique lodging concept. He standardized construction and operation of motels and eliminated the overhead cost of convention facilities and expensive lobbies.

Days Inn's value-oriented concept became a reality with the opening of the first Days Inn in Savannah Beach, Ga., in April, 1970. Days Inn became the "four-in-one-stop"—the first to provide the traveler with lodging, food, gasoline and a gift shop. Almost all properties include a swimming pool and children's playground.

Days Inns and Lodges do not sell alcoholic beverages. Each motel contains a chaplain on call to minister to the special needs of its guests, and provides a free Bible in each room for guests to take.

In 1978, at the young age of 44, Day died of cancer.

Richard C. Kessler succeeded him as chairman of the board, president and chief executive officer of Days Inns of America, Inc.

Marian U. (Deen) Day succeeded Day as chairman of the board of Cecil B. Day Companies, Inc. (the holding company for Days Inns and related real estate operations). She is guided by the corporate objective stated by her late husband in the first annual report of the Day Companies, which begins:

"The Company is committed to fulfilling its business responsibilities within the framework of Christian ethics, exerting a positive influence which strengthens the free-enterprise system."

Cecil B. Day, founder of Days Inns of America, Inc. (1934-1978)

Had it not been for the boll weevil, there might never have been a Delta Air Lines.

Invading the cotton fields of the South in the early 1900s, the insect had nearly destroyed the cotton industry, and the U.S. government was desperately seeking a way to stop the onslaught.

In 1916, however, Collett Everman Woolman, a young agriculture extension agent, and his colleague Dr. Bert Coad began looking for a method of dusting cotton crops with the poison calcium arsenate that would be faster than hand sprinkling.

Convinced that aerial dusting was the answer, Coad and Woolman worked for the next several years to perfect the dusting procedures.

C.E. Woolman got the break he needed in 1923 when George Post, an airplane manufacturing executive, convinced his management to start a new division—Huff Daland Dusters. Woolman left the extension service in 1925 to take charge of the new company's crop-dusting work.

Huff Daland Dusters' 18 planes comprised the largest privately owned aircraft fleet in the world. When the company sought to sell the dusting division in 1928, Woolman organized a group of Monroe, La., businessmen to buy the equipment. They changed the name to Delta Air Service (Delta from the Mississippi delta), with Woolman as general manager.

Although Delta was to continue dusting operations in the South until 1966, Woolman had bigger plans for the company. With the purchase of three six-passenger, 90-mile-per-hour Travel Air monoplanes, Delta began passenger service on June 17, 1929, over a route that extended from Dallas, Tx., to Jackson, Miss. Later, service was extended east to Birmingham and Atlanta, and west to Fort Worth.

Also developing in the 1930s were two other pioneer airlines, each destined to play a role in Delta's future: Chicago and Southern (C&S) Air Lines and in the Midwest and Northeast Airlines in New England.

Delta and C&S merged in 1953, and a new Delta took off, with Woolman as president and general manager.

Shortly after the merger, the DC-7 was introduced. Later, in lieu of purchasing the turbo-prop jet aircraft available in the late '50s, Delta chose to buy pure jets. Thus Delta became a jet leader among world airlines. Staying in the forefront of the jet age, Delta was the first to introduce the DC-8 and the Convair 880 jets, and later the DC-9.

In 1966, the airline's founder and driving force, C. E. Woolman, died. For the remainder of the decade, the company continued to progress under the guidance of Charles H. Dolson, one of Delta's pioneer pilots.

In the late 60s Northeast Airlines, facing financial problems, began to look for a merger partner, and on August 1, 1972, a merger between Northeast and Delta became effective.

When Delta moved its home office and overhaul base to Atlanta in 1941, the airline employed 400 people and had nine small planes. Today, the company is one of the world's largest carriers, employing more than 36,000, with a jet fleet in the hundreds.

The route system that started out carrying passengers between Texas and Mississippi now stretches from coast to coast and border to border, with international service to much of the Western Hemisphere and Europe, operating under the leadership of David C. Garrett, president and chief executive officer, and W.T. Beebe, chairman of the board.

Delta Air Lines' new, advanced fleet of aircraft, financial stability and strong competitive posture make it possible to look to the future with great confidence.

Delta Air Lines

Delta began passenger service in 1929 with the six-passenger, 90-mile-per-hour Travel Air monoplane.

The Boeing 767, scheduled to be placed into service by Delta late in 1982.

Eastern Airlines

Atlanta and Eastern Airlines grew up together.

Eastern began operations as Pitcairn Aviation, Inc., founded by aircraft manufacturer Harold F. Pitcairn to carry mail between New Brunswick, N.J., and Atlanta under a $3-a-pound Federal contract.

Because of an unanticipated backlog of mail, this first north-south airmail service had to operate a double schedule in both directions on opening day. Two planes left Atlanta on May 1, 1928, heading north; two others headed south out of New Brunswick.

Mail flights operated at night to compete with the railroads. Eugene R. Brown, a native of Decatur and a graduate of Atlanta's Tech High, piloted the first of the open-cockpit PA-5 Pitcairn Mailwings that left Atlanta. Brown took off from Candler Field, adjacent to the Candler auto racing track.

In an interview in 1978 in conjunction with Eastern's 50th anniversary celebration, Brown recalled that pilots used the racetrack for forced landings in those early days. Brown stayed with Eastern until he retired in 1964 after 37 years as the airline's senior pilot.

During his career Brown saw the fledgling mail carrier evolve into one of the world's major commercial airlines as aviation changed from novelty to accepted transportation mode.

In July, 1929, Pitcairn, after extending mail service from Atlanta to Miami, sold his airline to North American Aviation, Inc. In January, 1930, it renamed it Eastern Air Transport, Inc. Eastern began passenger service on August 18, 1930, between what is now New York's LaGuardia Airport and Richmond, Va.

On December 10 service was extended to Atlanta as Eastern became the city's first regularly scheduled passenger airline. Within a month, Atlanta-to-Miami passenger service was begun.

In January, 1935, the legendary Edward V. "Captain Eddie" Rickenbacker became general manager of Eastern. Three years later, with a group of associates, he bought the company for $3.5 million. Captain Eddie remained in charge at Eastern until 1963.

During this period, aviation came of age. Eastern's changing fleets reflected the advances in aeronautical design and technology—from the Douglas DC-2 through a succession of propeller-powered aircraft to the introduction in 1960 of the airline's first pure jet, the Douglas DC-8.

As Rickenbacker was retiring, the company was on the verge of becoming the first operator of Boeing 727s. In 1968 Eastern ordered 37 Lockheed L-1011 aircraft. On their delivery, the company became the first airline to put this jumbo jet into service.

Eastern gave Atlanta its first international service when a daily nonstop flight to Mexico City was inaugurated July 1, 1971. The Atlanta airport was renamed Hartsfield Atlanta International Airport and the U.S. Departments of Immigration and Customs were added.

The introduction of larger, faster, more sophisticated aircraft reflected the growth of air travel. In 1938, at the end of the decade, Eastern had 1,032 employees, operated 4,158 route miles and 34 daily scheduled flights, and owned 22 airplanes.

Fifteen years later, when Eastern celebrated its 25th anniversary, revenues were $136.5 million annually, and 25 million passengers had flown on Eastern. In 1977, however, Eastern carried more than that number.

The 31,302,000 passengers who chose the 50-year-old airline that year made it the free world's second largest airline in passengers boarded and in landings and take-offs. Revenues were $2.04 billion.

Three years later, revenues had climbed to more than $3.7 billion. In each of those years, Eastern carried more passengers than any other carrier in the free world.

Candler airfield and racetrack have long since been swallowed by what is now the world's largest terminal and the free world's second busiest airport. Of Eastern's 1,300 daily flight departures, about 300 operate from Atlanta, far more than the carrier's schedule from any of the other 122 cities on its broad route system.

Eastern uses 45 of the 138 gates in the new terminal, which opened in September, 1980. Eastern's gates, shortcut tunnel and other amenities at Hartsfield represent a $100 million investment in the new terminal. The company's activities in Atlanta employ 7,500 of its 38,500 employees.

Eastern's hostesses of about 50 years ago had at least two things in common with their contemporary counterparts: They were pretty and they smiled.

Emory University

Emory's 600-acre campus is a blend of traditional and modern architecture on a heavily wooded tract. Here, students enjoy the midday sun on the campus' Quadrangle.

Walking through Emory University's wooded 600-acre campus, one is impressed by buildings named for Atlanta business and professional leaders who have generously supported the development of the institution.

As a privately endowed research university, Emory remains closely associated with Atlanta, providing not only educational opportunities, but also offering programs and services geared to the needs of the community.

In fact, in large measure it was the active involvement by Atlantans that created Emory.

In 1914 the United Methodist Church decided to establish a university-level institution in the Southeast. Competition between cities for the facility was intense. The Atlanta Chamber of Commerce pledged $500,000 for the university to be located here, but the clincher was the promise of a $1 million donation by Asa G. Candler, founder of the Coca-Cola Co.

The University's roots, however, date from 1836, when the Georgia Methodist Conference established Emory College in Oxford, Ga., 40 miles east of Atlanta.

The first division to be housed on the Atlanta campus after Emory University was chartered in January, 1915, was the Candler School of Theology, named for Candler's brother, Bishop Warren A. Candler. Next came Emory College, which relocated from its original site in Oxford.

In time, the University added schools of law, medicine, dentistry, business administration and nursing, and a graduate school in the liberal arts. The Oxford campus became the site of Emory's Oxford College, a two-year degree-granting division.

By 1980, the University's enrollment ex-ceeded 8,000, with students from all parts of the country and many foreign nations. The faculty numbered approximately 2,500, including 1,300 voluntary faculty, most of whom practiced in the University Clinic.

Emory has always had a tradition of excellence in teaching. But it wasn't until the late 1940s and 1950s that research and service to the community began to assume larger roles. The University awarded its first Ph.D. degree in 1948. About the same time, the Woodruff Medical Center was established, quickly becoming one of the finest teaching, research and patient-care medical complexes in the country.

Several buildings on Emory's quadrangle are priceless examples of Italian Renaissance architecture and are listed on the National Register of Historic Places.

Much of the 1960s and 1970s were spent supplementing the University's facilities, rebuilding and modernizing the campus. Additions of stunning and sophisticated structures will continue through the 1980s, reconfirming Emory's commitment not only to building a fine university dedicated to higher education and service, but also to awakening a more creative, gracious community as well.

In 1979 Emory received a gift unprecedented in size in the history of private philanthropy. Robert W. Woodruff, former president of the Coca-Cola Co., and his brother George transferred to Emory the entire assets of the Emily and Ernest Woodruff Fund, Inc.—worth $105 million.

The Woodruff gift enables Emory University to look to the future with a sense of unity, a spirit of achievement and with the knowledge that Emory has the potential to join a select group of America's leading educational institutions.

In existence prior to the creation of the University, Emory College was situated near Covington, Ga., until 1916. The baseball team posed on the original campus for this turn-of-the-century photo.

The Equitable Life Assurance Society of the United States

The Equitable Life Assurance Society of the United States, the nation's third largest insurer, is well into its second century of providing security for millions of Americans. The company was founded in 1859 by Henry Hyde, a 25-year-old insurance company cashier who was convinced there was a need for larger amounts of insurance than his employer at the time was willing to write.

Headquartered in New York City since its founding, The Equitable was guided by Hyde until his death in 1899.

Since 1925, The Equitable has been a mutual company. Divisible surplus goes to policyholders in the form of annual dividends voted by the board of directors.

Always the innovator, The Equitable was the first to offer group insurance (1911), and later pioneered major medical insurance. In 1976 The Equitable became the first company to offer variable life insurance, and by 1980 the company had become the largest manager of pension funds in the country.

The Equitable issued its first policy to an Atlantan in 1860, just one year after its founding. As of January 1, 1982, the company was insuring 276,000 Georgians with benefits totaling $4.5 billion.

The Equitable has been a substantial investor in Atlanta's growth for more than 100 years. In 1892 the company financed and occupied the city's first "skyscraper" —an eight-story structure at 25 Pryor St. It was known as The Equitable Building until 1914, when it became the home of Trust Company of Georgia, and remained an Atlanta landmark until being razed in 1972 to make way for an addition to the current Trust Company building.

One of the first major companies to envision the expansion of Atlanta's business district, The Equitable in 1952 constructed a Southeastern regional headquarters building on West Peachtree.

The third—and current—Equitable Building in Atlanta, 100 Peachtree St., is on the site occupied for 62 years by the venerable Piedmont Hotel, which in its prime was one of the city's most handsome and fashionable spots.

The 100 Peachtree site is rich in history and tradition. It was part of a larger tract of land passed on by the state of Georgia to its citizens through a series of lotteries in 1826.

A Jackson County widow, Jane Doss, was the lucky winner of one parcel. The widow Doss sold her property for less than 25 cents an acre the same year. Had she not done so, her heirs would have become multimillionaires: The property was assessed at $10 million in 1920, and by the time The Equitable bought it in 1965, after several ownership changes, its strategic location in the heart of Atlanta's business and financial district had made it one of the city's most valuable sites.

The Equitable's 32-story, 590,666-square-foot building was opened in 1970 and immediately became one of Atlanta's prestigious business addresses, housing not only the company's Southeastern headquarters for various divisions but also the offices of a number of other major firms.

In 1982 The Equitable attracted the first major Japanese investment in Atlanta real estate by forming a joint venture to own The Equitable Building with the U.S. subsidiary of the Asahi Mutual Life Insurance Co. of Tokyo.

The Equitable's mortgage and real estate investments in Georgia now total more than $540 million and include office buildings, shopping centers, apartment complexes, residential subdivisions, industrial properties and other enterprises that add to the state's employment base. Total investments in Georgia, including stocks and bonds, are approaching $650 million.

Thus, The Equitable Life Assurance Society, with 950 Georgia employees and an annual payroll of more than $12 million, continues to be a major contributor to the economic growth of the city, state and region.

The Equitable Building

Richard Felker Company

Founder and president Richard Felker

Savings accounts, stocks and bonds are familiar to most investors, yet those investments frequently fall short of satisfying the investor's need for tax deductions, tax-free income and a growth rate at least equal to that of inflation.

In 1973 Richard Felker decided to do something about it. By forming a company that offered an alternative investment, he provided the missing link.

That alternative is an investment in a limited partnership established to own an Atlanta apartment complex. With the purchase of property through a partnership, it is possible even for a small investor to enjoy the tax benefits of ownership.

"The unique thing about our company," says Felker, "is that we give people who can invest only $5,000 to $10,000 an opportunity to benefit from multimillion-dollar purchases."

Richard Felker Company buys, upgrades and manages property, later reselling it for a profit. While the property is held, investors receive quarterly checks and progress reports from the Company. When the property is sold, usually after about three years, they receive a profit from the proceeds.

In 1981 Felker's company closed transactions in the purchase and sale of apartments for its partnerships in an amount exceeding $40 million.

That figure contrasts sharply with the Felker Company's first year, 1973, when business amounted to $400,000.

The Company's growth is further exemplified by its rapidly expanding staff. When Felker opened his first office, he had a staff of three. In 1982 there were more than 90 on the payroll.

Two other principals of the Company are John J. Cross and Pete T. Hobgood. Cross, formerly a senior vice president of The First National Bank of Atlanta, joined Felker in 1979 as a general partner. Hobgood, who has been with the Company since 1973, serves as president of RFC Management, Inc., a company wholly owned by Felker.

The parent Company's many apartment complexes have included Williamsburg Village, Lake Cumberland, Beau Rivage and Orleans North.

Richard Felker Company also owns the Habersham Hotel, described by Felker as a "quiet, quality, European-style hotel." The ten-story, 94-room property in downtown Atlanta has become a favorite of foreign business travelers who prefer its hospitality, reasonable prices and peaceful atmosphere.

The Company also buys apartments, improves them and converts them into condominiums. Among them are Brookwood Forest, Briarcliff Place and 4300 Roswell. From his office in The Equitable Building, Felker also oversees the progress of his other businesses: RFC Management, RFC Realty, RFC Equities, and Brookwood Marketing, Inc.

A native of Monroe and an Atlanta resident since 1952, Felker says he started his business because he wanted to be a part of Atlanta's exciting growth.

"I was motivated by the thought that I was living in one of the world's most dynamic cities," he says. "I couldn't just sit and watch all the progress without jumping into the real estate mainstream."

A graduate of Vanderbilt University, Felker is a past board member of the Atlanta Chamber of Commerce, past president of the Atlanta unit of the American Cancer Society, and the 1982 president of the Apartment Owners and Managers Association of Atlanta. He also teaches a course at the Emory University Continuing Education Center on real estate investing.

First Georgia Bank

First Georgia Bank is headquartered on Peachtree Street in the Candler Building, one of Atlanta's first skyscrapers and now on the National Register of Historic Places.

First Georgia Bank's major concern is meeting the needs of the people of metropolitan Atlanta, both personal and corporate.

For its individual customers it consistently offers the most complete and economical financial services program in the area.

To all its business customers, First Georgia gives top management attention.

To many, First Georgia may seem like a new bank in town, having operated under this name since 1972. However, the institution can trace its roots to three predecessor banks—two formed during the Depression of the Thirties to provide critically needed financing, and one that was started in the 1960s as the metropolitan region was undergoing unprecedented growth.

The highlights of First Georgia's history are:

1934: The Bank of Fulton County is organized by a group of East Point business people who were concerned that bank failures during the Depression would leave their community without a source of financing.

1935: The Peoples Savings Bank is chartered in Atlanta; in 1941 it is reorganized as a commercial bank.

1964: The American Bank of Atlanta is opened by a group that previously operated a consumer finance company in the city.

1968: The Peoples American Bank is formed by the merger of the two Atlanta banks. It is headquartered in the historic Candler Building.

1972: The Peoples American Bank changes its name to the First Georgia Bank to better identify the institution with the community it serves.

1973: The Bank of Fulton County is acquired. The combined institutions have a total of $78 million in assets.

1978: The First Railroad & Banking Co. of Georgia in Augusta acquires

Customers who visit First Georgia Bank's main office in the Candler Building enjoy the beautiful craftsmanship of its marble columns and crystal chandeliers.

President and chief executive officer Dick Jackson discusses First Georgia Bank's expansion plans with directors Deen Day, chairman of the board of the Cecil B. Day Companies, and Tom Cordy, president of AMC Mechanical Contractors, Inc.

majority interest in the Bank.

1978: First Georgia passes the $100 million in assets mark, making it the 22nd largest bank in Georgia.

1982: First Georgia exceeds $200 million in assets and becomes the 11th largest bank in the state.

The period of most rapid growth of the Bank began in 1975 when its new corporate strategy was introduced.

Conceived under the direction of Richard D. Jackson, president and chief executive officer, and former Georgia Governor Carl E. Sanders, the Bank's chairman, the program aims at the corporate middle market, with emphasis on locally-owned companies with annual sales of up to $50 million.

Bank services and financial packages are designed to meet the needs of these companies. Further, senior Bank officers service accounts, assuring customers direct access to the Bank's most experienced executives.

At the same time, the number of branch locations have been increased throughout Fulton and DeKalb Counties area, so that Bank officials are always conveniently available to both individuals and business customers.

As part of this strategy, First Georgia has continually revised and expanded its retail services. It became the first bank in Atlanta to offer simple interest consumer loans, and the first in the nation to offer a 12 per cent credit card. Its new Women's Banking Department, the first in the city, provides financial seminars, credit conferences and counseling to an increasing number of women in all walks of life.

With the success of these programs and the assets of First Railroad & Banking Company of Georgia behind it, First Georgia Bank looks forward to competing aggressively in providing the financial services to metropolitan Atlanta's citizens and businesses in the years ahead.

The First National Bank Of Atlanta

First Atlanta's three most recent chairmen: Thomas R. Williams, 1977-present (seated); Edward D. Smith, 1969-1977 (standing); and James D. Robinson Jr., 1952-1967 (in portrait)

In 1865 war-torn Atlanta needed a bank for loans to move crops and finance rebuilding.

Gen. Alfred Austell, respected because of his financial successes before the war, organized the Atlanta National Bank, the first national bank in the Southeast.

It was chartered Sept. 14, 1865. Only two months after opening, the Bank demonstrated faith in Atlanta's future by informing the City Council of its willingness to lend it money to pay the City's bills.

That was the beginning of The First National Bank of Atlanta and its parent, First Atlanta Corporation.

During the remainder of the century, the Bank and the city grew and prospered, surviving several periods of national financial crisis. As Atlanta flourished, there opened other banks that would eventually join First Atlanta: the Lowry Banking Co. in 1888, the American Bank and Trust Co. in 1889, and the American National Bank in 1891.

A series of mergers between 1916 and 1929 brought these banks together as The First National Bank of Atlanta, operating under the charter of the Atlanta National Bank and qualifying as the oldest national bank in the Southeast.

Following the merger and under the successive leadership of Robert F. Maddox, James D. Robinson and Edward D. Smith, the Bank was primarily known and respected as a leading regional bank serving major corporations throughout the U.S.

Then, in the late 1960s and early 1970s, it began to emerge as an innovator in banking services for the consumer, bringing Atlanta the Visa card, creating a highly successful check guarantee system and becoming a national leader in electronic banking with its network of Tillie, the Alltime Teller machines.

To position the company for continued growth, First Atlanta formed a holding company in the late 1960s, which today is First Atlanta Corporation. The new holding company became a major Southeastern consumer lender in 1972 when it acquired Gulf Finance Corp. and began providing financial services through its First Atlanta Mortgage Corp. and First Financial Life Insurance Co. subsidiaries.

In 1976 Thomas R. Williams, chairman of the Atlanta bank, was elected chief executive officer of the holding company. Under his guidance, First Atlanta undertook an aggressive statewide acquisition program by acquiring banks in Savannah, Augusta, Dalton, Macon and Calhoun, and in the adjoining metropolitan Atlanta counties of Cobb and Clayton.

As it entered the decade of the 1980s, First Atlanta's financial performance ranked it in the top 25 per cent among bank holding companies nationwide. With assets of approximately $4 billion, it is one of the nation's 100 largest bank holding companies. In 1981 it became Georgia's first bank holding company to be listed on the New York Stock Exchange.

First Atlanta Corporation has the size and expertise to handle financial requirements of multinational corporations as well as meet the daily needs of the citizens of Atlanta and Georgia.

The Atlanta National Bank was the first of four banks that would become The First National Bank of Atlanta. Chartered in 1865, Atlanta National was located on south Alabama Street, near the site of the present Connally Building. The pen-and-ink drawing is circa 1870.

379

Georgia Baptist Medical Center

The building in the center is the current West Wing of Georgia Baptist. Originally the surgical building, it was completed in 1926. The building just to the right of center was razed some years ago; a parking deck is now on the site.

This photo was made in 1948, during construction of the East Wing of the Hospital.

1901—On Thanksgiving Day, Dr. Len G. Broughton, a medical doctor and minister, along with a group of women from the Tabernacle Baptist Church in Atlanta, founded the Tabernacle Infirmary and Training School for Christian Nurses. The first building was a rented, five-room dwelling on Luckie Street in which three beds were available.

1902—Four students were enrolled in the first class at the Training School. They were graduated in 1904.

1913—The Georgia Baptist Convention assumed the accumulated debt of the Infirmary and rechartered it as Georgia Baptist Hospital.

1921—The Hospital moved from the Luckie Street location adjoining the Baptist Taberncle Church to the Boulevard address following the Atlanta fire. Several Baptist laymen had pledged their personal credit for acquisition of the new site. The first building was a School of Nursing Dormitory.

1922—Ownership of Georgia Baptist Hospital was transferred to the Executive Committee of the Georgia Baptist Convention.

1926—The Surgical Building, now the West Wing, was completed, bringing the patient capacity to 125.

1934—Sheffield Clinic, given to the hospital by I. M. Sheffield Sr., was the first cancer clinic in Georgia.

1937—One of five institutional founders of Atlanta Blue Cross under the leadership of administrator W. D. Barker Sr., who served from June, 1931, to January 14, 1946.

1950-51—East and North Wings were completed, increasing the patient capacity to 475 beds and 75 bassinets. Georgia Baptist Hospital became the largest private hospital in the state.

1956—An eight-floor professional building was opened for physician and dentist office space.

1959—The School of Nursing, the third largest diploma school of nursing in the nation, opened its present educational building.

1963—Warren P. Sewell Dormitory opened, providing a capacity for housing approximately 500 students.

1974—The 10-story patient Tower was completed, providing for the care of 523 patients and 43 infants. The Tower faces Parkway Drive which is now the main entrance to the Hospital. Overlooking the Atlanta skyline, the Tower provides many innovative facilities in keeping with our goals to offer maximum patient care.

1975—The Professional Building East opened, providing an additional six-story facility for physicians and dentists. This was the 11th construction project during the administration of Edwin B. Peel, who served from 1946 to 1978. Dr. Peel was the Hospital's longest-tenured chief executive officer, and led the Hospital in its evolution from a hospital into the Medical Center.

1979—The Medical Center became more aggressive in its continuing development into a Tertiary Medical Center (third stage or most advanced) under the leadership of administrator Robert L. Zwald, who also conceived the idea for development in Georgia for the establishment of the Georgia Baptist Health Care System. Under this registered trade name, it became the stated goal of our owners to extend the Christian ministry of healing to the people of Georgia and the region through operating, leasing and managing hospitals and diverse health care facilities.

1982—Harvest Heights Baptist Home

Center opened in DeKalb County, Ga. This Home Center is a 146-bed skilled and intermediate health care center for patients who no longer require the major facilities of a hospital but who still require nursing care. The management philosophy of the Home Center is an innovative approach of a "stepping stone" facility rather than a place of last resort.

1984—Projected opening of the Georgia Baptist Nursing Home. The Nursing Home will be at the corner of Parkway and Ralph McGill Boulevard, directly across from the Tower building of the Medical Center. The facility will be a four-story structure with 146 beds.

Completed in 1951, the East Wing sits in front of the West Wing, facing Boulevard.

A view of the Georgia Baptist Medical Center today: The building in the upper right is the School of Nursing, the third largest diploma-granting nursing school in the U. S. The area marked by dots (left foreground) is the site of the Georgia Baptist Nursing Home, scheduled to open in 1984.

Georgia Federal

Georgia Federal, one of the state's largest and strongest financial institutions, had a humble beginning in 1928 when the tallest building in Atlanta was 17 stories, women wore hats and white gloves to shop in the city, and the nation enjoyed prosperity.

At that time a group of professional and business men met daily for lunch at Mrs. Blackburn's Tearoom in downtown Atlanta, for conversation as much as the meal. Subjects ranged from politics to religion. They did not agree on all issues, but they did agree that most loans on real estate in Georgia came from out-of-state lenders and interest on those loans was not reinvested in Georgia.

From the luncheon forums came the idea to establish a mutual building and loan organization in Atlanta to encourage thrift and promote home ownership. It would contribute to the growth of the community through the construction of more homes, create employment and enhance the demand for building materials.

Rawson Collier, an executive with Georgia Power Company, was president of the newly formed Atlanta Building and Loan Association for the first three years, until business interests took him from the city. He was succeeded in 1931 by Walter McElreath, an eminent attorney and one of the founders of the Atlanta Historical Society. After Atlanta Building and Loan Association became Atlanta Federal in 1935, he continued to serve as its president until 1950, then as chairman until his death. McElreath was instrumental in bringing W.O. DuVall, the third president, into the organization.

DuVall has provided more than 50 years of extraordinary leadership. He served as legal advisor to the Association from its beginning, as secretary 1931-1949, as president 1950-1966, chairman 1966-1975, and now as chairman of the executive committee.

Other distinguished citizens who played significant roles in Georgia Federal's growth include Robert W. Davis, a food broker; E.H. Ginn, a General Electric vice president; W.L. Blackett, a retired oil executive; and Charles A. Adair, an appraiser and contractor.

Bill C. Wainwright joined the Association in 1945 and served as president from 1966 to 1977, and as chairman from 1975 until his retirement in December, 1981.

John B. Zellars, the current chairman and president, has provided outstanding leadership for 30 years, and has directed the firm's statewide expansion.

Statewide expansion began in 1972 when Home Federal of Augusta joined Atlanta Federal. Subsequent mergers of Glynn Federal in Brunswick, First Federal in Dublin, and Home Federal in Savannah brought into focus the need for a new name for the statewide, Atlanta-born institution. Thus, Atlanta Federal became Georgia Federal in 1976. Additional locations since have joined the growing Georgia Federal network of family banking centers: Columbus, Perry, Macon and Albany.

From modest assets of $46,471.51 in 1928, resources grew to more than $2 billion as of December 31, 1981.

Corporate headquarters were relocated in 1935 from 74 Plaza Way to the 22 Marietta Street Building, formerly occupied by the Third National Bank. The 17-story building was purchased in 1950, followed by purchase in 1958 of the adjoining building at 18 Marietta St., the old Fulton National Bank Building. In 1966, the two buildings were renovated and joined to become 20 Marietta Street.

Georgia Federal takes pride in its financial strength. For over 50 years the purposes of this financial institution have been to promote thrift and to encourage home ownership. Supplementing this heritage, the purpose today is to satisfy the full range of family banking needs.

Following in the footsteps of its past great leadership, Georgia Federal is committed to outstanding family banking, convenience and quality customer service. With dedicated and influential directors, vigorous and experienced officers, and a loyal and faithful staff, Georgia Federal is prepared and determined to meet the challenges of the future.

Looking west on Marietta Street at Five Points about 1928.

382

When the first electric streetcars appeared in Atlanta, replacing mule-drawn coaches, the Georgia Electric Light Company of Atlanta had been in business four years. Formed in 1883, the company was granted a charter to provide "electric lights for stores, dwellings, machine shops, depots, inside and out, or to introduce said lights wherever desired."

In 1891 the assets of the company were purchased by the Georgia Electric Light Company, which had just been organized by H.M. Atkinson, a newcomer to Atlanta.

In his acquisition, improvement and expansion of the properties owned by Georgia Electric Light and succeeding companies, Atkinson became the recognized leader of electric development in Georgia for the next four decades.

Atkinson organized the Atlanta Rapid Transit Company in 1901 and soon controlled all street railway, electrical and steam heat properties in the city.

Merging his companies in 1902, Atkinson formed the Georgia Railway and Electric Company. At that time, electricity in Atlanta was used primarily for street lighting, lighting homes and businesses in the central city, and powering small motors in elevators and manufacturing plants.

Atkinson served as board chairman and was joined on the board by several influential Georgians, including Thomas Egleston, founder of the Henrietta Egleston Hospital for Children.

Preston S. Arkwright, Atkinson's lawyer, became president of the new Company. Arkwright later coined the Georgia Power slogan, "A citizen wherever we serve."

The Company grew rapidly, and another merger in 1911 led to the formation of the Georgia Railway and Power Company. Seeking to meet the increased demand for electricity, the Company opened its first water-powered generating plant at Tallulah Falls in 1913.

The Georgia Railway and Power Company also pioneered in radio broadcasting, but it soon turned its station over to *The Atlanta Constitution*. The newspaper later gave the station to Georgia Tech, where it was operated as WGST for more than 50 years.

In the early 1920s an "energy crisis," caused by increased electricity demands during World War I, led to the construction of five more hydroelectric plants in north Georgia.

After the consolidation in 1927 of several power and railway systems across the state, the modern Georgia Power Company was formed. Atkinson became chairman of the board and Arkwright was named president and chief executive officer. Until his death in 1946, Arkwright personified Georgia Power in the public's eyes.

Today, Georgia Power Company is the dominant producer of electricity in the state, with 32 generating plants in service and three under construction. (The street

Georgia Power's energy-award winning headquarters in downtown Atlanta: This office tower has the largest solar system for climate control and water heating of any commercial building in the United States.

transportation systems were sold in the late 1940s and early 1950s.)

The Company's first nuclear generating facility went on line in 1978. Another is scheduled to begin operating in 1987.

Under the leadership of Robert W. Scherer, board chairman and chief executive officer, the Company continues its tradition of growth and progress. His vigor and foresight are major reasons a study ordered in 1981 by the Georgia Public Service Commission called the company's management "progressive and energetic."

The Company moved in 1981 into a new 764,000-square-foot, energy-efficient 24-story office tower. The new headquarters building at 333 Piedmont Ave. is expected to use only half of the energy consumed by most similar-sized structures. Its inverted pyramid shape reduces heat from direct sunlight in summer but allows the lower winter sun to generate natural heating.

Georgia Power, an investor-owned, taxpaying utility, is a unit of The Southern Company, which owns an integrated system of power companies across the Southeast.

Georgia Power Company

Workers had little more than muscle power to help them during the construction of Terrora Dam in 1925. This unit of the North Georgia Hydro Group is one of 18 hydroelectric dams owned and operated by Georgia Power.

The completed project has changed little in the last 40 years, so visitors today would see a sight very similar to this. The dam can produce a total of 16,000 kilowatts of electricity.

Georgia State University

A campus retreat in the middle of a bustling city: Georgia State University's Central Plaza

Since its inception in 1913, Georgia State University has become an integral part of the metropolitan region, providing 197 fields of study in 47 undergraduate and graduate degree programs, plus special services and research to businesses and government agencies.

From its modern campus adjacent to Atlanta's financial district, GSU offers an urban education experience for those who seek "a real world connection" between the classroom and the realities beyond.

GSU has grown to meet the increasingly demanding needs of the metropolitan region. And yet, without the strong support of numerous friends and alumni—in particular the leadership to two dedicated individuals—GSU might not have become the major university it is.

The first of these leaders was George M. Sparks, the University's first president. A former war correspondent and Macon newspaper editor, Dr. Sparks was asked in 1924 to teach a writing course for Georgia Tech's evening School of Commerce.

He was impressed by the serious-mindedness of students working to overcome great obstacles to get an education. He asked to be placed in charge of the program, and in 1928 was named its dean.

When he took charge, the School had an enrollment of 428. In the 1920s State schools were expected to make a profit from student fees, but there were times when Dr. Sparks had to use his own money to pay faculty salaries.

In 1933 Georgia decided the evening school should be an independent college. It was until 1947 when the regents incorporated the program into the University of Georgia.

By 1955 it was clear that a destiny of its own was in store for the school. The regents set the school on its own again, this time as the Georgia State College of Business Administration, with Dr. Sparks as president, a post he held until his retirement.

Dr. Noah Langdale Jr. became the second president, in 1957, a post he still holds. A Valdosta native and holder of law and graduate business administration degrees from Harvard, he worked tirelessly to gain public support to hire additional faculty, establish innovative programs and build a modern campus.

In addition to schools in Business Administration and Arts and Sciences, the institution under his leadership added Colleges of Education, Allied Health Sciences, Public and Urban Affairs and, beginning in 1982, Law. The institution granted its first doctorate degree in 1965. In 1969 the regents renamed it Georgia State University.

From 47 students and five instructors in its first year to more than 20,000 students and 800 fulltime faculty members, Georgia State University has become a premier urban university with a threefold mission of teaching, research and service.

A great urban university requires people of vision to lead it. At far left, Dr. George M. Sparks, Georgia State's first president; right, Dr. Noah Langdale Jr., current president.

Graphic Industries, Inc.

Graphic Industries, Inc., is the $50 million annual sales business that germinated from the seed of an idea of Mark C. Pope III.

Pope, a veteran of the printing industry, saw the possibility of Atlanta's becoming a southeastern center of printing and graphics when the city stood on the brink of its boom years at the end of the 1950s.

Already president of the successful Williams Printing Company in Atlanta, having succeeded founder Jesse R. Williams in 1955, Pope envisioned a conglomerate of graphic arts companies, each operating independently, each capable of complementing and supplementing the other affiliated companies.

Pope put his plan into action in 1962 when the opportunity arose to buy Atlanta Blue Print Co. Founded in 1919 as a blue print house, Atlanta Blue has diversified into one of the largest reprographic houses in the Southeast.

Atlanta Blue was the first graphics company in a string of firms that now make up Graphic Industries. During the ensuing 20 years, Pope engineered a succession of acquisitions, mergers and start-ups of firms that have joined the printing and graphics conglomerate.

Each company is a story in itself. Of the 10 companies of Graphic Industries, several are old-line Atlanta and Southeast printing and graphics houses.

Williams Printing Company, the firm Pope joined in 1949, was begun in 1922 in Atlanta by Jesse R. Williams as a one-man print shop in the old Austell Building on Forsyth Street; the building later housed *The Atlanta Journal* and became known as the Journal Building.

Williams got the Company started in the daytime while holding down a night shift as a printer on *The Atlanta Constitution*. When Pope started with the Company, there were 18 employees and the firm had an annual volume of $250,000. Over the years the printing firm grew, moved into its own building in 1959, then moved in 1971 to larger quarters on Spring Street, near downtown Atlanta, the Company's present location.

As the firm grew steadily, it incorporated the tremendous changes and technological advances of the printing industry during those years. Williams marks its 60th anniversary in 1982, and has more than 175 employees and a sales volume of more than $13 million annually.

In 1968 Pope formed Graphic Industries, Inc., as a holding company for all operations. He is president and chairman of the Atlanta-based company which operates over 70 printing presses in nine plant locations occupying 400,000 square feet of space, and is the largest commercial printing and graphic arts operation in the South. Graphic's five-year plan calls for doubling its sales to $100 million through acquisition and internal growth.

Other members of the conglomerate are Stein Printing Company, Inc., founded in 1924 by James S. Stein, who saw specialization as the key to success. Stein's firm began as printers of railroad tariffs; it was on the third floor of the old Loft Building at 57 Forsyth Street, NW, present site of Rich's Store for Homes Annex.

Besides building a national reputation for fine color printing of annual reports and other corporate material, Stein Printing Company pioneered financial printing for the investment banking community and SEC requirements for public companies in the Southeast. Today it is the acknowledged leader in this specialized field.

Ryco, Inc., formerly Rybert Printing Co., was founded in 1912 in Atlanta by Thomas F. Rybert Sr., who was succeeded by his son Thomas Jr. The company is a general commercial printer which still serves some of the same accounts—such as Sears, Continental Insurance Co. and the Salvation Army—which it has serviced for more than 40 years.

In 1981 Graphic purchased one of the oldest printing houses in the Southeast—111-year-old Edwards & Broughton Company, in Raleigh, N.C. Other companies of Graphic include Plunkett Graphics and General Color, in addition to operations in Charlotte, Greensboro and Jacksonville.

Mark C. Pope III has completed 33 years in the printing industry in Atlanta. He is proud that among Graphic's 700 employees are his three sons—John, Mark IV and Carter—and his daughter Patty, to insure the continuity of family involvement and private ownership of the Graphic operations through the next generation.

The growth of the Graphic companies attests to his commitment to the industry, and to Atlanta's importance as a Southeast printing center.

Jesse R. Williams (1932), founder of Williams Printing Company

Old Stein Printing Company building at 161 Luckie Street, NW, purchased in 1933 for $22,500.

Mark C. Pope III

Old Atlanta Blue Print building at 112 Spring Street, NW, in 1938; building was destroyed by fire in 1956.

389

Some Faces In Our Past

Photographed on the porch of their bachelor club at the northwest corner of Poplar and Fairlie are Joe Foster (left), J. C. Wayt (center) and Eustace A. Speer. The Skull and Cross Bones Club was given that name to discourage a burglar who had looted the place several times.

It's a bath house or a flooded basement—or.... At any rate, it's an amusing photo of two men taking a watery break.

Greenwood Cemetery

Tucked away behind the trees and gently rolling hills of Cascade Road, Greenwood Cemetery is not visible from any street or highway but it has been known to Atlantans for almost 80 years.

Greenwood was chartered on December 14, 1904, by James L. Mason, Atlanta city attorney, and William H. Bowen, a downtown merchant. The two displayed foresight in the early purchase of land: Despite its rapid growth, Greenwood today owns enough land to provide for its needs for generations to come.

The Cemetery's 200 acres, of which only about 100 are developed, make it the second-largest cemetery in the Atlanta area. Situated in West End, the crest of Greenwood's hills provides a clear view of the city skyline.

Gazing at the gardens and serene fountains of Greenwood Cemetery, one can hardly imagine that it was once the site of Confederate lines of defense during the Battle of Atlanta. The spot was located between the battles of Utoy Creek and Ezra Church, two of the fiercest of the Atlanta campaign.

Today, the only remaining evidence of the Civil War battle that raged more than 100 years ago lies in the undeveloped portion of the Cemetery where entrenchments and gun emplacements are still visible.

Just inside the Cemetery is Old Cascade Springs, once a popular weekend getaway for Atlantans. Greenwood's water supply, drawn in part from this source, is furnished through its own system of waterworks.

The Cemetery was landscaped by Bowen and Mayson to preserve its natural beauty. The park-like vistas and tree-lined drives are evidence of their careful planning.

After Bowen died in 1921, Mayson continued as the Cemetery's first president until his death in 1935.

For the next 20 years the Cemetery was developed and improved under the leadership of Dowse B. Donaldson, Mayson's son-in-law. He served as president until 1955, when Frank Bowen Jr. was named to succeed him.

Greenwood Cemetery is the resting place for a cross section of Atlantans representing all walks of life, including some of the city's pioneer families.

It is also known as a major ethnic cemetery. Included are a Greek section, two Chinese sections, and a Jewish section representing several congregations.

There is also a special section for a labor union.

In 1965 a group of Jewish survivors of the Holocaust erected a monument in Greenwood to honor Jews who died under Nazi persecution. A memorial service at the monument is held each April by the Eternal Life-Hemshech organization.

Though a comparatively young cemetery, Greenwood has gained broad public acceptance. Its tradition of sound business management, coupled with a well-staffed office, has resulted in controlled growth and financial stability.

A Jewish organization, Eternal Life-Hemshech, erected a monument at Greenwood to honor Jews killed during the Holocaust.

Greenwood Cemetery's horse-drawn wagon in 1915

Atlanta's skyline is clearly visible from the crest of Greenwood's rolling hills.

Hansell, Post Brandon & Dorsey

Hansell, Post, Brandon & Dorsey is one of the largest and, through its predecessors, one of the oldest law firms in Atlanta. Growing with Atlanta and the region, Hansell, Post now consists of more than 100 attorneys in three offices—First Atlanta Tower, Perimeter Center and Washington, D.C.

Hansell, Post was formed in 1962 through the merger of Crenshaw, Hansell, Ware, Brandon & Dorsey with Moise, Post & Gardner.

The Crenshaw firm had originally been formed in 1886 as Anderson & Roundtree by Clifford Le Conte Anderson, a graduate of Mercer University. On Anderson's death in 1933, Granger Hansell, a graduate of Emory University and Columbia Law School, became senior partner of the growing practice originally initiated by Anderson.

During his remarkable career, Hansell was active in law, business and the arts. In addition to forming Fulton Federal Savings & Loan Association as the first federally chartered thrift institution in Georgia, and participating in the organization of the Atlanta Arts Alliance, Inc., Hansell served on various corporate boards and was a trustee of Emory University.

The Moise firm had been formed in the mid-1940s by Warren Moise and Allen Post, each of whom received his legal education at Oxford University as a Rhodes scholar.

From the beginning of his practice in 1915, Moise was known as a legal scholar, noted for his analytic abilities and skillful written and oral arguments. Allen Post commenced his career in the Georgia attorney general's office and quickly became known as one of Georgia's finest trial lawyers.

After his practice broadened with the Moise firm and thereafter, Post's reputation for excellence in legal skills has continued. Moreover, Post has contributed his talent to many civic, charitable and political activities, in addition to serving as a director of various business organizations.

Post has maintained his active practice and is senior partner of the firm. The remaining name partners of Hansell, Post, Hugh M. Dorsey Jr. and Inman Brandon continue to contribute to the practice of the firm. Son of a former governor of Georgia, Dorsey has long been recognized as among the state's premier trial attorneys.

Shortly after the formation of Hansell, Post in 1962, the firm was saddened by the untimely deaths of Warren Moise and Emerson Gardner. The blending of skills and practices resulting from the merger, however, together with a diverse and strong client base, positioned the firm for growth and success.

As Atlanta and its legal practice grew during the 1960s and 1970s, Hansell, Post expanded apace, earning a position of pre-eminence in the Atlanta legal community.

The primary office of Hansell, Post has been situated in the First Atlanta Tower since 1967. Recognizing the significant business strength of suburban office locations, Hansell, Post opened an office in Perimeter Center in 1978. This office now provides a full range of legal services to the rapidly expanding business community in that area of the city. In 1980 the firm established an office in Washington, D.C., to further enhance the scope of the firm's capabilities.

As Hansell, Post has grown in locations and personnel, the diversity and nature of its practice developed similarly since 1962. This practice encompasses the full spectrum of sophisticated legal services required by the contemporary financial and commercial community.

Representing local, regional and national interests, the operations of the firm's clients are broad in scope, ranging from banking to commodities export, from newspaper publishing to manufacturing and from securities underwriting to brokerage to pharmaceuticals.

From Roundtree through Hansell, Post, Moise and Dorsey to its current partners, the firm and its members have been an integral part of the history of Atlanta and Georgia. Approaching the 100th year of this rich heritage, Hansell, Post enters the 1980s with eager anticipation and pride in its history. With 56 individual and professional corporation partners, the firm is administered by a management committee of 11 partners. The current chairman of that committee is L. Travis Brannon Jr.

Allen Post

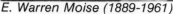

E. Warren Moise (1889-1961)

Granger Hansell (1901-1968)

Clifford L. Anderson (1862—1933)

Ira H. Hardin Company

The Ira H. Hardin Company home office building

Ira H. Hardin

At a very early age Ira H. Hardin knew he wanted to build things—houses, barns, warehouses—anything and everything. In fact, his father, surgeon and physician Dr. L. Sage Hardin, an 1898 graduate of Atlanta Medical College, fostered Ira's burning ambition by letting him build a walkway when he was only seven years old.

His ambition to build was fully realized after his graduation in 1924 from Georgia Tech. After 12 years of construction experience, he joined forces with a former Georgia Tech classmate to form the firm of Hardin and Ramsey.

In 1946 Hardin decided to go into business for himself, and the Ira H. Hardin Company was born. Since then he has been dedicated to providing his clients with the highest quality construction possible.

Hardin has been equally committed to maintaining high standards in the field of general contracting. He has served as president of the Georgia branch of the Associated General Contractors of America, and in 1965 he served as that organization's national president.

Ira Hardin's son, Allen Sage Hardin, joined the firm in 1955 and became president in 1968. In 1981 he became chairman of the board and chief executive officer of the Company, and Earl L. Shell Jr. was elected president and chief operating officer.

In addition to developing and expanding the Company's operations, Allen Hardin has been actively involved in the Atlanta community. He has served as president of the Atlanta Chamber of Commerce, president of United Way of Metropolitan Atlanta, and chairman of the Metropolitan Atlanta Rapid Transit Authority.

The Ira H. Hardin Company's early projects were mainly Atlanta residences, offices and industrial buildings. For many years the Company operated solely in and around Georgia.

In the mid-1960s the Hardin Company began working with some of the South's most prominent developers. As the size and number of their projects increased, the Company grew to become one of the largest general contractors in the Southeast.

Many Atlanta landmark projects were built by the Ira H. Hardin Company. They include the Trust Company Bank and office complex, the Atlanta Hilton Hotel and Atlanta Center complex, *The Atlanta Journal and Constitution* building, the Georgia Power Company headquarters, the Omni Arena, Phase I of the Georgia World Congress Center, the Coastal States Building, and the Omni International Hotel, office and retail complex.

Other Hardin projects in Atlanta have included three shopping malls—Northlake, Cumberland and Southlake—and numerous suburban office buildings.

Today, the Ira H. Hardin Company is a holding company with two construction companies—Hardin International, Inc., and Hardin Construction Company—and a service company, Hardin Associates.

With major projects throughout the Southeast and in major urban centers across the country, the Company specializes in office buildings, retail, hotel, institutional and multi-family projects.

The Atlanta Omni Arena, completed in 1972

Haverty Furniture Company

New stores are being added, like this one on Cobb Parkway in an Atlanta suburb.

The first Haverty Furniture Store, as it looked when it opened in 1885 at 117 Hunter Street

Reminiscing in his later years, J. J. Haverty recalled that when he opened the first Haverty Furniture Store in 1885 it was during the "Black Walnut Era."

The 10-piece bedroom set was in great demand: It included a Gothic bed, bureau, washstand, towel rack, rocker, four straight chairs and a center table.

It was enough to fill a convention hall, and required two horse-drawn wagons to haul it all.

James Joseph Haverty, the son of an immigrant from County Claire, Ireland, was 27 when he used his savings of $600 and a loan for another $600 to open that first store at 117 Hunter Street.

In 1889 he met and went into partnership with A. G. Rhodes, and they built a chain of Rhodes-Haverty Furniture Stores throughout the South and Midwest.

J. J.'s oldest son Clarence went to work for the company in 1898 at 16. In 1909 father and son, in a division of the company, took nine of the 17 Rhodes-Haverty stores and resumed business under the Haverty Furniture Co. name.

The Havertys believed it was important to build a professional management. As young people proved themselves, they were sent out to open Haverty stores. A holding company was formed to own the stores, but at each the manager was treated as a partner, sharing in his store's profits.

From 1909 until his death in 1939, J. J. Haverty worked closely with his son. The 50th anniversary of the firm was celebrated in 1935 in the middle of the Depression. Those were difficult years, particularly in the South, but the Company was sound.

There were 18 stores, and sales exceeded $5 million a year. Clarence Haverty was named president in 1938 and his brother-in-law Russell Bellman became vice president in 1946.

Clarence's son Rawson joined the company in 1941, only to be called for active duty in World War II.

The postwar period saw enormous growth and prosperity for the South. Spurred by Bellman, stores were remodeled and new stores added.

By 1955 Rawson Haverty was elected president. There were 39 retail stores in 10 Southern states, with annual sales of $16.8 million.

With the growth of the suburbs, Haverty's built stores in outlying areas while closing stores in older downtown locations. As tastes in home furnishings changed, the stores broadened their selections to include contemporary, Colonial and traditional stylings, and added furniture accessories.

As it approaches its 100th anniversary, Atlanta-based Haverty's has 67 retail stores, sales exceeding $122 million a year, and is the second largest independent furniture retailer in the nation.

Three generations of Havertys: J. J. (above, left); Clarence (center), and Rawson.

Historic Urban Equities

When Historic Urban Equities general partner James Cumming says, "There's just something about this old building," a listener detects a concern for more than square footage and leasing rates.

That is because Cumming, a Canadian whose interest in strategically located downtown properties led Historic Urban Equities to Atlanta in 1977 when it purchased and restored the Flatiron Building, has a fondness for sharing space with bygone generations.

"There's a tremendous satisfaction in it," he says about the rewards of returning older buildings to active business lives. "There's the satisfaction of working in a building that people were working in two or three generations ago. With the unusual shapes, there's a mystique that's awfully appealing, and it's difficult to define it exactly."

Historic Urban Equities has nonetheless taken something of a lead in retaining parts of Atlanta's past in the business life of her present. Also, others have found the mystique of old buildings appealing.

Lessors at the William-Oliver Building, a 1930 Art Deco-style structure that Historic Urban Equities bought and renovated in 1979, find this mystique in details like the carved granite facade and the marble and polished brass of the lobby, as well as the unique office space available.

Cumming tends to downplay his motives in reviving older, sometimes historic buildings. "Our basic interest is in key locations—downtown, highly visible prime sites," he says. "In many cases there is heritage-type property on these sites. But if there's not, it is not necessarily overlooked."

A case in point is Historic Urban Equities' recent purchase of the Allied-Cathcart building on Houston Street, a moving company's former storage space, for renovation into loft-type working and living quarters.

Motivations aside, Historic Urban Equities' investments in Atlanta's past have helped the city's downtown retain a sense of tradition amid the newer skyscrapers of glass and concrete. It has done the same elsewhere.

For 10 years the company had flourished in Toronto, Canada, as the Historic Properties Group. Starting with a block of row houses resembling those on Atlanta's Baltimore Place, the company successfully brought forgotten or over-looked historic properties back to life, and won widespread acclaim and awards for its contributions to preservation of Canadian heritage.

The move to Atlanta came when company principals learned, through ownership of Toronto's Flatiron Building, that its Atlanta counterpart was for sale.

The English-American Building, known also as the Flatiron, under construction in 1897

The building, designed by Bradford Gilbert in 1897 and surviving as the oldest commercial high-rise in the city, offered the requisite prime location.

Stripped to bare brick and its 11 floors completely renovated, the Flatiron Building was successfully converted into the Georgia Justice Center housing the State Bar of Georgia, the Judicial Council and the Georgia Trial Lawyers Association, among others.

In addition to owning and managing the Flatiron and William-Oliver Buildings, Historic Urban Equities is constantly in search of prime downtown structures with potential for conversion into office or living space. The company actively seeks out buildings which are pleasing and which, when cleaned up and modified, are interesting to others as well.

Historic Urban Equities applies a similar formula to all its investments, carefully selecting underutilized buildings in prime downtown locations and putting together a mix of retailers and other tenants to provide an economically feasible blend of uses.

The company has done restorations in eight cities in the United States and Canada, but now is concentrating its efforts in Atlanta.

M. D. Hodges Enterprises, Inc.

M. D. Hodges

Mark Durward Hodges had made a name for himself as an entrepreneur by the time he was 21. As a young man in Milledgeville, he began developing and owning a variety of enterprises from candy manufacturing to textiles, and he had also begun to acquire large holdings of Middle Georgia timberland.

In the early Fifties he saw Atlanta as a city about to boom, and decided to expand his operations there.

In 1958 he established what is now M. D. Hodges Enterprises, Inc., a commercial and industrial development and construction firm.

Hodges continues as owner and president of the company, and is totally involved in the day to day operations of his firm. He has set company policy and guided his corporation according to the ethics and standards of quality of design and construction which are a large part of his working philosophy.

In the past two decades, M. D. Hodges Enterprises has concentrated most of its construction projects in metro Atlanta. The company has designed and constructed millions of square feet of commercial and industrial space and currently builds more than one million square feet of space a year.

These buildings are constructed mostly for speculation; however, some structures are for specific users. The company's policy is to have a large variety of space in inventory, available for tenant lease.

With the foresight and vision that have marked Hodges as a successful entrepreneur, he has recognized Atlanta as a national distribution center and has built to fill that need in the area.

While M. D. Hodges Enterprises may occasionally sell one of its buildings, the company usually retains ownership of its properties, and the firm leases to more than 300 of the top U. S. corporations as well as to individuals and partnerships.

The detailed use of brick on the building exteriors is one of the company's trademarks, as is the design of fewer column obstructions within the building, special emphasis on office facades, attention to subsurface and surface drainage including concealment of metal downspouts, and a focus on energy conservation.

The company has in-house capabilities for design, planning and construction to develop a project from site selection through finance to building maintenance.

Headquarters of M. D. Hodges Enterprises, 300 Great Southwest Parkway

Holder Construction Company

Colony Square

Since its birth in 1960 the Holder Construction Company's growth has paralleled that of Atlanta.

"We're a product of Atlanta's dramatic economic growth," says Robert M. Holder Jr., the Company's founder, chairman and chief executive officer. "This is a company of the present and the future."

Working in 1960 in the Atlanta office of a national construction company, Holder started his business "from scratch." His first project was a large industrial plant for American Home Products Corporation.

That first year, the Company's total volume of business was $2 million. By contrast, 1981's business amounted to more than $75 million.

Holder started out with a staff of three; today that number has grown to around 500.

A relative newcomer to the Atlanta market, Holder has established itself as one of the largest construction companies in the region and is ranked by *Engineering News-Record* as one of the top 400 general contractors in the nation.

Among the company's clients are Delta Air Lines, Saks Fifth Avenue, Chase Manhattan Bank, IBM and The Equitable Life Assurance Society.

In 1975, the Company opened a new division, Holder Management Services. With a staff of 30 and a branch in Houston, the division specializes in construction management and consulting, development management and property management. Today, this division ranks among the largest construction management firms in the United States.

The division's customers include virtually all of the money-center banks in New York, Chicago, Houston, Dallas and San Francisco. Also, it was the construction manager for The Martin Luther King Center in Atlanta.

Holder Construction Company was a key partner in the construction of the new Hartsfield International Airport midfield project, building 10 of its major jobs including the international terminal and concourse. Another airport project was Delta Air Lines' maintenance hangar, the second-largest clear-span structure in Georgia.

The Management Services division also played a major role in the development of the new airport, acting as the airlines' representative for the entire midfield project.

While Holder has constructed Atlanta-area projects such as Colony Square and Phipps Plaza, it builds in all regions of the United States. Its Tiara Tower at Singer Island, Fla., is the state's tallest condominium tower.

Holder says that although profit is the Company's main goal, "people are our most important resource.

"We treasure our reputation for skill and integrity," he says. "The only way to preserve that reputation is to train, support and develop our managers and leaders to the fullest, and through them achieve outstanding performance."

According to Holder, his company is an enthusiastic, aggressive, young business.

"We're a first-generation company dedicated to top quality achievement and growth for the future."

Phipps Plaza

Hudgins & Company, Inc.

For more than a half century, Hudgins & Company, Inc., and its predecessors have been demolishing buildings in Atlanta and the Southeast. In fact, every major hotel and most of the rest of Atlanta's best-known edifices stand on sites cleared entirely or in part by Hudgins.

Some prominent properties have been cleared twice by Hudgins. The Atlanta Hilton hotel, for instance, sits on land once occupied by the old Atlantic Brewery, which Hudgins razed in the mid-1950s, and later the Heart of Atlanta motel, demolished by Hudgins in 1973.

The city's first major demolition project was carried out by Hudgins in 1930 with the leveling of the Aragon Hotel. Forty-one years later the Collier Building was razed by Hudgins at the same site. The Georgia-Pacific Center occupies that site as well as the site of the DeGive Building/Loews Grand Theatre, demolished by Hudgins in 1978.

All told, more than 50,000 structures have been demolished by Hudgins crews since the firm was founded in 1925. Most of those numbers were accounted for in massive clearing efforts for the city's public housing projects and for freeway building here and all about the state.

The firm's founder, J.H. Hudgins, was born in DeKalb County in 1899. As a youth, he worked with a surveying party and as a postman. He bought an aging truck to haul sand and gravel, which he loaded and unloaded by hand because dump trucks had not yet been invented.

Over the years the business grew into the Hudgins Transfer Company with a fleet of about 100 trucks. A second firm, Hudgins Contracting Company, was formed as Hudgins expanded his operations to excavation and construction.

His son, H.T. Hudgins, began work as a water boy at clearance sites in the late '30s. "I fell through my first roof when I was 13," Hudgins recalls with a mixture of pride and amusement. After graduation from the University of Georgia in 1949, the younger Hudgins formed his own excavation company. In 1954 father and son joined forces to form the present Company. Seventeen years later, the elder Hudgins died, and the firm passed to his son. In 1977 the third generation of Hudgins became involved in operations.

From 1928, when demolition activities were begun, to the present, the Hudgins family has been in the forefront of the

The 1974 implosion of the Henry Grady Hotel on Peachtree Street, positioned four inches from Davison's department store. The Peachtree Plaza hotel is now on the old site of the Grady.

demolition industry. The Company was the first in this region to purchase and utilize bulldozers, loaders and cranes. In the early '60s, Hudgins became the first Southern company to use explosives to demolish highrise structures. The first and most spectacular instance of this technique in Atlanta occurred in 1974 with the implosion of the Henry Grady Hotel to clear the site for the Peachtree Plaza hotel.

With the advent of the preservation movement, demand increased for the interior demolition so as to preserve handsome old exteriors. Again, Hudgins earned a reputation as an innovator and was chosen to do the interior demolition required for the renovation of the historic Florida state Capitol in Tallahassee.

In 1980 Hudgins took on the extremely delicate task of removing the rear wall of the Cyclorama building in Atlanta to gain access to the huge and badly deteriorated Civil War painting inside. The work involved demolition of walls as close as 12 inches to the fragile mural.

Among the most notable landmarks razed by Hudgins over the past 54 years are the Kimball House, the Peachtree Arcade, the Aragon and Henry Grady hotels, Terminal Station, the Atlanta Journal-Constitution Building, St. Joseph's Hospital, and the Century Building, commonly known as the Three Sisters Building. All these and many others have worn the familiar banner which proclaims "Hudgins Was Here!"

Preparation in the early stages for the 1959 demolition of the Kimball House, Atlanta's premier hotel for many years. It was situated between Decatur, Pryor and upper Wall Streets. Note the trackless trolley wires.

The Aragon Hotel (1930), on the southeast corner of Peachtree and Ellis Streets, was Hudgins' first major demolition project.

International Group

In the complex world of business it is rare to find an organization that both advises its clients on alternative courses of action and accepts complete responsibility for implementing chosen alternatives. Such an organization is International Group.

A full-service business, management and computer organization, International is a closely knit, tightly controlled cooperative of independent companies and individuals whose myriad business services are augmented by an even larger network of carefully chosen associates.

International believes that every company should have a business adviser it can call on for in-depth knowledge in many fields, and on whose resources it can draw for assistance and advice. That, in essence, is International's relationship to its clients.

Its role is similar to that of a law or accounting firm, except that International's services and expertise are not limited to one or two relatively narrow fields. The organization is composed of six primary groups with capabilities in broad business areas. Within each group are a number of more specialized units.

International's organizational structure, its business philosophy and its concept of both advising and implementing are virtually unique. The range of services and expertise the group offers is unavailable from any other single source.

International is based in Atlanta, but its scope is national, and its reach, as the name implies, is worldwide. The same thought and care that go into all of the firm's business decisions led to choosing Atlanta as its headquarters city. Atlanta's intrinsic vibrancy, diversity and potential for continued growth as a business and financial center were among the criteria.

International began in 1975 with a carefully devised 12-year program. The first three years were devoted to selecting top individuals and companies in various fields, and to laying plans for testing its concepts in the marketplace. In short, International's founders in those three years put into place a business entity of a type that had not previously existed.

The organization and planning period complete, International in 1978 entered the testing phase of its plan. Among the early clients were American Express, National Data, Curtis 1000, Cox Broadcasting, the Atlanta Regional Commission, Georgia Institute of Technology and numerous agencies of Federal, state, local and foreign governments including Saudi Arabia and Nigeria. Today, International continues to accelerate the expansion of its client base and its resources across the country and throughout the world.

The diversity of International's projects —from creating a pilot nationwide telecommunications system to brokering huge fertilizer and oil contracts—demonstrates the group's extraordinary versatility and its ability to handle all or any part of almost any assignment a company cannot or does not choose to handle with its existing resources.

By combining the knowledge, experience and expertise of its staff with that of associated groups, International can provide any organization—large or small— with full management or special assistance in the financial-legal-accounting area, sales and marketing, personnel education and training, all types of computer-related activities and other technological services, and administrative services of all types.

The firm's primary purpose is to provide whatever expertise and assistance is necessary to enable an organization to function efficiently and profitably.

Like the concept on which International was founded, the firm's organizational structure is markedly different from that of most businesses. Each of the several hundred persons associated with the group is a partner, and each shares in the partnership's profits in proportion to his or her contributions. This includes not only professional and management personnel, but also support personnel such as secretaries and clerks.

Partners—firms and individuals—are chosen on several criteria, including proven performance and professionalism, the potential for independent growth, and compatibility with International's needs. Partners include lawyers, accountants, printing firms, public relations professionals, travel agencies, an executive services organization and an array of data processing and management experts.

All work together within the organizational structure, yet each partner is encouraged to grow independently in order to preserve the entrepreneurial creativity that is the firm's driving force.

Privately owned by its partners, International has no plans or need to raise capital by traditional means. Instead, the firm has adopted other, more effective means of raising capital. The firm's founders believe this is the way many organizations will be and should be structured and operated in the future.

Johnson and Higgins

Henry Ward Johnson (1821-1881)

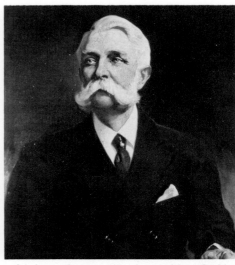

Andrew Foster Higgins (1831-1916)

Johnson & Higgins was founded in New York City in 1845 by two young marine-loss adjusters, Henry W. Johnson and Andrew F. Higgins. They saw a need to fill the void in professional assistance in settling losses.

In providing this service, the two men also found themselves negotiating insurance contracts for clients. Their activities led them to establish the first insurance brokerage firm in the United States.

Previously, a buyer had to handle insurance matters directly with the insurance companies. Service to the client, rather than allegiance to one particular company, remains the hallmark of Johnson & Higgins.

As a marine-oriented firm, the new insurance brokers' business from the outset was tied to the marine industry, and soon they opened a second office on the West Coast. Over the years, however, the firm has expanded into all areas of insurance and established a network of offices in major cities throughout the country.

In 1956 the firm made the decision to enter the Southeastern insurance market. The area was emerging as a fast-developing region of the country and was attracting an increasing number of businesses.

Since Atlanta was the transportation hub as well as an important business and financial center, firm officials decided to initiate service to the Southeast through an Atlanta location, a move which no doubt would have pleased founder Andrew Higgins, a native of Macon, Ga.

To open the Atlanta office, Johnson & Higgins merged with the firm of Dubose-Egleston, a well-established local agency which had been founded in 1876, only 31 years later than Johnson & Higgins. The principal of the agency, Beverly M. Dubose Jr., was named head of the newly created subsidiary, Johnson & Higgins of Georgia, Inc.

The Southeastern territory included eight Southern states from Virginia to Florida and Louisiana. The firm quickly determined the need for the many services provided by a major insurance brokerage firm in the Southeast, and it became apparent that more offices would be required to carry out the pledge of providing the best service.

In the 1960s and 1970s, offices of Johnson & Higgins were established in Richmond, Va.; New Orleans, Miami and Charlotte, N.C.

In 1968 the Atlanta office acquired the important local firm of Lipscomb-Ellis, which had been founded in 1898, thus merging Atlanta's two oldest agencies into one. Charles Sims Bray, president of Lipscomb-Ellis, became president of Johnson & Higgins of Georgia, Inc., and Beverly DuBose Jr. was elected chairman of the board.

As the Atlanta office continued to grow, more services were provided. The Johnson & Higgins organization became a major U.S. broker in the international field, with a network of more than 36 overseas offices. Access to those facilities was offered to clients in the Southeast.

The Atlanta office typifies the Johnson & Higgins goal to provide full service in insurance in each of the company's offices throughout its system. This was a goal set in 1845 when the company was founded.

As a firm, Johnson & Higgins pioneered in several areas of service such as employee benefits and actuarial consulting. The founders strove to remain in step with the times, and today the company still follows their example.

In 1980 an office was opened in Birmingham, Ala., and a year later an office was created in Nashville to serve Tennessee.

The Atlanta branch, now led by Albert S. McGhee, has developed into a major branch of the Johnson & Higgins system. After almost a century and a half, the oldest and only major privately held insurance brokerage firm in the country looks forward to the challenge of the future.

Jones, Bird & Howell

Jones, Bird & Howell is a law firm engaged in the general practice of law in its own building, the Haas-Howell Building, next to the home of the newly-established United States Court of Appeals for the Eleventh Circuit in downtown Atlanta.

The firm began in the early 1900s, when Robert P. Jones established an Atlanta firm engaged in the general practice of law. In 1925 F. M. Bird began practicing law in Atlanta after returning from Washington, D.C., where he had served Senator Hoke Smith. In 1945 Arthur Howell became Mr. Bird's partner, and in 1959 Bird & Howell merged with the Jones firm to become Jones, Bird & Howell. The labor law firm of Wilson & Wilson joined the firm in 1976.

Robert Tyre Jones Jr., better known as Bobby Jones, winner of the Grand Slam of golf during the Golden Age of Sport, was a member of the firm until his death in 1971.

Lawyers in the firm have a tradition of involvement not only in the professional activities of the Atlanta and Georgia bar but also in the cultural and civic life of Atlanta.

Robert T. Jones Jr. (1902-1971)

Francis M. Bird

Arthur Howell

Kennesaw Life And Accident Insurance Company

An early home of Kennesaw Life: 165 Luckie Street

Kennesaw Life and Accident Insurance Company was the brainchild of two Marietta insurance agents, A. G. Haskins and Hugh M. Morris. An organizational meeting for the fledgling Company, described by the *Cobb County Times* as "Marietta's first home-grown insurance company," was held January 1, 1954. The goal of the organizers was to raise $200,000 from the sale of stock.

On February 2, 1954, Haskins, J. F. Shaw Jr., Harry O. Hames, H. A. Pontius and Frank D. Holcombe petitioned for incorporation, with each petitioner to own 250 shares of common stock. Hugh Morris was not one of the original petitioners, but later records list him as a vice president and member of the board of directors.

The new Company received its charter on March 3 and was licensed by the State on May 10. The following day its first insurance policy was sold to Marietta resident George LeCroy.

Initially, the Company wrote only health and accident insurance. Its first life policy was written in October, 1954, on Virginia Carole Fricks, an infant.

By the end of its first year the Company's office staff had grown to 13, and its agency force numbered 42. The number of insureds had reached 43,172, and life insurance in force was $4,291,954. A first-anniversary open house was held in the Company's headquarters on Atlanta Street, in a building bought in December and converted into modern office facilities. A. G. Haskins was president and James E. Berry, Cobb County tax commissioner, was chairman.

In 1957, only three years after its founding, the Company had assets of $400,000, and $8.4 million of life insurance in force. The board of directors then decided that Kennesaw Life was to be developed into a major insurance company, and devised a plan providing for internal growth as well as external growth through mergers and acquisitions.

To implement the plan, the board in 1958 elected an experienced insurance executive, Fred W. Lagerquist Jr., as president. Much of the first year under Lagerquist was devoted to reorganization. Even so, assets increased more than 46 per cent, and life insurance in force by 25 per cent.

By the time another year had passed, the Company's agency force had reached 190, insurance in force stood at $90 million, and premium income was $1.75 million. As the Company enlarged, investor interest grew, and in 1959 the Company had 7,500 shareholders.

In 1959 the Company moved its headquarters to Buckhead Avenue in Atlanta, where it remained until it bought a building at 165 Luckie St. In 1966 the Company acquired its present home office building, 1447 Peachtree St.

True to the plan set forth by the board in 1957, Kennesaw Life sought growth through mergers as well as internal development. From 1958 through 1963, for example, it acquired five life companies. These and later mergers contributed greatly to the Company's emergence as the major insurance company envisioned by its leadership.

Lagerquist continued as president of the Company until his death in 1977. He was succeeded by William J. Ruth Jr., who serves as president of LifeSurance Corporation, a holding company for Kennesaw Life and other subsidiaries. By 1982 Kennesaw Life was licensed to do business in 35 states, an increase of 22 over the previous 10 years.

Today, the LifeSurance companies have assets totaling more than $50 million, and life insurance in force of about $900 million—an impressive record for what began as "Marietta's first home-grown insurance company."

The Company keeps pace with rapidly changing economic conditions by offering insurance products tailored to meet consumer needs: payroll-deduction whole life, cancer and loss-of-time insurance; credit insurance and annuities as well as ordinary life.

Present home of Kennesaw Life: 1447 Peachtree Street

Life of Georgia began in classic Atlanta fashion as the Reconstruction-era dream of two former farmboys with a little cash and a large dream.

Now, nine decades after its founding in an Atlanta boardinghouse, the company that began by providing "a piece of paper and a promise" to industrial workers has become one of the largest insurers in North America, with $8 billion of life insurance in force.

Life Insurance Company of Georgia's annals reflect the growing fortunes of its Southeastern base. As the region's economy changed and its population prospered, the company's policies have evolved from a single weekly premium sickness and accident policy to a full line of ordinary insurance (added in 1946) and group insurance (added in 1957), as well as a growing annuity business.

In accord with market trends, the company offered ordinary insurance exclusively to all life policyholders beginning in 1981. This completed the phase-out of industrial insurance that had once been Life of Georgia's cornerstone.

Matching the Sunbelt success of the company's marketing appeal to Southern families has been its investment strategy. Life of Georgia is a major source of capital for suburban homes in Southern cities, for shopping centers on the Florida Gold Coast, warehouses in the oil-boom cities of Texas and Oklahoma—even the jetways that funnel passengers into planes along the vast concourses of Atlanta's Hartsfield International Airport.

Its roots, however, are undeniably modest. Shortly after its founding in 1891 as the Industrial Aid Association (it became the Industrial Life and Health Insurance Company in 1903 and assumed its present name in 1947), the division of labor was precise.

Founder John McEachern administered the home office in rented quarters in the old state Capitol in Atlanta (destroyed by fire in 1893). Founder I. M. Sheffield recruited and trained the field force.

Now, the company has 120 offices in 11 Southeastern cities, staffed by 3,800 employees (1,000 in metro Atlanta). Headquarters are in Life of Georgia Tower, a 29-story building at West Peachtree and

North Avenue. (Previous company-owned home offices were at 91-93 Walton Street and at Linden Avenue and West Peachtree Street, now Doctors Memorial Hospital of Atlanta.) A new home office is planned on a heavily wooded site in north Fulton County by 1985.

Throughout its growth, in economic depression and boom times, Life of Georgia has nurtured the reputation engendered in its early surname, "The Old Reliable," a role strengthened by its present position as the major component of GeorgiaUS Corporation.

This financial-services company in 1981 acquired First of Georgia Insurance Group of Augusta, which offers property and casualty protection in 24 states. GeorgiaUS Data Services, Inc., a computer time lease firm in Atlanta, is the other component of the parent company.

GeorgiaUS Corporation is the largest North American holding of Nationale-Nederlanden, N.V., the worldwide insurance group headquartered in The Hague. Life of Georgia was acquired by N-N for $360 million in 1979 and continues as an independently managed company.

These twins were more than a couple of cute kids on Life of Georgia's billboards in the early Sixties; they represented the company's $2 billion insurance in force. Present coverage in force exceeds $8 billion.

Life Of Georgia

Life of Georgia policies over the years reflected the changing face of the South—and the company's broadening range of insurance protection.

Co-founder and first president of Life of Georgia, John Newton McEachern, was a native of then-rural (and distant) Cobb County. He recalled hearing Sherman's guns as a boy near Kennesaw Mountain.

Life of Georgia co-founder Isham Mallie Sheffield: His shift from tobacco to insurance foretold the massive transformation which the former agricultural center of Atlanta was to undergo as it evolved into the financial hub of the Southeast.

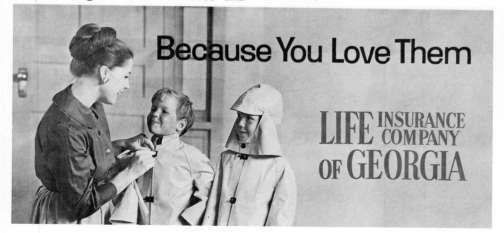

Because You Love Them

LIFE INSURANCE COMPANY OF GEORGIA

Maier & Berkele, Inc.

As Atlanta's oldest jewelers, Maier & Berkele, Inc., has assisted Georgians in celebrating the traditional rites of the family —marriages, anniversaries, births and birthdays—for four generations.

Battles around Kennesaw raged outside Atlanta as H. Armin Maier was born at the corner of Alabama and Forsyth Streets on June 2, 1864. The son of John Maier, a painter whose portraits hang in the State Capitol and Governor's Mansion, and Maria Anna Berkele Maier, Armin Maier was to build a family tradition and lay the foundation for one of the outstanding jewelry firms in the South.

Maier & Berkele became the region's first jewelry store to qualify as Registered Jewelers with the American Gem Society, the first to develop a bridal registry and the first to import fine china and watches.

The firm became a leader in the national gemological education movement of the Thirties, with Armin Maier Sr. serving as one of the first governors of the Gemological Institute of America. A half century later, his grandson Frank H. Maier Jr. was elected to the industry's highest professional office, the American Gem Society presidency.

Armin Maier Sr. began the family tradition as a jeweler's apprentice while in his teens. By 23, he had bought an interest in A. L. Delkin, a wholesale tool store, and added diamonds, watches, jewelry and silverware to his stock. Three years later, in 1890, he convinced his uncle John Berkele to buy out Delkin and open the first Maier & Berkele store, on Whitehall Street. Berkele, a locksmith retired from Heinz & Berkele, was a member of the City Council and Board of Street Commissioners. He was also chief engineer of the city's volunteer fire department.

Maier housed his goods in mahogany display cases beneath elaborate chandeliers, and also operated a wholesale and catalog division and artware stores. He bought wares throughout Europe, and commissioned original designs, among them a silver and enamel souvenir teaspoon for the Cotton States and International Exposition of 1895.

From the turn of the century, Maier set industry standards by selling the highest quality diamonds, watches and jewelry. Meanwhile, he established his personal business philosophy: "I want Maier & Berkele to be a place that a little girl can get just as good a value as the shrewdest horse trader."

The family business grew quickly in size and reputation. It was Maier & Berkele craftsman J. W. Kreeger who engraved the Great Seal of Georgia in 1914, and presented it to Gov. John M. Slaton. The company hit its pre-World War II sales peak in 1920, selling such popular merchandise as silver, diamonds, swagger stocks, "stomachers" and grandfather clocks.

In 1928 Maier & Berkele moved to 111 Peachtree Street; in 1934 Maier's son Frank H. opened a Savannah branch. Silver was the company's stock and trade, and Maier & Berkele designed the silver service for the cruiser Savannah. Atlanta became known as the "goblet center of the universe." White-gold wedding rings surrounded by diamonds sold for as little as $50, sterling teaspoons for $1 and goblets for $5.

Facing diminished interest in jewelry during the Depression, Maier & Berkele opened extensive china, crystal and stemware departments in the Thirties, wooing brides by selling silver flatware by the place setting and introducing a bridal registry.

By 1946 the company opened Maier & Berkele-Charles Willis Associates, operating until Willis went into business independently.

Maier & Berkele's headquarters at 3225 Peachtree Road opened in 1963; a Decatur store was established as the result of purchasing the Myron E. Freeman jewelry firm in 1964. New stores were opened in Cumberland (1973), Southlake (1976) and Perimeter (1982) Malls.

Traditionalist and innovator, Maier & Berkele continues to build on its founder's philosophy: "The reputation we have earned is something that is our privilege to give. It must never be charged for."

Maier & Berkele's store at 31 Whitehall Street about 1916

The Midnight Sun

In 1968, while Atlanta was still gasping with wonder at John Portman's glass bubble elevators, walkways in the sky and street sculptures taller than buildings, he awed the city with another architectural innovation—a restaurant as unique as his own city-within-a-city, Peachtree Center, where the restaurant was built.

The Midnight Sun opened in August, 1968. It was a Scandinavian restaurant, complete with Stig Jorgensen, general manager, 20 chefs and staff members imported from Denmark.

As Atlanta's honorary Danish consul, Portman felt a deep affinity and affection for Denmark and the Scandinavian countries. He had long been attracted to their impeccable sense of contemporary design. He also admired their unique and skillful preparation and presentation of food. He felt Atlanta would share his enthusiasm for a restaurant equal to the best in Scandinavia.

And so it did. The Midnight Sun was a triumph. Atlantans loved it, as did visitors from all over the world.

Built around a large marble tiered fountain open to the sky, the restaurant was the height of contemporary opulence. The banquet rooms were equally as grand. Every detail of the restaurant was designed and decorated by Portman, even the table linens and matchbook covers.

Through the years, The Midnight Sun continued to receive the world's highest awards for cuisine, design and decor. Simultaneously, Atlanta was growing at mind-boggling speed. Suddenly it became a top convention city, an international city, and its visitors and residents were acquiring an appetite for international cuisine.

Anticipating the broadening taste of its clientele, The Midnight Sun seized the opportunity again to be an innovator in fine dining in Atlanta. Hence, plans were made to change The Midnight Sun.

The restaurant was closed early in 1981 for renovation—to embellish further the palatial setting and to enhance the warmth and intimacy of the atmosphere. Fred Halimeh, a veteran of The Four Seasons Restaurant in New York and one of the country's foremost restaurateurs, became general manager. He added top chefs and waiters to his staff—primarily European—because The Midnight Sun was soon to become a European restaurant.

Today, The Midnight Sun is comparable to some of the finest restaurants abroad. It is the epitome of European dining in the grand manner. Even the most sophisticated, well traveled guest is impressed with the quality and imaginative preparation of the cuisine, the finesse of the service and the congeniality of the staff.

As for the wine list, it is Georgia's finest, and one of the largest in the Southeast. Halimeh intends to make it one of the best in the country, which he is presently doing. By attending some of the world's most acclaimed wine auctions, notably the Annual Heublein Premier National Auctions of Rare Wines, he has acquired vintages of such rarity and stature that his purchases have received international news coverage.

The Midnight Sun's banquet facilities have also been changed, thereby attracting some of the most prestigious convention groups and parties in the country.

Should one wonder what Portman thinks of today's Midnight Sun, it should be noted that not only did he revitalize the restaurant's design and decor, inspire the revision of the menu from Scandinavian to European, and initiate the expansion of the wine cellar to limitless proportions, but he also created a traditional European sidewalk cafe adjoining The Midnight Sun. This is where Portman dines almost every day.

George Muse Clothing Company

George Muse, founder

William F. Clark, Muse's president and chief executive officer

The George Muse Clothing Company, a 103-year-old employee-owned clothing firm, is considered an Atlanta institution.

Founder George Muse, after working for five years in a store owned by Dr. R. P. Kimbro, at the age of 20 bought the business in 1879. It has remained in the heart of downtown, while expanding to seven other suburban locations.

His philosophy of hard work and community involvement, combined with personal service and quality men's clothing at a fair price, was the cornerstone of the firm's success.

Moving in 1921 from Whitehall Street to the present location at 52 Peachtree Street (site of the old Confederate Arsenal) enabled Muse's to add women's departments. In 1923 a public contest and poll reassured management that its quality merchandising approach was correct, and continues to this day. Customers also enjoy the benefits of one of the Southeast's finest alterations department, which now employs a staff of more than 45 skilled craftsmen.

Through the foresight of then-president James Harry Alexander, the concept of employee ownership was conceived. His will directed that his stock be made available to the employees. He felt those who worked hard for the Company's success should share in the rewards and its future, while encouraging personal dedication and a sincere appreciation of their customers.

Today, more than 40 employees share the ownership, with no individual having majority control. A profit-sharing plan was begun in 1945. Much of this accounts for the fact that in Muse's long history, there have been but six presidents, all promoted from within:

George Muse	1879-1917
William W. Orr	1917-1927
James H. Alexander	1927-1944
Oby T. Brewer	1944-1966
E. Brannon Morris	1966-1974
William F. Clark	1974-present

At a time when large corporations have bought up most small companies, Muse's has remained staunchly independent. It enjoys the luxury of making its own decisions and determining policies designed to assure good customer and employee relations. Muse's employees have served many Atlanta families for three and four generations.

The following list of stockholders with more than 30 years service indicates the direction and contribution of what is referred to as the store family:

Retired Stockholders

	Years of Service
Carl Hood	48
Clyde Hughes	39
Charles Jackson	48
D. Homer Yarn	39
Olin Babb	44
Pauline Mitchell	32
Cliff Ray	48
John Stell	47

Active Stockholders

	Years of Service
Charles McClain	43
Ed Haney	35
John Ruff	33
Mildred Mewborn	32
Sal Vitale	30

Although many downtown merchants through the years have closed or moved to shopping centers, Muse's has remained in its seven-story building at the center of Atlanta's historic Five Points. Muse's ability to survive the economic swings of more than 100 years attests to its strength of management and its strong customer base. Bill Clark feels, as did his predecessors, that "Downtown has a great future and we look to the excitement of Atlanta's growth, and Muse's next 100 years."

Muse's downtown store, built in 1921

The National Bank of Georgia today is a leader in offering innovative financial services to Atlanta citizens and businesses. A comparative banking newcomer, having been founded in 1911, it nonetheless holds a unique place in banking history: It was one of the first organized specifically to lend to working people.

These days when banks compete for car, vacation and other loans to individuals, it's hard to believe there was a time not long ago when banks wouldn't lend to ordinary people. If the average person needed a loan, about the only place he could go to was a loan shark, and nowhere was the evil of loan sharking worse than in Atlanta.

One Atlantan who for years battled the loan sharks was W. Woods White. His fight against loan sharking was the reason why he was so excited when he met a young attorney who had successfully opened an experimental bank in Norfolk, Va., to make credit available to the average person.

That lawyer was Arthur J. Morris, the founder of consumer banking. With Morris' assistance, a similar bank was organized by White and others here. It opened in June, 1911, as the Atlanta Loan & Savings Company, later to be the Morris Plan Company of Georgia, the Bank of Georgia and, finally in 1965, The National Bank of Georgia.

The experimental banks in Norfolk and Atlanta were so successful that soon Morris Plan banks were operating in 127 cities in 30 states. It didn't take long for the other commercial banks to realize that consumer lending was good business.

By the 1930s consumer banking was adopted throughout the industry. At the same time, the Atlanta bank was being approached by its customers who had gone or desired to go into business and who wanted their bank to make loans for that purpose. Just as other banks had expanded into consumer lending, the forerunner of today's NBG entered the field of commercial lending.

The period of the Bank's greatest growth began in the late 1970s when ownership passed to Dr. Ghaith R. Pharaon, an American-educated Saudi Arabian investor. In 1978 he named international banker Roy P. M. Carlson as the Bank's president.

Carlson set as NBG's goals to continue as a leader in the Bank's traditional area of consumer service, to aggressively seek new corporate clients among Georgia's small-to-medium size companies and to open markets for Georgia products and services through consulting and financing for international trade.

In addition, Carlson undertook a program to expand NBG beyond Fulton and DeKalb Counties to other communities in metropolitan Atlanta. In 1982 a holding company was formed, NBG Financial Corporation, to facilitate the acquisition of other banks. It became the parent company of the Atlanta bank and the NBG banks of Cobb, Clayton and Gwinnett. In the first three years under Carlson's leadership, the NBG organization has substantially more than doubled in size and earnings.

Just as Atlanta has changed over the years, The National Bank of Georgia has expanded from a pioneer in consumer lending to a leader in promoting Georgia products throughout the world. It has been an exciting time and NBG looks forward to continued service to its community.

The National Bank Of Georgia

Roy P. M. Carlson

The Bank of Georgia building (now NBG) under construction in 1960

An NBG "mini-branch," one of many ways in which NBG makes banking more convenient

National Service Industries, Inc.

As a conglomerate, National Service Industries is known less by its corporate name than by the logotypes of its components. Most Atlantans will recognize readily the logos reproduced here, which are of Atlanta-born companies. They are Atlantic Envelope Co. (AECO), established in 1893; Selig Chemical Industries (1895), National Linen Service (1919), North Brothers Co. (1934), Zep Manufacturing Co. (1937) and Lithonia Lighting (1941).

By all accounts, few Atlantans are aware that their city is the home of one of America's most successful corporate giants, a company which is forecast to become a billion-dollar operation by 1984, if not sooner. The company is National Service Industries, Inc., and its lack of public notoriety has in no way detracted from its astounding performance over the past 20-odd years.

Headquartered in a handsome, Georgian-style building at the bustling intersection of 14th and Peachtree Streets, NSI is the almost-unseen parent corporation of 10 widely diversified companies.

The most prominent of these are Lithonia Lighting, National Linen Service and Zep Manufacturing, all long time Atlanta firms that have prospered and grown enormously as major divisions of NSI. In no small part this derives from NSI's fundamental policy that its member companies should retain a large measure of operational autonomy.

The emergence of NSI as a major conglomerate can be traced directly to National Linen Service and the aggressive expansion pursued by its founder, Atlanta businessman I. M. Weinstein.

Founded in 1919, National Linen bought out many of its competitors in succeeding years, so that by 1958 it was by far the largest linen service company in the nation. Facing anti-trust action by the Justice Department, National entered into a consent decree which limited its acquisitions within the industry.

The action turned out to be a blessing in disguise for it resulted in the decision to expand through diversification. By this time the presidency of the firm had passed to the founder's son, Milton Weinstein, whose first acquisition was the Zep Manufacturing Co., a chemical specialty manufacturer founded here in 1937.

The year was 1962 and Zep was headed by Weinstein's friend, Erwin Zaban. As part of the merger agreement Zaban joined National as executive vice president. From that point on the die was cast, and National's long-term prosperity was assured.

In 1964 National acquired another of the city's senior firms, the Atlantic Envelope Co., founded in 1893. Renamed National Service Industries, Inc., in 1965, NSI subsequently brought in two more local companies: North Bros. Co., an insulation supplier, and Selig Chemicals, which was merged into the same division with Zep.

NSI completed what was to be one of its most successful acquisitions in 1969. In that year NSI brought in Lithonia Lighting, already a potent competitor in the industrial and institutional lighting industry. Lithonia Lighting and its divisions now constitute the largest manufacturer of fluorescent lighting fixtures in the world.

The late Sixties and early Seventies saw the acquisition of several smaller firms, including DeVille Furniture, Marketing Services, National Recreation, Certified Leasing, and Block Industries, a clothing manufacturer.

In addition to these diversifications, NSI has expanded greatly through the acquisitions of related firms for its divisions. Lighting, Linen Service and Chemicals account for more than 70 per cent of NSI's gross sales, now approaching $900 million annually.

In 1975 Weinstein retired from the company, and Zaban led NSI as both president and chairman. In 1978 Sidney Kirschner was named president and chief operating officer. Zaban remains as chairman and chief executive officer.

Since its first diversification in 1962, NSI never has had a losing year and its record of profitability is among the highest among major U.S. corporations.

According to the latest *Fortune 500* listings, NSI ranks 343rd in the nation in sales, 113th in return on equity, and 68th in total return to investors. Furthermore, the company, which now employs more than 17,000 persons in the U.S. and Canada, is virtually debt-free.

"It is a record we're rather proud of," Zaban says with characteristic understatement.

Oglethorpe University

One of the South's oldest educational institutions, Oglethorpe University was established in 1835 at Milledgeville. It was named after the founder of Georgia and modeled, architecturally and academically, on his *alma mater,* Corpus Christi College, Oxford. The University is firmly rooted in the British tradition of undergraduate education.

During its long history Oglethorpe has produced more than it share of distinguished graduates in business, education, medicine, law, religion and other fields. Perhaps its most illustrious alumnus is Sidney Lanier—Class of 1860—the noted Southern poet who also taught English at the University.

After the Civil War the young college moved to Atlanta which, by then, was becoming the commercial and cultural center of the state. In 1915 the University was re-established in its present location on the residential north side of Atlanta, near Brookhaven. Its rolling and wooded campus is one of the most beautiful in the Southeast.

During the 19th Century Oglethorpe was closely associated with the Presbyterian Church. In this century it has been an independent, private institution, drawing its students and faculty from many religious backgrounds. Though originally a men's college, Oglethorpe became co-educational in 1920, and its student body of 1,000 is now divided almost equally between men and women.

Its students are drawn from a wide geographical area; in 1981-82 Oglethorpe undergraduates came from 26 states and 33 foreign countries.

Among those who have contributed notably to the development of the University during its long history are Samuel K. Talmage, Thornwell Jacobs, Philip Weltner, Donald C. Agnew, George Seward, and Paul K. Vonk, all former presidents; Joseph Le Conte and Wendell Brown, revered professors; and J. T. Lupton, Emma Markham Lowry, William Randolph Hearst and Robert W. Woodruff, generous donors.

Through the years Oglethorpe has come to have certain distinctive characteristics: a personal approach to education with close relationships among faculty and students; strong emphasis on the skills of communication and the fundamental fields of the arts and sciences; a substantial core of studies required of all students, regardless of their specialized interests; a well-trained and well-compensated faculty; selective admissions, resulting in a student body that is cosmopolitan and well above the average in intellectual ability; a remarkable record of success in preparing students for professional schools, especially of medicine, law and business; a policy of not accepting Federal grants for institutional support, and increasingly generous financial support from corporations, foundations and alumni.

Chemistry laboratory at Oglethorpe

Lupton Hall

413

Oxford Industries, Inc.

Oxford's present home, 222 Piedmont Avenue

Oxford's first home (recent photo), 151 Spring Street

Oxford Industries, Inc., was founded by the Lanier brothers: left to right, Thomas, Hicks and Sartain. Thomas was one of a number of Atlanta leaders who perished in the Orly (Paris) plane crash in 1962.

Oxford Industries began in 1942 when the three Lanier brothers—Hicks, Sartain, and Tommy—bought a partnership in Oxford of Atlanta, a small merchandising/sales firm for men's sports shirts and slacks.

A year later Oxford of Atlanta became Oxford Manufacturing Company and acquired its first plant, in Rome, Ga., to produce men's slacks and shirts.

Today, Atlanta-based Oxford Industries, Inc., manufactures and sells a full line of men's wear and women's wear to mass merchandisers, department stores and specialty shops, and under designer, private or Oxford labels.

The $400 million-a-year apparel company employs more than 11,000 people, and owns 42 manufacturing plants. All except two plants in Mexico are in the Southeast, with 24 in Georgia.

To give credit for the success of Oxford is to credit its founders, the Lanier brothers. They considered hard work and integrity as important as the business acumen they displayed in a highly competitive business.

From the Company's modest beginnings, the Laniers built the business through acquisitions and by broadening its apparel lines. By 1950 sales had reached the $3.5 million mark. With the addition of new products in men's outerwear, net sales grew to $10 million by 1954, and the following five years saw Oxford expanding production substantially and continuing to add to its product lines.

Oxford made its first entry into the women's apparel market in 1959 with the manufacture of ladies' man-tailored shirts.

In succeeding years the Company continued its successful growth through acquisition and a knack for choosing the right products to fill out its lines. The period was marred by the untimely deaths of Oxford president Thomas Lanier and his wife Nell, victims of the Paris plane crash in 1962 that claimed the lives of 120 Atlantans.

Oxford constructed its present corporate headquarters at 222 Piedmont Avenue in 1965 and consolidated the various offices previously scattered throughout the city.

The Atlanta company was among the first manufacturers to test and adopt the use of permanent-press fabrics, which revolutionized the apparel industry and consumer home care of apparel.

By 1966 sales had exceeded $100 million. A year later Oxford Manufacturing changed its name to Oxford Industries, Inc.

Lanier Business Products was acquired by Oxford in 1968 through a merger. The office-machine manufacturing and distributing company was organized in 1934 as a partnership of the three Lanier brothers in Nashville. Hicks, the eldest brother, directed Lanier before its acquisition by Oxford, and continued in an advisory role until his death in 1974. Lanier Business Products operated as a part of Oxford until 1977 when the company was spun off into a separate entity.

In 1960 Oxford went public, selling 240,000 shares of stock, and shortly thereafter was listed on the American Stock Exchange. The stock is currently listed on the New York Stock Exchange.

J. Hicks Lanier became chairman of the Company in 1981 upon the retirement of his father, Sartain, one of the founders. Oxford has reported record-breaking sales, profit and growth during the last few years.

Peachtree Bank

In the years before 1971 the major Atlanta banks were restricted from branching into suburban areas like DeKalb County. To get a competitive edge for the time when the laws changed, the big banks would assist local business people in chartering suburban banks, with the idea of eventually merging these institutions.

This was the case when the Peachtree Bank was organized in Chamblee in 1960 with the help of the Trust Company of Georgia. But in 1971, when Georgia's branching laws were relaxed and the Trust Company sought to acquire Peachtree, the U.S. Antitrust Division objected. It argued that the Peachtree had built a solid reputation for personal service and community involvement, and that such a merger would seriously reduce competition in DeKalb County.

Few customers realized there was any link between their Bank and a big Atlanta institution. But they did know about the friendly and efficient service they received and how the Bank had become an important source of funding for local businesses and consumers. In the same way, they saw how involved the Bank and its officials had become in DeKalb civic and cultural affairs.

The directors of Peachtree Bank recognized a court battle would take years, while blocking the Bank from opening branches and raising capital to meet the needs of rapidly growing DeKalb County. In addition, if they lost the case, Peachtree would still be a one-location bank, while the Atlanta banks would have branched all over the County.

In October, 1971, the Trust Company shares were purchased by friends of the Bank in the Chamblee community. President Charles B. Ginden, a former Trust Company officer and for the four previous years head of Peachtree Bank, began the task of leading the institution as it entered an era of intense competition from the other DeKalb and Atlanta banks, now including the Trust Company.

When Peachtree Bank became independent, it had assets of $24 million and two offices in northeast DeKalb. In the next decade it increased its financial resources five-fold, built and/or acquired seven additional branches, and became the largest independent bank headquartered in DeKalb County.

A major event in its growth occurred in 1974 when it acquired the Citizens Bank of Georgia in Stone Mountain, permitting it to expand its service area into that fast-growing part of the County. Another important step took place in 1980 when it organized its own bank-holding company, Peachtree Bancshares, to facilitate expansion.

In the 1980s the growth and profitability of the Peachtree Bank continued. Total assets exceeded $160 million, and through its holding company it acquired in 1982 the Bank of Woodstock in fast growing Cherokee County.

Throughout this period, president Ginden, the officers and staff have strived to maintain the close community identification and personal service to all customers, individual and commercial, both large and small. This personalized service impressed even Washington bureaucrats back in 1970, and led to the Bank's having remained independent.

Charles B. Ginden as president guided the institution through its transition into a major independent bank.

The opening of the Peachtree Bank in 1960: William Oliver, chairman; James Sibley, representing the Trust Company of Georgia; Frederick G. Storey, director; Woodie Malone, director and Chamblee mayor; Davis Fitzgerald, president; and Ralph Wright and James D. Chesnut, directors.

Handsome branches with contemporary exteriors in earth tones have been built throughout DeKalb County, such as the Winters Chapel Branch shown here.

415

Peachtree Center

Peachtree Center, Atlanta architect/developer John Portman's prototype for modern multi-use urban development throughout the world, is a hub for business, conventions, shopping and entertainment, conceived to meet downtown Atlanta's business and social needs.

Designed and built by Portman, the Center's 10 buildings in 1982 drew thousands of people to shop, dine and work.

The development, which covers 10 acres in downtown Atlanta on either side of Peachtree Street between Baker and Ellis Streets, represents an investment of approximately $350 million, with planned growth expected to reach $700 million by 1990.

Peachtree Center is the product of Portman's desire to create an urban village environment in which everything the resident needs is within walking distance. The Center incorporates the architectural qualities of Denmark's Tivoli Gardens and other people-oriented complexes that encourage inhabitants to interact with their surroundings.

The first component of Portman's urban village —the Atlanta Merchandise Mart— opened in 1961 at Peachtree and Harris Streets as a wholesale facility for furnishings, floor coverings, decorative accessories and apparel. It was followed in 1965 by the Peachtree Center Building at 230 Peachtree, a 27-story structure with 360,000 square feet of space for office and retail use.

In 1967 and 1969, respectively, the Atlanta Gas Light Tower and the South Tower expanded the complex on the east side of Peachtree Street. Each 24-story facility added 299,000 square feet of office and retail space.

The heart of Peachtree Center and Portman's village concept, the Shopping Gallery, opened in 1974. The three-level mall encompasses shops, boutiques, restaurants and cafes situated among open-air atriums, courtyards, fountains, sculpture and greenery.

The design is similar to European marketplaces and "encourages a relaxed pace where people leisurely shop, dine and just watch other people," Portman said. The Center's international flavor also is evident in the cuisine of its restaurants and cafes, and in the merchandise of its stores and boutiques.

Peachtree Center's Cain and Harris towers opened their doors in 1974 and 1976, respectively. The 27-story buildings each house 360,000 square feet of office and retail space.

The 1,100-room Peachtree Center Plaza Hotel made its debut on Atlanta's skyline in 1976 on the onetime site of the governor's mansion, at Peachtree Street and International Boulevard. At 73 stories, the structure is the world's tallest hotel, and Atlanta's tallest building.

The development added the Atlanta Apparel Mart in 1979. The 1.2 million-square-foot showcase for wholesale apparel further enhances the Center's stature in the convention business.

An expansion of Peachtree Center underway includes Atlanta's largest hotel, two office towers and retail stores on the former site of St. Joseph's Hospital.

A complex of retail stores, restaurants and offices, Peachtree Center is a focal point for social and business gatherings in Atlanta.

416

Peachtree Corners, Inc.

Greeting residents, workers and visitors has been this signpost which, in keeping with the community's concern for the environment, combines both natural and man-made elements.

Peachtree Corners, Inc., under the leadership of founder Paul Duke, has evolved from a developer of the award-winning Peachtree Corners planned community into a major diversified-services organization.

The company began in the late 1960s by assembling 2,000 acres in southwest Gwinnett County for a planned community. A 12-year master development program was prepared by professional planners who paid particular attention to environmental preservation.

In the first 30 months, the company invested $10 million in on-site improvements, including a private sewer system, underground utilities and nine miles of four-lane roadway. The expenses of planning and improvements quickly paid off as some of the nation's largest and most prestigious corporations developed or leased space there, creating jobs and expanding the County's tax base.

By 1974 the project was advancing rapidly, having attracted several other major developers, including a joint venture between Kaiser Aluminum and Aetna Life Insurance Co. for an industrial center; the investment group which created Technology Park/Atlanta; Texas financier Lamar Hunt's Peachtree World of Tennis, one of the world's foremost recreation and residential complexes; and Cousins Properties, Inc., which developed the Corners Shopping Center.

Several single and multi-family projects were completed; others are under construction.

In 1975 the company and the community were hard hit by the economic downturn. But the company continued to function, and began preparing a restructuring program to be carried out when the economy rebounded.

During this period the company realized two things. First, when a developer has served its community and built a reputation for fair dealings, it retains the clients it has served. Second, when one begins with an exceptional concept—that is, private enterprise and state and county governments working together to benefit one community—the chances of success are increased, even when adversity is experienced.

By the late 1970s the company's restructuring was in place. It was keyed to diversifying beyond real estate into insurance, financial services and other lower-risk businesses.

Peachtree Corners, Inc., is now a holding company for these growing subsidiaries:

Financial Risk Services, Inc., and Peachtree Insurance Associates, two companies which offer integrated risk services including expertise in reinsurance, risk management, international insurance coverages, management services to independent agents, export credit coverage and advice in trade finance.

Peachtree Corners Realty, Inc., a major real estate brokerage company specializing in sales and leasing of commercial and industrial properties, with special emphasis on income-producing properties.

Peachtree Corners Development Company, which concentrates on developing suburban office parks with individual buildings clustered in a controlled environment to maximize appreciation for investors.

The parent company's five-year business plan calls for the acquisition or start-up of additional companies under the leadership of proven professional managers who will share in the ownership.

Not surprisingly, Peachtree Corners, Inc., remains an integral part of the community it founded. It and the others there enjoy the benefits of the balanced living, working and playing environment carefully created just a few years ago.

417

Peat, Marwick, Mitchell & Co.

A chance meeting in the United States between two young Scots who had known each other at the University of Glasgow led to a partnership that eventually became the world's foremost public accounting firm.

The year was 1897; the men were James Marwick and S. Roger Mitchell, and they opened their office in the financial district of New York City.

Within nine years the firm of Marwick, Mitchell & Co. had offices in Chicago, Minneapolis, Pittsburgh and Philadelphia. By 1911, it had more than a dozen offices in the United States and Canada and three overseas. On a transAtlantic voyage that year, Marwick met another Scottish accountant, William Barclay Peat. An international affiliation was formed, and in 1924 the firm became Peat, Marwick, Mitchell & Co.

Today, the firm has more than 23,000 employees, 300 offices in 72 countries, and earns professional fees in excess of $1 billion annually.

Marwick, Mitchell & Co. became a part of the Atlanta business community on December 1, 1922, when an Atlanta CPA, William H. James, opened an office in Room 904 of the Atlanta National Bank Building at Whitehall and Alabama Streets.

James became a partner in Peat, Marwick, Mitchell & Co. in 1925, but resigned in 1927 to return to his own accounting practice. He retired from active practice in 1972 at the age of 83. At 93, he is the oldest living former partner of Peat Marwick, Atlanta—and possibly of the firm.

At the time James resigned, Peat Marwick's Atlanta office, which had moved to the Hurt Building on Edgewood Avenue, had 22 employees, many of whom were working on matters for Alabama Power Company, which had become a major client, and Atlanta Laundries. Later, the growing firm moved to The First National Bank Building at Marietta and Peachtree Streets.

Subsequent managing partners include M.F. Pixton (1929-1941), Wayne Traer (1941-1959), Jack Kramer (1960-1970), and Norman E. White (1970-1982). In July, 1982, E. Harold Stokes succeeded White as managing partner.

Stokes, a native Atlantan, joined Peat Marwick's Atlanta office in 1962 upon graduation from Georgia State University, and was admitted to partnership in 1972.

An apropos Atlanta historical anecdote during Pixton's reign: Peat, Marwick, Mitchell & Co. received membership certificate No. 95 to the Atlanta Athletic Club on January 23, 1931, just a few scant months after Bobby Jones, also a member of the Club, had completed the only Grand Slam of golf.

Currently, the Atlanta office of Peat Marwick has 220 employees including 21 partners. The firm provides accounting and auditing, tax and management consulting services to a diverse list of more than 2,200 clients.

The firm is situated in the Peachtree Center South Tower, where it celebrates the 60th anniversary of the Atlanta office opening, on December 1, 1982.

UNITED STATES		CANADA	EUROPE
NEW YORK	ATLANTA	MONTREAL	LONDON
NEWARK	NEW ORLEANS	TORONTO	PARIS
BOSTON	MINNEAPOLIS	WINNIPEG	MARSEILLES
WORCESTER	KANSAS CITY	MOOSE JAW	BRUSSELS
PHILADELPHIA	TULSA	CALGARY	
PITTSBURGH	DALLAS	VANCOUVER	
DETROIT	SAN ANTONIO		
MILWAUKEE	SALT LAKE CITY	CUBA	
CHICAGO	PORTLAND	HAVANA	
INDIANAPOLIS	SAN FRANCISCO		
ST. LOUIS	LOS ANGELES		
LOUISVILLE			

MARWICK, MITCHELL & CO.
ACCOUNTANTS AND AUDITORS

We have pleasure in announcing that we have acquired the business of William H. James & Co., Certified Public Accountants, Atlanta, Ga., and have opened a Branch Office at the Atlanta National Bank Building, Atlanta, Ga., under the management of Mr. William H. James, C. P. A.

MARWICK, MITCHELL & CO.

New York,
December 1, 1922.

The announcement of the opening of the Atlanta office of Marwick, Mitchell & Co. in 1922. An original of the announcement hangs in Peat Marwick's office.

Perry Communications, Inc.

Perry Communications, Inc., has grown over the past half century from a youth training program to a state-of-the-art printing, design and publications firm serving national as well as Metro Atlanta customers.

Its reputation for superb full-color and black-and-white printing, enhanced by one-stop typesetting, engraving, design and writing services, has made it a leading house for jobs demanding uncompromising craftsmanship.

Perry's walls are lined with awards for its broad range of projects, which have included creative corporate reports, handsome magazines, technically demanding point-of-purchase advertising materials, critically acclaimed books and high-impact brochures.

The company also operates a travel agency, Perry Travel, Inc., in Dunwoody. With the help of computers, the agency specializes in corporate travel in addition to handling vacation, group and incentive travel.

Today's modern printing operation, with some 140 employees and a 100,000-square-foot plant, evolved from a small Atlanta job shop and from an in-house training program for young men at the Georgia Baptist Children's Home in Hapeville, Ga.

Brown Tyler established the training program in the Thirties to serve the Children's Home printing needs and to teach young men a usable trade. Later he was given permission to seek work outside the Home, and still later to convert to commercial operation as Tyler & Co.

After Tyler's death, the business was purchased in 1949 by two local businessmen, George F. Longino and Bradley T. Porter. Their growing company, Longino & Porter, was purchased in 1960 by John H. Perry Jr., a Florida newspaper publisher, oceanographer, submarine designer and real estate developer.

Under his ownership, the company launched a program not only to expand volume but to convert from letterpress to offset printing. In the ensuing years it has stayed in the vanguard of the industry by adding modern phototypesetting equipment, color quality control monitoring, five-color sheet-fed presses and an eight-page web press that is the only one of its kind in Georgia.

In addition to high-quality work for its clients, Perry has produced several full-color showcase publications, including a hard-cover photographic portrait of Atlanta, a lavishly illustrated profile of The Coca-Cola Company, an Atlanta guidebook, a history of the Fox Theatre and a much-acclaimed promotional series called "Perrygrafs."

In 1968, the progressive company purchased a competitor with even older roots in Atlanta: Higgins-McArthur, Inc. It was started in 1924 when veteran Atlanta printer Charles Higgins bought a small local operation. Two years later, it became Higgins-McArthur when Higgins was joined by Richard McArthur, who had been advertising manager for a major Chicago type foundry. The firm established a solid reputation for typographic excellence and quality printing.

The combined firm operated under the name Higgins-McArthur, Longino & Porter until 1976, when it was changed to the simpler Perry Communications, Inc. When the company's Marietta Street plant in downtown Atlanta was bought to make way for the Omni International complex the firm moved to its present plant at 2181 Sylvan Road in Southwest Atlanta.

Today, Perry's chief executive officer and principal stockholder is Christopher Evans, a British-born American citizen with broad experience in journalism and printing.

Current officers and directors are Evans, president; Tommy L. Walker, vice president-sales; M. Floyd Morris, vice president-production; Matt Phelan, senior vice president-marketing; John H. Perry Jr., vice president; M. Alan Lowe, treasurer; Norman V. Werling, secretary, and Haywood Waters, plant manager.

Perry directors (from left) are Norman V. Werling, accountant; Haywood Waters, production; Tommy L. Walker, sales; M. Floyd Morris, production; Chris Evans, president; Matt J. Phelan, marketing, and M. Alan Lowe, treasurer.

John Portman & Associates

John Portman & Associates is the pivotal operating company within a comprehensive architectural, engineering and real estate development organization formed by Atlanta architect/developer John C. Portman Jr.

Two other companies, Portman Properties and Peachtree Purchasing, perform functions that complement JP&A's design role.

The development of the Portman organization began in the late Fifties when Portman, a native Atlantan, became discontent because of his inability to control the fate of his architectural designs. His first major real estate development was the Atlanta Merchandise Mart, which was occupied in July, 1961. The growth of the Mart, both physically and in number of activities, has been a major factor in making Atlanta the merchandising hub of the Southeast.

The next milestone in the development of the Portman organization and of Portman's reputation as an innovative architect/developer, was the design of the Hyatt Regency Hotel. It introduced the atrium into modern hotel design along with other features such as exposed, glass-enclosed elevators and rooftop restaurants.

The Hyatt Regency, which has been expanded twice since completion in 1967, was joined on the Atlanta skyline in 1976 by the Peachtree Center Plaza Hotel, another innovative Portman design and the world's tallest hotel.

In the long list of Portman-designed projects, Atlanta's Peachtree Center is one of four major urban multiple-use complexes. Started in 1967 as a complement to the Atlanta Merchandise Mart and the Hyatt Regency Hotel, this complex of office towers and retail functions pioneered modern development of the upper Peachtree area between Ellis and Baker Streets. The others are Renaissance Center in Detroit, Embarcadero Center in San Francisco, and Marina Centre in Singapore.

In the development of the Portman companies, JP&A is the oldest and the largest, reflecting Portman's primary role as an architect. Organized in 1969, it is the successor to earlier design firms in which Portman was involved as a principal.

In addition to emphasis on architectural design, JP&A has full capabilities in interior space analysis and planning, construction evaluation, urban design and planning, architectural model fabrication, and graphics. Because structural components are integral to Portman's architectural expression, JP&A includes a large structural engineering design group.

Although JP&A executes commissions for a variety of outside clients, much of its work is generated by Portman Properties, which focuses on property development and management.

Organized in 1971, Portman Properties performs market analysis and feasibility studies, financial analysis and packaging, project accounting, property management and project marketing and programming. It also performs a range of administrative services associated with project development and management.

Peachtree Purchasing buys furniture, fixtures and equipment for hotels and other commercial buildings on a contract basis.

Two additional Portman companies manage Portman's business activities in Atlanta. Peachtree Center Management Company handles the property management aspects of Peachtree Center; the Atlanta Market Center manages the Atlanta Merchandise Mart, the Atlanta Apparel Mart and the Atlanta Decorative Arts Center.

Architect/developer John C. Portman Jr. explains a design point to one of the designers in his firm.

John Portman & Associates' designs contributions—from the Hyatt Regency Hotel (lower right) to the cylindrical Westin Peachtree Center Plaza Hotel, the world's tallest—changed the shape of Atlanta's skyline.

Rich's has been called "the store that married a city" and "a bundle of staggering statistics." She is a Southern institution comprising 19 stores and more than 350 departments in which millions of people seek everything from suits to silver, seven days a week.

For more than a century people have gathered at Rich's to shop, to celebrate and, oftentimes, to seek sustenance. They have even written poetry and letters to her as if Rich's were a member of the family.

From her beginnings, Rich's set out to be more than a collection of merchandise, showcases and cash registers—to make people a motivating force in her business.

Morris Rich, a Hungarian emigrant, was 20 years old—the same age as Atlanta—when he borrowed $500 from his brother William to open a small retail store on Whitehall Street.

On opening day, May 28, 1867, he laid boards over the red clay mud to protect the footwear of the customers he hoped would come—and they did. Here, with five employees, the store's volume was $5,000 that first year.

Rich's brothers Emanuel and Daniel joined him in M. Rich & Bros. in 1877, and in 1882 they moved to 56 Whitehall Street, the store being described as a "bazaar of fashion...filled with the leading ladies of the city." Of the Rich brothers, *The Constitution* wrote: "It is due to such men that Atlanta is what she is."

By 1906 Rich's had launched a mail-order business and its third store, featuring such innovations as plate glass windows, elevators and a loading area where "a half dozen wagons may be loaded or unloaded at the same time."

The Riches' civic-mindedness was foremost. The brothers had helped bail out the debt-ridden Cotton States and International Exposition in 1895. When cotton prices dropped in 1914, and Georgians were caught with unsold surpluses, Rich's took up to 5,000 bales in exchange for merchandise at above the market price as its "duty and privilege."

In 1930 Walter Rich loaned $645,000 to the City Council to help meet the teachers' payroll. Again, in 1945, Dick Rich, grandson of the founder, opened the store's safe on the Sunday before Labor Day to pay a detachment of troops at Fort McPherson whose funds were time-locked in the Fort's vaults.

The Rich family's vision has been as big as its heart. When "Rich's Palace of Commerce" opened at the corner of Alabama and Broad Streets in 1924, the 52-year, $4,242,000 lease was said to be the biggest deal of its kind in the community's history. Likewise, the store was to become the first in the country to be completely air conditioned.

Other Rich's "firsts" have become annual traditions: the Lighting of the Great Tree atop Rich's Crystal Bridge downtown on Thanksgiving eve, the street fair of Georgia produce, the spring birthday party for those 80 years old and up, and the fashion extravaganza, Fashionata.

Rich's policy—"the customer is always right"—undergirds her reputation. Rich's traditionally has made refunds, exchanges and adjustments based on what her customers felt was honest and fair, even when it meant occasionally accepting altered or outdated goods.

Rich's has shared its profits with the community, too. In 1943 the store made its first large gift for a business school at Emory University. Rich's also contributed a radio station to local schools, a computer center and lab to Georgia Tech, a ward to Georgia Baptist Hospital and a wing to St. Joseph's Infirmary.

Since the 1950s, Rich's has grown rapidly, beginning its branch store expansion at Lenox Square in 1959. In 1980 Rich's opened Richway, its discount division. In 1976 Rich's became a division of Federated Department Stores, Inc., and Richway was made a separate division of Federated in 1980.

As she looks ahead to her second century of service, Rich's—Atlanta's institution—retains her heritage as the most famous mercantile establishment in the South.

Rich's, Inc.

An Atlanta tradition: the "Lighting of the Great Tree" at Christmas time

Robert and Company

Atlanta Municipal Auditorium, 1925

Atlanta Civic Center, 1968

William B. Hartsfield Airport Terminal, 1958

Hartsfield Atlanta International Airport, 1981 (joint venture of Robert and Company, Howard Needles Tammen and Bergendoff, and Williams-Russell & Johnson, Inc.)

Georgia Tech Grant Field, 1924

Georgia Tech Arthur B. Edge Jr. Intercollegiate Athletic Center, 1982

Grady Memorial Hospital, 1957

Emory Hospital, 1975, and Emory School of Nursing, 1971

For all but the last six years of its 65 year history, the story of Robert and Company was centered around one man— L. W. "Chip" Robert Jr.

From the time he founded the architecture, engineering and planning firm in 1917 until his death in 1976, Robert was a leader in the industrialization of the Southeast.

In 1926 *Atlanta Journal* headlines read, "Greatest Textile Deal in World's History Brought About By L. W. Robert, Jr....Considered Forerunner of Big Industrial Expansion."

Robert's particular interest in transportation development for Atlanta led him around the world 17 times before 1964. The knowledge he attained and the belief he shared with Mayor William B. Hartsfield resulted in construction of Atlanta's first major air transportation center, fully designed and engineered by Robert and Company.

Over the years, the firm has been involved in many dimensions of the development of Atlanta. In education, Robert and Company has designed numerous buildings at Robert's *alma mater*, Georgia Tech, and on the fine campuses of Emory and Georgia State University.

In Atlanta's cultural development, projects include the old Municipal Auditorium, the Civic Center and the original Atlanta Art Museum; in health, Grady Memorial Hospital, Emory Hospital additions, the Yerkes Primate Research Center and the Communicable Disease Center.

In transportation, both the old Hartsfield and portions of the new Hartsfield Atlanta International Airport were designed by Robert and Company. And in industry, the firm during World War II designed Marietta's original Bell Bomber plant, now known as Lockheed.

In a 1935 editorial *The Atlanta Journal* said, "Whatever buildings are erected under Chip Robert's supervision will be honestly built and represent the full value of whatever they may cost."

For the firm which began with a handful of employees in downtown Atlanta and today has more than 150 people on staff with regional offices in Auburn, Tampa and North Palm Beach, those basic principles still hold true.

robert+
Company

Robinson-Humphrey/ American Express, Inc.

Justus C. Martin Jr., current chairman of the board and chief executive officer, with a portrait of his predecessor, Alexander Yearley IV

Robinson-Humphrey / American Express, Inc., Atlanta's full-service investment banking and brokerage firm, has been both a cause and beneficiary of the growth of the Southeast since 1894.

Roby Robinson founded the firm that year primarily to market municipal bonds. Barely eight years later he and William G. Humphrey incorporated the firm as The Robinson-Humphrey Company, Inc. Robinson was succeeded as president in 1921 by the late Henry B. Tompkins, who guided the firm through the Great Depression and into the 1960s.

Alexander (Sandy) Yearley IV became president in 1965, attracting to the growing firm a cadre of talented, youthful people. Yearley was named chairman of the board and chief executive officer in 1971 and Justus C. Martin Jr. became president. Martin earlier had spearheaded the firm's successful drive to secure investment in Southeastern stocks and industries from outside the region, particularly from overseas.

From the first, Robinson-Humphrey encouraged business in the South. As the region has grown, so has the company. It opened its first branch office in 1947 in Columbia, S.C., and now has almost 40 branches in seven states: Georgia, New York, North Carolina, South Carolina, Florida, Tennessee and Alabama.

By the time of its merger in mid-1982 with American Express, the firm was the region's premier financial services firm. Its grassroots contacts through its branch offices gave Robinson-Humphrey an unsurpassed knowledge of Southeastern business. Direct association with the individuals, businesses and industries that drive the Southeastern economy is supported by one of the largest research departments of any regional financial firm in the nation.

Scrutiny of securities only glanced at by New York firms causes many institutional investors in the nation's financial centers to rely on Robinson-Humphrey to advise them of investment opportunities before they are discovered on Wall Street. This knowledge of its home territory also means that the company creates the over-the-counter market for the stocks of leading Southeastern banks, corporations and utilities.

Robinson-Humphrey's growth has put the full range of financial services at the doorstep of individuals and businesses in the Southeast, a position further reinforced by affiliation with American Express.

For example, many firms now look no farther than the company's Corporate Finance Department for investment banking services. And in offering major bond issues, Robinson-Humphrey has served as the managing underwriter for issues by MARTA, the region's largest construction project since TVA; the Municipal Electric Authority of Georgia; the South Carolina Public Services Authority; and the City of Atlanta for Hartsfield International Airport.

This activity reflects the firm's knowledge, resources and capabilities in assisting industrial development, bond issues, advising on fixed income securities, developing employee benefit plans, trading listed blocks of stock, appraising real estate investment opportunities and planning personal financial strategies.

As new financial vehicles develop, Robinson-Humphrey also is at the forefront in incorporating them into its services to clients. For example, the company, a member of all leading securities exchanges, was a charter member of the Chicago Board Options Exchange, and owns the first broker-sponsored money market fund.

As the decade unfolds, Robinson-Humphrey/American Express no doubt will continue to provide the same leadership in Southeastern financial markets as it has since 1894.

Rollins, Inc.

R. Randall Rollins, president and chief operating officer (left); O. Wayne Rollins, co-founder, chairman and chief executive officer of Rollins, Inc. (center); and Gary W. Rollins, vice president of Rollins, Inc., and president of the Orkin termite and pest control subsidiary

Rollins' presence in Atlanta was established in 1926, when its Orkin termite and pest control subsidiary opened Atlanta offices in the Candler Building. At the time, Orkin was celebrating the 25th anniversary of its founding and, even then, was described by the Atlanta Chamber of Commerce as "a distinct asset to the city." Orkin later became part of Rollins.

Within a week of Orkin's arrival in the city, *The Atlanta Journal* reported that the "systematic business of ridding Atlanta buildings and homes of rats, roaches and other pests is under way," including a contract "for ridding a nationally-known Atlanta company's place of rats."

The Journal went on to proclaim that efforts of cats, and even the mythical prowess of the famous Piper of Hamlin, do not compare with the accomplishments mentioned in scores of endorsements of Orkin by public health officials, officers of the United States Army Engineering corps, the governor of Virginia, department stores and other public and private concerns.

Orkin offices were strategically relocated to other sites in Atlanta over a period of almost four decades.

In 1963, on a five-acre site on Piedmont Road, N.E., just north of Interstate 85, was built what was to become new headquarters offices for Orkin and the far-flung Rollins empire. The well-landscaped structure of contemporary design, with high, arched windows, soon emerged as an Atlanta landmark.

It was described by the Atlanta Beautiful Commission as an outstanding contribution to the increasing beauty of the city, and a citation accompanying its award to the firm was presented by Atlanta mayor Ivan Allen Jr. in 1965.

Rollins acquired its Orkin subsidiary in 1964 for $62.4 million when Rollins' revenues were $9 million. The transaction was a modern-day example of American financing ingenuity that captured the imagination of Wall Street: Institutional lenders put up the bulk of the purchase price and willingly looked beyond assets to lend against potential earnings growth.

Orkin is believed to be responsible for many firsts in the giant pest control industry. Among them, in the early Fifties, were the development of a specialized service to the food processing industry, and tent fumigations (with nylon tents) to control drywood termites.

Orkin was the first pest control company to establish a technical department, and the first to use phosphate insecticides against resistant insects. Orkin was instrumental in developing the concept of providing continuous preventive control of pests and termites through regular, periodic inspection and treatment.

Rollins' termite and pest control subsidiary has expanded from revenues of $34 million to approximately $200 million between 1962 and 1982, with operations in 45 states and the District of Columbia. Orkin, with a history of more than 80 years' service, is the largest in the world in that industry.

Atlanta became headquarters for Rollins businesses established between 1950 and 1961: cable television, radio and television broadcasting and outdoor advertising operations that range from Massachusetts to California.

A Rollins subsidiary, Dettelbach Pesticide Corporation, which supplies proprietary formulations to Orkin, was incorporated, with offices in Atlanta, in 1960.

Atlanta was the site of the formation in 1969 of Rollins Protective Services

Company, a firm which became the largest in the country in residential security, with 48 branch offices in 24 states.

In 1973, even before an energy crisis was commonly accepted as a likelihood in the United States, Rollins entered the oil and gas field services business. By 1982 the revenues of this burgeoning segment of Rollins had grown from about $10 million to approximately $200 million.

Rollins Lawn Care, with offices in six cities, was established in Atlanta in 1977, to provide fertilization and weed control for residential and commercial customers.

The company, co-founded by O. Wayne Rollins, a native of Ringgold, Ga., who is chairman and chief executive officer, is listed on the New York Stock Exchange. R. Randall Rollins succeeded his father as president and chief operating officer in 1975. His brother, Gary W. Rollins, became president of the Orkin subsidiary in 1978.

Rollins was designed to provide essential services for homes and businesses. The familiar diamond trademark of the company, known throughout most of the country, signals many notable accomplishments of the Atlanta-based diversified services firm.

Since going public in 1960, Rollins has increased its earnings every year. Rollins revenues have grown from slightly more than $4 million to approximately $525 million between 1960 and 1982.

A Rollins stockholder, when its common shares were first traded in 1960, made an $800 investment to acquire 100 shares. Those shares, held to June 11, 1982, through stock splits and a stock dividend, had grown to 2,317 shares with a market value of $31,858.

By fiscal 1982 year end, Rollins' dividend payments per share to stockholders had been increased 88½ times since 1960. Rollins has increased its dividend each year during its 22 years as a public company. Accordingly, the stockholder's original $800 investment was paid off, by Rollins' dividend payments, as early as 1971.

The Rollins College Scholarship program instituted in Atlanta in 1968 to provide assistance to the sons and daughters of company employees attending colleges, universities and trade schools, has made awards totaling more than $308,000.

Rollins' 12 Atlanta area office locations employ about 900 of the firm's 10,000 employees. Since its inception, company management has dedicated itself to the vital work of ensuring customer satisfaction as well as security and opportunity for all its employees.

The customers of Rollins' subsidiaries are serviced today from some 5,600 vehicles, believed to be one of the largest motor vehicle fleets in the country.

The termite and pest control subsidiary of Rollins has been providing service to its customers since 1901.

H. J. Russell Construction Company

Herman J. Russell was once quoted in *Atlanta* magazine as saying that there should be no such thing as a "white business" or a "black business," that it ought to be "just business."

Yet Russell's firm, H. J. Russell Construction Co., has come to symbolize the growth of black-owned enterprises in Atlanta. In 1962 Russell became the first black businessman to join the Atlanta Chamber of Commerce, despite the vehement protests of a few die-hard segregationists. Ironically, he became president of the Chamber in 1981.

Russell's business enterprises, which now constitute what might be called a miniature empire, had modest beginnings. His father, the late Rogers Russell Sr., had for many years owned a small plastering firm that employed at most a dozen persons.

As a boy and a young man, Herman learned the value of hard work, toiling in the family's plastering business as a hod carrier, mortar mixer and laborer. He also learned the value of property ownership. As a high school sophomore, he invested $250 in a small lot near his home in Summerhill. During his senior year in high school, with the help of friends he began building a duplex on the lot.

As a student at Tuskegee Institute in Alabama, Russell earned extra money by using his skills as a plasterer, enlisting the aid of some classmates in subcontracting on local construction jobs.

He was graduated from Tuskegee in 1953 with a major in construction engineering. Returning to Atlanta, he again worked in his father's business, all the while acquiring additional properties near his home.

When the elder Russell died in 1957, the plastering business went to Herman, then 27 and a building entrepreneur.

In 1962 Russell formed H. J. Russell Construction Co. and soon began to bid successfully on major construction jobs. Among the early successes was a $1 million subcontract for all the plastering and drywall work in the new Equitable Building. The firm also worked on Atlanta-Fulton County Stadium and a number of large commercial projects.

In the early 1960s Russell began some apartment developments and other projects for his own account.

Over the last two decades the construction Company and the plastering Company, which at various times have been separate and combined, were involved with numerous well known projects in and around Atlanta. Among them are the Atlanta Life Insurance Co. building, the new terminal at Hartsfield International Airport, the Martin Luther King Center, the Georgia-Pacific Building, MARTA stations, Benjamin Mays High School and the Atlanta University Library.

Today Russell's construction business has an annual volume of more than $50 million. In addition, he presides over a business empire that includes a beverage distributor, an insurance agency, a construction management firm, a television station, an airport concessionaire, and an apartment management company. With the construction and plastering firms, these enterprises employ more than 700 persons, mostly in Atlanta.

Managing these businesses allows Russell little free time, but he does work with various civic and professional organizations.

Two of the major projects in which H. J. Russell Construction Co. has been involved: the Martin Luther King Jr. Community Center and the new terminal of Hartsfield International Airport.

Scripto, Inc.

Among the most senior of Atlanta's corporate citizens is Scripto, Inc. Founded in 1923 as the Atlantic Manufacturing Co. by M. A. Ferst, an innovative graphite manufacturer, the company recorded first-year sales of $5,170 in 1924 and was renamed Scripto Manufacturing.

Ferst's idea was to make an inexpensive pencil with replaceable eraser and lead. To this day Scripto remains the preeminent producer of mechanical pencils, for which the M. A. Ferst Co. of Atlanta still produces lead and eraser refills.

For 40 years Scripto grew and prospered as a leader in the increasingly competitive writing instrument industry. Within five years of its founding, annual sales had soared to $250,000. In 1942 production was temporarily halted while Scripto manufactured ordnance materials for the nation's war effort.

Scripto resumed pencil manufacturing and also founded its export department in 1945. It was the beginning of a golden era for the company, now renamed Scripto, Inc. In 1948 Scripto introduced its first ball point pen to America and then solidified its position in the mushrooming market in 1953 by producing a ball point that sold for $1. For the first time, sales topped the $10 million mark.

In 1955 Scripto committed to the production of a third major line, the cigarette lighter. It was a natural development for the pen and pencil manufacturer because of common channels of marketing and distribution. The VuLighter, Scripto's first entry in the lighter market, was well received and in 1956 Scripto went public with its first offering of a Class A common stock. Sales in 1957 exceeded $20 million.

It was in the mid-1960s that the difficult years for Scripto began. Diversification had become synonymous with corporate strength in those days. In Scripto's case, however, the acquisition of several unrelated businesses diverted the firm's energy and attention when Scripto was being severely tested by its larger competition in the writing instrument and lighter markets. In 1964, for the first time in 40 years, sales lagged significantly, and by 1968 the company was operating in the red.

Wilkinson Sword, Inc., the New Jersey razor manufacturer, purchased controlling interest in Scripto in 1974. Scripto closed its aging plant and headquarters in downtown Atlanta and moved to its present location in DeKalb County in 1977. The move was a momentous occasion, coming when Wilkinson was still paring losing operations and searching for new leadership to restore Scripto's fortunes and competitive position.

Finally, in 1978, the right man for the job was found. The entry of K. Douglas Martin, a gregarious Kentuckian with an outstanding record in consumer products, signaled the beginning of a truly remarkable turnaround for Scripto.

Scripto's first home

As Scripto's new president and chief executive officer, Martin completely overhauled management and marketing operations. New cost-accounting procedures revealed weak product lines, which were quickly eliminated. Manufacturing procedures were streamlined. The company's retail distribution and trade support networks also were rejuvenated by product improvements and aggressive marketing efforts in the U.S. and abroad.

In short, within two years of Martin's arrival, the company was in the black again. Then came April, 1980, when Scripto stunned the ball point industry by introducing a disposable erasable pen, which sold for almost a dollar less than the competition's non-disposable version. Backed by the most extensive advertising campaign in the company's history, sales of Scripto's disposable erasable pen enormously increased the firm's profitability.

In 1981 controlling interest in Scripto passed to Allegheny International, Inc., of Pittsburgh, when Allegheny acquired Wilkinson Sword. In 1982 Allegheny transferred operational control of Wilkinson and the Eddy Match Co. of Canada to Scripto. About the same time, Scripto signaled its reemergence in the lighter field with the introduction of a new, sleekly designed lighter, the Ultra Lite™ disposable lighter.

Scripto has continued its advance with a diversified portfolio of new products and timely expansion into international markets. At present, approximately 1,000 persons are employed nationwide.

Scripto's current headquarters

Selig Enterprises, Inc.

Chairman Simon S. Selig Jr. (right) and President S. Stephen Selig III pose with a portrait of the company's founder, the late Benjamin J. Massell.

No story on Atlanta real estate and development would be complete without mention of the saga of Selig Enterprises, Inc., which started its history in 1942 as CMS Realty Company, named after its major stockholder, Caroline Massell Selig.

The name was changed to Selig Enterprises, Inc., in 1968, when Simon S. Selig Jr., its present chairman, and his son, S. Stephen Selig III, the current president, took over the complete management of its operation.

CMS Realty Company was founded by Ben J. Massell, father of Caroline M. Selig, and operated by him until his death in 1962. Massell was known to all Atlanta as "the father of Atlanta's skyline."

He was called "a one man boom" by the late Atlanta Mayor William B. Hartsfield. During his lifetime Ben Massell was responsible for construction of more than 1,000 buildings of all sizes from a one-story, single-tenant structure to today's Merchandise Mart on Peachtree Street.

When Ben Massell died in 1962, son-in-law Simon Selig divided his time between the Massell Company and Selig Chemical Industries, a budding giant in the chemical specialties field. The dual responsibility was too much.

Selig sold the chemical company to National Service Industries and went full time with CMS Realty Company, the operating company Massell had started. Upon his death, Massell's holdings were divided between the Massell Company (then operated by Ben Massell Jr.) and CMS Realty Company.

CMS Realty Company, under Simon Selig's direction, eventually reacquired all of the properties which were divided at the time of Massell's death. It was Selig's guidance, leadership and business acumen that enabled CMS Realty (ultimately Selig Enterprises, Inc.), through countless acquisitions and new developments, to spark a growth the like of which had not been seen in the Atlanta real estate community in many years.

In 1982 the burgeoning Selig Enterprises empire, a constellation of office buildings, office parks, industrial complexes and shopping centers, not only polka-dots the Atlanta landscape but stretches as well from North Carolina to Tennessee and from Florida to Puerto Rico. Acquisitions and developments are the rule rather than the exception.

The company's dramatic growth is shown by the increase in the number of properties developed or acquired over the past several years. These have an occupancy rate of approximately 95 per cent.

Selig Enterprises, Inc., today is a real estate holding company with its corporate headquarters in one of its modern office buildings, at 1100 Spring St., N.W. Its senior staff consists of officers heading up its financial, leasing, administrative, development, construction, property management and appraisal operations.

Selig Enterprises, Inc.'s, "secret word" is growth—to grow with Atlanta and to help Atlanta grow. Both Simon and Steve are quite active in the arts, civic affairs and charitable and political activities in the Metropolitan Atlanta area. In fact, Steve spent four years (1976-1980) in the White House as deputy assistant to President Jimmy Carter.

Thunder River, the new whitewater rafting adventure, simulates a wet and splashing ride down a free-spirited wild water river. The quarter mile trip takes about four minutes, and one thing is for sure: "You're gonna get wet."

Since Six Flags Over Georgia opened here in June, 1967, some 35 million persons have entered its gates, and every year since then the enormous theme park has kept its promise to offer at least one new attraction.

The park, which operates approximately 180 days per year, first opened with six main sections named for the British, American, Spanish, French, Confederate and Georgia flags that have flown over the state.

In 1973, Six Flags unveiled its new Cotton States Exposition section, the centerpiece of which is the Great American Scream Machine, a towering roller coaster which remains one of the park's most popular attractions.

The overwhelming success of the Scream Machine was widely publicized, and ignited a nationwide revival of roller coaster construction. Six Flags added a second roller coaster, the Mind Bender, in 1978. The Mind Bender was then the world's only triple-loop roller coaster.

Other thrill rides at Six Flags include the Runaway Mine Train and the Great Gasp, the aptly named parachute drop added in a major expansion of the U.S.A. section in 1976.

Over the years Six Flags has become virtually synonymous with wholesome family fun, and it ranks easily as one of Atlanta's most alluring attractions for tourists and conventioneers. More than half its visitors come from out of state, and the park has drawn customers from more than 30 nations.

From the massive 54-acre parking lot

The log flume, one of Six Flags' first rides in 1967, continues to be one of the most popular family rides at the park.

to all points inside, park patrons are guided and greeted by young, effervescent hosts and hostesses. At night the park takes on a glittering, almost-magical ambience. Day or night, the grounds, restrooms and many dining areas are kept spotlessly clean. Among the most popular family rides are the two log flumes, the Flying Dutchman and Thunder River, the white water raft ride added in 1982.

With a summer season staff of 3,000, Six Flags has the distinction of being the state's largest single-unit employer of youths. The most sought-after positions at Six Flags are the performers' roles in the live stage shows presented at the park's two theaters, the Crystal Pistol Music Hall and the Ship-Shape Theater.

Aspiring actors and actresses from all over the Southeast compete in auditions for parts in the Broadway-type revues and variety shows. The park also employs an ever-changing array of puppeteers, magicians, professional bands, make-believe costume characters and gunfighters who perform all about the grounds. A perennial favorite show features the performing dolphins. To witness all the live entertainment offered at Six Flags in one day would take six hours or more.

There are more than 100 rides, shows and attractions. Since its opening, the park proper has grown from 60 to 196 acres, and the overall property has expanded from 276 to 330 acres. So the park's unofficial motto has become, "Six Flags will never be completed."

Six Flags Over Georgia is a subsidiary of Six Flags Corp., which owns and operates five other major theme parks across the nation: Six Flags Over Texas, founded in 1961 midway between Dallas and Fort Worth; Six Flags Over Mid-America in St. Louis, AstroWorld in Houston, Tx., the Great Adventure in Jackson, N.J., and Magic Mountain in Valencia, Calif. The Corporation also owns and operates two wax museums—the Stars Hall of Fame in Orlando, Fla., and the Movieland Wax Museum in Los Angeles.

Six Flags Over Georgia

Thrill seekers love the Great American Scream Machine. The old-timey wooden roller coaster features a 100-foot first drop with the train reaching speeds of 60 miles per hour.

John Smith Co.

The fourth generation—John E. Smith II—with one of the firm's carriages outside the Company's Cobb Parkway showroom

At the turn of the century, the John Smith Co. was making and repairing carriages—and soon, automobiles—from this Broad Street plant.

When Atlanta was rising from the ashes of the Civil War in 1869, John M. Smith, a 34-year-old Irish immigrant, came to Atlanta and opened a blacksmith shop on Broad Street for the manufacture of carriages for Atlanta's pioneer families. Within a few years everyone came to know that a John Smith Carriage, in the words of one writer, "was one with every bolt of steel and every spoke of hickory."

By the Gay Nineties Atlanta had risen to become the commercial hub of the South. In those days nothing was more exciting than an afternoon drive behind spirited horses. The price of carriages from John Smith Co. ranged from $150 for a surrey to $2,500 for a brougham.

Their quality design and construction won 45 awards and diplomas from major expositions and fairs. It was a John Smith-built brougham made for the Henry Hunter Smiths that carried President and Mrs. Grover Cleveland to Atlanta's International Cotton States Exposition in 1895.

In the same year John E. Smith, after his graduation from Georgia Tech and a special course in carriage design in New York, joined his father in the business. Soon it became evident to him that the stately victoria, the dignified brougham and the popular rockaway and surrey were on their way out and the future was in the new motor car.

Soon the Company was repairing automobiles, and in 1904 John Smith Co. actually toyed with the idea of becoming a manufacturer, building one electric and two gas-engine cars. But technical advances were being developed too rapidly for a small manufacturer to stay up to date.

So, from 1906 to 1913 the Company became a dealer for other makers and sold Reos, Pierce Arrows, Hudsons, Chalmers, Hatfield High Wheelers, Apperson Jack Rabbits, Saxons and Chandlers. By 1913 the era of the carriage was over and the last of them kept at the Company's shop, then at 122 Auburn Ave., were burned as kindling.

As the auto industry stabilized, the John Smith Co. cast its lot with General Motors in 1913 as a Buick dealer. In 1924 it became exclusively a dealer for GM's Chevrolet division.

John E. Smith was invited to become a member of the original General Motors President's Dealer Advisory Council in 1935. Later his son, Hal L. Smith, succeeded his father as head of the Atlanta dealership and he, too, was asked to join GM's President's Council.

In 1921 the Company relocated to 530 West Peachtree St., where it remained for 55 years.

It moved once more, to make way for Atlanta's rapid-rail system and, in 1976 opened on an 8.5-acre site at 2155 Cobb Parkway. Just two years prior to that, a fourth generation, John E. Smith II, succeeded his father Hal as president.

The John Smith Co. is now the oldest family-owned and operated company in metropolitan Atlanta.

The Company has come a long way since that Irish carriage maker started the firm over a century ago. Over that time Atlantans have come to refer to John Smith Chevrolet as "The Old Reliable." That would make the original founder proud, knowing even if it were automobiles and not carriages, those who followed him were carrying on his tradition of providing quality transportation for their customers.

Spelman College

"I am building for a hundred years hence, not only for today," said Sophia Packard, one of the founders of Spelman College, over 100 years ago. Spelman, now a four-year liberal arts college primarily for black women, celebrated its 100th anniversary in April, 1981.

Spelman has come a long way from its beginnings in the damp basement of Atlanta's Friendship Baptist Church. There, with $100 and 11 students, two New England schoolteachers, Sophia Packard and Harriet Giles, labored against overwhelming odds to provide education for Southern black women. Within three months of its opening, the school had 80 students. By the next year 200 women between the ages of 15 and 52, many of them former slaves, were enrolled.

Lack of money was a constant problem, but a fund-raising trip to the North brought Spelman's founders together with John D. Rockefeller, who became a major benefactor of the school.

A milestone in the progress of the then-named Atlanta Baptist Female Seminary was the procurement of nine acres of property that had been used as drill grounds for Federal troops after the Civil War. The property included five frame buildings which became classrooms and dormitories.

But for a school that depended on donations, the property's $15,000 note was a problem. Again Mr. Rockefeller helped. In April, 1884, he with his wife and her mother, Mrs. Harvey Spelman, visited the Seminary. Before leaving, Mr. Rockefeller paid off the note. At the suggestion of a grateful Miss Packard, the school's name was changed to Spelman Seminary in honor of Mrs. Rockefeller's mother.

The Rockefeller gift, the first of a long tradition of philanthrophy from the Rockefeller family and foundations, not only alleviated a shaky financial situation, but also created a recognition of Spelman that otherwise may have taken years to achieve. Financial backing came in from a number of new sources. In 1886 a $40,000 gift from Mr. Rockefeller resulted in the first major construction—Rockefeller Hall.

Two year later the school was granted a State charter, and Miss Packard became Spelman's first president. At her death in 1891, Spelman Seminary had 800 pupils, 30 teachers and property valued at $90,000. Harriet Giles then became president and served 18 years, during which time the school provided training for its students in domestic arts, religion, vocational training for teaching, nursing and home economics.

During Lucy Hale Tapley's presidency (1901-1927), Spelman qualified as a teacher's college, and on June 1, 1924, its name was changed to Spelman College. Florence Read, the next president, saw it as more than a teacher's college, and worked to develop Spelman as a liberal arts school. One of the most significant moves under Ms. Read came in 1929: Spelman agreed to affiliate with Morehouse College and Atlanta University. The affiliation developed into the Atlanta University Center, a consortium of six institutions that share resources and activities.

During the 1930s the fine arts were added to the College's curriculum, and Spelman developed rapidly as a center for fine arts and culture in Atlanta.

In 1953 Ms. Read retired and Dr. Albert E. Manley became the first black to serve as Spelman president. Under Dr. Manley, Spelman women were encouraged and prepared to broaden their roles in society and to enter the fields of medicine, law, engineering, business and industry, Dr. Donald M. Stewart, Spelman's second black president, assumed the presidency in 1976.

Today Spelman is committed to providing a strong liberal arts experience and to preparing competent, well educated, problem-solving black women for leadership positions. In only three years, under Dr. Stewart's leadership the College doubled its endowment by raising over $12 million. This important effort was stimulated by a major challenge grant from the Rockefeller Brothers Fund and was greatly enhanced by the participation of James E. Robinson III, a native of Atlanta and chairman and chief executive officer of the American Express Company.

At the threshold of its second century, Spelman looks to new challenges and to positioning itself competitively and distinctively among the strongest and best liberal arts colleges in the United States.

Spelman founders Sophia B. Packard and Harriet E. Giles

First graduating class of Spelman Seminary, 1887

Storey Theatres, Inc.

Storey Theatres, Inc., was chartered August 6, 1952, in a division of theaters owned by an earlier partnership.

Of Storey's original 11 theaters—nine neighborhood houses and two drive-ins—only one, the Rhodes, still is operating, although under different ownership.

Most of the others have fallen victim to the trend away from single, neighborhood theaters and toward multi-screen theaters in shopping centers. Some, particularly the drive-ins, became far more valuable as real estate than as businesses.

The opening of the Glenwood Drive-In Theater in August, 1955, signaled the beginning of Storey's expansion. The next 10 years saw the acquisition of the Gwinnett Drive-In, and the construction of the Fulton Boulevard and North 85 drive-ins.

In April, 1963, the Rhodes, completely remodeled, modernized and equipped for roadshow attractions, opened *Lawrence of Arabia* on a reserved-seat basis.

Storey Theatres' first shopping center facility, the North DeKalb, opened in July, 1965. Fifteen months later, the second opened in Lakewood Mall, which became the Lakewood Twin in August, 1974. The North DeKalb became a twin theater in 1976. The National Triple Theater opened in October, 1971; it added a fourth auditorium at Christmas 1978. The newest in the Storey circuit, the Shannon Four, opened at Shannon Mall in Union City on August 1, 1980.

In 1956 the company entered the Gainesville market, in partnership with John Thompson of that city, with the Skyview Drive-In. To this were quickly added the Lanier Drive-In Theater and the Sherwood Theater. The Blueridge Cinemas—a three-theater complex—was added in March, 1978. In December, 1980, the Gainesville partnership was dissolved, and Storey Theatres assumed complete control of the theaters.

In July, 1972, after having managed it for Modular Cinemas, Inc., for some time, Storey Theaters acquired the Brainerd Theater in Chattanooga. The following year the Plaza Theater was added to the company's Chattanooga holdings.

As the company grew, a separate corporation—United Vendors, Inc.—was established to manage and centralize purchasing for the concession operations. Kent Advertising Agency was established to handle advertising for Storey Theatres.

In 1952 the original 11 screens managed by Storey Theaters, Inc., turned in a combined gross income of $400,000. In 1981, with 24 screens, the company's theaters grossed over $5 million in admissions and concession sales.

Officers of the corporation are Frederick G. Storey, chairman of the executive committee; James H. Edwards, president and chief of operations; Manuel F. Rodriguez, vice president, buying and booking; and Coley W. Hayes, vice president, secretary and treasurer.

The 1950s saw the industrialization of the South. The new factories required the sophisticated support services traditionally available in the older industrialized regions. One of these service firms to expand into the South during this period was Arthur Young & Company, the international accounting, tax and management consulting firm.

Arthur Young established an Atlanta office in December, 1951, at the urging of its client, the Lockheed Corp.

Lockheed was reopening the Bell Bomber Plant in Marietta as the Lockheed-Georgia Co. and required not only an audit but also an extensive work-utilization study that would take several years to complete. Arthur Young's Atlanta office opened with 20 professionals.

From 1951 until 1955 the major work in the office was Lockheed and referral assignments from other Arthur Young offices. Then, in 1956, it combined practices with a firm which audited another major Georgia company, West Point-Pepperell, Inc.

Gradually, the firm gained other clients, and by the end of the decade its professional staff had grown to 40. Still, Atlanta was Arthur Young's only office south of Washington, D.C., and the staff was kept busy handling an increasing number of assignments as the international firm's clients established operations in the region.

Finally, in 1963 the Birmingham, Ala., office was opened, and this was followed over the years by offices in 10 other major Southern cities.

In those early years Arthur Young's Atlanta office acquired a reputation as the auditors only for big, publicly-held companies. However, by the 1970s the office had developed a local practice that included many of the metropolitan region's growing and emerging companies.

A significant development occurred in 1980 when Arthur Young combined practices with Libby, Thomas and Braxton, a major independent Atlanta accounting firm with particular expertise in advising on financing.

It now is the Small Business Department — a firm within a firm, providing the close, personalized service generally found in a small firm but with the resources and expertise of a major international firm.

Trucking and related transportation services have historically been important to Atlanta's economy, and Arthur Young has developed extensive expertise to assist companies in this field in financial management.

This newest department joins the Audit and Tax Departments which provide auditing, accounting and tax planning and preparation services for corporations and individuals, and the Management Services practice, which provides a broad range of consulting services including the evaluation and selection of computer systems.

These four divisions serve a broad range of clients with specialized expertise in several fields, including health care, transportation, high technology, textiles, financial services, manufacturing and government services.

Arthur Young in Atlanta has grown over the years to a level of more than 130 professional and support personnel, including 15 partners and directors, led by William C. Merrick as managing partner.

It occupies two floors in Peachtree Center's Gas Light Tower and a connecting floor in the Harris Tower. As part of a major worldwide firm, it has worked to maintain Arthur Young's reputation, as described by *Fortune* magazine, as a "widely respected and super-professional" firm.

Arthur Young & Company

William C. Merrick is managing partner of the Atlanta office of Arthur Young.

Arthur Young provides accounting and a wide range of consulting services to numerous hospitals and health-care facilities throughout the area.

Lockheed-Georgia Corp. was Arthur Young's first major Atlanta-area client, and remains one of its largest accounts.

The Indexes

For the benefit of the reader, *ATLANTA: Triumph Of a People* contains two indexes: One is arranged by subject matter in the main historical text; the other is for illustrations.

The subject index, which begins on the following page, is selective. That is to say, the authors have not indicated every page on which Five Points is mentioned or *The Atlanta Intelligencer* quoted, for example. It is believed, however, that the page references will assist readers interested in finding most subjects which are mentioned in substance, rather than in passing.

The same is true of the index to illustrations.

INDEX TO HISTORY

Index to Illustrations

Photo and Illustration Credits

The sources of the photographs and illustrations are noted below, arranged in alphabetical order and by page numbers.

The photographs and illustrations which appear within the corporate and institutional profiles (pages 341, 342 and 344 through 447) were provided by those entities and are not indexed. Photographs on pages titled "Some Faces In Our Past" are from the Atlanta Historical Society.

The authors thank the following who gave permission to use the illustrative material herein.

ATLANTA HISTORICAL SOCIETY: 9 (top), 10, 11, 12 (bottom), 14 (bottom), 15, 16 (bottom), 18 (bottom), 20, 21, 22, 24 (bottom), 25, 26, 28 through 38, 40, 42, 43 (top and bottom), 47 (bottom), 48 (bottom), 50 (top), 51 (top), 54, 56 (bottom), 58 (top and right), 59, 60 (bottom), 61 (bottom), 65, 66 (bottom), 67 (bottom), 72, 76 (bottom), 80 through 83, 84 (bottom), 85 (top center, right and bottom), 87 (top left and right), 89, 90, 91 (top left and bottom), 92 through 98, 99 (top), 100 through 108, 109 (left), 112 through 116, 118 through 127, 128 (top), 129 through 139, 141 through 149, 154, 155 (top), 156 through 161, 163, 164 (top and middle), 165 (top), 166 (bottom), 167, 168, 169 (bottom), 170, 171, 172 (top three and two in middle column), 173 through 181, 183 through 196, 198 through 200, 201 (all except top right and lower left), 202 through 209, 210 (top left and bottom), 212 through 215, 218, 219, 221, 222 (bottom), 223, 224, 226, 227, 229 (bottom), 238, 239, 248, 251, 259, 260 (bottom), 266, 275, 276 (lower right), 279, 280, 351, 355, 385, 390, 421.

ATLANTA HISTORICAL SOCIETY (by permission of Franklin Garrett): 27.

ATLANTA HISTORICAL SOCIETY (by permission of Wilbur Kurtz, artist): 13, 14 (top), 16 (top), 17, 19 (top), 23, 24, 53, 56 (top), 68, 140 (bottom).

ATLANTA HISTORICAL SOCIETY (by permission of Kenneth Rogers): 165 (bottom).

ATLANTA HISTORICAL SOCIETY (by permission of Willis M. Timmons): 421

ATLANTA JOURNAL-CONSTITUTION: 221, 222 (top), 229 (top), 234, 235, 238, 239 (top), 241 (upper right and left, and lower right), 252, 255, 256, 257, 260, 261, 263, 264, 270, 271, 273, 285, 305, 309, 312 (bottom), 319 (bottom left), 320.

BARTON & LUDWIG/COLDWELL BANKER: 281.

CAPRICORN CORP. (from *The Fabulous Fox At 50,* Copyright, 1979, Capricorn Corporation): 231, 232.

CAPRICORN CORP. (from *The Million-Dollar Legends: Margaret Mitchell and Gone With the Wind,* Copyright, 1972, Capricorn Corp., courtesy of the Estate of Margaret Mitchell): 240, 241 (upper top), 242, 243, 244, 245.

CARTER & ASSOCIATES: 279 (top).

CYCLORAMA: 64.

EASTERN AIRLINES: 220, 228, 229 (bottom), 236, 237.

EDGAR ORR: 233.

EDGAR ORR/KILE STUDIO: 230, 233.

ELIZA PASCHAL: 172 (lower left), 201 (top right and bottom right), 256, 250 (top).

EMORY UNIVERSITY LIBRARY/SPECIAL COLLECTIONS: 247 (upper and lower), 265, 269 (permission of Jack Kanel).

FOX THEATRE: 250 (bottom).

HARTSFIELD INTERNATIONAL AIRPORT: 322.

JOHN SMITH CO.: 216-217 (bottom).

KIRK KINGSBURY: 249, 317, 321.

LANE BROTHERS PHOTOGRAPHY: 242.

LIBRARY OF CONGRESS: 61 (top), 62, 63, 71 (bottom), 74, 75, 76 (top).

LOCKHEED-MARIETTA CO.: 306.

NORMAN SHAVIN: (woodcuts from *Harper's Weekly*): 12 (top), 18 (top), 19 (bottom), 39, 43 (middle, left and bottom), 44 through 46, 47 (left, top and middle), 48 (top), 49, 50 (bottom), 51 (bottom), 52, 55, 57, 58 (middle left and bottom), 60 (top), 66 (top), 67 (top), 69, 70, 71 (top), 73, 77 (bottom), 78, 79, 84 (top), 85 (top left), 86, 87 (top center and bottom), 88, 91 (top right), 99 (bottom), 109 (right three), 110, 111, 117, 128 (left), 140 (top two), 155 (bottom), 162, 164 (bottom), 169 (top), 182, 197, 210 (center right), 216 (upper six), 217 (top three), 225, 229 (top), 262, 284, 286, 287, 307 (top), 308, 309, 311, 312 (top), 313 through 316, 318, 319 (top, and bottom right), 320 (left), 337, 338, 339.

PERRY COMMUNICATIONS (from *Atlanta: A Celebration;* photography by Chipp Jamison. Copyright, 1978, Perry Communications): 276 (upper and lower left), 277 (bottom), 279, 281, 289 through 304, 310, 323 through 336.

ROBERT & CO.: 249, 258.

SIX FLAGS OVER GEORGIA: 307 (bottom).

TRUST COMPANY BANK: 166 (top), 282-283 (by Lane Brothers).